RECORDS OF ST. PAUL'S PARISH

THE ANGLICAN CHURCH RECORDS OF
BALTIMORE CITY
AND
LOWER BALTIMORE COUNTY
[MARYLAND]

EARLY 1700S THROUGH 1800

VOLUME 1

Bill and Martha

Reamy

HERITAGE BOOKS
2007

HERITAGE BOOKS

AN IMPRINT OF HERITAGE BOOKS, INC.

Books, CDs, and more—Worldwide

For our listing of thousands of titles see our website
at
www.HeritageBooks.com

Published 2007 by
HERITAGE BOOKS, INC.
Publishing Division
65 East Main Street
Westminster, Maryland 21157-5026

International Standard Book Number: 978-1-58549-108-X

TABLE OF CONTENTS

Undated Postcard, requiring 1 cent postage
Maryland Historical Society, Church Files

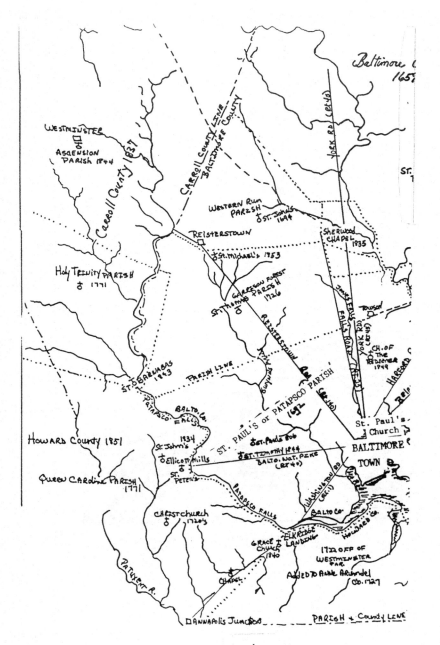

iv

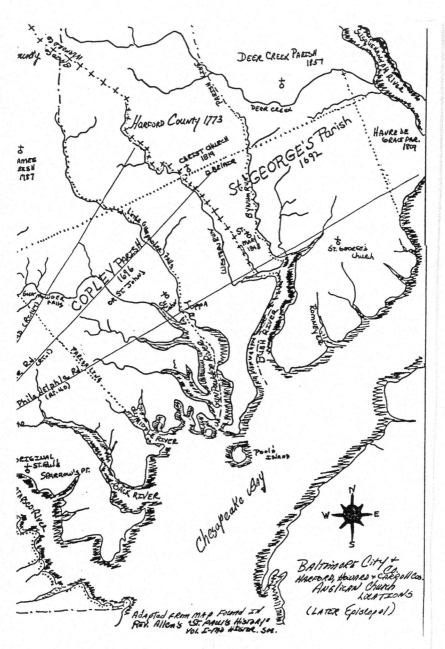

Baltimore City & Co.
Harford, Howard & Carroll Cos.
Anglican Church Locations
(Later Episcopal)

Adapted from map found in
Rev. Allen's "St. Paul's History"
Vol. I—Md. Histor. Soc.

This book is part of a series* of church registers of the Church of England (Episcopal) in Maryland published by Family Line Publications, and the first to be published on St. Paul's, Baltimore City and County. We plan to publish a second volume covering a subsequent period. A third volume is planned describing the burying ground of St. Paul's Parish, listing decedents. This cemetery is the oldest in the City of Baltimore and still in existence. Volume three will include not only tombstone inscriptions, but also genealogical information found in the Hayward-Deilman newspaper clipping file at the Maryland Historical Society pertaining to those burials.

*Previously published by Family Line: St. John's & St. George's, Harford County, MD, Henry Peden; St. George's, Harford County, MD, Reamy (picks up where Peden's leaves off); St. James, Baltimore County, Maryland, Reamy; St. Thomas, Baltimore County, MD, Reamy.

INVENTORY

Some of the records of St. Paul's Church are held in the Maryland Historical Society, Manuscript Division. They are contained in record group #1727 and consist of 12 boxes of materials.

Box 1: St. Paul's Protestant Episcopal Parish, Baltimore City. Register I 1710-1788; births 1710-1789, marriages 1716-1787, burials 1722-1789. The last page of the book includes vestry minutes June 7, 1777.

Register II 1786-1796.

Register "N.B. The Irregular Entries of Births, Marriages and Burials from the Year [sic] till December 1721 are exactly copied from the Old Register kept by John Gay, Col. John Thomas &c." [actually births apparently entered in 1723, and as early as 1710, and up to 1732.]

Marriages 1793-1794, burials 1791-1794, baptisms 1790-1794.

Box 2: Register III, Baptisms, Marriages & Burials Celebrated Commencing January 1, 1792 (through 1877).

Box 3: Register IV, May 1832 - July 1878; baptisms 1832-1878, marriages 1836-1878, burials 1837-1878.

Register, 1859-1870, baptisms October 1864 transcribed in Register IV [see above].

Box 4: Register of Baptisms 1856-1865 (transcribed in Register IV).

Register 1871-1876 (transcribed in Register IV).

Register 1870-1876, marriages 1871-1876 (transcribed in Register IV) Baptisms December 1, 1870-1876, confirmed 1871-1876, communicants 1873-1874 and burials 1870-1876.

Box 5: Register of baptisms, marriages and deaths 1878-1935.

Box 6: Full-name index of all celebrations (births, burials, marriages) held from the beginning of the parish contained in the many registers 1710-1933.

Box 7: [In folder] "This is in the handwriting of Thomas Chase, Rector of St. Paul's, Baltimore from 1744 to his death in 1777. Appears to be a list of marriages only received for ceremonies, probably for a notebook kept by him."

[Moneys rec'd. for pews for 25 September 1784 to 14 January 1787.]

Loans made to Vestry November 1819.

Test Book 1785-1836 [Oaths disclaiming allegiance to King of Great Britain & support to U.S. Federal Government] Vestry-men and date of signatures.

Book of accounts and receipts 1798-1812.

Vestry records September 16, 1878 - February 14, 1905, with index.

Box 8: Vestry Letter Book 1903-1904 (correspondence).

Register of Voters 1906.

Box 9: Vestry Proceedings October 11, 1915 - February 22, 1931 & Vestry Records March 1905 - June 23, 1915

Box 10: Record of Services May 29, 1904 - May 7, 1910. Date, name of members, offerings, records of marriages, baptisms, communicants, state of the weather, etc.

Box 11: Record of Services 1910-1916.

Box 12: Record of Services 1916-1923.

St. Paul's, located in downtown Baltimore and still an active parish, has an extensive collection of Anglican Church records, preserved in excellent condition. The bulk of the collection is held at the Maryland Historical Society in their manuscript department, some records are still retained by the church, and a considerable amount of papers have found their way to Duke University in North Carolina. These records will also be abstracted for genealogical information for the time period covered and will be included in Volume II.

Our thanks go to the staff of the Maryland Historical Society, especially to Karen Stuart, Head Librarian, Francis P. O'Neill and Kate Sampsell, Librarians, Susan Weinandy and Romel Showel of the Manuscript Division. Special thanks to Mr. F. Garner Ranney, Archivist of Library of the Episcopal Diocese of Maryland, whose office and collection are housed at the Maryland Historical Society. It was he who made us aware of the micro-filmed records held by the Diocese Library regarding St. Paul's Parish, which records are housed at Duke University, North Carolina.

Bill & Martha Reamy

ST. PAUL'S PARISH

INTRODUCTION

by

Robert Barnes

This transcription of the parish registers of St. Paul's Parish was taken from the first three volumes of the original registers, which until recently have not been available to researchers. They are found in manuscript collection MS.1727 at the Maryland Historical Society, which spans the years 1710-1935, and fills twelve boxes. Until now researchers at the Maryland Historical Society have had to rely on the transcription made by Lucy H. Harrison in 1894. In checking the original records, the compilers of this volume found a page containing approximately fifteen marriages performed by Rev. Thomas Chase either at his home or the home of one of the contracting parties. Because the marriages were not performed in the church, or for some other reason they were not entered in the actual parish registers, and hence were overlooked by Miss Harrison when she made her copy of the registers.

According to J. Thomas Scharf, the boundaries of the parish as originally laid out extended from the Pennsylvania Line on the north to the Patapsco River and Falls of the Patapsco on the south, from the western boundary of Baltimore County to the Chesapeake Bay, Middle River and Big Gunpowder Falls on the east. The boundaries of the parish were changed in the 1740's when Saint Thomas' Parish was established.(1)

The first vestrymen were chosen in 1692 when the parish was first established. Although no record remains of that first meeting to choose vestrymen, their names are found in a Baltimore County Court Proceeding of 1693. By 1694 the parish contained 231 taxable inhabitants who were assessed 8240 pounds of tobacco. (2)

The first known rector of the parish was Rev. William Tibbs, whose tenure lasted from 1702 until his death in 1732. A graduate of Merton College, Oxford, he did not enjoy the respect of his parishioners.(3)

He was followed by Rev. Joseph Hooper, who served from 1732-1739 (Hooper is omitted by Weis).(4)

The next rector was Rev. Benedict Bourdillon, probably of Huguenot origin, who served Somerset Parish on the Eastern Shore from 1735-1739, and then Saint Paul's Parish from 1739 to his death in 1745. His widow, Mrs. Jane Bourdillon, advertised a sale of property at his house in February of 1746 and Jane and his sons--Andrew Theodore, William Benedict, and Thomas Jacob--

authorized Daniel and Walter Dulany to sell additional property in April of 1764.(5)

Bourdillon was followed by Rev. Thomas Chase, who served from 1745 until his death in 1779. His obituary stated he was a gentleman of great learning and urbanity.(6)

Chase's two successors were Rev. William West, who died in 1791, and Rev. John Joseph Bend whose ministry lasted from 1791 to 1812.(7)

The compilers have included sections on Historical Notes of the Parish, and a detailed inventory of the records deposited at the Maryland Historical Society.

Readers will note that entries in this transcription are followed by brackets in which are enclosed the page numbers to Harrison's transcript, designated by H, or the page numbers of the three volumes of original registers, designated by R1, R2, or R3.

For a fuller history of the parish, see Francis F. Beirne, St. Paul's Parish, Baltimore, A Chronicle of the Mother Church (Baltimore: Horn-Schafer Company, c.r. 1967).

1. J. Thomas Scharf; History of Baltimore City and County (1881); Repr. Baltimore: Genealogical Publishing Company, Inc., 1971, pp. 516-617.

2. Ibid.

3. Frederic L. Weis; The Colonial Clergy of Maryland, Delaware, and Georgia (1950); Repr. Baltimore: Genealogical Publishing Company, Inc., 1978, p. 66.

4. Scharf, pp. 518-519.

5. Weis, p. 34; The Annapolis Maryland Gazette, issues of 4 February 1746 and 12 April 1764.

6. Weis, p. 38; Scharf, p. 518; Maryland Journal and Baltimore Advertiser, 6 April 1779.

7. Scharf, pp. 518-519.

"The irregular entries of births, marriages and burials from the early 1700s until 1721 are copied exactly from the Old Register kept by John GAY, Col. John THOMAS, etc."

Henry & Elizabeth, twins, born 14 June 1715; Susanna b. 13 7br 1717; Youroth b. 13 August 1719; Sophia b. 4 October 1721; s/o & d/o Henry & Susanna BUTLER.   {R-I-2} {H-1}
Samuel s/o Simon & Sarah PERSONS b. 2 March 1723.
Mary d/o Nicholas & Aberilla GOSTWICK b. 14 December 1722.
Humphrey b. 26 April 1723 s/o James & Elizabeth CHILCOAT.
John b. 2 April 1722 s/o William & Mary CONNELL.
Richard b. 20 May 1723 s/o Daniel & Elizabeth STANSBURY.
William b. 27 July 1720 s/o William & Elizabeth REAVES.
Thomas s/o Thomas & Mary BIDDISON b. 2 October 1721.
Sarah b. 8 January 1721 d/o Thomas & Tabitha SHEREDINE.
Amon b. 22 July 1723 s/o Henry & Susanna BUTLER.   {H-2}
Thomas b. 5 9br 1722 s/o William & Mary SMITH.
William b. 16 Xbr 1721 s/o Joseph & Ann FOREMAN.
Thomas b. 13 Februray 1716 & Joseph b. 26 February 1718, s/o
    Thomas ALDER.
Ruth b. 26 October 1722 d/o John & Jane RUTLEDGE.
John b. 5 Xbr 1722 s/o John & Mary RYSTONE.
Ruth b. 15 July 1722 d/o William & Eleoner GRIMES.
Elizabeth b. 5 July 17-- d/o William & Elizabeth REEVES.
Merriman b. 22 January 17-- s/o Jacob & Elizabeth COX.
Mary b. 1 March 1722/3 d/o Benjamin & Sarah BOWEN.   {R-I-3}
George b. 9 October 1718; Ruth b. 23 May 1721; s/o & d/o John &
    Jemima EAGER.   {H-3}
Temperance b. 24 February 1712; Richard b. 10 March 1710; John b.
    5 March 1713; Thomas b. 22 January 1716; Benjamin b. 2 9br 1719;
    s/o & d/o Richard & Rebecca COLEGATE.
William b. 24 May 1723; Benjamin b. 8 xbr 1717; s/o John & Sarah
    PALLEN.
Rachel b. 22 February 1715; Jonathan b. 25 Februay 1717; d/o &
    s/o Jonathan & Anne PLEWMAN.
Elizabeth b. 16 November 1722 d/o Edmund & Mary BAXTER.
John b. 23 December 1718 s/o Margaret CANNADAH.
George b. 28 February 1720; Amey b. 21 7br 1722; s/o & d/o
    Charles & Margaret GREEN.
John WATTS s/o Edward & Mary WATTS b. 5 December 1722.
Rebecca b. 13 February 1717; Elizabeth b. 29 August 1720; Jacob
    b. 2 December 1722; children of Jacob & Elizabeth MORRIS. {H-4}
Nathaniel b. 16 February 1722 s/o Nathaniel & Elizabeth DARBY.
Ann b. 25 September 1719; Henry b. 29 Xbr 1722; d/o & s/o Henry &
    Amey PEREGOY.   {R-I-4}
Margaret b. 12 March 1723/4 d/o Philip & Jemima JONES.
Charles b. 28 September 1723 s/o John & Martha MERRYMAN.
James b. 11 April 1720; Rebecca b. 18 January 1723; s/o & d/o
    James & Elizabeth POWELL.
Richard b. 17 October 1718; Robert b. 4 Xbr 1721; s/o John &
    Elizabeth CARTER.
Ruth b. 25 October 1723 d/o Jacob & Honor PEACOCK.
Elizabeth d/o John & Alice MERRIMAN b. 11 September 1721.
Samuel b. 12 November 1721 s/o Samuel & Mary MERRYMAN.
Anne b. 27 March 1724 d/o Zachariah & Mary GRAY.   {H-5}
Philip b. 16 December 1720; Pressusocia b. 27 October 1723; s/o &
    d/o Robert & Anne BURGAN.

Joseph b. 9 January 1716; John b. 16 August 1720; Susanna b. 6
   September 1723; children of Robert & Susanna GREEN.
Anne b. 17 December 1723 d/o Nicholas & Ebarilla GOSTWICK.
Ebarilla b. 24 April 1724 d/o Thomas & Elizabeth GOSTWICK.
Isaac b. 1 September 1721; Robert b. 25 March 1723; s/o John &
   Mary GREEN.
Absalom b. 2 October 1722 s/o William & Mary BARNEY.
Benjamin b. 17 September 1721; Mary b. 17 January 1723; s/o & d/o
   Thurlo & Cicelia BRYAN.
Mary d/o Benjamin & Sarah BOWEN b. 1 March 1722/3.
Anne b. 14 April 1720; Elizabeth b. 16 August 1721; Mary b. 15
   January 1723; d/o Matthew & Elizabeth HAWKINS.   {R-I-5} {H-6}
Richard b. 15 November 1721 s/o Richard & Elizabeth SMITH.
William b. 5 July 1720 s/o William & Catherine GAIN.
Abraham b. 7 September 1722 s/o Edward & Jane CORBAN.
Kedermath b. 23 March 1717; Mary b. 27 March 1719; d/o Charles &
   Jane MERRIMAN.
Sarah b. 10 February 1714; Margaret b. 23 October 1716; d/o
   William & Sarah HARRIS.
Anne b. 23 March 1722 d/o John & Mary WHITE.
Jeremah b. 24 November 1716; Margaret b. 7 June 1719; James b. 12
   May 1721; Eleoner b. 16 February 1723; s/o & d/o Patrick &
   Sarah NEAL.
Abarillah b. 9 October 1723 d/o Tobias & Honor STANSBURY.
John b. 17 January 1723 s/o James & Rebecca DURHAM.   {H-7}
Benjamin b. 22 March 1722/3 s/o Thomas & Alice DURHAM.
Abarilla b. 15 September 1724 d/o James & Mary RIDER.
Chloe b. 25 August 1724 d/o Hugh & Ann JOHNES.
John b. 3 October 1716; Catherine b. 17 September 1718; Ruth b.
   22 January 1720; s/o & d/o William & Sarah HAMILTON.   {R-I-6}
Sarah b. 1 Xbr 1724 d/o Edward & Eleanor RISTONE.
Susanna Mead b. 27 April 1723 d/o Stephen & Susanna BODY.
Penelope Mead d/o Stephen & Elizabeth BODY b. 27 November 1724.
Susannah BIDDISON b. 13 March 1724 d/o Thomas & Mary BIDDISON.
William ARRUNDAL b. 20 June 1719.
Samuel b. 25 January 1724 s/o William & Ann INGLE.
Nicholas b. 20 May 1721 s/o Nicholas & Eleanor ROGERS.   {H-8}
James Lloyd b. 17 July 1724 s/o Lloyd & Eleanor HARRIS.
Sarah b. 2 March 1724 d/o James & Rebecca DURHAM.
Alleridge b. 15 March 1724 d/o Matthew & Elizabeth HAWKINS.
George b. 25 September 1724 s/o Richard & Elizabeth SMITH.
George b. 13 March 1713 s/o George & Elizabeth COLE.
Solomon b. 18 December 1724 s/o Benjamin & Sarah BOWEN.
Thomas b. 24 April 1714; Dixon b. 6 December 1720; s/o Thomas &
   Jane STANSBURY.
Ruth b. 15 March 1724 d/o Jacob & Elizabeth MORRISS.
Moses b. 8 November 1723 s/o Thomas & Easter RUTTER.
Edmond b. 13 January 1724 s/o Thomas & Jane STANSBURY.
Phillis Anna b. 12 May 1725 d/o Edward & Jane CORBAN.   {H-9}
Neal b. 21 December 1718; Henry b. 25 March 1721; s/o Nicholas &
   Frances HALE.
Nicholas b. 2 November 1724 s/o Nicholas Jr. & Ann HALE.
Martha d/o Patrick & Martha LINCH b. 28 January 1725.   {R-I-7}
Philip b. 29 June 1725 s/o James & Rebecca POWELL.
Jemimah HARRIMAN b. 19 October 1724 d/o John & Alis HARRIMAN.
Mary b. 9 September 1724 d/o Richard & Elizabeth HUETT.
Elizabeth b. 18 September 1724 d/o John & Matthew [sic] LACY.
Robert b. 21 September 1724 s/o John & Mary RYSTON.
Hester b. 8 April 1725 d/o William & Mary CONNELL.

2

Jemimah b. 20 August 1725 d/o Philip & Jemima JONES.
Lidia b. 7 August 1725 d/o Richard & Sarah HINDON.
Lidia HALL d/o Thomas & Ann HALL b. 16 January 1724.
Thomas b. 17 April 1722; Joseph b. 9 July 1724; s/o Thomas &
   Dorcas SUTTON.   {H-10}
Phillis Ann b. 9 July 1725 d/o Edmund & Mary BAXTER.
Betty b. 3 January 1725 d/o William & Patience BUCKNER.
Jacob b. 7 July 1725 s/o Jacob & Elizabeth COX.
Richard b. 22 February 1725 s/o Daniel & Elizabeth STANSBURY.
Comfort Plat b. 12 April 1712; Bray b. 6 April 1716; s/o & d/o
   Bray Plat & Elizabeth TAYLER.
Martha b. 7 June 1725 d/o Luke & Ruth TROTTON.
Roger b. 3 January 1720; Aquilla b. 9 May 1723; s/o Christopher &
   Ann RANDALL.   {R-I-8}
Uroth b. 15 October 1713; Susanna b. 15 9br 1711; John
   b. 9 July 1719; Samuel b. 21 July 1721; Benjamin b. 3 October
   1723; Mary b. 27 March 1726; s/o & d/o John & Margaret WHIP.
John b. 3 July 1726 s/o Christopher & Ann RANDALL.   {H-11}
Elizabeth b. 11 Xbr 1717; Mary b. 9 July 1719; John b. 10 7br
   1721; Eleoner b. 20 8br 1723; Sarah b. 24 7br 1725; children of
   John & Mary WOODEN.
Joseph b. 14 April 1726 s/o John & Martha MERRIMAN.
John b. 26 September 1721; Daniel b. 13 September 1724 s/o
   Charles & Margaret PAR.
Mary b. 23 May 1725 d/o Edward & Mary WATTS.
Margaret b. 25 July 1722; Elizabeth b. 20 February 1724; d/o
   Lewis & Mary JGON.
Mary b. 20 August 1714; Martha b. 16 January 1715; Danceybell b.
   26 February 1718; Luencyde b. 8 August 1721; Elisabeth b. 13
   January 172-, in the morning; children of George & Elisabeth
   WITH.   {H-12}
Jane d/o John & Elizabeth ENSER b. 29 January 1725.   {R-I-9}
Abraham b. 7 Spetember 1726 s/o Robert & Susanne GREEN.
Tibetha b. 23 February 1726 d/o Jonas & Rosanha ROBINSON.
Rhoda b. 5 February 1726 d/o James & Mary RIDER.
Nicholas b. 11 December 1726 s/o John & Sarah MERRIMAN.
Daniel b. 3 January 1724; Thomas b. 27 March 1726; s/o Thomas &
   Tabitha SHEREDINE.
Mary d/o Edward & Sarah TURBELL b. Sat., 29 April 1727, 11 p.m.
Mary b. 6 June 1727, bap. 14 July, d/o Martin & Mary PARLETT.
Edward b. 17 April 1726 s/o William & Christan TELL.   {H-13}
Mary b. 5 January 1726/7 d/o Thomas & Ann HARRIS.
William b. 1 April 1727 s/o Thomas Francis & Comfort ROBERTS.
Sophia b. 9 March 1726/7 d/o Matthew & Elizabeth HORKINGS.
Easter b. 21 October 1726 d/o Thomas & Easter RUTTER.
Tobias b. 11 February 1726/7 d/o Tobias & Honor STANSBURY.
Thomas b. 27 March 1727 s/o John & Jane ROGERS.
Providence b. 26 June 1727 d/o Edward & Jane CORBEN.
William b. 21 June 1727 s/o William & Mary CONNELL.
Mary b. 4 June 1729 d/o John & Hannah PRICE.
Betty b. 25 October 1727 d/o William & Patience BUCKNER. {R-I-10}
William b. 14 January 1722 s/o Ellinor ORGAINE.
John b. 19 March 1722 s/o John & Prisceller SEMMKINES.   {H-14}
Nicholas b. 8 February 1727 s/o Samuel & Mary MERRYMAN.
Temperance b. 17 June 1726 d/o Henry & Susanha BUTLER.
Jane b. 14 September 1722; John b. 14 January 1724; Absolam b. 22
   March 1726/7; children of John & Hannour PRICE.
Aquiler PAULING s/o Sarah PAULING b. 25 October 1727.
Elisabeth b. 6 March 1728 d/o Luke & Ruth TROTTEN.

Dorothy b. 1 February 1727 d/o John & Amie TOWNSEND.
William b. 15 September 1725; Ellinor b. 12 March 1727/8; s/o &
    d/o Richard & Mary MARCHENT.
Susannah d/o Nicholas Jr. & Anne HAILE Junr. b. 26 December 1727.
Ruth b. 20 January 1728 d/o Luke & Jane STANSBURY.   {H-15}
John b. 18 April 1728 s/o Jacob & Elizabeth MORRIS.
Richard b. 25 September 1728 s/o Jacob & Constance ROWLES.
Elizabeth b. 21 May 1728 d/o Thomas & Tabitha SHEREDINE.
Absolom b. 8 January 1728 s/o Henry & Susanha BUTLER.
Matthew b. 13 June 1728 s/o Alexander & Feby MAC MILLON.
Roger b. 21 January 1725; Margaret b. 9 January 1728; s/o & d/o
    William & Elizabeth REIVES.
Aquiler b. 3 December 1726 s/o Thomas & Elizabeth GORSWICK.
Robuck LINCH s/o Patrick & Martha LINCH b. 23 July 1728 about 2
    hours before day.   {R-I-11}
Frances Holland b. 19 October 1728 d/o Edward & Mary WATTS.
Mary b. 8 June 1728 d/o John James & Sarah DERYDOR.
Edmundniah b. 23 May 1728 s/o Edmund & Mary BAXTER.   {H-16}
Thomas b. 9 March 1726 s/o John & Mary REYSTONE.
Margaret b. 30 September 1728 d/o John & Amie TOWNSEND.
Kerenhappuck b. 3 October 1728 d/o George & Sarah BAILEY.
Ruth b. 18 June 1726; Benjamin b. 24 September 1728; d/o & s/o
    Thomas & Darkus SUTTON.
Rosannah b. 4 June 1729 d/o Jonas & Rosannah ROBISON.
Sophia b. 29 September 1727 d/o John & Mary WOODEN.
Benjamin b. 26 June 1729 s/o Robert & Susannah GREEN.
Mary b. 7 March 1729 d/o Thomas Francis & Comfort ROBERTS.
Matthew b. 21 August 1729 s/o Matthew & Elisabeth HORKINGS.
Moses b. 27 January 1728 s/o John & Mary EDWARDS.
William Green b. 4 March 1728 s/o Thomas & Anne Green HALL.
Moses b. 4 October 1729 s/o Robert & Margrett MAXFIELD.   {H-17}
Elinor b. 18 May 1728 d/o James & Rebecca POWELL.
George b. 23 November 1729 s/o George & Elizabeth GOODWEIN.
Samuel b. 30 July 1728 s/o Samuel & Elizabeth SMITH.
Benjamin b. 26 August 1726 s/o John & Mary SING.
Anne b. 18 March 1729 d/o Patrick & Matha [sic] LINCH.
Henry b. 21 March 1729 s/o William & Hannah GREEN.
Lettis b. 4 June 1730 d/o Thomas & Lettis TODD.
Mary b. 4 June 1728 d/o Thomas & Ailce MILLES.
Mary b. 19 September 1729 d/o John & Mary RISTONE.   {R-I-12}
Mary b. 16 August 1730 at midnight d/o John & Mary EDWARDS.{H-18}
John Oystain b. 10 April 1729 s/o Thomas & Elizabeth GOSWICK.
Jeremiah b. 31 July 1730 s/o Jacob & Elizabeth MORRICE.
John b. 19 August 172- s/o Richard & Rachell DEMMETT.
Charles b. 7 September 172-(?) s/o Charles & Sarah WELLS.
Unity b. 2 March 1730 d/o Edward & Jane CORBEN.
Edward b. 26 October 1730 s/o Edward & Mary WATTS.
Thomas Harris b. 10 March 1727; Mary b. 13 October 1729; s/o &
    d/o John & Elizabeth GREGORY.
George b. 19 April 1728 s/o George & Anne HARRYMAN.
James b. 11 January 1730 s/o Thomas & Ruth FRANKLAND.
Nathen s/o Rebecca HAWKENS b. 16 November 1722.
Elizabeth b. 13 January 1727; John b. 16 September 1730; d/o &
    s/o William & Rebecca GAIN.   {H-19}
Luke b. 30 January 1729 s/o Luke & Ruth TROTTEN.
Mary b. 7 July 1730 by Nicholas & Anne HAILE.
Mary b. 2 August 1730 d/o Soloman & Elizabeth HILLEN.
Henry b. 8 September 1730 s/o Jacob & Elizabeth BELL.
Soloman b. 31 August 1730 s/o Thomas & Easter RUTTER.

Rebecca b. 20 February 1728; John b. 2 January 1730/31; d/o & s/o
   John & Rachell MOALE.
Josious b. 22 December 1729 s/o Benjamin & Sarah BOWEN.
Violetta b. 15 March 1729/30 d/o William & Patience BUCKNER.
Zackariah b. 30 June 1730 s/o Zachariah & Rebecca GRAY.
Allanson b. 13 August 1730 s/o Stephen & Elisabeth BODY.   {H-19}
Ruth b. 4 June 1730 d/o Jonathan & Ann HUST.   {R-I-13}
Elisabeth b. 7 June 1731 d/o Robert & Frances NORTH.   {H-20}
Elisabeth b. 9 August 1726; Richard b. 27 July 1728; John b. 4
   April 1730; children of John & Mary MILLER.
Mary b. 1 January 1730 d/o William & Mary CONNELL.
Sarah b. 12 May 1729 d/o John Jr. & Sarah MERRYMAN.
John FORSTER s/o Patience FORSTER b. 22 January 1730.
Ann b. 15 January 1730 d/o James & Mary LENOX.
Greenbury b. 11 February 1731 s/o Edmund & Mary BAXTER.
Martha d/o Mary WILLIAMS b. 31 June 1731.
Jemima b. 19 July 1727 d/o Thomas & Jane STANSBURY.
Zackens s/o Dorithy RICHARDS b. 17 October 1716.
Ruth d/o Mary SING b. 24 August 1729.
John b. 14 December 1727; Charles b. 25 January 1730; s/o John
   HARRYMAN.
Ann b. 19 August 1726 d/o Robert & Ann BURGAIN.   {H-21}
Elinor b. 16 November 1724; Mary b. 15 October 1727; John b. 3
   July 1730; children of John & Sarah WATTS.
Daniel b. 23 July 1727; Elisabeth b. 21 October 1730; s/o & d/o
   Daniel & Elizabeth STANSBURY.
Abraham b. 7 June 1728 s/o John & Elisabeth CARTER.
Samuel b. 6 March 1730 s/o William & Elisabeth RAYMAN.
Mary b. 20 February 1720; John b. 15 July 1726; Nathan b. 5 April
   1731; d/o & s/o Mary FITCHPATRICK.
Tobitha b. 20 February 1731 d/o Benjamin & Sarah BOWEN.
Mathew b. 20 May 1732 s/o Richard & Rachell DIMMETT.
Benjamin b. 8 May 1731 s/o Patrick & Mary KELLY.
Thomas b. 14 July 1732 s/o Jacob & Elisabeth BELL.   {H-22}
Robert b. 24 July 1732 s/o Edward & Mary WATTS.
George b. 3 July 1732 s/o Tobias & Honnor STANSBURY.
Mary b. 24 July 1732 d/o John & Mary MILLER.
Ruth b. 30 January 1732 d/o Robert & Mary GREEN.
Mary b. 2 August 1732 d/o John & Mary GREEN.
Job b. 18 March 1730; Mary b. 18 March 1730; s/o & d/o Job & Mary
   EVANS.
Solomon b. 7 December 1729; Keziah b. 12 October 1731; s/o & d/o
   John & Mary WOODEN.
Mary b. 22 February 1730 d/o William & Mary BARNEY.
Ebarilla b. 23 May 1726 d/o Charles & Judah ROBISON.
Cornelious b. 4 June 1729 s/o Cornelious & Barbary ANGLEN.
Alice b. 18 June 1730 d/o John & Mary EDWARDS.   {H-23}
John b. 23 June 1731 s/o Edward & Sarah LEWIS.
Elisabeth b. 4 July 1731 d/o John & Julytha SPICER.
Patience b. 16 September 1731 d/o James & Elizabeth BOSLEY.
Thomas b. 15 January 1731 s/o Thomas Francis & Comfort ROBERTS.
Mary b. 14 December 1728; John b. 24 April 1731; d/o & s/o John &
   Elinor GOLDSMITH.
Mary b. 1 December 1731 d/o Henry & Jane YOSTIAN.   {R-I-14}
Elisabeth b. 4 December 1728 d/o James & Elisabeth CHILCOAT.
Thomas b. 13 July 1732; Sarah b. 19 September 1725; William b. 4
   January 1726; Samuel b. 29 January 1727; children of Samuel &
   Ann DURBIN.
Sarah b. 20 July 1732 d/o Solomon & Sarah WOODEN.   {H-24}

Elisabeth b. 2 July 1732 d/o Patrick & Honnor HARN.
Rachel b. 8 January 1732 d/o John & Honnor PRICE.
Elisabeth b. 3 June 1730; Sophia b. 21 June 1732; d/o Samuel &
    Elisabeth SMITH.
Austain b. 6 November 1716; Christopher b. 12 August 1720;
    Richard b. 8 November 1772; Mary b. 5 October 1724; Zabrit b.
    19 March 1730; children of Christopher & Flora CHOATE.
William b. 22 August 1729; Mary b. 30 September 1731; s/o & d/o
    Lewis & Mary IGOUE(?).
John b. 8 May 1732 s/o John & Susannah BERRY.
Prudance b. 26 January 1727 d/o Stephen & Elisabeth GILL. {H-25}
Allinor b. 25 February 1728; Ruth b. 26 March 1731; d/o Samuel &
    Comfort HARRYMAN.
MERRYMAN daugher (-ursocey?) born to William & Margret MERRYMAN
    24 November 1726.
Margaret b. 24 February 1727; William (MARRYMAN) b. 11 April
    1729; d/o & s/o Margret & William MERRYMAN.
Mary b. 5 September 1732 d/o Joseph & Elisabeth CROSS.
Elisabeth b. 12 July 1721; John b. 25 September 1723; Jane b. 29
    January 1725; Abraham b. 5 February 1727; Joseph b. 11 April
    1730; Temperance b. 19 September 1732; children of John &
    Elisabeth ENSOR.   {H-26}
Sarah b. 21 March 1721; Charles b. 12 October 1725; Barbary b. 20
    December 1726; Benjamin b. 17 October 1730; children of Charles
    & Sarah GORSUCH.
Mary b. 30 August 1731 d/o Richard & Elisabeth RICHARDES.
Edward b. 25 June 1731 s/o Benjamin & Ann RICHARDES.
Elisabeth b. 3 February 1732 d/o Charles & Sarah GORSUCH.

"The following is what is Baptized by the Reverend Joseph HOOPER
& sum give in to the Regester that was baptized before and
neglected entering."

John b. 9 March 1731 s/o John & Elisabeth GREGORY.
Mary b. 1 September 1731 d/o John & Elisabeth RICHARDES.
Rechal(?) b. 30 December 1732 d/o Robert & Margrett MAXFIELD.
Elisabeth b. 13 September 1731 d/o Mertin & Mary PARLETT.
Flora b. 11 February 1732 d/o Patrick & Matha LINCH.
Elisabeth b. 13 December 1732 d/o Thomas & Elinor TODD.
Ruth b. 28 January 1732 d/o William & Mary BARNEY.   {H-27}
Prudance b. 9 January 1732 d/o John & Catherine EVENS.
Elinor b. 15 February 1732 d/o Richard & Mary BOND.
Ann b. 20 December 1732 d/o Nicholas & Ann HAILE.
Thomas b. 16 February 1732 s/o Robert & Francies NORTH.
Margrett b. 27 April 1732 d/o Robert & Mary DEBUTTS.
Hannah b. 12 May 1732 d/o Peter & Jane SORTER.   {R-I-15}
Henrietta b. 18 August 1728; Philip b. 2 March 1729; Rachel b. 22
    April 1732; children of Philip & Ann JONES.
Hannah b. 25 February 1732 d/o William & Elisabeth RAYMAN.
Jonathan HANSON baptized 12 June & 10 of next September will be
    23 years of age - 1733.
John HAWKINS baptized 12 June 1733.   {H-28}
Daniel b. 9 February 1732 s/o Dutten & Dianah LAINE.
Rebeccah b. 2 May 1733 d/o Edmund & Ruth HOWARD.
John b. 2 August 1732; Rebeccah b. 14 February 1728; s/o & d/o
    Michal & Rachel GLADMAN.
Violetta b. 4 July 1731; Richard b. 2 September 1729; d/o & s/o
    Christopher & Sarah GIST.
Zeporah b. 24 December 1732 d/o Nathanel & Mary GIST.

Thomas b. 30 October 1731 s/o Thomas & Mary BUCKINGHAM.
Comfort b. 27 February 1731 d/o William & Ann LOGGSTONE.
John b. 21 October 1732 s/o John & Susannah BELL.
Nathael b. 14 November 1730 s/o Thomas & Hannah BROTHERS.
Rebeccah b. 9 January 1732 d/o Thomas & Elisabeth GREEN.   {H-29}
Solomon b. 30 October 1731 s/o Edward & Catherine STOCKDELL.
Ruth b. 27 April 1733 d/o Benjamin & Ann RICHARDS.
Mary b. 10 January 1731 d/o William & Margrett HARWAY.
Mary b. 6 May 1733 d/o Alexander & Elisabeth GRANT.
Samuel b. 17 August 1733; Bail b. 9 May 1731; s/o Samuel & Urath
    OWINGS.
Mordicah b. 10 March 1732 s/o Thomas & Keziah GRAYHAM.
Ruth b. 16 June 1733 d/o Luke & Ruth TROTTON.
Charles b. 22 May 1733 s/o Charles & Milison MERRIMAN.
Samuel b. 4 October 1732 s/o Richard & Sarah LAINE.
Ann b. 1 August 1729 d/o Edward & Ruth NORWOOD.
Thomas b. 17 December 1732 s/o Thomas & Esther RUTTOR.
James b. 22 November 1724; Samuel b. 7 September 1727; Joseph b.
    26 July 1730; s/o Samuel & Hannah MAXFIELD.
Rechal b. 8 June 1732 d/o John & Mary REYSTONE.
Sarah b. 24 December 1732; Martha b. 5 September 1729; d/o Thomas
    & Mary CAMPE.
Elinor b. 4 September 1732; Lloyd b. 10 November 1729; d/o & s/o
    Doctor George & Elinor BUCHANAN.   {R-I-16}
Thomas b. Wednesday, 11 January 1726/7 about 7 p.m.; Christopher
    b. Thursday, 25 September 1729 about 2:00 a.m.; William b.
    Wednesday, 18 August 1731 about 10 p.m.; Rebekah b. 27 ?? 1733,
    Thursday, about 4:00 p.m.; s/o & d/o Christopher & Katherine
    RANDALL.   {H-31}
William b. 17 November 1733 s/o Matthew & Elizabeth HAWKINS.
John b. 13 October 1732 s/o Thomas & Ann SHAREWELL.
Ann b. 20 July 1733 d/o George & Ann GOODWIN.
Ann b. 5 February 1733 d/o William & Sarah FELL.
Rebekah b. 9 September 1733 in Westminster parish in Anne
    Arundale County, d/o John & Susanna ORRICK.
Gilbert MARSH s/o John & Ann MARSH baptized 17 March 1733/4 & was
    then 11 years old the 16th February Last from this date.
John b. 14 August 1733 s/o John & Rebekah GRIFFIN.
Benjamin b. 17 August 1731 s/o Matthew & Elizabeth HAWKINS.
John b. 4 October 1733 s/o Abraham & Charity EAGLESTONE.
Jonathan b. 22 February 1733/4 s/o Jonathan & Sarah HANSON.
Ruth b. 8 July 1727 d/o Joseph & Elisabeth BEASMAN.   {H-31}
Benjamin b. 8 March 1732/3 s/o Thomas & Kiturah PRICE.
Joseph b. 21 March 1733 s/o William & Ann WELLS.
Mary b. 4 April 1734 d/o Thomas & Mary BOREING.   {H-32}
Mesha b. 27 September 1733; Morris b. 13 July 1731; s/o Zebediah
    & Keturah BAKER.
Ellenor b. 15 December 1733; Mary b. 7 December 1730; Sarah b. 24
    January 1728; d/o William & Elizabeth LITTLE.
Elizabeth b. 6 November 1732 d/o Solomon & Elizabeth HILLING.
Ruth b. 9 February 1715; Samuel b. 10 May 1718; Sarah b. 19
    January 1722; Elizabeth b. 11 May 1724; Richard b. 15 May 1726;
    Cassandra b. 1 August 1728; Anthony b. 19 March 1731; children
    of Richard & Sarah GOTT.   {R-I-17} {H-33}
Ann b. 18 January 1729; Mary b. 25 January 1731; Abraham b. 18
    January 1733/4; d/o & s/o Alexander & Katherine TANSEY
Edward b. 22 May 1729; Elizabeth b. 2 December 1731; Richard b. 7
    December 1733; children of Richard King & Rachel STEVENSON.

Thomas b. 14 February 1718; Johannah b. 28 May 1720; Sarah b. 15
  August 1722; Broad b. 12 August 1725; Abraham b. 10 January
  1727/8; Mary b. 12 May 1730; Elizabeth b. 13 February 1733/4;
  children of Thomas & Sarah COALE.   {H-34}
Susanna b. 2 November 1714; Mary b. 10 December 1716; William b.
  20 February 1718; Sarah b. 26 February 1721; Thomas b. 13
  December 1724; John b. 12 March 1726/7; Joshua b. 18 May 1729;
  Edward b. 20 December 1730; children of John & Eliza. COCKEY.
Joseph HOOPER son of Rev. Mr. Joseph HOOPER, Rector of St. Paul's
  Church & Eliza. his wife b. 5 December 1733, baptized the 13th.
Elizabeth b. 23 February 1733/4 d/o Jonas & Rosanna ROBISSON.
Jemina b. 29 March 1734 d/o Job & Mary EVANS.
Nathaniel b. 15 October 1733 s/o Christopher & Sarah GIST.
Leah b. 7 October 1733 d/o John & Rebekah PRICE.   {H-35}
Elizabeth b. 20 July 1733 d/o William & Ann RUTTER.   {I-R-18}
Edward b. 6 November 1725; William b. 1 February 1731; Sarah b.
  23 April 1733; s/o & d/o Edward & Susanna STEVENSON.
Thomas b. 19 March 1727; Elizabeth b. 4 April 1729; Margrett b.
  13 December 1733; children of William & Margett HARVEY.
Martha b. 26 November 1726; Caziah b. 10 April 1729; Mary b. 14
  February 1730/1; Jeminah b. 19 March 1733/4; children of Jabez
  & Mary MURREY.   {H-36}
Thomas b. 15 April 1714; John b. 5 November 1720; William b. 28
  February 1721; Benjamin b. 18 December 1723; Mary b. 6 February
  1725; Lloyd b. 10 November 1727; Mordecai b. 19 December 1729;
  Stephen b. 15 October 1731; children of Thomas & Leah FOARD.
Prescilla b. 2 January 1733/4 d/o John & Mary HAWKINS.
Elizabeth b. 18 December 1733/4 d/o Samuel & Comfort HARRYMAN.
Jethro Linch b. 23 February 1732 d/o Philles WILKESSON.
Patience b. 5 February 1733/4 d/o George & Ann HARRYMAN.
Edward b. 6 May 1734 s/o Edward & Sarah LEWIS.
William b. 13 December 1733 s/o John & Mary WOODEN.
James b. 15 April 1725; Elliner b. 1 November 1727; Edward b. 15
  August 1729; Providence b. 27 August 1731; children of Turler &
  Cissill BRIANT.
John b. 8 October 1732 s/o James & Mary LENOX.   {H-37}
Absalom b. 20 October 1733 s/o Zachariah & Rebekah GRAY.
Sarah b. 19 November 1733 d/o Henry & Susannah MAYNER.
Ann b. 13 February 1733 d/o William & Ann LAGSDON.
Mary b. 27 July 1734 d/o Richard & Mary MARCHANT.
Thomas b. 10 August 1734 s/o Gabriel & Mary HOLLAND.
Rebekah b. 4 March 1733/4 d/o John & Katherine STINCHCOMB.
Elizabeth b. 13 June 1734 d/o John & Sarah MERRYMAN.
Dutton b. 15 July 1730 s/o Richard & Sarah LAINE.
Martha b. 28 February 1718; Ann b. 25 May 1721; Moses b. 2
  September 1723; Solomon b. 10 March 1724/5; Isaac b. 1 October
  1728; children of William & Martha WHEELER.   {H-38}
Daniel b. 4 August 1734 s/o John & Alice DARBY.
Rachel b. 31 July 1732 d/o Laurance & Eballia HAMMOND.
William b. 26 December 1733 s/o William & Rebekah GAIN.   {R-I-19}
William b. 16 October 1732; James b. 10 July 1728; Elizabeth b. 8
  September 1729; Shadrath b. 7 September 1731; children of
  Josephus & Ruth MURREY.
Benjamin b. 8 July 1734 s/o William & Sarah ROGERS.
John b. 30 November 1734 s/o John & Katherine EVANS.
Lucy b. 24 August 1731; Christopher b. 13 January 1733; d/o & s/o
  William & Ann FELL.
Moses b. 21 June 1734 s/o Robert & Susanna GREEN.
Tidings b. 30 August 17-- s/o Richard & Sarah LANE.   {H-39}

Mary b. 29 December 1734 d/o James & Barbara DIMMETT.
Edward b. 1 January 1734 s/o John & Mary EDWARDS.
Nicholas Tempest b. 10 May 1728; William b. 15 March 1731;
    Eleanor b. 25 February 1729; children of William & Sarah
    ROGERS.
Elisabeth b. 15 March 1721; Jacob b. 11 February 1723; Susannah
    b. 17 July 1726; Sarah b. 17 November 1728; William b. 14 May
    1730; Mary b. 31 March 1734; children of William & Elizabeth
    COX.
Elizabeth b. 5 August 1734 d/o John & Hannah PRICE.
William b. 9 February 1734 s/o Thomas & Sophia SLIGH.   {H-40}
Naomi b. 22 November 1734 d/o John & Elizabeth ENSOR.
Tego b. 25 October 1728; John b. 26 May 1733; Benjamin b. 14
    April 1730; children of Tego & Katherine TRACY.
David b. 2 March 1734 s/o Charles & Sarah GORSUCH.   {R-I-20}
Abraham b. 20 December 1734 s/o Abraham & Charity EAGLESTONE.
James b. 9 September 1734 s/o John & Elizabeth GREGORY.
John b. 30 November 1734 s/o John & Katherine EVANS.
Sarah b. 19 February 1734/5 d/o Benjamin & Sarah BOWEN.
John b. 6 December 1734 s/o William & Elizabeth BAUSLEY.
John b. 29 October 1734 s/o John & Mary REAGAN.
William b. 18 December 1733 s/o William & Sarah JOHNSON.
James THOMAS baptized 13 April 17-- by Rev. Mr. Joseph HOOPER &
    was then 25 years & 11 months old.   {H-41}
Agnes b. 1 June 1731 d/o Dr. George & Mary WALKER.
Ruth b. 5 December 1734 d/o Richard & Mary BOND.
Jemina b. 4 January 1734 d/o John & Mary MILLER.
Laurance b. 16 October 1734 s/o Henry & Jane YOSTON.
William b. 21 March 1734/5 s/o John & Elliner GOLDSMITH.
Rachel b. 20 June 1732; Ruth b. 20 March 1734/5; d/o Christopher
    & Ann RANDALL.
Laban WELSH s/o Ann WELSH b. 22 August 1734.
Christopher b. 21 September 1734 s/o Nathaniel & Mary GIST.
William b. 30 December 1734 s/o Michael & Sarah HOGSKISS.
William b. 12 September 1733 s/o William & Alice SMITH.
Mary b. 17 March 1734 d/o Edward & Susanna STEVENSON.   {H-42}
Katherine b. 4 November 1731; Anna b. 22 May 1733; d/o James &
    Mary GARDNER.
William b. 6 March 1734/5 s/o William & Mary BARNEY.
James b. 2 February 1734; Mordecai b. 5 May 1729; Warnol b. 14
    February 1732; children of James & Mary WOOD.
John b. 20 April 1734 s/o Peter & Jane JARTOR.
Sarah b. 25 November 1734 d/o Henry & Ann FISHBOUGH.
Sarah b. 16 November 1734 d/o John & Margrett MACKLAND. {R-I-21}
Margrett b. 6 October 1734 d/o Edward & Katherine STOCKSDALE.
Ann b. 25 September 1731 d/o Henry & Ann FISHBOUGH.
Rosannah b. 15 June 1733 d/o Paul & Rosannah YOUNG.
Thomas b. 22 September 1726 s/o Thomas & Ann HALL.   {H-43}
Edward b. 27 October 1728 s/o Jonathan & Elizabeth TIPTON.
George b. 25 October 1734 s/o William & Margrett MERRYMAN.
Ann b. 23 July 1735 d/o Richard & Sophia RUTTER.
Mary b. 28 January 1734 d/o Charles & Milisant MERRYMAN.
John b. 14 July 1734 s/o Solomon & Elizabeth HILLING.
Sarah b. 10 February 1733 d/o William & Frances JAMES.
Rachel b. 9 March 1734/5 d/o Jacob & Elizabeth BELL.
Anna b. 14 June 1735 d/o Thomas & Ann JONES.
Elizabeth b. 2 August 1730; Ann b. 3 November 1732; William Mills
    b. 14 August 1734; d/o & s/o Thomas & Tabitha SHEREDINE.
Prescilla b. 3 July 1735 d/o William & Elizabeth BOND.   {H-44}

9

Joseph & Rebekah, twins, born 20 July 1735 s/o & d/o William & Mary CONNELL.

Henry b. 18 September 1735 s/o Edward & Rachel REESTON.

Elizabeth b. 9 April 1735 d/o Peter & Mary JOHNSON.

Ebarilla b. 11 March 1734/5 d/o Robert & Elizabeth HARRYMAN.

John b. 31 July 1735 s/o William & Mary HALL.

Elisabeth b. 19 August 1735; Thomas b. 26 July 1736; Hannah b. 19 January 1731; children of Roland & Alice WILLIAMS.

Shadrach b. 7 September 1735 s/o Nicholas & Ann HAILE. {R-I-22}

Joseph b. 3 December 1726; Betty b. 5 November 1729; Nicholas b. 9 June 1731; George b. 16 June 1735; children of Nicholas & Ebarilla GOSTWICK. {H-45}

Benjamin b. 23 May 1735 s/o John & Mary RYSTON.

Sarah b. 1 June 1735 d/o Elias & Sarah DOD.

Betty b. 1 July 1728 d/o John & Elizabeth THORNBURY.

Sarah b. 14 April 1735 d/o Tego & Katherine TRACEY.

Rachel b. 20 September 1735 d/o George & Mary OGG.

Christopher b. 18 July 1727 s/o Mary SLYDER.

Esther b. 3 April 1729; Peter b. 5 February 1732; Rachel b. 29 October 1735; children of Peter & Mary MAYJORS.

Edward b. 14 February 1730; Mary b. 10 February 1732; John b. 24 April 1735; s/o Richard & Honour FOWLER.

Peter b. 11 March 1734 s/o John & Elizabeth COCKY. {H-46}

Kerby b. 5 March 1728; Ebarilla b. 18 May 1730/1; children of Thomas & Sarah DEADMAN.

Edward b. 23 October 1732; Elizabeth b. 25 August 1734; children of Robert & Sarah SWEETING.

John b. 11 January 1735 s/o John & Jemina BOARD.

Mosts b. 2 July 1735 s/o William & Ann RUTTER.

Edward b. 3 February 1735/6 s/o William & Sarah FELL.

William b. 20 March 1718 s/o William & Elizabeth BARNEY.

William b. 19 February 1735 s/o Thomas & Elizabeth BOREING.

Henry b. 2 February 1735 s/o Abraham & Charity EAGLESTONE. {R-I-23}

Ann b. 10 January 1735/6 d/o Benjamin & Margrett HAMMOND.

Susanna b. 25 February 1734; Ureth b. 23 March 1735/6; d/o Alexander & Phebe MACKMILLIAN. {H-47}

Joshua b. 26 November 1735 s/o Edmond & Ruth HOWARD.

Norman b. 26 September 1735 s/o John & Katherine STINCHCOMB.

Amos b. 20 February 1735 s/o Job & Mary EVANS.

Rachel b. 2 May 1736 d/o Samuel & Ureth OWINGS.

Flurre b. 24 March 1736 d/o Dr. Buckler & Jane PARTERIDGE.

Ruth b. 15 September 1735 d/o Henry & Jemima STEVENSON.

George b. 26 May 1736 s/o Passtohr & Pattey AVERLY.

Thomas b. 30 January 1735/6 s/o John & Alice HARRYMAN.

Jesper b. 11 May 1725; Elisha b. 3 April 1730; Darcus b. 3 October 1728; Sarah b. 28 July 1731; Ruth b. 3 November 1734; Benjamin b. 11 May 1736; children of Jesper & Sarah HALL.

Jemima b. 7 March 1735 d/o Richard & Sarah LANE.

Ann b. 13 October 1735 d/o William & Mary MILLS.

Joseph b. 16 December 1735 s/o John & Mary OSBAN.

George b. 16 February 1735 s/o George & Elizabeth HAILE.

George b. 18 March 1735/6 s/o Richard & Subbimer COALE.

Caroline b. 13 March 1735/6 d/o Emmanuel & Katherine TEEL.

George b. 12 April 1724; Sarah b. 5 September 1726; Katherine b. 15 July 1728; Mary b. 10 October 1730; Rebekah b. 16 October 1732; children of George & Mary OGG. {R-I-24} {H-49}

John b. 7 April 1736 s/o Thomas & Mary GIBBINS.

ST. PAUL'S CHURCH REGISTER

Mary b. 18 February 1717; William b. 27 February 1719; Thomas b.
8 March 1721; Jonathan b. 2 September 1723; John b. 6 July
1726; Luke b. 24 January 1728; Solomon b. 17 March 1732; Sarah
b. 17 July 1734; children of Thomas & Sarah TIPTON.
Mary b. -- November 1719; Sarah b. -- January 1720; William b. --
February 1722; Elizabeth b. -- February 1723; Benjamin b. --
April 1725; Rachel b. -- August 1728; Hannah b. -- January
1731; Keturah b. -- October 1732; children of William & Mary
KNIGHT.   {H-50}
Cassia b. 15 February 1735/6 d/o Gaberiel & Mary HOLLAND.
John b. 14 June 1736 s/o William & Ann CARTER.
Joseph b. 15 April 1736 s/o John & Mary COALE.
Sarah b. 20 June 1736 d/o Samuel & Elizabeth MEREDITH.
Jane b. 26 June 1736 d/o John & Ann STANSBURY.   {R-I-25}
Samuel GRAY b. 2 April 1695.
Katherine b. 11 July 1736 d/o Francis & Roseen CLAPLATEL.
John b. 13 November 1735 s/o John & Mary CHINOARTH.
William TOWSON s/o Darius TOWSON b. 23 January 1735.
Ediff b. 8 August 1728; Ureth b. 25 November 1731; Dennis b. 9
December 1734; children of Dennis & Rachel COALE.
Ann b. 26 December 1735 d/o Daniel & Elizabeth STANSBURY. {H-51}
Greenbury b. 4 October 1735 s/o John & Mary BAXTER.
Charles Merryman b. 5 December 1734 s/o Samuel & Elisabeth SMITH.
James b. 28 January 1735 s/o John & Alice DARBEY.
Elizabeth b. 16 July 1736 d/o John & Elizabeth ROBINSON.
Margaret b. 6 May 1736 d/o Nathaniel & Mary DAVIS.
Bethiah b. 24 February 1734 d/o Elizabeth THORNBURY.
Ann b. 4 September 1736 d/o Edward & Rachel REESTON.
Samuel b. 26 September 1736 s/o Peter & Susanna BOND.
William b. 19 February 1736 s/o Thomas & Elizabeth BOREING.
Ruth b. 13 January 1736 d/o John & Mary WOODEN.
William b. 25 September 1736 s/o George & Ann HARRYMAN.   {H-52}
John b. 15 August 1730; Sarah b. 12 August 1734; William b. 30
August 1736; children of Jonathan & Mary TIPTON.
Rebekah b. 13 August 1736 d/o Jonas & Rosanna ROBISSON.
William b. 8 December 1735 s/o John & Sarah WATTS.   {R-I-26}
Elizabeth b. 28 June 1733; Katherine b. 6 August 1736; d/o Thomas
& Mary WRIGHT.
Samuel b. 13 May 1721; Sarah b. 3 October 1722; Mordecai b. 18
April 1724; children of William & Hannah TIPTON.
John b. 15 September 1736 s/o Thomas & Rebekah SPICER.
Elizabeth b. & June 1736 d/o Thomas & Mary WOODWARD.
Johannah b. 15 October 1736 d/o William & Margrett MERRYMAN.
Ezekiel b. 28 December 1736 s/o William & Ruth TOWSON.   {H-53}
Elliner b. 7 January 1736 d/o Thomas & Mary CORKRAM.
Elizabeth Russell b. 12 July 1734 d/o Stephen & Deborah ONION.
Hannah b. 27 October 1736 d/o Christopher & Katherine RANDALL.
Charles b. 24 January 1736 s/o Thomas & Hannah STANSBURY.
Cuzsiah b. 4 March 1735 d/o Jonathan & Sarah HANSON.
Sarah b. 10 November 1736 d/o John & Katherine EVANS.
Samuel b. 8 February 1736 s/o Samuel & Jane LANE.
Charles b. 22 May 1733; Millisant b. 7 December 1736; s/o & d/o
Charles & Millisant MERRYMAN.
Elisabeth b. 14 February 1736 d/o Thomas & Susannah GIST.
William b. 1 July 1735 s/o James & Elizabeth BANSLEY.
Elijah b. 20 June 1736 s/o George & Sarah BAILEY.   {H-54}
William b. 8 November 1736 s/o Edward & Mary SWEETING.
Zeporah b. 16 June 1729; Susannah b. 6 October 1732; Richard b. 1
April 1734; d/o & s/o Nathaniel & Mary DAVIS.   {R-I-27}

11

Richard b. 26 March 1737 s/o Abraham & Charity EAGLESTONE.
Samuel b. 11 December 1736 s/o John & Elizabeth SARGEANT.
Sarah b. 12 July 1736 d/o Samuel & Comfort HARRYMAN.
Mary b. 2 September 1736 d/o William & Elizabeth RAWLINGS.
Robert b. 12 March 1736 s/o Robert & Elizabeth HARRYMAN.
Mary b. 16 August 1736 d/o Henry & Amey PERRIGO.
Charles b. 6 January 1736 s/o Charles & Jane HESSY.
Mary b. 25 December 1736 d/o Richard & Mary BOND.   {H-55}
Jemima b. 7 January 1736 d/o Henry & Jemima STEVENSON.
Thomas b. 20 June 1736 s/o Robert & Jane ELLSAM.
William b. 12 January 1736 s/o William & Margarett HARVEY.
Hector b. 14 September 1736 s/o John & Margrett MACKLANE.
Thomas b. 2 April 1736 s/o Thomas & Elliner PORTER.
Solomon & William, twins, s/o Wadkins & Mary JAMES b. 6 March
    1734.
John Cockey b. 11 January 1736 s/o Joshua & Mary OWINGS.
Luke b. 9 March 1736 s/o John & Elizabeth ENSOR.
Mary b. 11 March 1735 d/o Hugh & Sarah JONES.
Mary b. 16 December 1736 d/o James & Prudence KELLY.
Elizabeth b. 26 April 1737 d/o John & Elizabeth GREGORY.
Judeth b. 30 June 1736 d/o Thomas & Mary DAVIS.   {H-56}
Mary b. 18 September 1729; John b. 22 July 1735; children of
    William & Elizabeth BANKS.
Francis b. 26 June 1737 s/o Thomas & Elizabeth WELLS.   {R-I-28}
James b. 27 January 1716; Prudence b. 16 March 1720; Richard b.
    15 March 1722; Alexander b. 12 March 1727; Ann b. 17 February
    1729; Honour b. -- October 1724; children of James & Ann WELLS.
Elliner b. 21 October 1736 d/o John & Elliner GOLDSMITH.
Elizabeth b. 2 November 1736 d/o Prudence HARRYMAN.
Henry b. 28 April 1737 s/o Valentine & Mary CARBACK.
Thomas b. 30 January 1735/6 s/o John & Alice HARRYMAN.
John b. 25 May 1736 s/o James & Mary GARDNER.   {H-57}
James b. 28 January 1735 s/o John & Alice DARBEY.
Mary b. 4 June 1736 d/o Robert & Margrett MAXFIELD.
Margrett b. 11 July 1736 d/o Samuel & Ann DURBIN.
Esther b. 25 April 1736 d/o Edward & Susanna DAVIES.
Garanhappuk b. 9 August 1736 d/o Josephus & Ureth MURREY.
Mary b. 31 May 1737 d/o William & Mary HALL.
Abraham b. 10 July 1737 s/o John & Mary ROYSTON.
Mary b. 20 May 1737 d/o Robert & Ann LOVEPITSTOE.
John b. 14 December 1737 s/o John & Alice DARBY.
William b. 10 August 1736 s/o Robert & Rachel WILKINSON.
John b. 16 February 1736/7 s/o John & Sarah MERRYMAN.   {R-I-29}
Joseph b. 22 May 1736 s/o Mary FRANKLIN.
Janet b. 20 February 1736 d/o William & Sarah FELL.   {H-58}
Mayberry b. 12 August 1735, baptized 20 April 1738 s/o Mayberry &
    Anne HELMS.
Luke b. 9 March 1736/7 s/o John & Elizabeth ENSOR.
Abner b. 19 November 1737 s/o Samuel & Elizabeth SMITH.
Luke Stansbury b. -- April 1733 s/o William & Elizabeth BOND.
John b. 23 January 1737/8 s/o John & Anne STANSBURY.
Timothy b. 9 February 1737/8 s/o Jonathan & Sarah HANSON.
Stephen b. 11 March 1737/8 s/o John & Mary WOODEN.
Mary b. 1 November 1737 d/o Charles & Sarah GORSUCH.
Rachel b. 11 March 1737/8 d/o William & Anne CARTER.
Athaliah b. 21 February 1737/8 d/o James & Barbara DEMMITT.
Henry b. 27 June 1737 s/o Edward & Susan STEVENSON.
Ezekiel b. 19 January 1733; Urath b. 4 November 1734; Daniel b. 4
    November 1736; s/o & d/o Daniel & Sarah RAGAN.   {H-59}

Elizabeth b. 8 January 1735/6; Mary b. 22 February 1737/8; d/o
    Peter & Jane SARTER.   {R-I-30}
Hezekiah b. 7 November 1736 s/o Edward & Sarah LEWIS.
Nathan b. 20 October 1737 s/o Joseph & Flora PARREGOY.
Francis b. 30 September 1737 s/o Francis & Elizabeth PETTY.
Robert Newman PAULIN s/o Elizabeth PAULIN b. 18 April 1734.
Joshua b. 29 November 1735; John b. 18 August 1728; s/o Richard &
    Rachel DEMMIT.
Mesheck b. 19 August 1738 d/o Nicholas & Anne HAILE.
Mary b. 26 June 1738 d/o Francis & Anne RIDER.   {H-60}
Sarah b. 7 March 1739 d/o Thomas & Hannah STANSBURY.
Henry b. 2 March 1739 s/o Henry & Jemima STEVENSON.
Edward b. 20 August 1731 s/o John & Anne ROBERTS.
Epictetus b. 8 March 1738/9 s/o John & Dorcas HUNT.
Urath b. 26 June 1738 d/o Samuel & Urath OWINGS.
Robert b. 7 June 1738 s/o Nathaniel & Mary DAVIS.
Ruth b. 2 February 1730; John b. 1 March 1731/2; Thomas b. 1
    January 1733/4 d/o & s/o Nathaniel & Rhoda AYERS.   {R-I-31}
Michael b. 3 July 1736; Thomas b. 5 February 1738/9; Rebecca
    b. 14 February 1728/9; John b. 3 August 1733; children of
    Michael & Rachel GLADMAN.
Thomas b. 29 March & baptized 12 May 1739 s/o John & Mary
    MEDCALF.
Benjamin b. 21 August 1736 s/o Joseph & Susannah ARNALL.
Ruth b. 27 March 1738 d/o Richard & Sarah OWINGS.
William b. 1 July 1738; Ann b. 29 May 1736; s/o & d/o William &
    Sarah WILLSON.
Anne b. 2 May 1738 d/o William & Sarah HAMILTON.
Richard b. 13 November 1738 s/o Joshua & Mary OWINGS.
Mary b. 25 October 1736; Margaret b. 12 March 1737/8; d/o David &
    Sarah DEHAY.   {H-62}
Delilah b. 14 November 1738 d/o Endimion & Cathrine BAKER.
Mary b. 6 July 1736 d/o John & Mary MEDCALF.
Sarah b. 10 November 1728 d/o Lawrence & Margaret BLUNDELL.
John b. 4 February 1738/9 s/o John & Margaret MACCLAN.
Mary b. 23 April 1737 d/o Philip & Mary JARVIS.
Sarah b. 25 September 1738 d/o Ezekiel & Sarah WALKER.   {R-I-32}
John b. 22 November 1738 s/o Thomas & Susannah GIST.
Ann b. 3 April 1739 d/o Richard & Mary BOND.
Elizabeth b. 25 February 1739 d/o John & Ann STANSBURY.
Ann b. 26 November 1737; Stale b. 10 April 1740; d/o & s/o Stale
    & Mary DURHAM.   {H-63}
Mary b. 11 October 1739 d/o Jonathan & Sarah HANSON.
Richard b. 11 January 1739; Rachel b. 17 July 1737; s/o & d/o
    John & Rachel MOALE.
Elizabeth b. 20 July 1740 d/o John & Margrett TAYLOR.
Actia b. 20 July 1740 d/o Samuel & Elizabeth MERREDITH.
Edward b. 24 March 1737/8; Belinda b. 25 March 1740; children of
    Emmanuel & Katherine TEAL.
Ann b. 9 June 1739 d/o John & Mary ROBINSON.
Sophia b. 12 September 1727; Hannah b. 2 December 1729; Caleb b.
    18 March 1731/2; John b. 25 January 1734; Rachel b. 11 November
    1737; children of John & Hannah OWINGS.   {H-64}
Edward b. 17 June 1739 s/o Edward & Achsah FOTRELL.
James b. 6 September 1738 s/o James & Mary GARDNER.
Jane b. 27 October 1739; Catherine b. 18 April 1741; d/o John &
    Sidney HAMILTON.
Nathan b. 4 May 1744 s/o Edward & Sarah LEWIS.
Jemima b. 11 August 1740 d/o John & Mary WOODIN.

Elizabeth b. 4 May 1740 d/o Francis & Ann RYDER.
Rowland b. 21 October 1740 s/o Rowland & Alice WILLIAMS.
Nathaniel b. 7 November 1734; Patience b. 22 September 1736; John
  b. 25 Jan. 1738/9; children of Nathaniel & Patience STINCHCOMB.
Ellin b. 29 April 1740 d/o Robert & Frances NORTH.{R-I-33} {H-65}
Priscilla b. 22 March 1725/6; Venetia b. 16 October 1728; Sarah
  b. 28 January 1730/1; Elizabeth b. 16 August 1733; Kezia b. 25
  April 1735; Margaret b. 18 January 1738/9; Francis b. 23 June
  1741; d/o & s/o Francis & Elizabeth DORSEY.
Rebecca b. 19 August 1739 d/o John & Hannah PRICE.
On Saturday 29 October 1740 about 2 o'clock in the morning was b.
  in St. Paul's Parish in Baltimore County, William Benedict, son
  of the Rev. Benedict BOURDILLON & Johanna Gertruy JANSSEN his
  wife; & was baptized by his father in St. Paul's Church on
  Sunday the 18th of October 1741.   Capt. John AMLER & Mrs.
  Frances NORTH stood by Proxy for William JANSSEN Esqr. his
  Godfather & Mrs. Henrietta JANSSEN his Godmother.
Thomas b. 18 October 1740 s/o Samuel & Urath OWINGS.   {H-66}
Phebe b. 26 August 1741 d/o James & Mary GARDNER.
Solomon b. 22 October 1737; Nathaniel b. 12 March 1739/40; s/o
  Solomon & Elizabeth HILLEN.
On Friday, 6 August 1742 was b. in Baltimore County Thomas s/o
  the Rev. Benedict BOURDILLON & Johanna Gertruy JANSSEN his
  wife & was baptized by his Father in St. Paul's Church on
  Sunday, 3 October 1742.   Messrs. Jam. RICHARD & David
  BOURDILLON & Mrs. Molly HANSON stood by Proxy for His
  Excellency Thomas BLADEN, Esqr. Governor of this Province & the
  Rev. Mr. Jacob BOURDILLON his Godfathers, and Mrs. Barbary
  BLADEN his Godmother.
Francis b. 1 August 1741 s/o Ducal & Grace MACQUAIN.
Christopher b. 13 July 1741 s/o Samuel & Ann DURBIN.
Henry b. 12 December 1739 s/o Henry & Mary CROSS.
John b. 10 June 1741 s/o John & Mary HARRISSON.   {H-67}
Martha b. 28 May 1741; Benjamin b. 9 October 1738; d/o & s/o
  Thomas & Ann WHEELER.   {R-I-34}
Elizabeth b. 12 August 1741 d/o Jonathan & Sarah HANSON.
John b. 19 March 1737; Martha b. 18 January 1739; s/o & d/o John
  & Mary EDWARDS.
Cloe b. 28 February 1741 d/o William & Margrett MERRYMAN.
John b. 9 April 1737; Benjamin b. 25 May 1739; Elisha b. 18
  January 1741; s/o John & Hannah JONES.
Pricilla b. 3 February 1738; Rachel b. 26 January 1740; d/o
  Robert & Elizabeth HARRIMAN.
Mary b. 5 April 1740; Sarah & Elane, twins, b. 24 February
  1741/2; children of John & Helen BAILEY.   {H-68}
Elizabeth b. 26 September 1736 d/o Robert & Katharine MORGAN.
Martha b. 8 June 1738 d/o Richard & Margret HUTCHINSON.
Nicholson b. 23 April 1741 s/o Alexander & Zipporah BAKER.
John b. 17 October 1736; Thomas b. 8 April 1739; Henry b. 20
  September 1741; s/o Cowper & Hannah ORAM.
Sarah b. 3 January 1741/2 d/o John & Mary ROBINSON.
Benjamin b. 28 August 1740 s/o William & Sarah ROGERS.
George b. 12 October 1728; John b. 2 September 1730; Ruth b. 8
  March 1732; William b. 28 October 1735; Benjamin b. 22
  September 1739; Mary b. 4 April 1741; children of George & Mary
  BAILEY.   {H-69}
Jemima b. 23 April 1741 d/o Richard & Mary BOND.
Benjamin b. 17 November 1737; William b. 5 January 1739; s/o
  Francis & Elizabeth PETTEY.

Hannah b. 20 April 1743 d/o Thomas & Hannah STANSBURY.   {R-I-35}
Ann HARRIMAN b. 2 June 1742 d/o George & Ann HARRIMAN.
Mary b. 9 September 1742 d/o Hughes & Cathrine DEBARY.
Benjamin b. 15 November 1738; Elizabeth b. 27 October 1742;
  children of John & Elizabeth SARJANT.
Sarah BUTLER b. 8 April 1741, grand-daughter of Henry & Susannah
  BUTLER.
William b. 27 January 1742/3 s/o John & Sydney HAMILTON.
Hannah b. 17 April 1743 d/o Samuel & Urath OWINGS.   {H-70}
Joseph b. 4 October 1737; Elizabeth b. 1 March 1740; s/o & d/o
  John & Sarah PERRY.
Nathan b. 7 December 1738; Solomon b. 15 September 1742; s/o
  Robert & Susanah GREEN.
Urath b. 10 September 1742 d/o Benjamin & Sophia BOND.
Elizabeth b. 15 February 1735/6 d/o Matthew & Elizabeth HAWKINS.
Andrew b. 22 October 1734; Archibald b. 12 May 1737; George b. 23
  June 1740; Elizabeth b. 28 June 1742; children of Dr. George &
  Eleanor BUCHANAN.
Ann b. 27 July 1740; Joseph b. 29 November 1742; d/o & s/o
  William & Ruth BAZEMAN.
Rachel b. 16 February 1741/2 d/o Emmanuel & Catharine TEAL.{H-71}
Abednego b. 12 August 1741; John b. 13 September 1743; s/o
  Nicholas & Ann HAILE.
Johanna b. 2 October 1742 d/o Solomon & Elizabeth HILLEN.
John b. 6 November 1740; Ruth b. 22 January 1742; s/o & d/o
  Alexius & Martha HILLEN.
Edith b. 24 April 1734 d/o Thomas & Eleanor HOOKER.   {R-I-36}
Sarah b. 18 October 1737; Richard b. 24 May 1739; Ann b. 9 July
  1741; children Richard & Johanna JONES.
John b. 22 November 1738; Thomas b. 30 March 1741; Mordecai b. 22
  February 1742/3; s/o Thomas & Susannah GIST.
Nickodemus b. 25 July 1743 s/o Richard & Mary BOND.
John b. 27 February 1742/3 s/o John & Mary METCALFE.   {H-72}
Kerrenhappuck b. 26 February 1742/3 d/o Peter & Susanna BOND.
Sarah b. 19 March 1742/3 d/o Stephen & Sarah OWINGS.
Robinson b. 8 December 1739; James b. 4 June 1741; John b. 30
  March 1743; s/o John & Margaret CHILCOAT.
Agnes b. 18 March 1742/3; James b. 4 October 1738; children of
  William & Jemima SEABROOK.
Rachel b. 11 December 1742 d/o Samuel & Jane MERRYMAN.
Amon b. 3 January 1743/4 s/o John & Hannah PRICE.
John & Ann, twins, b. 11 January 1732; James b. 5 March 1740;
  William b. 18 December 1743; children of John & Jemima BOARD.
Sarah b. 24 September 1741; Mary b. 5 September 1743; d/o
  Nathaniel & Patience STINCHCOMB.
Thomas b. 15 May 1743 s/o Edward & Ann MEACHAM.   {H-73}
Sarah b. 29 January 1738/9; William b. 30 November 1741; Thomas
  b. 27 September 1744; children of Thomas & Phebe BOND.
Hill SAVAGE s/o Sarah was b. 22 December 1738.
Sarah b. 22 March 1743/4 d/o William & Sarah ROGERS.   {R-I-37}
Rachel b. 9 January 1744/5 d/o Michael & Rachel GLADMAN.
John b. 16 August 1744 s/o John & Mary ROBINSON.
Sarah b. 9 September 1744 d/o James & Mary GARDNER.
Stephen Gill b. 5 December 1743 s/o John & Susanna WOODEN.
Rachel b. 8 May 1743 d/o Samuel & Elizabeth MEREDITH.
Stansbury b. 15 April 1744; Presbury b. 15 April 1744; s/o Thomas
  & Sophia DEMMITT.   {H-74}
Dinah b. 18 February 1743/4; John b. 5 October 1745; d/o & s/o
  John & Rachel WALKER.

Rebecca b. 28 August 1741; Sarah b. 20 December 1742; William b. 7 March 1743; Thomas b. 27 February 1744; children of William & Sarah HAMMOND.

Samuel b. 12 September 1742; John b. 4 February 1744/5; s/o John & Mary HISER.

Samuel b. 3 December 1745 s/o Cooper & Hannah ORAM.

Larkin b. 17 May 1746 s/o William & Sarah HAMMOND.

James b. 24 July 1744; Katherine b. 4 August 1746; s/o & d/o George & Eleanor BUCHANAN.   {R-I-38} {H-75}

George b. 27 February 1743; John b. 10 March 1746; s/o Emmanuel & Katherine TEAL.

Obed b. 17 June 1746 s/o Alexander & Zipporah BAKER.

Samuel BLACK s/o Margaret b. 28 June 1740.

Luzana b. 27 April 1741; Vashti (dau.) b. 1 January 1743; Daniel b. 29 October 1745; d/o & s/o Zachariah & Margret LETT.

Benjamin b. 2 January 1744; Aquila b. 17 November 1746; s/o Roger & Rachel RANDALL.   {H-76}

Mary b. 26 May 1736 d/o James & Kathrine BARTON.

Lewis b. 24 February 1736/7; Greenberry b. 6 November 1739; Hazael (son) b. 14 April 1741; Selah (son) b. 10 February 1743; Joshua b. 22 November 1745; children of Selah & Comfort BARTON.

Elizabeth b. 15 July 1746 d/o John & Mary CONNELL.

Susannah b. 19 October 1737; Ann b. 20 August 1742; d/o Edward & Mary HUBBARD.   {R-I-39}

Henrietta Maria b. 26 February 1746, baptized by Rev. Thomas CRADDOCK 24 April 1747, d/o Tobias & Mary STANSBURY.

Edward b. 6 April 1739; Isaac b. 25 December 1740; Jacob b. 14 February 1746; s/o Angell & Sarah ISRAELLO.

Elizabeth b. 9 January 1747 d/o William & Sarah HAMMOND.

Joseph b. 17 September 1740; John b. 24 February 1743; Sarah b. 30 September 1746; children of John & Susan HAIGH.

Charles b. 28 March 1746; Eleanor b. 5 January 1747; s/o & d/o Eleanor ROGERS.   {H-78}

Mary b. 16 February 1747 d/o Thomas & Mary PEARSE.

William b. 19 June 1747 s/o Richard & Mary CRISWELL.

Rachel b. 9 February 1745; Charles b. 28 August 1748; d/o & s/o John & Ann CONNAWAY.

James Lloyd b. 5 July 1748 s/o Nicholas & Henrietta ROGERS.

Charles b. 27 January 1745; Alexander b. 7 February 1747; s/o William & Mary LOWE.   {R-I-40}

Maurice b. 8 July 1748 s/o Alexander & Zipporah BAKER.   {H-79}

Joseph b. 2 August 1748 s/o Joseph & Jane BARDWELL.

Ann b. 9 October 1748 d/o John & Mary CONNELL.

James b. 29 May 1743 s/o William & Ann FERGUSON.

Priscilla b. 20 October 1734; Seneca b. 31 July 1736; Onesiphorus (son) b. 19 February 1740; Christiana Eberhardina b. 20 February 1742; children of John & Dorcas HUNT.

Warner b. -- February 1731 s/o John & Dorcas TOWARD.

William b. 7 July 1748 s/o George & Eleanor BUCHANAN.   {H-80}

Rachel b. 22 April 1732; Rattenbury b. 3 March 1733; Thomas b. 2 March 1735; Nicholas b. 2 May 1738; Hannah b. 3 March 1742; Ann b. 3 August 1746; John b. 12 August 1748; children of Philip & Ann JONES.

Nancy b. 17 December 1748 d/o Thomas & Esther GRIFFEN.   {R-I-41}

Ann b. 7 February 1748 d/o Cooper & Hannah ORAM.

William b. 18 January 1745 s/o Thomas & Mary ROE.

Ruth b. 10 September 1732; Mordecai b. 20 July 1734; William b. 17 July 1738; Elizabeth b. 2 February 1739; Mary b. 13 December 1740; Patrick b. 14 December 1742; Emmanuel b. 29 May 1745;

Gilbert b. 1 March 1746; Ann b. 6 November 1748; children of
Patrick & Mary KELLY.   {H-82}
Elizabeth b. 10 June 1731; Sarah b. 13 October 1734; Charles b. 6
January 1736; Henry b. 24 April 1739; Keturah b. 11 October
1742; Mary b. 4 June 1745; children of Charles & Jane HISSEY.
Elizabeth b. 12 February 1738; John b. 15 August 1743; d/o & s/o
John & Comfort MARSH.   {R-I-42} {H-83}
Edward b. 5 August 1730; Urath b. 14 February 1732; Elisha b. 27
October 1735; Pleasance b. 3 January 1737; Henry b. 27 January
1739; John b. 8 December 1743; Charles b. 27 September 1746;
children of Henry & Keturah (Comfort) LEWIS.
Elizabeth b. 13 January 1744; Gideon b. 13 August 1747; d/o & s/o
John & Mary PERVEAL.
Ruth b. 20 January 1748 d/o Henry & Jemima STEVENSON.
Charles b. 23 February 1747 s/o Benjamin & Ann RICHARDS.
Ann b. 20 April 1749 d/o Abraham & Charity EAGLESTONE.   {H-84}
Ann b. 8 October 1742 d/o William & Mary LOW.
Benjamin b. 11 September 1749 s/o Roger & Rachel RANDALL.
Sarah b. 23 April 1737; John b. 6 July 1739; Hannah b. 10 January
1740; Nathaniel b. 22 March 1742; Anna b. 2 September 1745;
William b. 11 November 1746; Aquila b. 7 May 1749; children of
John & Katherine STINCHCOMB.   {H-85}
Mary b. 13 September 1745 d/o Humphry & Sarah CHILCOTE.
Elizabeth b. 25 August 1744; Martha b. 28 December 1745; Urath b.
27 February 1747; d/o John & Mary PENINGTON.   {R-I-43}
Ruth b. 26 February 1736; Phillip b. 29 December 1737; John b. 29
July 1740; Thomas b. 25 September 1742; Joseph b. 18 January
1745; Sarah b. 17 May 1747; Benjamin b. 18 October 1749;
children of William & Sarah JOHNSON.
William b. 17 October 1745; Thomas b. 15 April 1747; Edward b. 21
August 1748; Garrett b. 16 January 1749; s/o Garrett & Rosanna
WILSON.   {H-86}
Greenberry b. 10 March 1729 s/o Greenberry & Mary DORSEY.
Mary b. 30 July 1747; George b. 30 March 1750; d/o & s/o John &
Rachel WALKER.
Agnes b. 18 December 1749 d/o Thomas & Althea FENLEY. {R-I-44}
Elizabeth b. 11 March 1749/50 d/o Dixen & Elizabeth BROWN.
Rachel b. 7 November 1726; Sarah b. 7 February 1729; Hilyard
(son) b. 20 April 1735; children of Hillard & Mary BOSTON.
John b. 11 July 1745; Roger b. 10 July 1748; s/o Roger & Mary
HOLEBROOK.   {H-87}
Jacob Hurd b. 15 November 1748; Samuel b. 10 July 1747; s/o
Edward & Sarah LEWIS.
John b. 4 August 1741; Ann & Ruth, twins, b. 29 August 1744;
Thomas b. 6 May 1747; William b. 31 August 1749; s/o & d/o
Nathaniel & Mary YOUNG.
Sarah b. 2 July 1736; William b. 11 June 1739; Elenor b. 27 April
1742; Belender b. 8 June 1743; Ann b. 18 March 1744/5; Richard
b. 10 June 1748; children of John & Ann ROBERTS.
Patrick b. 21 March 1749/50 s/o Benjamin & Sarah KELLEY.
Joseph b. 8 June 1742; Rachel b. 16 January 1744; Jacob b. 14
November 1747; Matthew b. 11 April 1750; children of Mathew &
Rachel TURNER.   {H-88}
Elenor b. 15 September 1749 d/o John & Elenor LONG.
Ruth b. 28 April 1744; William b. 4 April 1746; d/o & s/o William
& Elizabeth STANSBURY.
Joseph b. 16 February 1750 s/o Richard & Rebeka CARTER. {R-I-45}
Margarett b. 14 November 1749 d/o Christopher & Ann MC KUNE.
Rachel b. 4 April 1750 d/o Abraham & Elizabeth GREEN.

William b. 20 April 1750 s/o Henry & Elizabeth GREEN.
Sarah b. 7(11?) October 1747; Ann b. 28 February 1749/50; d/o
    John & Mary GREGORY.   {H-89}
Sarah b. 28 July 1749 d/o Joseph & Ruth SUTTON.
Luke b. 24 August 1747; Jane b. 14 April 1750; s/o & d/o Thomas &
    Hannah STANSBURY.
Mary b. 12 June 1748; Sarah b. 12 May 1750; d/o William & Sarah
    PARLOT.
John b. 12 November 1745 s/o Benjamin & Abarilah CURTIS.
Sarah b. 26 June 1750 d/o Thomas & Mary VESTERMAN.
James & Joseph, twins, b. 19 December 1742; Daniel b. 5 April
    1744; s/o Joseph & Flora PERRIGO.   {H-90}
Ann b. 17 October 1737; John b. 1 January 1739/40; d/o & s/o
    Henry & Jane YOSTEN.
Mary b. 24 May 1750 d/o Moses & Catherine WHEELER.   {R-I-46}
Sarah b. 27 March 1745 d/o Richard & Subinah COLE.
Eleaner b. 14 August 1749 d/o Richard & Mary CRISWELL.
William b. 1 September 1749 s/o John & Mary COOK.
Poesocia b. 22 May 1750; Jarvice b. 14 September 1747; children
    of Thomas & Ann BIDDERSON.
Frederick b. 27 July 1747; Ann b. 17 March 1747/8; children of
    Conduice & Persocia GASH.   {H-91}
Thomas b. 27 November 1738 s/o Thomas & Elenor TODD.
Sarah b. 5 November 1741; William b. 18 February 1742; Joshua b.
    25 April 1745; Deborah b. 26 October 1746; Nella b. 25 February
    1747; Ann b. 14 January 1749; children of William & Elenor
    LINCH.
Martha b. 15 June 1748; Patrick b. 17 May 1750; d/o & s/o Robuck
    & Jemima LINCH.
Joseph Ward b. 24 November 1749 s/o Richardson & Mary STANSBURY.
Edward Allison b. 24 March 1749; John b. 21 January 1747; s/o
    John & Ann WATTS.   {R-I-47} {H-92}
Martha b. 20 January 1749/50 d/o Peter & Martha ROBERSON.
Philip b. 20 August 1740; Henry b. 13 May 1742; John b. 31
    October 1744; Abraham b. 21 November 1747; s/o Solomon &
    Elizabeth SHIELS.
William b. 17 December 1743; James b. 10 April 1748; Elizabeth b.
    2 May 1750; children of John & Ruth BUSK.
Sabra SHAW d/o Mary b. 10 September 1739.   {H-93}
Mary b. 15 January 1749/50 d/o John & Mary PERVEAL.
Nicholas b. 5 August 1750 s/o Henry & Keturah LEWIS.
Jane b. 14 December 1747; Sarah b. 13 May 1749; d/o Amos & Hannah
    HOLEBROOK.
Cloe b. 6 July 1750 d/o Benjamin & Deborah JONES.   {R-I-48}
John b. 12 February 1750 s/o Francis & Elizabeth PETTY.
Edward Spicer b. 21 February 1742/3; Joshua b. 2 October 1745;
    Amon b. 13 Feb. 1747/8; children of Jonathan & Sarah HANSON.
Elizabeth b. 31 August 1750 d/o Daniel & Mary POWEL.   {H-94}
Rachel b. 13 August 1750 d/o George & Sarah HARRIMAN.
Abraham b. 10 July 1750 s/o William & Elizabeth ENSOR.
Phillip b. 4 December 1745; Samuel b. 9 July 1748; s/o Samuel &
    Elizabeth SINDAL.
Elizabeth b. 28 August 1750 d/o Nicholas & Jane MERRIMAN.
John b. 6 March 1749 s/o Joseph & Elizabeth MERRYMAN.
Isaac b. 17 February 1749 s/o Abraham & Ann SOLLERS.
Peggy b. 20 August 1749 d/o William & Frances BARNEY.
Margret b. 5 August 1749 d/o Dorothy TOWNSEND.
Lloyd b. 25 October 1750 s/o Emmanuel & Catherine TEAL.
Benjamin b. 18 August 1750 s/o Edmund & Dorcas TALBOTT.   {H-95}

Thomas b. 5 January 1750/1 s/o Charles & Sarah GORSUCH.
William b. 1 January 1750/1 s/o Henry & Jemima STEVENSON.
Mary b. 20 April 1750 d/o John & Mary PENNINGTON.
Phillis Baxter b. 23 March 1750 d/o Susanah GREEN.
Eve b. 10 March 1750/1 d/o Andrew & Mary CAPHORT.   {R-I-49}
Gilbert b. 16 January 1750/1 s/o John & Ann ROBERTS.
Elizabeth b. 3 January 1748; James b. 3 February 1750/51; d/o &
   s/o James & Sarah ROGERS.
Cooper b. 13 September 1750 s/o Cooper & Hannah ORAM.
Henry Smith b. 8 September 1750 s/o Leonard & Mary JARRET.
John & James, twins, b. 22 December 1751 s/o John & Aberila CARY
   (CAREY).   {H-96}
George b. 22 November 1751 s/o Thomas & Mary ROE.
Mary b. 26 October 1751 d/o William & Mary SIM.
William b. 31 March 1752 s/o George & Barbry PICKETT.
Elizabeth Crosby b. 18 May 1752 d/o John Crosby & Sarah HODSON.
Henry b. 29 October 1751 s/o Henry & Elizabeth GREEN.
Dorcas b. 30 June 1752 d/o Charles & Sarah GORSUCH.
William b. 7 July 1752 s/o John & Mary GREGORY.
William b. 31 December 1746 s/o Heighe & Rosanna SOLLERS.
Benjamin b. 28 June 1752 s/o Thomas & Hannah STANSBERY.
Mary b. 13 January 1752 d/o Richard & Ann HAILE.
Mary Ann b. 14 July 1752 d/o William & Sarah JOHNSON.   {R-I-50}
John b. 13 January 1753 s/o John & Elenor LONG.   {H-97}
Elizabeth b. 14 January 1752 d/o Robuck & Jemima LYNCH.
Mathew b. 3 April 1740; John b. 15 August 1742; Anne b. 2 January
   1745; William b. 20 June 1748; Mary b. 11 February 1750; Thomas
   b. 4 November 1752; children of Thomas & Anne COOK.
Joseph LANGLEY was b. 10 December 1753.
Benjamin Robinson b. 1 October 1754 s/o Edmund & Rebecca TALBOTT.
Florah b. 26 June 1752; Lydia b. 23 April 1754; d/o John &
   Florah MORGAN.
Elizabeth b. 11 June 1755 d/o George PICKET & his wife.
Jobe b. 31 March 1755 s/o Henry & Elizabeth GREEN.
Charles b. 1 February 1753; Benjamin b. 29 April 1755; s/o
   Charles & Sarah GORSUCH.   {H-98}
Susanah b. 2 May 1755 d/o William & Jane LOCK.
Charles North b. 23 June 1752 s/o Christopher & Elizabeth CARNAN.
Charles b. 20 October 1755 s/o Lyke & Sophia CHAPMAN.
Asabell b. 16 December 1754; George b. 27 March 1756; children of
   William & Mary SIM.
John b. 1 April 1756 s/o Amoss & Hannah HOLEBROOK.
Samuel b. 17 June 1745; Mary b. 13 June 1749; Action b. 26
   December 1751; Marice (son) b. 9 March 1754, children of Samuel
   & Jane (Jean) MERRYMAN. (Samuel only listed as parent for last
   son.)
Elisha b. 21 January 1757 s/o Charles & Sarah GORSUCH.
Sarah b. 11 July 1755 d/o John & Cathrine LEWIS.   {H-99}
John b. 27 December 1757 s/o John & Vinity WISHER.
Sarah b. 20 December 1756 d/o John & Anne MACLOUR.
David b. 27 January 1757 s/o Thomas & Sarah STANSBURY.
Thomas b. 18 January 1757 s/o John & Elizabeth WOODARD.
Nathan b. 4 May 1740 s/o Edward & Sarah LEWIS.
Tobois b. 23 March 1718/19 s/o Luke & Angian STANSBURY   {R-I-51}
   (born in Baltimore County & was m. to Mary HAMMOND 27 April
   1746.)
Henrietta b. in St. Pauls Parish 26 February 1747/8; Cathrine b.
   28os/17 March 1759 ns; Rebecca b. 22 os/11 April 1751; Jean b.
   6 os/9 June 1753 ns; Mary & Sarah, twins, b. 12 September 1755

ST. PAUL'S CHURCH REGISTER

ns; children of Tobies (Tobias) & Mary STANSBURY. (os=old
style; ns=new style)
Sarah RUTER b. 6 July 1757 d/o Henry & Elizabeth RUTER.
Nicholas b. 5 July 1757 s/o William & Margret JISOP.
Jeane b. 6 October 1756 d/o John & Alner LONG.
Dickson b. 10 December 1757 s/o Richard & Elizabeth BROWN
   (BROWNE).
Benjamin b. 24 March 1758 s/o Benjamin & Elizabeth JAVIOUS.
Alnar & Mary, twins, b. 20 January 1758; children of William &
   Rosanah POUTANY.   {R-I-53}
Elizabeth b. 13 January 1750; John b. 30 October 1758; Thomas b.
   11 November 1753; William b. 2 November 1755; children of
   William & Lusanah EDWARDS.
Mary b. 10 March 1758 d/o Job Jr. & Mary EVINS.   {H-101}
Sarah b. 3 September 1758 d/o John & Mary HISER.
Sarah b. 7 October 1756 d/o Job Jr. & Mary EVINS.
Jeams Vaine Bonfeald ENSOR s/o Orphy ENSOR b. 27 Dec. 1757.
Benjamin b. 10 February 1758 s/o Conduce Gash & Proseliah GATCH.
William b. 8 March 1758 s/o William & Elizabeth SANDEL.
Naomah b. 15 March 1758 d/o Solomon & Temperance BOWEN.
David b. 20 July 1757 s/o Jacob & Elizabeth SANDEL.
Solomon b. 19 March 1758 s/o William & Anne CARTER.
Orphy b. 21 April 1758 d/o Thomas & Mary TIPTON.
William b. 12 March 1758 s/o William & Ruth SHOY.
Alenr. b. 9 --- 1758 d/o John & Mary DUGLES.
Mathew b. 21 April 1758 (dau?); Thomas Ward b. 8 July 1755;
   children of Thomas & Jean SHEPARD.   {H-102}
Henry b. 8 September 1758 s/o Lenord & Mary SMITH.   {R-I-54}
Hustice b. 13 October 1746; Elizabeth b. 26 May 1748; children of
   Lenord & Mary GARROD.
Sarah b. 15 October 1748 d/o John & Elizabeth WOODWARD.
Richard Gardner STANSBURY b. 21 February 1758 s/o Robert
   STANSBURY & Sarah GARDNER.
Sarah b. 2 February 1757; John b. 5 October 1758; d/o & s/o John
   & Flora MORGAN.
Eleanor b. 1 August 1759 d/o Lloyd & Rachel BUCHANAN.
Ann b. 24 July 1758 d/o Alexander & Sarah STEWART.
Philip b. 23 November 1749; Nicholas b. 7 October 1753; Ann b. 12
   July 1758; s/o & d/o Nicholas & Henrietta ROGERS.   {H-103}
George b. 6 August 1753 s/o William & Agnes LUX.
John b. 26 January 1759 s/o Dixon & Elizabeth BROWN.
Joshua b. 20 April 1759 s/o Charles & Sarah GORSUCH.
Daniel b. 8 May 1759 s/o Thomas & Hanah STANSBURY.
William b. 15 September 1757 s/o Christopher & Judith DUKES.
Mary b. 1 December 1758 d/o George & Barbara PICKETT.
Elizabeth b. 1 April 1758 d/o John & Caroline ORRICK.
Thomas Cockey Deye FORD b. 26 July 1758; Caroline FORD b. 27 June
   1759; s/o & d/o Thomas FORD & Charlotta Cockey FORD.
Samuel b. 18 January 1760 at 5 minutes after 5 AM s/o Samuel &
   Mary SEED. (SEEDHIS?)
Charles b. 6 November 1759 s/o William & Margaret GESUP. {H-104}
Rebecca b. 12 January 1760 d/o Thomas & Ester GRIFFITH.
Sarah b. 9 July 1759 d/o Joseph & Elizabeth PATRIDGE.   {R-I-55}
James b. 1 October 1759; Mary b. 12 July 1754; s/o & d/o Joseph &
   Elizabeth BANKSON.
Sarah b. 15 October 1758; Charles b. 26 March 1760; children of
   John & Elizabeth WOODWARD.

20

Elin b. 6 January 1743; Ann b. 2 September 1745; Mary b. 6
January 1750; John b. 13 November 1752; Joseph b. 15 December
1750; children of Joseph & Elin SOLLERS.

John b. 29 March 1760 s/o John & Caroline ORRICK.   {H-105}

Jane b. 30 April 1760 d/o William & Jane LOCK.

Moses b. 13 January 1758; Joseph b. 15 March 1760; s/o Joseph &
Mary MERRYMAN.

Luisa b. 26 October 1756; Elizabeth b. 1 March 1760; d/o Andrew &
Mary STIGAR.

Sarah b. 21 December 1750; Ruth b. 21 March 1753; Ann b. 20 March
1755; John b. 11 July 1757; Susanna b. 12 July 1760; d/o & s/o
John & Ann CONAWAY.

William b. 3 June 1760, baptized 27 July 1760 s/o William & Agnes
LUX.   {R-I-56}

Catherine b. 24 September 1758 d/o John & Catherine LEWIS.{H-106}

Catherine b. 14 May 1760 d/o John & Margaret GARDNER.

Anne b. 29 October 1760 d/o Ephraim & Mary GRAY.

Sarah b. 13 February 1761 d/o Luke & Rachel JOHNSON

Anne b. 16 October 1759; George Henry b. 20 March 1761; d/o & s/o
John Henry & Elizabeth MIER.

Pleasant b. 4 March 1759; Rebecca b. 8 December 1760; d/o John &
Ureth YOUNG.

Belinda b. 25 July 1754; Charles b. 24 October 1756; d/o & s/o
Emanuel & Cathrine TEAL.

Francis b. 11 January 1761 s/o Dixon & Elizabeth BROWN.

Richard b. 11 April 1761 s/o Henry & Elizabeth RUTTER.

Joshua b. 13 May 1759 s/o John & Eleanor LONG.   {H-107}

Elizabeth b. 19 October 1760 d/o Henry & Elizabeth GREEN.

Sarah b. 28 --- 1758; Elizabeth b. 20 April 1761; d/o Francis &
Anne TURNER.

Ruth b. 2 July 1760 d/o Thomas & Sarah SIMS.

Mary b. 18 November 1754; Henry b. 16 March 1758; d/o & s/o
Nathaniel & Mary YOUNG.

Cathrine b. 6 April 1753; Anne b. 20 June 1755; John b. 14
December 1758; Sarah b. 10 January 1760; children of William &
Mary MILLER.   {R-I-57}

Elizabeth b. Saturday 8 September 1759; John b. Sunday 17 May
1761; children of John & Ellin MOALE.

Richard b. 19 October 1760 s/o Joshua & Anne DEMMITT.

Edward b. 4 August 1757; Jane b. 2 May 1761; s/o & d/o Amos &
Hannah HOLEBROOKS.   {H-108}

Ruth b. 19 November 1760 d/o George & Mary STANSBURY.

Elizabeth Key b. 30 September 1760 d/o Robert & Elizabeth
DAVIDSON.

James b. 19 December 1760 s/o Ambrose & Elizabeth GAUHAGAN.

Rosanna b. 31 May 1760 d/o William & Rosanna PUTANY.

John b. 21 January 1746; Edward b. 24 March 1749; Penellope b. 5
April 1751; Josias b. 3 January 1757; Dickerson b. 17 March
1758; Beale b. 21 February 1760; children of John & Sarah
WATTS.

Elizabeth b. 3 November 1753; Jacob b. 21 July 1756; Rachel b. 6
March 1759; Anne b. 6 March 1761 children of Richard & Anne
ROWLES.   {H-109}

Ruth b. 14 November 1754; Luke b. 14 July 1756; Rachell b. 18
March 1758; Susannah b. 31 May 1761; children of Luke &
Susannah TROTTEN.   {R-I-58}

George b. 2 January 1760; William b. 19 June 1758; s/o Thomas &
Patience JACKSON.

William b. 22 September 1760 s/o William Jr. & Elizabeth SMITH.

Elizabeth b. 27 April 1745; Margrett b. 2 June 1747; Peggy b. 21
August 1749; John Holland b. 24 July 1752; William Stevenson b.
28 December 1754; Mary b. 20 August 1757; Joshua b. 6 July
1759; children of William BARNEY & Frances Holland, his wife.
Elizabeth b. 1 April 1761 d/o William & Charity WILLIAMS.
Susanah b. 3 September 1756 d/o Edmond & Rebecca TALBOT.   {H-110}
Charllotte MC KINSIE d/o Anne MC KINSIE b. 23 March 1761.
Mary b. 2 June 1751 d/o William & Hannah THACKHAM.
Mary b. 6 February 1761 d/o Zachariah & Sarah MC CUBBIN.
Elizabeth b. 28 February 1757 d/o Edward & Ruth SWEETING.
Edward b. 29 July 1755; Daniel b. 31 December 1757; Thomas b. 4
March 1760; s/o Thomas & Nancy SMITH.
Jemima b. 10 January 1761 d/o Henry & Jane STEVENSON.
Ezekiel b. 16 March 1757; Joshua b. 16 March 1757; s/o Elizabeth
STORY.   {R-I-59}
Cathrine b. 4 July 1754; Sarah b. 20 October 1756; Nathaniel b.
10 March 1759; children of Tobias Jr. & Blanche STANSBURY.
Anne b. 19 September 1761 d/o Edward & Ruth LEWIS.   {H-111}
Nicholas b. 14 January 1761 s/o James & Mary BRYAN.
Elizabeth b. 28 April 1754; Eleanor b. 19 November 1755; Frances
b. 14 December 1757; Mary b. 20 November 1759; d/o John Jr. &
Eleanor ENSOR.
William b. 11 September 1761 s/o Thomas & Hannah STANSBURY.
Casandra b. 13 April 1761 d/o Richardson & Mary STANSBURY.
William b. 22 October 1761 s/o Robert & Elizabeth SWEETING.
Susannah b. 24 August 1761 d/o William & Margret ENGLE.
Robert b. 7 September 1757; Rosanna (or Mary) b. 8 October 1761;
children of Alexander & Mary GILCOAT.
Flora b. 24 December 1758 d/o Nathan & Rebecca PERIGO.
John b. 13 July 1746 s/o James & Elizabeth SLAYMAKER.   {H-112}
Mary b. 12 July 1754; James b. 1 October 1759; Joseph b. 23 March
1761; children of Joseph & Elizabeth BANKSON.
Jeremiah Townley b. 23 May 1748 s/o Richard & Catharine CHASE.
Anna b. 9 September 1762 d/o Robert & Catharine MANLEY.   {R-I-60}
Hannah b. 20 January 1762 d/o Richard & Rebecca CARTER.
Charles Ridgely s/o John & Achsa CARNAN of this Parish &
Grandson of Charles & Prudence CARNAN of Reading in the County
of Berks in England, b. 6 December 1760, Christened 2 August
1761. John CARNAN & Daniel CHAMIER Jr. proxys for Thomas DICK
& Charles RIDGELY Jr. Godfathers & Francis CHASE & Elizabeth
GOODWIN Godmothers.
Mary b. 26 July 1762 d/o John & Elizabeth WOODWARD.
Esther b. 21 May 1762 d/o William & Margret JESSOP.
Ann b. 4 April 1762 d/o William & Sarah HODGES.
John b. 7 December 1762 s/o Edward & Mary MORRIS.   {H-113}
William b. 30 September 1762 s/o Samuel & Mary SEEDS.
Mary Elizabeth b. 31 March 1762 d/o Philip & Catharine BARNHOUSE.
Margarett b. 7 December 1762 d/o James & Rebecca KELSO.
Elizabeth b. 19 July 1763 d/o Jacob & Sarah LEBE.
Eleaner b. 3 June 1763 d/o John & Margaret GARDNER.
Hannah b. 2 March 1763 d/o John & Elizabeth SIMPSON.
Sarah b. 25 May 1763 d/o Francis & Baley RIDER.
John b. 28 May 1763 s/o William & Mary BENNETT.
Margarett b. 13 August 1763 d/o Septimus & Ruth NOEL.
William Horatio BULL s/o Constantine BULL of the Parish of St.
Georges Lombland in the City of Norwich in the County of
Norfolk in England & Catherine his wife of Dalton in Yorkshire
(whose Maiden name was WALKER) was b. 20 May 1764 & baptized 1
July 1764.   {R-I-61}

Elizabeth Margaret HICK d/o William HICK of Aeaster Selby in the Ainsty of the City of York in Yorkshire & Ann HICK of the City of Worcester in England (whose Maiden name was LOWE) was b. 21 January 1764. {H-114}

Ann CHASE d/o the Rev. Mr. Thomas CHASE, Rector & Ann his wife b. 21 August 1764 & Christened 6 September 1764.

Moses b. 17 November 1747 s/o Richard & Sophia RUTTER.

John b. 15 December 1760 s/o John & Esther JONES.

Susanna b. 22 June 1764 d/o George Ernst & Susanna Catharine LINDENBERGINN.

Catharine b. 20 October 1764 d/o William & Catharine HOFFMONON.

Rebecca b. 15 March 1763; Richard b. 28 January 1765; children of John & Ellin MOALE.

Rachel b. 14 June 1765 d/o Joseph & Chloe TURNER. {H-115}

Thomas b. 11 December 1765 s/o Rev. Thomas & Ann CHASE.

John b. 8 December 1761 s/o John & Mary GERMON. {R-I-62}

Sarah b. 27 March 1766 d/o Samuel & Elizabeth SYNDAL.

Alexander b. 27 January 1766 s/o James & Temperance MAIDWELL.

Abraham b. 18 March 1766 s/o William & Margarett JESSUP.

Mary b. 18 September 1765 d/o Edward & Sarah TEEL.

John b. 18 October 1764 s/o Samuel & Sarah BOWEN.

Greenbury b. 15 August 1762 s/o Abraham & Elizabeth GREEN.

John b. 7 January 1766 s/o Richard & Sarah ACTON.

Ann b. 18 January 1766 d/o John & Ann SHECKLE.

William b. 16 February 1766 s/o Esther & William HAMMOND.

Mary b. 29 December 1765 d/o John & Margarett GARDNER. {H-116}

Shadrick b. 11 February 1766 s/o John & Rachel CRADOCK.

Joshua b. 30 March 1766 s/o John & Elizabeth BOREING.

William b. 8 December 1765 s/o John & Martha BROWN.

George b. 6 December 1765 s/o George & Ann CHARD. {R-I-63}

Elizabeth b. 26 November 1765 d/o James & Mary GALLOWAY.

Thomas Evrett Royal b. 2 December 1765 s/o Richard & Jane ROGERS.

William b. 13 September 1765; Eleanor b. 3 June 1764; s/o & d/o Benjamin & Ann ROGERS.

Charles b. 26 December 1760; Ephraim b. 25 November 1762; s/o William & Lusandy (Lusindy) EDWARDS.

Thomas b. 22 April 1767 s/o Thomas & Ariana SOLLERS.

Elizabeth b. 8 September 1767 d/o Rev. Thomas & Ann CHASE.

Ann b. 19 September 1762; Elizabeth Waugh b. 14 May 1764; d/o Thomas & Elizabeth JONES (in Patapsco Neck). {R-I-64}

John b. 4 November 1764 s/o Robert & Catharine MANLY.

Hnriatta [sic] Maria b. 4 April 1766 d/o Thomas & Elizabeth JONES (in Patapsco Neck). {H-118}

Dorothy b. 18 February 1762; George b. 19 September 1763; Alexander Pitt b. 5 June 1765; Andrew b. 29 July 1766; children of Andrew & Susannah BUCHANAN.

William b. 30 June 1767 s/o Robert & Catharine MANLY.

Eliz Burgis b. 25 February 1765; Susannah b. 1 February 1767; d/o Benjamin & Margret LELSON. {R-I-65}

Mary b. 11 March 1766; Rebecca b. 16 November 1767; d/o Abraham & Rebecca CAZIER.

Elizabeth b. 8 June 1765; William b. 6 June 1767; children of Britingham & Catharine DICKINSON. {H-119}

John b. 11 August 1765; Rebecca b. 23 April 1767; children of John & Mary LEES.

Elenor b. 17 --- 1766 d/o John & Sarah ADDAIR.

Sarah b. 1 September 1767 d/o Daniel & Rachel BROOKE.

Henry b. 9 October 1767 s/o William & Sarah HODGES.

James b. 13 September 1767 s/o James & Elizabeth CALDWELL.

James b. 19 October 1766 s/o Robert & Catharine MATHEWS. {R-I-66}
Cecilius b. 29 December 1767 s/o John & Sarah CALVERT.   {H-120}
Charles b. 8 June 1768 s/o Elias & Pleasance BARNABY.
Elizabeth b. 15 September 1766 d/o Charles & Pleasance BARNABY.
Eleanor b. 14 May 1767 d/o Luke & Susanna TROTTON.
Ann b. 28 April 1768 d/o John & Susannah CHRISTOPHER.
Andrew b. 20 September 1762; Elizabeth b. 7 April 1764; children
   of Charles Frederick & Elizabeth WIESENTHAL.
Thomas Waters b. 15 April 1767 s/o Benjamin & Rachel GRIFFITH.
Deborah b. 23 June 1768 d/o John & Rebecca PERIGO.   {H-121}
Thomas b. 4 May 1766; John b. 21 July 1768; s/o Charles &
   Elizabeth STANSBURY.   {R-I-67}
Catherine Rogers b. 9 September 1768 d/o Addison & Sarah SMITH.
Martha b. 25 March 1768 d/o George & Hannah CHILDS.
Mark Alexander b. 25 May 1766; Rebecca b. 31 May 1768; s/o & d/o
   James & Mary COX.
Absalom b. 21 August 1757; Elizabeth b. 2 January 1760; William
   b. 29 January 1762; Elenor b. 2 February 1764; Greenberry b. 14
   February 1766; Thomas b. 26 March 1768; children of William &
   Elenor JOHNSON.   {R-I-68}
Richard b. 14 November 1768 s/o John & Martha MAYBURY.
Joshua b. 22 March 1761 s/o John & Ruth MURRAY.
John b. 26 January 1764; Ruth b. 10 September 1767; s/o & d/o
   Joshua & Ruth MURRAY.
Margaret b. 22 July 1768 d/o John & Margaret GARDNER.   {H-123}
Elizabeth b. 19 September 1768 d/o Samuel & Mary ARROWSMITH.
Joseph Few b. 28 May 1769 s/o John & Margaret HOOPER.
Ellin b. 30 September 1768 d/o Thomas & Mary BOND.
Mary Margaret b. 29 September 1766 d/o John & Margaret HOOPER.
Ruth Jane b. 15 May 1769 d/o Samuel & Ruth BUNGEY.   {R-I-69}
Charlotte b. 14 May 1768 d/o Thomas & Anne DEN.
Edward b. 26 October 1769 s/o William & Eve BELL.
George Birch Russell b. 25 January 1770, baptized 8 February
   1770, s/o Rev. Thomas & Ann CHASE.
John b. 8 November 1769 s/o Samuel & Susanna CROSS.
George b. 23 April 1770 s/o John & Sarah Elizabeth LEE. {H-124}
John DAY b. 26 June 1770 s/o John & Mary DAY; grandson of Stephen
   DAY of Baconsields in Buckingshire in England.
Richard b. in Philadelphia 3 May 1766; Elizabeth b. 5 July 1769
   in Baltimore; William b. 11 Nov. 1770 in Baltimore, children of
   William & Mary SPENCER.
Rebecca b. 11 September 1770 d/o John & Barbara WILKINSON.
(The above 4 entries registered 14 January 1771 per William
   SPENCER, Regr.)
Eleanor b. 18 February 1771 d/o Andrew & Sarah WHITE.   {R-I-70}
William Monk b. 24 June 1770 s/o William & Sarah O'BRIAN.
Barnabas b. 13 January 1760; Mary b. 20 January 1765; s/o & d/o
   Miles & Hannah LOVE.   {H-125}
(The above four entries registered 6 April 1771 per William
   SPENCER, Regr.)
Thomas b. 2 September 1770 s/o Richard & Sarah STANSBURY.
George b. 18 April 1771 s/o George & Mary STANSBURY.
(Above 2 entries registered 2 May 1771 per William SPENCER, Reg.)
Campbell b. 1 January 1771 (reg'd. 10 June 1771) s/o John & Ann
   CANNON.
Anna b. 25 April 1768; Mary b. 30 July 1771; d/o Richard ALLEN &
   his wife.
Christopher HANSON b. 17 October 1759.
Mary b. 16 March 1755 d/o Benjamin & Elizabeth JERVIS.

24

John Thomas b. 2 January 1762 s/o Thomas & Ruth HOLLAND. {R-I-71}
William b. 6 March 1772 s/o Thomas & Ann DEN (DOW?).   {H-126}
William b. 17 October 1768; Elizabeth b. 12 September 1770; s/o &
   d/o James & Mary SEDDON.
Rachel b. 8 January 1772 d/o Cealidge & Ann BARTON.
William Bowen b. 14 April 1772 s/o Edmond & Kathrine EASTON.
William b. 29 March 1772 s/o Thomas & Mary HODGES.
James b. 20 October 1745 s/o John & Margret SEDDON.
Lloyd b. 19 October 1768 & departed 18 April 1769; Elizabeth b. 5
   September 1770; Archibald b. 22 September 1772; children of
   Andrew & Susannah BUCHANAN.
William b. 6 March 1772 s/o Thomas & Ann DEW (DEN?).
William b. 17 October 1772; Elizabeth b. 12 September 1770; s/o &
   d/o James & Mary SEDDON.   {H-127}
Rachel b. 8 January 1772 d/o Cealidge & Ann BARTON.
William Bowen b. 14 April 1772 s/o Thomas & Catharine EASTON.
William b. 29 March 1772 s/o Thomas & Mary HODGES.   {R-I-72}
Ann b. 8 February 1772 d/o William & Flora BOSWELL.
Daniel b. 13 February 1772 s/o John & Ann MC CLURE.
William Denniferd b. 8 March 1771 s/o William & Elizabeth FINN.
Patrick b. 2 December 1768 s/o Thomas & Bridget FORD.
Elijah b. 21 August 1768 s/o Joseph & Elizabeth JOICE.
Samuel b. 22 February 1772 s/o Samuel & Elizabeth BALL.
William b. 6 April 1744; Richard b. 1 September 1746; s/o William
   & Sarah BELL.
George b. 2 April 1770; William b. 6 March 1772; s/o William Jr.
   & Eve BELL.   {H-128}
Lydia b. 11 March 1755; Rachel b. 17 January 1752; Nicholas b. 7
   June 1757; children of Lancelot Sr. & Rachel TODD.
Elizabeth b. 13 March 1772 d/o David & Achsah WALTEEN (WALEEW?).
Joseph b. 17 June 1772 s/o Richard & Sarah STANSBURY.   {R-I-73}
George Gilpin b. 29 August 1759 in Cecil County, baptized 7
   October 1772 by Rev. Thomas CHASE, Rector of St. Paul's
   Parish in Baltimore County, MD, s/o Isaac & Mary GUEST.
Sarah b. 2 February 1772 s/o John & Rebecca PERIGO.
Sarah b. 14 March 1772 d/o --- & Sarah BARTON, his wife.
Nicholas b. 6 January 1771 s/o Benjamin & Rebecca BAXTER.
Sarah b. 17 September 1770 d/o Daniel & Rachel DAVY.   {H-129}
Thomas b. 3 February 1772 s/o Aquila & Elizabeth SERJEANT.
Benjamin b. 17 October 1770; William b. 2 January 1772; s/o
   George & Hannah CHILDS.
Rachel b. 3 January 1772 d/o Richard & Rebecca COALE.
Elizabeth b. 17 September 1771 d/o Nathan & Sophia WRIGHT.
Elizabeth b. 19 August 1772 d/o William & Orpha MARSHALL.
William b. 14 June 1772 s/o Joseph & Eleanor CAPBLE.
Elizabeth b. 1 April 1772 d/o Nicholas & Mary GRIMES.   {R-I-74}
Sarah b. 16 August 1772 d/o James & Mary SEDDON.
Prudence b. 3 May 1772 d/o Henry & Elizabeth PENNY.
Susanna b. 9 October 1771 d/o James & Susanna CHAMBERS.
John b. 29 December 1772 s/o William & Catharine STACEY.
Sophia b. 2 August 1772, baptized by Rev. Thomas CHASE, Rector of
   St. Paul's Parish in Baltimore County, MD, 15 August 1772, d/o
   Harry Dorsey & Prudence GOUGH.   {H-130}
John b. 4 November 1767; Elizabeth b. 1 June 1772; s/o & d/o
   William & Susanna HUNT.
George William b. 9 October 1769; s/o Thomas & Mary Sophia
   MARSHALL.
Mary Sophia d/o William (?) MARSHALL b. 18 December 1771.

Alexander b. 30 October 1766; Christian (dau.) b. 6 May 1769; children of Henry & Elizabeth PENNY.

Francis Norton b. 2 January 1773 s/o John & Ann FRISBY. {R-I-75}

John b. 18 September 1772 s/o Thomas & Catharine GOLDSMITH.

Mary b. 17 January 1773 d/o Barney & Catharine RAU. {H-131}

John b. 25 December 1770 s/o Francis & Alice SMITH.

Elizabeth b. 1 April 1772 d/o Notley & Mary GRIMES.

Rachel b. 13 November 1763 d/o Joshua & Hannah DEMITT.

Mary b. in 1772 d/o William & Mary PULLEN.

George Crispin b. 2 January 1769 s/o Joseph Hamilton & Rachel DOUGLASS.

Hannah b. 12 February 1773 d/o Richard & Rosanna HILL.

Elizabeth b. 16 October 1771 d/o Rezin & Elizabeth GRIMES.

Thomas b. 9 January 1773 s/o Thomas & Mary ROBINSON.

Penelope b. 17 April 1772 d/o Henry & Mary ARBACK.

John b. 29 November 1772 s/o Richard & Mary WILLIAMS.

Elizabeth b. 24 March 1773 d/o John & Elizabeth WALKER.

John b. 3 April 1773 s/o John & Easter GARDENER. {H-132}

Richard b. 9 February 1773 s/o William & Dorothy KING.

Richard Hugh b. 12 September 1771, baptized 31 May 1773, s/o John & Margrate HOOPER.

Edward b. 2 March 1773 s/o Josiah & Jemima PENINGTON.

Darrel b. 3 October 1772; Ealner b. 12 November; s/o & d/o Thomas & Hannah READING.

Mary b. -- January 1772 d/o James & Temprance MEADWELL. {R-I-76}

Thomas Wells b. 8 August 1772 s/o Jonathan JOYCE.

Nathaniel b. 19 March 1773 s/o Christian & Elizabeth DAVIS.

Ann b. 2 April 1773, baptized 20 June 1773, d/o John & Duret GRAVES.

Thomas b. 10 June 1773 at 1/2 past 6 PM s/o James & Mary CHRISTE.

Danel b. 8 October 1772 s/o Danel & Sarah STAINSBUAREY.

Joshua b. 15 December 1771 s/o Robert & Sarah LYNCH. {H-133}

Sarah b. 3 April 1773 d/o John & Cathrein READ.

Nickloss b. 26 July 1773 s/o John & Susannah CHRISTOPHER.

Action b. 8 July 1773; George b. 30 May 1771; d/o & s/o George & Elizabeth SANK.

Elizabeth b. 24 July 1773 d/o Thomas & Celices PLACE.

Patrick Read b. 22 April 1773 s/o Elizabeth ANDREWS, wife of William ANDREWS then deceased.

Sarah b. 1 November 1772 d/o Joseph & Ruth HILL.

Sarah b. 1 October 1771; Ann b. 27 March 1773; d/o William & Sarah WRIGHT.

Darcous b. 3 March 1773 d/o Robert & Mary FITCH.

John Donford b. 2 November 1764 s/o William & Elizabeth FINN.

Frances b. 20 May 1772 d/o John & Margrete MARTEN. {R-I-77}

George b. --- s/o Joel & Mary HICKINGBOTTOM. {H-134}

Henry b. 20 June 1772 s/o John & Tabaitha HUGHS.

Richard Diver b. 20 August 1772 s/o Abraham EGELSTONE.

Samuel b. 19 July 1773 s/o Samuell & Cloe SMITH.

John b. 26 September 1771 s/o Luke & Susanah TROUGHTON.

James b. 10 May 1771 s/o Mary COLLERS.

Margrate b. 6 July 1773 d/o Alexander & Mary WALKER.

Rebekah b. 11 August 1773 d/o Thomas & Ann BURGAN.

Sarah b. 6 August 1773 d/o Thomas & Margret SUMMERS.

Samuel b. 26 August 1772 s/o James & Mary STOKES.

Gratvill (Grabill?) b. 13 December 1772 s/o Adam & Sarah CORNER.

William b. 12 October 1773 s/o James & Ann DAGG.

Richard Thomas b. 19 November 1773 s/o John & Mary DAY. {H-135}

Thomas b. 4 December 1773 s/o William & Ann WILKISON.

Ann b. 1 December 1772 d/o Zarack & Comfort GRAY.
Elizabeth b. 5 December 1772 d/o James & Sarah FOX.
Samuel b. 26 July 1773 s/o John & Maria SPARKS.
George b. 25 January 1774 s/o Ann SMITH.
William b. 6 January 1774 s/o John & Mary PATERSON.
Thomas b. 1 January 1774 s/o Henry & Elonor WRIGHT.
Thomas b. 21 September 1773 s/o James & Elizabeth LEGETT.
Roseana b. 11 October 1773 d/o William & Cathreen HARRIS.
Elizabeth b. 10 November 1767 d/o Mary WARD.   {R-I-78}
Joshua b. 13 January 1775 s/o Josias & Jemima PENNINGTON.
James b. 30 May 1776 s/o James & Sarah WOOLFE.   {H-136}
Ann b. 28 July 1774 d/o Sarah ISRAELO.
Elizabeth b. 22 January 1777 d/o John & Sarah PARISH.
Ann b. 14 February 1775 d/o John & Elizabeth WILLIAMS.
William b. 30 August 1774 s/o William & Elizabeth BARKER.
Agnes b. 12 September 1774 d/o William & Agnes YOUNG.
Ann b. 4 October 1774 d/o Richard & Mary WILLIAMS.
Ann b. 5 October 1774 d/o William & Mary PULLEN.
John b. 5 October 1774 s/o George & Susanna SHELLY.
Stephen b. 9 January 1773 s/o William & Mary SPENCER.
Florence b. 23 June 1775 s/o [sic] Daniel & Anne KEITH.
Martha b. 12 March 1775 d/o Rezin & Elizabeth GRIMES.
Richard b. 30 March 1774 s/o William & Eve BELL.   {H-137}
Jane b. 3 October 1775 d/o Edmund & Keziah STANSBURY.
William Pulteney b. 5 December 1774 s/o Thomas & Susanna LOGAN.
Joshua b. 16 August 1775 s/o Christian & Elizabeth DAVIS.
Susanna b. 23 July 1774 d/o John & Catharine BELL.   {R-I-79}
John b. 2 October 1774 s/o James & Mary SEDDON.
Thomas b. 4 April 1776 s/o John & Ann CLAY.
Mary b. 19 June 1776 d/o Job & Christian GREENE.
William b. 6 May 1776 s/o William & Elizabeth SMITH.
Benjamin b. 29 December 1775; Richard b. 25 March 1762; Thomas b.
    27 February 1761; John b. 9 July 1769; s/o Richard & Mary
    FOWLER.   {H-138}
William b. 16 January 1776 s/o James & Ruth EDWARDS.
Job b. 22 April 1776 s/o Samuel & Chloe SMITH.
Cecilia b. 12 November 1775 d/o Thomas & Margaret CONNOLLY.
John b. 1 August 1776 s/o John & Elizabeth WILLIAMS.
Frances b. 28 August 1776 d/o Richard & Mary COUGHLAN.
Elijah b. 15 November 1776; James b. 28 June 1764; Ann b. 25
    April 1767; children of John & Susanna CHRISTOPHER.
John b. 19 January 1777 s/o John & Margaret HEWLETT.
Mary b. 25 March 1777 d/o Henry & Ruth CLAY.
David b. 23 April 1777 s/o John & Jane HALL.   {R-I-80}
Mary b. 10 December 1776 d/o James & Mary SEDDON.   {H-139}
Sarah b. 6 April 1777 d/o Thomas & Elizabeth HIGNOTT.
Mary Ann b. 26 August 1777 d/o Thomas & Margaret CONNELLY.
Morgan b. 11 September 1777 born in Baltimore Town & baptized by
    Rev. CHASE, s/o Francis & Elizabeth LEWIS, late of New York.
Thomas b. 5 January 1777 s/o Thomas & Susanna LOGAN.
John b. 1 January 1774, christened 30 August 1778; Sophia b. 5
    August 1778; christened 30 August 1778; s/o & d/o John &
    Catherine TAYLOR.
Susanna Maria b. 2 October 1773 in the City of Annapolis at 9:30
    a.m., d/o William & Mary JACOB.
Rinaldo William b. 12 June 1776, baptized 30 August 1778; s/o
    William & Mary JACOB.   {H-140}
Catherine b. Baltimore Town 21 December 1777 d/o James & Jane
    SMITH.

Elenor b. 4 January 1778 d/o Daniel & Marh CALLEGAN.

Charles b. 13 January 1778 at Baltimore Town s/o Charles & Ann REILEY.

Henry b. 7 January 1778 in Baltimore Town s/o Henry & Hannah LAWRENCE.   {R-I-81}

Leonora b. 27 July 1778 in Baltimore Town, Monday between 4 & 5 a.m., baptized by Rev. CHASE 6 September 1778, d/o John & Martha MORRISSON.

Ann b. 10 October 1778 (registered 8 October 1778?) d/o Ambrose & Barbara CLARK.

Catherine b. 28 June 1777 d/o John & Ann BILSON (registered 8th October 1778).

John b. 17 August 1778 Fells Point, Baltimore Town s/o John & Priscilla BARNARD.   {H-141}

Jacob Robert b. 24 January 1778 s/o Thomas & Mary CONSTABLE.

Elizbeth b. 8 January 1778 in Baltimore County d/o James & Isabella ROSS.

Anna b. about 24 December 1777 d/o Thomas & Jinet GIBBONS.

Charlotte b. 13 March 1778 in Baltimore Town d/o Lewis & Elizabeth LEVENEAU.

John b. 16 June 1776 in Baltimore County s/o Arthur & Rebecca DUN.

John b. Saturday 18 April 1778, 11 p.m. in Baltimore Town & christened 14 May 1778, s/o Job & Christian GREENE.

Elizabeth b. 12 August 1774 in Annapolis, Ann Arundel County, christened 14 June 1778, d/o Bright & Eleanor SULLIVAN.

Alexander b. in Baltimore Town 7 June 1775, christened 14 June 1778, s/o Benjamin & Elizabeth JAMES.

John Jeremiah b. 20 October 1778 in Baltimore Town about 2 p.m., s/o William & Mary JACOB.

Samuel b. 10 July 1779 s/o Philip & Elizabeth SIDNAL.   {H-142}

Margaretta Clara b. 22 June 1779, baptized 6 December 1779 d/o Charles & Margaret CARROLL.   {R-I-82}

Elizabeth b. 21 April 1781 d/o Christopher & Peggy HUGHES.

John Ensor b. 20 February 1781, baptized by Rev. William WEST 19 September 1781; s/o Nicholas Jr. & Deborah MERRYMAN.

Eleanor Addison b. 14 November 1766; Catherine Rogers b. 9 September 1768; Rebecca b. 4 June 1770; Richard b. 26 March 1772; William Rogers b. 21 November 1774; children of John Addison & Sarah SMITH.

John MERRYMAN b. 3 November 1778; Benjamin Rogers b. 27 October 1780; Anne b. 8 November 1782; s/o & d/o John & Sarah (formerly wife of John Addison SMITH) MERRYMAN.   {H-143}

John Lawless b. 1 March 1784; James b. 1 June 1779; s/o Thomas & Catherine JAFFREY.

Elizabeth b. 17 October 1784; John b. 14 December 1785; d/o & s/o John E. & Frances GIST.   {R-I-83}

Ann b. 9 November 1786, baptized 11 April 1787; Elizabeth b. 15 August 1784; d/o John & Mary MILLER.   {H-144}

Thomas b. 22 September 1766; William North b. 1 November 1768; Robert b. 10 October 1769; Robert North b. 22 January 1771; Samuel b. 4 January 1773; Rachel b. 5 February 1775; Frances b. 10 February 1777; William b. 14 January 1779; George Washington b. 19 January 1780; Randle Huls b. 26 January 1782; Mary North b. 5 September 1783; s/o & d/o John & Ellin MOALE.   {R-I-84}

Ann b. 25 August 1781; Frances Moale b. 6 October 1782; John Moale b. 5 March 1784; Alexander b. 6 December 1786; Thomas b. 23 October 1789; children of Thomas & Rebecca RUSSEL.   {H-145}

28

William b. 14 August 1763; Thomas b. 3 September 1764; John b. 9
February 1769; children of William & Elizabeth ASQUITH.
Edward b. 11 December 1778; Elizabeth b. 25 February 1780;
children of William & Tabitha ASQUITH.

MARRIAGES - ST. PAUL'S PARISH

Thomas WAINEWRIGHT m. Pleasance DORSEY 30 November 1722-L.{H-146}
Richard MARCHENT m. Mary SWEETING 28 July 1723. B   {R-I-97}
William CONNEL m. Mary ROBINSON 2 April 1721. B
Matthew TALBOTT m. Mary WILLIAMSON 5 June 1722. B
Benja KNIGHT m. Jane MERRIMAN 6 August 1723. B
Thomas HOWARD m. Cathrine JOHNSON 4 July 1723. L
Samuell DURBIN m. Ann LOGDEN 4 July 1723. B
Philip JONES m. Jemimah EAGER (widow) 29 May 1723. L
Jacob ROWLES m. Anne LYNCH 27 January 1723. L
Edward WATTS m. Mary MORGAN (widow) 18 February 1721. B
Nathaniel DARBY m. Elizabeth DEMITT (widow) 10 April 1721. B
Henry PEREGOY m. Amy GREEN 16 February 1716. B   {H-147}
John GOLLOHANN m. Frances PEREGOY 16 February 1723. B
Robert MUNGUMERY m. Alice SMITH (widow) 12 August 1718. B
Jacob PEACOCK m. Honor HARDEN (widow) 26 October 1720. B
Zachariah GRAY m. Mary DEMITT 19 December 1719. B   {R-I-98}
Nicholas GOSTWICK m. Ebarilla YANSTONE -- December 1720.
Thomas GOSTWICK m. Elizabeth YANSTONE -- September 1717.
John GREEN m. Mary SAMPSON -- December 1720.
Samuel HARRIMAN m. Jane SMITH 18 August 1723.
Jacob COX m. Elizabeth MERRIMAN 25 September 1722. L
Joseph CROUCH m. Mary LYNCH 3 January 1719. L
John WHITE m. Mary RENCHER -- -- 1722.
William BUCKNER m. Mrs. Patience COLEGATE 20 September 1724.
Edward RISTONE m. Eleanor NEAL -- February 1723. B
Stephen BODY m. Susannah LONG 3 April 1722. B
Stephen BODY m. Elizabeth ---- 10 February 1728.
Lloyd HARRIS m. Eleoner ROGERS (widow of Nicholas ROGERS) 4 July
   1721. L   {H-148}
Thomas ADDAMS m. Margaret CAMBEL 28 March 1725. B
John PHIPPS m. Mary WITTIS (widow) 28 Xbr 1719. B
Nicholas HALE Jr. m. Ann LONG 25 December 1723.
Patrick LINCH m. Martha BOWEN -- -- 1722.
Richard WHEELER m. Rebeccah --- 31 October 1725. L
Richard HINDON m. Sarah GARDER 8 June 1723.
Thomas HALL & Ann GREEN were married by Mr. George ROSS, Minister
   of the North East Parish, Cecil County, 23 September 1723.
George HARRIMAN & Anne WILKINSON m. 30 March 1725.   {R-I-99}
John MERRIMAN m. Sarah ROGERS 30 December 1725.
Morick MEACK m. Eleanor WARIN 7 August 1726. B
John WOODEN m. Mary GILL 27 January 1716.
Simon WARD m. Margaret LOBB, widow of Joseph LOBB, 3 7br 1723.
Edward TURBELL m. Sarah GAY 10 April 1727. B
John EDWARDS m. Mary MERREMAN 23 January 1727. B
Jacob BELL m. Elisabeth ROWLES 18 February 1727. B   {H-149}
Jacob ROWLES m. Constance SAMPSON 4 January 1727. B
Samuel HARRYMAN m. Comfort TAYLOR 3 June 1728. B
Robert GARDNER m. Mary ANGLEING 5 January 1728. B
William SMITH m. Eilce SMITH 22 May 1729. B
William GREEN m. Hannah HAILE 21 August 1729. B

B = Banns   L = License

Edward GWYN m. Easter FFEILD 15 November 1728. B
George WALKER m. Mary HANSON 14 November 1728. L
Soloman HILLEN m. Elizabeth RAVEN 7 October 1729. L
William MAINER m. Martha TUCKER 14 December 1729.
Jonathan HURST m. Ann GORE 29 December 1729.
John MITCHENDER m. Mary CHANLOR 8 February 1729.
Thomas FRANKLAND m. Ruth WILLMOTT 26 October 1729. L
George GOODWINE m. Anne RUTTER 29 March 1730.
Robert MAXFEILD [sic] m. Margrett JARVISS 1 February 1728.
James THOMPSON m. Sarah MILLER 28 June 1730.
Joseph CROSS m. Elisabeth MERRYMAN 13 September 1730.
Richard FOWLER m. Honour LOGSDON 13 September 1730.
Thomas PARKER m. Anne CRAIN 13 September 1730.
Jonathan ROBERTS m. Johanna THOMAS 13 September 1730.
Peter MAJOR m. Mary SLIDER 27 October 1730.
Thomas PILLES m. Margrett FINEX -- September 1730.   {R-I-100}
Partrick [sic] KELLE m. Mary MASH (no date).
Edward MUNGER m. Mary SINGDALL 28 July 1730.
Selah BARTON m. Rebecca BEDDESON 27 December 1730.
John BROWN m. Anne TURNER 29 November 1730.   {H-150}
William SINKLEN m. Mary HINES 26 November 1730.
James BOSLINE b. Elizabeth PARISH 26 November 1730.
John GOLDSMITH m. Elinor HAMBLETON 28 October 1730.
John COLE m. Mary CHARFINCH 25 December 1730.
Thomas LAX m. Martha PORTER 20 December 1730.
Abraham EAGLESTONE m. Charity JOHNES 20 December 1730.
Charles MARRYMAN m. Milleson HAILE 2 February 1730.
William GAIN m. Rebecca HARKENS 1 August 1727.
Alexander GRANT m. Elisabeth COLE 16 February 1730.
Thomas BOREING m. Mary HAILE 21 January 1730.
Samuel OWINGS m. Urath RANDALL 1 January 1730.
Robert OWINGS m. Hannah FORQUER 23 December 1730.
John BERRY m. Susannah LEE 11 July 1731.
John MILLER m. Mary GAIN 11 February 1725.
Thomas HUGHS m. Catherine DENICE 5 December 1731.
Robert SWEETING m. Sarah LAINE 5 December 1731.
John EVENS m. Catharine COOK 19 December 1731.
Thomas GREEN m. Elisabeth CARTER 11 August 1732.
Benjamin PRICE m. Elisabeth HEWETT 22 June 1730.
Henry YOSTAIN m. Jane RIDER 24 January 1730.
Samuel SMITH m. Elisabeth COX 3 September 1727.
Edward SWEETTING m. Mary WATTS 21 December 1732. L
Jonas HEWLING m. Ann BOWEN 20 December 1732. L
Daniel RAGON m. Sarah LEWIS 26 December 1732.
John SERGANT m. Elisabeth GOSSTWICK 4 February 1732.
Robert FROST m. Francies TYE -- February 1732.
John OSBURN m. Mary SULLIVAN 24 December 1732.
Joseph THOMAS m. Darkes SUTTON 4 February 1732.
George ELLIOTT m. Patience BUCKNER 12 January 1732. L   {H-151}
James DIMMETT m. Barbary BROAD 27 March 1733.
Paul YOUNG m. Rosehannah MASH 20 May 1733.
Philip JONES m. Ann RATTENBARY d/o Dr. John & Margarett 2 October
1727.
Daniel WARD m. Ann BOYED 27 May 1733.
Jonathan HANSON m. Sarah SPICER 12 June 1733.
John HAWKINS m. Mary SIMKINS 12 June 1733.
John STENCHCOME m. Katherine MACCLEANE 23 July 1733. L   {R-I-101}

B = Banns   L = License

30

John THORNBURY m. Elizabeth STONE 7 August 1733. L
John HARRISON m. Johannah MORRIS 4 September 1733.
George ARNOLD m. ---- TUMBLETON 2 September 1733.
William JOHNSON m. Mary Ann POALING 22 September 1733.
John DARBY m. Ailce(?) GAY 3 December 1733.
Edward THOMAS m. Sarah HERBERT 17 December 1733.
John PARRISH m. Elizabeth THOMAS 2 January 1733.
John BOARD m. Jemina HENDERSON 13 January 1733.
Richard PINKHAM m. Phillis NOBLE 26 November 1733.
Nathaniel YOUNG m. Ann BUTTLER 25 December 1733.
James RAMSEY m. Elizabeth MILAM 3 January 1733.
John MACKLANE m. Margett TAYLOR 14 January 1733.
Nathaniel STINCHCOMB m. Patience ROWLS 15 January 1733.
John REAGAN m. Mary MORRICE 21 January 1733.
Robert HARRYMAN m. Elizabeth SIMKINS 24 January 1733.
Selah BARTON m. Comfort ROBERTS 24 January 1733.
William FELL m. Sarah BOND 8 January 1732, by the Rev. Mr.
  COTHERNE, Minister at Joppa.
William RAWLINGS m. Elizabeth GREEN 28 April 1734.
Thomas PRICE m. Keturah MERRYMAN 1 July 1732 by Rev. Wm. TIBBS.
Thomas SLIGH m. Sophia WILKISSON 17 April 1734. L   {H-152}
Richard SAMPSON m. Ann EMPEY 15 May 1734.
Christopher TREAGLE m. Mary ROWLES 27 May 1734.
Thomas BYWATERS m. Eddy WOOD 2 June 1734.
William KIBBLE m. Mary PLOWRIGHT -- March 1734. L
John BAKER m. Mary HILLIARD 16 April 1734.
Laurance HAMMOND m. Ebarilla SIMPKINS 21 June 1734. L
Richard BOND m. Mary JONES 5 August 1731.
James BOREING m. Rebekah GAIN, widow 5 August 1734.
Isaac CHAPMAN m. Mary FITCHPATERICK 27 October 1734.
William HALL m. Mary MERRYMAN 17 December 1734.
William WILEY m. Margrett SING 23 December 1734.
William WORTHINGTON m. Hannah CROMWELL 30 June 1734. L
John SHAW m. Frances BOYS 2 July 1734.
John Martin CARBACK m. Frances MAHORN 14 July 1734.
Capt. George URIEL m. Elliner WELCH 24 July 1734. L
William NEWMAN m. Mary GAIN 25 July 1734.
John GLASSINGTON m. Mary JORDAN 1 August 1734.
Henry SMITH m. Katherine ORGAN 24 September 1734.
John GILES m. Sarah BUTTERWORTH 16 October 1734. L
Joshua DORSEY m. Flora FITSIMMONDS 3 November 1734.   {R-I-102}
Isaac BENNETT m. Eliz. KERSEY 5 November 1734.
Simon THOMPSON m. Savory LETT (negroes) 10 November 1734.
Edward ORSLER m. Ruth OWENS 21 November 1734.
Edward ABBETS m. Katherine WORTON 24 November 1734.
William BROOKS m. Sarah JONES 10 December 1734.
Bazaliel FOSTER m. Mary MEAD 24 December 1734. L
Emmanuel TEALE m. Katherine JOHNSON 24 December 1734.   {H-153}
Thomas DIMMETT m. Sophia STANSBURY 26 December 1734.
James COBB m. Ruth ELLEDGE 21 January 1734.
John CARPENTER m. Mary MATTHEWS 27 January 1734.
Mabry ELMS m. Ann PUNTANY 6 February 1734. L
William FLOWERS m. Mary KILLEY 8 February 1734. L
Reece THOMAS m. Martha GRAY 5 January 1734.
John STANSBURY m. Ann ENSOR 12 February 1734.
Thomas BOREING m. Elizabeth WELCH 3 February 1734.
Thomas GIBBONS m. Hannah SHARP 6 April 1735.

B = Banns   L = License

Benjamin HAMMOND m. Margett TALBOTT 6 April 1735. L
James THOMAS m. Mary ADAMS 13 April 1735.
Edward PARRISH m. Elizabeth GILL 3 May 1735.
James SPURR m. Judeth WILLIAMS 26 May 1735.
Timothy HURLEY m. Katherine GAYER 16 February 1734.
Staley DURHAM m. Mary PARLETT 18 February 1734/5.
Thomas WHETTS m. Rachel FLOYD 13 April 1735.
James AVIS m. Mary STEVENS 19 April 1735.
Richard COALE m. Subbiner HAILE 15 May 1735.
Henry STEVENSON m. Jemina MERRYMAN 19 June 1735. L
James BOSTON m. Katherine BANNAKER (negroes) 22 May 1735.
Edward CHOATE m. Elliner SAVAGE 22 May 1735.
William PEARCE m. Mary CRAWFORD 3 June 1735.
Edward DAVIS m. Susannah COPE 4 June 1735.
Thomas GIST m. Susannah COCKEY 2 July 1735. L
Peter BOND m. Susannah BUTTLER 1 August 1735.
William RAWLINS m. Elizabeth GREEN 28 April 1735.   {H-154}
William CARTER m. Ann HAILE 18 September 1735.
William MILLS m. Mary KENT 5 October 1735.
George COALE m. Elizabeth BAKER 26 October 1735.   {R-I-103}
John STEVENSON m. Mary TIPTON 13 November 1735.
Anthony CHAMNIS m. Sarah COALE 24 November 1735.
John SAYTH m. Sarah RICH 15 July 1735.
William MACKUBBIN m. Clara PHIPS 11 August 1735. L
William HAMMOND m. Eliza. RAVEN 26 August 1735. L
James KILLEY m. Prudence LOGSDON 2 September 1735.
Patrick MACKGUGIN m. Elizabeth MACKDANIEL 21 September 1735.
Luke TROTTON m. Elizabeth LENOX 3 October 1735. L
John LOGSDON m. Margrett WOOLLEY 9 October 1735.
George NORTON m. Margrett WRIGHT 7 November 1735.
Anthony CAFFREY m. Johannah HEARN 26 November 1735.
Edward GRACE m. Patience FOSTER 9 December 1735.
William HUGHS m. Hannah BANKSTON 11 December 1735. L
William ROBERTS m. Elliner MAYHAM 11 December 1735.
John TYE m. Presotia HITCHCOCK 11 December 1735.
Robert ELLSOM m. Jane TAYLER 15 December 1735.
Nicholas PEDDICOAT m. Ann JACKS 23 December 1735.
Robert WILKISSON m. Rachel LENOX 8 June 1736.
Thomas SPICER m. Rebeckah MERRYMAN 1 January 1735.
George HAILE m. Elizabeth CHAWFINCH 17 January 1735.
John BAYLEY m. Ann WELCH 19 January 1735.
Thomas COCKRAN m. Mary BARNETT 31 January 1735.
Samuel MEREDITH m. Elizabeth COOK 3 February 1735.
Philip CORDIMAN m. Ann SAMPSON 5 February 1735.   {H-155}
Joshua BULLEVENT m. Mary BUTTLER 7 February 1735.
Joseph PARAGY m. Flora RYDER 17 February 1735.
Hugh JOHNES m. Sarah KEMP 19 February 1735.
William TOWSON m. Ruth GOTT 24 February 1735.
Thomas STANSBURY m. Hannah GORSUCH 2 March 1735.
John GORSUCH m. Mary PRICE 4 March 1735.
John LONG m. Elliner OWENS 8 March 1735.
Paul GARRISSON m. Elizabeth FRAZER 8 March 1735.
Joshua OWINGS m. Mary COCKEY 9 March 1735.
John PLOWMAN m. Sarah CHAMBERS 3 May 1736.   {R-I-104}
Henry SMITH m. Katherine DUNN 3 May 1736.
Thomas BOND m. Phebe THOMAS 9 May 1736.
Arthur DUNN m. Margrett FISHPAW 2 June 1736.

B = Banns   L = License

Thomas KELLY m. Mary MUSHGROVE 4 June 1736.
Robert CONSTABLE m. Judeth COOK 7 June 1736.
Joseph CLUTTERBUCK m. Mary WALKER 7 June 1736.
Thomas LEVERLY m. Elizabeth HENDERSON 7 June 1736.
Richard LOVINGTON m. Martha WARREN 14 June 1736.
George OGG Sr. m. Mary POTEE 22 August 1722.
Edmond HOWARD m. Ruth TEALE 27 February 1728.
William TIPTON m. Tabitha WRIGHT 25 November 1736.
James BOREING m. Martha WHEELER 25 December 1736.
Robert WILKINSON m. Rachel LENORE 8 June 1736.
Thomas HALL m. Sarah MARLER 15 June 1736.
John SIAHS m. Mary CHAMBERS 21 June 1736.
Robert CRAGGHEAD m. Katherine WARD 24 June 1736.
Robert CHAPMAN m. Elizabeth TAYLOR 30 June 1736.
John PILLY m. Mary WHEELY 8 July 1736.
Joseph ARNOLD m. Susannah CHAPMAN 20 July 1736.
Thomas WELLS m. Eliza. HOWARD 16 September 1736.
Robert LOVEPITSTOW m. Ann ROYSTON 23 September 1736.
Thomas WHEELER m. Ann HAWKINS 20 October 1736.
Thomas MATTHEWS m. Elizabeth MATTHEWS 7 November 1736.   {H-156}
Samuel WHITE Jr. m. Sarah WITCHCOAT 1 December 1736.
George ASHMAN m. Jemina MURREY 9 December 1736.
Charles MOTHERBY m. Rebekah NEWMAN 14 December 1736.
John CHINWORTH m. Jane WOOD 16 December 1736.
John Valentine CARBACK m. Mary HARRYMAN 19 December 1736.
John CLAUSY m. Mary SING 29 December 1736.
Suel YOUNG m. Margrett ACTON 13 January 1736.
David DEHAY m. Sarah TILBURY 13 January 1736.
Stepto CLARK m. Elizabeth ANDERSON 8 February 1736.
George COALE m. Ann JONES 20 February 1736.
Joseph SMITH m. Mary MORGAN 11 April 1737.   {R-I-105}
James MASH m. Margrett HARRIS 25 September 1737.
Roger HOLEBROOK m. Mary BOSTON 3 April 1738.
Jeremiah AYERS m. Mary FRANKLIN 2 April 1738.
Richard DEAN m. Elizabeth MARSH 3 January 1739.
William HARRISON m. Elizabeth LANGAM 12 May 1740.
Paul YOUNG m. Mary DAVIS 24 April 1743.
William HAMMOND m. Sarah SHEREDINE 9 March 1739.
Roger RANDALL m. Rachel STEVENS 26 December 1742.
William JESSOP m. Margaret WALKER 25 June 1748.
Nicholas ROGERS m. Henrietta JONES 18 August 1745.
Thomas ROE m. Mary WILLIAMS 15 April 1745.
Philip MASHAM m. Mary NEWMAN 3 June 1745.   {H-157}
Robert WICKINS m. Jemima HOLAWAY 3 June 1745.
Thomas TOMLINSON m. Elizabeth WILKENSON 3 June 1745.
William DARLINGTON m. Ann HIND 4 June 1745.
Abraham SUTTON m. Martha HARROWSMITH 3 July 1745.
John OLIVER m. Alice TWELVES 6 July 1745.
Feiters HARTWAY m. Elizabeth PARNETSON 27 July 1745.
Thorny BUSH m. Elisha PIKE 24 August 1745.
Francis AGHEN m. Lydia PRICE 8 September 1745.
James SLEMAKER m. Elizabeth GILES 15 September 1745.
James BROWN m. Frances CHARTRES 22 September 1745.
Jonathan TIPTON m. Eleanor BRYANT 24 September 1745.
William PONTANEY m. Sarah WOODEN 29 September 1745.
John SEDDON m. Margaret EVANS 3 October 1745.   {H-158}
John RATTENBURY m. Margaret JONES 3 November 1745.   {R-I-106}
Zachariah MACCUBBIN m. Sarah NORWOOD 7 November 1745.
Alexander MC COLLUM m. Elizabeth BEESTON 12 November 1745.

Josiah MARSH m. Sarah BREESET 17 November 1745.
Jonathan KEMP m. Margaret BARNET 2 December 1745.
John MILLER m. Eleanor SMITH 14 December 1745.
Merryman COX m. Honour HALL 26 December 1745.
Abraham TOWSON m. Elizabeth MAHORN 1 January 1745.
Jacob GROSS m. Mary RICHARDS 9 January 1745.
Garret WILSON m. Rosanna SMITH 21 January 1745.
Francis CUTLER m. Eleanor WOODEN 30 January 1745.
Henry WARRILL m. Juliatha SPICER 30 March1746.   {H-159}
Rev. Thomas CRADDOCK m. Katherine RISTEAU 31 March 1746.
Leonard DECAUSSE m. Mary HAWKINS 31 March 1746.
Samuel ORMOND m. Ann LAMBETH 19 May 1746.
Richard CRISWELL m. Mary WOODEN 28 May 1746.
Dennis DUN m. Jane CRUMP 15 June 1746.
Dickson BROWN m. Elizabeth TROTTON 17 June 1746.
John CHAPMAN m. Mary HALL 17 July 1746.
Charles CROXALL m. Rebecca MOALE 23 July 1746.
John GREGORY m. Mary PARLET 27 July 1746.
Jacob ROWLES m. Mary SCARF 28 September 1746.
James SMITH m. Charity LETT 6 October 1746.
Edward NORWOOD m. Mary FITZSIMMONDS 9 November 1746.   {H-160}
John BRADLEY m. Elizabeth JONES 15 December 1746.
Thomas FINLEY m. Althea KIDD 22 July 1747.
Edward WANN m. Prudence MARSH 23 July 1747.
Roebuck LINCH m. Jemima STANSBURY 16 August 1747.   {R-I-107}
Christopher MC EUEN m. Ann WALKER 6 September 1747.
Henry JOHNSON m. Ann BONE 24 September 1747.
Abraham RUTLIDGE m. Penelope RUTLIDGE 13 October 1747.
Thomas WALTON m. Elizabeth WILLIAMS 26 October 1747.
Thomas JOYCE m. Eleanor THORNTON 1 December 1747.
Thomas EDNEY m. Constant PENINGTONE 3 December 1747.
Charles CONNAWAY m. Sophia WOODEN 17 December 1747.
William ARNOLD m. Sarah LEE 26 December 1747.   {H-161}
Thomas PIERCE m. Mary HUMPHRIES 28 December 1747.
Jacob BOND m. Frances PATRIDGE 28 December 1747.
Thomas SMITH m. Mary GOLDSMITH 20 January 1747.
Charles SMITH m. Ann CONNELL 28 January 1747.
John TIPTON m. Martha MURRAY 18 February 1747.
Gilbert MARSH m. Lavina BUCKNAM 20 February 1747.
William HARTEGIN m. Mary SAWELL 9 April 1748.
John ROBESON m. Lucy MURRAY 10 April 1748.
John COLLINS m. Mary HUGHES 10 July 1748.
John PARKS m. Sarah LINCHFIELD 10 September 1748.
John BAYS m. Eleanor HARRYMAN 12 September 1748.
William PAGE m. Esther MILLER 3 October 1748.   {H-162}
William HOUCHINS m. Hannah GWIN 29 November 1748.
Richard CROXALL m. Eleanor BUCHANAN 12 December 1748.
Robert WILMOT m. Sarah MERRYMAN 15 December 1748.
Thomas WHEELER m. Elizabeth HILLEN 21 December 1748.
Zachariah GRAY m. Mary LINCH 22 December 1748.   {R-I-108}
Moses WHEELER m. Katherine GARDNER 23 December 1748.
George LETHERLAND m. Margaret THOMAS 24 December 1748.
Thomas PRESBURY m. Ann WOODWARD 29 December 1748.
John COOK m. Mary PRICE 29 January 1748.
Thomas ROE m. Mary JONES 30 January 1748.
Samuel MEREDITH m. Jemima TAYLOR 2 February 1748.
Richard HOOD m. Mary OXFORD 5 February 1748.   {H-163}
Samuel JONES m. Isabella DOUGLAS 19 February 1748.
Richard HUTCHINSON m. Sarah HARRISON 22 February 1749/50.

Luke TIPTON m. Sarah BOSTON 26 December 1749.
Edward WEGLEY m. Jane FISHER 2 January 1749/50.
Christian DAVIS m. Frances COLEMAN 2 January 1749/50.
Aquila GOSWICK m. Elizabeth STANSBURY 14 January 1749/50.
Nicholas BAKER m. Mary STEVENS 18 January 1749/50.
Zebediah BAKER m. Hannah BAKER 28 January 1749/50.
Abraham GREEN m. Elizabeth BAXTER 28 January 1749/50.
Thomas NEWSTER m. Ann FREEMAN 4 February 1749/50.
David BELAMY m. Mary HANNS 27 February 1749/50.
John WALKER m. Rachel BOSTON 23 January 1742.   {H-164}
William NICKOLDSON m. Mary CONNELL 24 April 1750.   {R-I-109}
William STANSBURY m. Elizabeth ENSOR 14 February 1739/40.
Richard RUTTER m. Mary BARNEY 3 June 1750.
John CUSTIS s/o Benjamin & Abiather his wife b. 12 November 1745.
William LINCH m. Elinor TODD 6 September 1740.
William HANCOCK m. Honour STRINGER 29 September 1750.
John BARRATT m. Margarett NEWELL 26 September 1750.
George PRESGRAVES m. Mary HOLBROOK 30 September 1750.
Thomas TRUMAN m. Elizabeth DIGHTON 1 October 1750.
Abraham ENSOR m. Mary MERRIMAN 30 January 1750.
William SHAW m. Ruth HARRIMAN 17 September 1750.
William THACKER m. Hanner COX 14 February 1750/1.   {H-165}
Jonas BOWEN m. Elizabeth WHITH 14 February 1750/1.
Edmund TALBOTT m. Darcas HALL 26 October 1749.
William SIM m. Mary LOW 17 June 1750.
Edmund TALBOTT m. Rebecca ROBINSON 18 June 1752.
Thomas COOK m. Ann WHEELER 3 October 1739.
Christopher CARNAN m. Eliza NORTH 13 June 1751.
Nicho. Ruxton GAY m. Ann LUX 21 September 1751.
William LUX m. Agnes WALKER 16 July 1752.
Warnell WOOD m. Thamer SMITH 28 May 1754.
Benjamin Robinson TALBOT s/o Edmund & Rebecca his wife b. 1
   October 1754.
John Dickson STANSBURY s/o Thomas & Hanner his wife b. 19
   December 1754.   {R-I-110}
Risdell SMITH m. Hanner CHETTLE 26 November 1755.
William GISSUP s/o William & Margaret his wife b. 28 July 1755.
Tobies STANSBURY m. Mary HAMMOND 27 April 1746.   {H-166}
Elizabeth HELMS d/o Mayberry Jr. & Mary b. 27 September 1757.
John ORRICK m. Caroline HAMMOND 20 February 1757.
Joseph BANKSON m. Elizabeth SLEMAKER widow of James 16 January
   1752.
John CONAWAY m. Anne NORWOOD 14 May 1744.
John Henry MIER m. Eliza COLE 11 January 1758.
John WATTS m. Anne BODY 15 April 1743.
John WATTS m. Sarah EAGLESTONE 20 April 1756.
Richard ROWLES m. Anne GORSWICK 30 January 1753.
Luke TROTTEN m. Susannah LONG 10 February 1754.
Edward SWEETING m. Ruth TROTTEN 6 June 1756.
William SMITH Jr. m. Eliza. SHAW 19 February 1759.
William BARNEY m. Frances Holland WATTS 26 January 1743. {H-167}
William JOYCE m. Sarah LEE 25 May 1760.
John ENSOR Jr. m. Eleanor TODD 6 March 1753.
James WOOD m. Elizabeth DAVIDSON 27 January 1762.
Moses GREEN m. Eliza. HARRIMAN 25 March 1762.   {R-I-111}
Nathan PERIGO m. Rebecca EVANS 7 December 1757.
Elisha HALL m. Mary NICHOLSON 13 May 1762.
Michael HAMET m. Ann HUNT 9 January 1763.
Thomas BARCLAY m. Margaret COLE 26 March 1763.

John ANDERSON m. Lydda RICHARDS 28 March 1763.
The Rev. Thomas CHASE & Miss Ann BIRCH, eldest daughter of Mr.
Thomas BIRCH, Chirurgeon & Man Midwife in the Town of Warwick,
in the County of Warwick in that part of great Britain called
England, were m. by the Rev. Mr. William WESTMINSTER of
Westminster Parish 19 July 1763.   {H-168}
John YEARLY m. Margarett PHILIPS 4 March 1754.
William BLACK m. Esther BANNCKER 22 September 1744.
John MC CONIKIN m. Eleoner LONG 20 September 1762.
John WARD m. Mary KELLEY 21 December 1766.
John GUY m. Margaret HARPER 13 July 1766.
John ROBINSON m. Elizabeth BUTHAEY 2 September 1767.
James GALLOWAY m. Mary Ann GOOCH 29 August 1767.   {R-I-118
John MC CONNICAN m. Mary DARBY 26 February 1753. {Register pages
Andrew BUCHANAN m. Susannah LAWSON 20 July 1760. 112-117 missing)
James COX m. Mary WHITE, widow, whose maiden name was ALEXANDER,
15 August 1765.
John DAY s/o Stephen DAY of Bacon Fields in Buckinghamshire m.
Mary EVANS 26 June 1765.   {H-169}
William SPENCER s/o William SPENCER of New Castle m. Mary
WHITACKER d/o Thomas WHITACKER of Inniskilling in Ireland, 30
June 1765.
Dogulass SPENSE m. Catherine MOONEY 20 June 1770.
William MARKLAND m. Orpha EDENFIELD d/o John ENSOR Senior 19
November 1770. L
Patrick KENNEDY m. Hannah FRENCH, widow of Baltimore Town, 6 June
1772.
George PAYNE m. Elizabeth SMITH, widow, 25 April 1772.
Capt. James RIDDEL m. Ann PLUMBER 1 January 1773. L
William PARLETT m. Elizabeth DEW 1 February 1773. L
Conrad APPLEBY m. Ann CREAGUE 19 January 1773. L
Jacob SUMMERS m. Eleanor QUEA 28 February 1773. B   {R-I-119}
John SOMMERS m. Mary LASHFORD 28 February 1773. B   {H-170}
Samuel BUTLER m. Alice BURGESS, widow of Hugh, 2 August 1772.
George DAFFIN m. Mary BANKSON 13 February 1773. L
Joseph Hamilton DOUGLASS m. Rachel BAYARD 4 April 1768.
William SCOVEE m. Hannah HANSON 15 June 1769. L
Josiah PENINGTON m. Jemina HANSON 24 February 1771. L
James STUART m. Cathreene MATHEWS 1 August 1773. L
Thomas WELLS m. Alice WIGNALL 15 June 1772. B
Samuell BUNGEY, widower m. Mary MULL, widow 22 August 1773. L
John WILLIAMS m. Ann SEYMER 10 June 1770.
James MECOMBES m. Eloner JONES 12 September 1773. B
Joseph STANSBURY m. Jane LONG 12 December 1773. L
George LEVLY m. Chartine MULL 1 January 1770. L
Francis MANING m. Patience GRIFES 30 January 1774. B   {H-171}
Job GREENE, b. in New Port Rhode Island in New England, m.
Christian PIERCE 13 July 1772 at said Job GREENE's House in
Baltimore Town by Rev. Mr. CHASE, Rector of this parish. L
Thomas LOGAN b. in City of Aberdeen in that part of Great Britain
called Scotland, m. Miss Susanna DALY, late of the City of
Dublin in the Kingdom of Ireland, 13 February 1774, by Rev.
Thomas CHASE. L
Esau OAKLEY m. Jane SMITH 15 October 1774. L   {R-I-120}
Benjamin DAVIDSON m. Elizabeth BAKER 16 October 1774. L
Joseph TRAINSWORTH m. Sarah ELLIS 22 October 1774. B
John WILLIAMS m. Elizabeth PERSON 2d Saturday in January 1755.

B = Banns   L = License

Francis CLARK m. Eleanor HASE 10 April 1775.
James EDWARDS m. Ruth STANSBURY 9 March 1775. L
John CURRY m. Elizabeth WILSON 4 November 1775.   {H-172}
Robert WATERS m. Mary IRELAND 11 July 1775.
Alexander MC MULLAN m. Hannah STRINGHAR 1 June 1776.
William WILLOX m. Dorcas BARRATT 2 March 1776.
Patrick KEITH m. Esther REDMAN 9 December 1776.

The following records were found among loose papers in Box vii
and are included here. They are records of Rev. Thomas CHASE.
4 Nov. 1776, Richard PARISH m. Sarah BAKER by Banns at my house.
5 Nov. 1776, John DEVER m. Rebecca TALBOT by License at his
    house.
6 Nov 1776, Isaiah WAGSTER m. Mary WARRELL by License at my
    house.
7 Nov. 1776, Stephen VELIN m. Sarah PICKET by License at my
    house.
10 Nov. 1776, Michael JORDAN m. Elizabeth DEVERIS by License at
    my house.
10 Nov. 1776, John Dixon WEATHERBURN m. Catharine LITTLEJOHN by
    License in St. Paul's Church.
18 Nov. Samuel CHESTER m. Mary COURSEY by License at my house.
19 Nov. Patrick SCOCHNEJOY m. Catharine COTTER by Banns at my
    house.
11 Nov. Nicholas PERIGO m. Eleanor SHERMEDINE by License at my
    house.
21 Nov. 1776, Hugh GIBSON m. Elizabeth KELLEY by License at my
    House (Rev. Thomas CHASE).
23 Nov. 1776, Samuel MACUTTER(?) m. Margaret POCOCK by License at
    my house.
28 Nov. 1776, Andrew GETZELMAN m. Mary STEWARD by License at my
    house.
9 Dec. 1776, Patrick KEITH m. Esther REDMONDS by License at my
    house.
11 Dec. 1776, James MATTHIAS m. Magdalen BUTTON by Banns at my
    house.
12 Dec. 1776, Loyd RAWLINGS m. Elizabeth BROTHERS by License at
    my house.

Walter PERDUE m. Martha WATSON 3 October 1776.
Richard TAYLOR m. Margaret WELSH 6 February 1777.
John GORMAN m. Mary SHEPHERD 24 February 1777.
Thomas HARRISON m. Mary WHITE 16 April 1777.
James WRIGHT m. Ann CASSEY 7 January 1777.   {H-173}
Samuel STANSBURY, Sr. m. Anne CULLESON 24 May 1777.   {R-I-121}
Michael MORE m. Bridget MACARTER 31 March 1777.
James LITTLE m. Rachell CONOWAY 24 May 1777.
Thomas WOOLHEAD m. Caroline HILL 25 May 1777.
George COOPER m. Ann SOUTHERN 16 June 1777.
Robert JOHNSON m. Alice PETERKIN 3 September 1777.
George RANKIN b. in that part of Great Britain called England m.
    Mary BULL d/o Constantine BULL 25 February 1771.
Marmaduke GRANT m. Eleanor REILEY 15 May 1776, both of Baltimore
    Town.   {H-174}
Thomas BRANNEN m. Mary SHEPPARD 16 May 1778.
William JACOB of the City of Annapolis & Province of Maryland,
    5th s/o Zachariah JACOB of Anne Arundel County in the aforesaid
    province m. Mary MONK d/o Rinaldo MONK, late of the City of
    London in that part of Great Brittain called England by Rachel

37

his wife (who was widow & Relict of Edward RISTON of Baltimore
County, Deceased). William & Mary were married 19 July 1772 in
Rangers Forest in the County aforesaid on Sunday 19 July 1772
by Rev. William EDMINSTON at about 3 o'clock p.m.
George DENT m. Susannah DAVIS 28 January 1779.   {R-I-128*}
Joshua DUDLEY m. Catherine STEWART m. 9 April 1777.
  marriage sworn to in affidavit given 12 June 1779 by Ann {H-175}
  SMITH, Edward MC LURE & Sarah MC LURE who stated they were
  present at their marriage, both then of Baltimore Town, by Rev.
  Thomas CHASE, deceased, late Rector of St. Paul's & they lived
  as man & wife during said DUDLEYs residence in Baltimore Town,
  which was until November last past.   {R-I-129}
John MILLER m. Mary HILL -- September 1777. This marriage sworn
  to in affidavit given 12 July 1779 by Mary SMITH & James MC
  DONALD. They stated both were of Baltimore Town & married by
  late Rev. Thomas CHASE; lived together as man & wife until said
  MILLER went on a voyage to sea in a vessel called Thetis
  commanded by Capt. CREAGUE in April last.   {H-176}
Philip HALL m. Sarah FRAZIER about 2 June 1772. This marriage
  sworn to in affidavit given 25 October 1779 by Mathew PATTON &
  Aubrey RICHARDSON; marriage performed by the late Rev. Thomas
  CHASE.   {H-177}
Samuel STREET m. Elizabeth HALMONAY 20 November 1779.   {H-178}
Charles MUNSTAN m. Ann FITZGERALD 20 November 1779.
John KANNADAY m. Ann PERRY 11 July 1779.
John TIMBLIN m. Elizabeth JOHNSON -- November 1774. February 21,
  1780 Michael CAIN made oath that the above marriage was
  performed by the late Rev. Thomas CHASE. Same date affidavit
  signed by Thomas GIST. Also: "This is to Certify that Edward
  JOHNSON & Margaret his wife lived near me & informed that John
  TIMBLIN had married their Daughter Elizabeth & TIMBLIN lived
  with his father in law some time before he went to the Camp.
  Witness my hand this 21st Day of February 1780. Nicholas
  ORRICK."   {H-179}
John LEGARD m. Mary CILESTIN 8 February 1780.
Andrew KNIGHT m. Elizabeth LIDGET 26 March 1780.
John HAGERTY m. Sarah COOPER 16 May 1780.
* {Register pages 122 through 127 & 129 through 132 missing}
Alexander MELVELL m. Elionor EVANS 10 June 1780.   {H-180}
William MILLAR m. Elizabeth SMITH 15 July 1780.
William AGGIS m. Ann ANDERSON 28 July 1780.
John TRITTON m. Lucy MC CARTY 7 August 1780.
Patrick MC NAMARA m. Sarah GLESON 15 August 1780.
John HAYS m. Rebecca WILLIAMS 23 October 1780.
Isaac STOKEHAM m. Mary MC GREGORY 14 November 1780.
Evan THOMAS m. Ruth ARNOLD 27 February 1781.
George HUSSEY m. Rachel HAYWARD 11 January 1781.   {R-I-133}
William JACOB s/o Zachariah JACOB of Baltimore Town m. Mary
  GODFREY, formerly of town of Portsmouth, state of Virginia, 27
  March 1781.
Richard HAISLIP m. Mary BABINGTON 27 March 1781.   {H-181}
Edward BENNET m. Mary WARD 10 June 1780.
Francis BOLTON m. Margaret HOWSER 16 April 1781.
Peter CLARK m. Elizabeth WADLEY 4 July 1781.
John PEACOCK m. Elizabeth SMITH 5 July 1781.
Thomas LOWRY m. Catherine BRIAN 17 January 1774. 10 July 1781
  James LONG & Catherine LONG gave sworn affidavit that they were
  present at the marriage on or about date given, which was
  performed by Rev. CHASE.   {R-I-134}

Barnaby CONROY m. Jane SPICER 17 July 1781.   {H-182}
John CONLY m. Honor KEMP 11 August 1781.
William SMITH m. Frances GREENE 25 April 1780.
William WILCOXON m. Esther TAYLOR 10 November 1781.
Christopher HANSON m. Airy ROLLS 28 October 1781.
Thomas MAY m. Cathrine BEAMER 27 December 1781.
11 January 1782 Frances SKILEHORN made oath confirming marriage
   of Thomas LOWRY & Catherine BRIAN on or about 17 January 1774
   (see above).   {R-I-135}
Charles FENTON m. Dolly DANILY 2 March 1782.   {H-183}
John IRISH m. Mary HALL 2 April 1782.
Rennick FRANCES m. Ann RODDY 15 May 1782.
George HILAND m. Catherine SMITH 30 May 1782.
Thomas SPICER m. Elizabeth LLOYD 17 August 1782.
Peter FITE m. Mary CLAYER 23 August 1782.
Zachariah FOWLER m. Elizabeth JONES 19 September 1782.
Francis RONDET m. Margaret CELESTON 20 August 1782.
John VITRIE m. Mary LOCKERMAN 4 June 1780.
Samuel HULL m. Margaret HOLLIS 27 October 1782.   {H-184}
Nicholas PLISHO m. Mary MILLER 23 December 1779.
Stephen SEGUR m. Elizabeth RICHARDS 29 May 1780.   {R-I-136}
James BARBER m. Sarah ROGERS 19 May 1782.
James HARDY m. Mary CALDRON 7 January 1783.
Cornelius WELLS m. Charlotte CRAIGHEAD 13 February 1783.
Captain John Addison SMITH m. Sarah ROGERS d/o late William
   ROGERS of Baltimore Town deceased, 17 October 1765.
John MERRYMAN of Baltimore Town, Merchant, m. Sarah SMITH, widow
   of Capt. John Addison SMITH, 9 December 1777.
James BOWEN m. Margaret ROBISON 1 January 1783.
John HENDERSON m. Michal ? BARTON 17 April 1783.
Peter PRICE m. Mary HARCOURT 22 April 1783.   {H-185}
Thomas COOPER m. Margaret SUMMERS 7 July 1781.
John KENNEDY m. Bridget PEARSON 26 May 1783.
John ANDERSON m. Susanna BROWN 26 May 1783.
Moses SINCLAIR m. Mary JEMMISON 29 December 1782.   {R-I-137}
Nicholas FLORANCE m. Pamela WOOLEN 19 August 1783.
James SPICER m. Elizabeth SCOVEY 25 September 1783.
Henry STEWARD m. Catherine MUMFORD 7 September 1783.
Thomas WOODIN m. Martha GOTT 5 October 1783.
Capt. Jacob STOBO m. Sarah HUGHES 12 October 1783.
William BUCHANNAN m. Catherine MYERS 27 August 1783.
William THOMASON m. Margaret BAXTER 16 October 1783.
Benjamin SHEARMAN m. Rebecca SPENCER 7 December 1783.   {H-186}
John BEACHEM m. Elizabeth STICKER 25 December 1783.
Joshua HOLMES m. Arit SELMAN 25 December 1783.
Henry CROCKET m. Anne MERRICK 18 February 1784.
Hugh DRUMMOND m. Elizabeth CADLE 24 February 1784.
Richard REAVES m. Margaret WEST 6 April 1784.   {R-I-138}
Thomas GRIFFEN m. Elizabeth JONES 29 April 1784.
James WEBB m. Eleanor ROW in 1778. 4 May 1784 Catherine HOLLAND
   of Baltimore County made oath that she was present when Rev.
   CHASE solemnized the above marriage in 1778.)
Clodius BESSE m. Margaret MEALY 15 April 1784.   {H-187}
Charles CONNOWAY m. Catherine GARDENER 9 May 1784.
Peter FIVEASH m. Charlotte PARKS 12 May 1784.
Philip RENSHAW m. Ruth GERMAN 12 March 1784.   {R-I-139}
John TRYABLE m. Sarah KIRBY 25 May 1784.
William MARR m. Aney OWINGS 17 June 1784.   {H-188}
Matthias BONNER m. Ann Maria NICHOLSON 27 December 1779.

John WILLIAMS m. Catherine TUCKER 28 June 1784.
John STANLEY m. Margaret MAXWELL 1 October 1783.
George James LE AIGEAU m. Rachel ADAMS 10 July 1783.
William DEAVER m. Rachel CHINEA 27 July 1784.
Ephraim LAMBAUGH m. Elizabeth TWIST 31 July 1784.
James SANDERS m. Ruth ANDREWS 11 February 1782.
Adam BARNES m. Ruth SHIPLEY 5 August 1784.
Nathaniel PORTER m. Rebecca MASON 31 August 1784.
John FRIOR m. Catherine CALLAHAN 19 September 1784.
John SHRIER m. Anne OLDIS 29 August 1782.
Edward CONNER m. Rachel FORBES 13 December 1783.   {H-189}
John DENTON m. Margaret MAY 18 November 1784.   {R-I-140}
George FITE m. Rosanna POUTANY 8 October 1783.
William MAYCOCK m. Phebe MILES 5 September 1784.
Henry OYSTON m. Margaret POUTENAY 1 February 1785.
John HARRYMAN m. Mary EAGLESTONE 17 February 1785.
William PACKER m. Elenor WRIGHT in 1776.   27 May 1785 John
   WILLIAMS made oath that he was present when Rev. Thomas CHASE
   solemnized above marriage sometime in 1776 and they "lived
   together as man & wife untill he, the said William PACKER, was
   unfortunately Drowned. . .")
Jonathan PELLING m. Margaret KEYS 29 May 1785.   {H-190}
William WILLIBY m. Jane CAIN 24 July 1785.   {R-I-141}
Frances Haly d/o Stephen STEWARD & Elilzabeth his wife was born
   11 February 1783.
Stephen STEWARD s/o Stephen STEWARD & Elizabeth his wife b. 7
   April 1784 & departed this life 7 June 1784.
Robert CUNNYNGHAM m. Elizabeth ADAMS 23 May 1783.
Ambrose DAVIS m. Elizabeth GROVER 25 August 1785.
John WOOD m. Ann SHRIER 17 April 1785.
William HOWE m. Elizabeth MAXWELL 23 October 1784.
Edward SYNNOTT m. Ann CONDREN 3 November 1785.
Zechariah GRAY m. Sophia HOLMES 22 February 1781.
William MATTHEWS m. Elizabeth SHORTERS 9 April 1786.   {H-191}
John E. GIST m. Frances TRIPPE 13 November 1783.
John CLARKE m. Hannah MAYDWELL 29 April 1783.
Robert LAKING m. Mary LANGLY 24 May 1783.
Ephraim SMITH m. Beddy SMITH 30 May 1786.
Joseph THOMPSON m. Jane BLACK 5 September 1786.   {R-I-142}
Hugh TAYLOR m. Elizabeth CURREY 13 September 1786.
Robert WOOD m. Jane DUNN 19 May 1783.
Robert Crawford WOODS m. Catherine O'BRIEN 17 September 1786.
Charles MC ALLISTER m. Ann SAMPSON 21 October 1786.
Zebulon WEATHERS m. Ann COATS 16 November 1786.
Joseph HAWKINS m. Ann SHIPLEY 22 April 1787.
James TAYLOR m. Mary JONES 17 June 1784.   {H-192}
Robert TOWNSEND m. Margaret WILLSON 1 September 1787.
John MOALE, Esquire m. Ellin NORTH d/o Capt. Robert NORTH 25 May
   1758.   They were married at Mr. Christopher CARNAN's in
   Baltimore Town.
Thomas RUSSEL & Rebecca MOALE were married at Green Spring in
   Baltimore County by Rev. William WEST 12 October 1780.
Elizabeth HUGHS d/o Christopher & Peggy HUGHES was b. 25 April
   1781.
William ASQUITH m. Elizabeth CONNELL 2 May 1762.   {R-I-143}
NOTE: Register pages 143-172 are blank.

John EAGER d. 11 April 1722.   {H-193}
John PALLEN d. 14 April 1722.   {R-173}
Charles MERRIMAN d. 17 May 1722.
Johanah RISTONE wife of Edward d. 10 January 1723.
Sarah DURHAM d/o James & Rebeccah of Back River d. 23 Oct. 1725.
Jemimah JONES wife of Philip JONES Jr. d. 17 September 1725.
Jacob COX d. 1 November 1724.
Capt. Charles MERRIMAN of Patapsco d. 22 December 1725.
Hester CONNELL d/o William & Mary d. 8 April 1726.
Anne GOSTWICK d/o Nicholas d. 26 July 1726.
Joseph LOBB d. 14 February 1723.
Edward TURBELL d. 17 April 1727.
John HILLEN d. 2 April 1727.
Ann JOHNES d. 1 March 1727.
Edward COOKE d. 4 March 1727.
Hugh JOHNES d. 22 March 1727.
Mary MERRYMAN wife of Samuel d. 26 March 1728.
Joseph GOSWICK d. 30 March 1728.
Ann ROWLS wife of Jacob d. 30 April 1727.
John NORTON d. 24 March 1726/7.
Jane HARRYMAN wife of Samuel d. 30 March 1727.
Philip POWELL d. 2 December 1728.
Jonas BOWEN d. 25 December 1728.
Ruth MORRIS d/o Jacob & Elisabeth d. 23 February 1728.
Samuell GAIN s/o William & Catherine d. 18 January 1728. {H-194}
Mary RIDER wife of James d. 4 April 1729.   {R-I-174}
Sarah DERYDOR wife of John James d. 2 January 1728.
Elisabeth RIDER d/o James d. 15 April 1729.
Betty BUCKNER d/o William & Patience d. 16 April 1727(9?).
Robert MUNGUMRY d. 21 March 1726.
Elice MUNGUMRY d. 22 March 1726.
Thomas SUTTON d. 2 July 1729.
Moses EDWARDS d. 6 August 1727.
Richard HEWETT d. 20 February 1729.
Charles MERRYMAN s/o John Sr. d. 15 December 1729.
William HAMMILTON d. 17 April 1730.
Lettes TODD wife of Thomas at North Point d. 10 June 1730.
Ruth FRANKLAND wife of Thomas d. 31 January 1730.
Nicholas HAILE Sr. d. 29 March 1730.
William BUCCKNER d. 17 August 1731.
John DENASKEY drowned in Patapsco River, falling out of a flat of
   Capt. John RANDELL 7 August 1731.
Alice EDWARDS d. 20 December 1731.   {H-195}
Elisabeth THORNBURY wife of John d. 12 March 1731.
Mary BROWN wife of Dr. John BROWN d. 8 September 1732.
Rev. Mr. William TIBBS, Rector of this parish d. 11 October 1732.
Thomas WEEKS d. 16 December 1732.
Barbary BROAD Sr., aged 79 years 5 March next d. 19 January 1732.
Sarah BOWEN d/o Benjamin d. 26 January 1732.
Joyce SAITH wife of John d. 9 March 1732.
Elisabeth MORRIS wife of Jacob d. 14 February 1732.
Robert GORSUCH d. 19 March 1732.
Violetta BUCKNER daughter of William d. 8 November 1732.
Jemima JONES first wife of Philip d. 18 September 1725.
Jemima JONES d/o Philip & Jemima d. 18 November 1729.
Ruth TROTTON wife of Luke, aged 43 years, died 22 November 1733.
Hannah MAXFIELD wife of Samuel d. 1 February 1731.
Mary BOREING wife of Thomas d. 14 April 1734.
Thomas STONE d. 18 December 1733/4.

Richard SAMPSON d. 26 October 1734.
Katherine COOK d. 17 December 1734.
Christopher RANDALL d. 2 February 1734.   {H-196}
Presotia BOREING late wife of Capt. John d. 2 February 1734.
Stephen GILL d. 17 February 1734.
Rosannah YOUNG d. 16 June 1733.
Elizabeth COALE wife of George d. 14 September 1735.
Luke STANSBURY s/o Luke d. 26 December 1735.
William CONNELL d. 9 May 1736.
Enoch BAILEY s/o of George buried 2 July 1736.
Mary CONNELL d. 3 October 1736.
William COCHRAN, merchant, d. 4 October 1736.
Patrick WISE, sailor with Capt. GRAY, d. 15 September 1736.
John HILLING s/o Solomon HILLEN(?) d. 11 October 1736.
Sarah FULKS wife of Joseph d. 13 November 1736.
William ROSE buried 27 November 1736.
Jesper BARWELL d. 27 November 1736.
William TIPTON d. 6 May 1726.
Mary TIPTON d. 6 December 1736.
Jemima MERRYMAN d/o William d. 13 August 1736.   {H-197}
Margrett MERRYMAN d/o William d. 5 August 1736.
Elizabeth STONE wife of Thomas buried 2 February 1736.
Margrett DENNIS d. 29 January 1736.
Margrett YOUNG d. 2 February 1736.
Hannah OWINGS wife of John d. 22 January 1738.
Capt. Richard GIST d. 22 August 1741.
Sarah GARDNER d/o James & Mary d. 12 December 1744.
Mary GARDNER wife of James d. 21 August 1745.
Lloyd HARRIS d. 23 August 1742.
Easther RUTTER d. 16 January 1749/50.
Dinah HALL d. 2 January 1749/50.
Isiah OCUSSON with his wife Margaret OCUSSON d. 25 January
    1749/50.
Ann RUTTER d/o Richard & Sophia d. 6 January 1749/50.
Sophia RUTTER wife of Richard d. 16 January 1749/50.
James FURGUSON s/o William d. 9 August 1750.   {H-198}
Capt. Darby LUX d. 14 October 1750.
Darcas TALBOTT wife of Edmd.; 23 years, 3 months, 4 days old, d.
    7 January 1752.
Benjamin TALBOTT s/o Edmd. & Darcas; 1 year, 4 months 23d, d. 11
    January 1752.
Kathrine LOCK d/o William & Jane; 2 years, 3 months, 12 days, d.
    23 January 1752.
Rottenberry JONES s/o Philip & Ann in Anteagna d. 11 Sept. 1754.
Nicholas ROGERS s/o Nicholas & Eleanor d. 7 May 1758.
Jane LOCK d/o William & Jane d. 20 September 1760.
Margret BARNEY d/o William BARNEY & Frances HOLLAND his wife, d.
    24 September 1748. Also daughter Mary BARNEY d. 29 Aug. 1758.
William NICHOLSON d. 29 June 1761.
William ROGERS d. 11 June 1761.   {H-199}
Mary Catharine HOFFMONON wife of William d. 7 November 1764.
Catharine HOFFMONON d/o William & Catharine d. 27 October 1764.
Thomas PALSER d. 22 Decembber 1765.
Joshua LONG s/o John d. 11 November 1764.
Eleanor LONG d/o John d. 22 November 1764.
Elizabeth TROTTEN d. 11 November 1765.
Joshua BODY s/o Peter d. 9 November 1765.
Thomas STANDSBURY d. 4 May 1766.
Joshua STANSBURY s/o John d. 18 September 1767.

William FRY, late of City of London, Sail-maker, d. 8 July 1768.
Bernhardt DE HAMM d. 14 November 1765.
Robert PATTERSON s/o John d. 5 June 1772.   {H-200}
Elizabeth JOICE wife of Joseph d. 3 October 1772.
Richard ADAMS, merchant late of Dublin, d. 3 December 1772.
Joseph Hamilton DOUGLASS d. 8 July 1769.
Catherine Rogers SMITH d/o John Addison SMITH & Sarah his wife d.
    18 August 1769.
Capt. John Addison SMITH d. 8 Mary 1776.
Elizabeth GIST d/o John E. & Frances, aged 8 days, d. 25 October
    1784.
John GIST s/o John E. & Frances, aged 8 months, 3 hours d. 14
    August 1786.
Joseph GIST s/o Joseph Sr. & Elizabeth d. 15 December 1786.
Ruth NOEL wife of Septimus d. 1 April 1787.
William ASQUITH s/o William & Elizabeth d. 6 December 1764.
Elizabeth ASQUITH wife of William d. 26 November 1772.   {H-201}
John ASQUITH s/o William & Elizabeth d. 14 July 1785.

REGISTER OF BIRTHS, MARRIAGES & BURIALS
by Rev. William WEST
ST. PAUL'S PARISH
Commencing from the year 1786 - Second Book

James TAYLOR m. Mary JONES 7 June 1784.   {R-II-1} {H-203}
Robert TOWNSEND m. Margret WILLSON 1 September 1787.
William COWAN m. Catherine STEWART 17 November 1787.
Anthony SCOLLARD m. Ann CAMPBELL 11 December 1787. Witnesses:
    Edward WALSH, Edmund JOHNSON, Margaret JOHNSON & Mary KEATING,
    Larn WRIGHT, Reg.)
James MELDRUM m. Hannah COOK 12 December 1787.
John WESCOTT m. Sarah JOHNSON 22 September 1787. Witnesses:
    Daniel LEARY, Edward JOHNSON, Anthony SCOLLARD, Ann SCOLLARD,
    Mary JOHNSON & Larn WRIGHT, Reg.)
Ann MILLER d/o John & Mary b. 9 November 1786; bapt. 11 April
    1787.   {R-II-2}
Elizabeth MILLER d/o John & Mary b. 15 August 1784; bapt. 11
    April 1787.   {H-204}
Mary LEE d/o William & Ann b. 12 April 1787; bapt. 21 Oct. 1787.
Thomas CROW s/o William & Sarah b. 7 September 1787; bapt. 28
    September 1787.
Sussana SINDELL d/o Philip & Elizabeth b. 8 June 1787; bapt.
    11 November 1787.
Joshua POCOCK s/o Joshua & Ann b. 6 November 1787; bapt. 9
    December 1787.
Jemima POCOCK d/o James & Rebecca bapt. 6 November 1787 at age
    4 months.
John FIELDS s/o William & Elizabeth bapt. 13 April 1788 at 4 mo.
Thomas HARVEY m. Hannah THORNTON 31 December 1787. Witnesses:
    Arthur DUNN & Rachel THORNTON.   {R-II-3}
Benjamin HALL m. Rachel POMFREY 3 January 1788. Witnesses:
    William CAPEL [sic] & Hanah CAPLE.
Thomas GLYNN m. Catherine DRISKELL 6 January 1788.   {H-205}
Samuel COOPER m. Martha ROBERTS 13 July 1788. Witnesses: Edward
    MC DONALD, Nicholas OTTWAY, Hannah HENNESSY, Mary HOGDEN &
    Catherine DESMOND.
James SLADEN m. Eleanor MURPHY 21 July 1788. Witnesses: Thomas
    WALL & Elizabeth WALL.

John SPRAY m. Mary SUMMERS 31 July 1788.   {R-II-4}
George Carr GRUNDY bapt. 12 June 1785 at 1 month, 13 days; Eliza.
    Catherine GRUNDY bapt. 27 August 1786, at 4 weeks, 1 day; Mary
    GRUNDY bapt. 4 May 1788, b. 1 April 1788; children of George &
    Mary GRUNDY.
Henry bap. 1 June 1788 at age 4 1/2 months, s/o John & Margaret
    STEPHENSON.
John son of Jane COLE reported by said Jane to belong to Zebulon
    HOLLINGSWORTH christened 1 June 1788 at 5 months.   {H-206}
Robert s/o Robert & Ann BAKER bapt. 16 May 1788 at 3 months.
Ann Osburn TAYLOR d/o John & Ann bapt. 8 June 1788 at 1 month.
George bapt. 8 June 1788 at 3 months; John bapt. 8 June 1788 at 3
    years s/o Henry & Sarah EVANS.
William bapt. 8 June 1788 at 9 months; James bapt. 8 June 1788 at
    3 years; John bapt. 8 June 1788 at 5 years; s/o John & Hannah
    HARTER.
Phebe d/o Samuel & Cosiah MEALY bapt. 8 June 1788 at 2 1/2
    months.   {R-II-5}
Mary d/o James & Ann STARR bapt. 22 June 1788 at 9 months.
John s/o John & Rebecca HOLMES bapt. 29 June 1788 at 8 months.
Joseph WAIT s/o Thomas & Eleanor bapt. 29 June 1788 at 1 month.
James s/o William & Patty RICHEY bapt. 6 July 1788 at 8 months.
Hannah d/o Michael & Mary JONES bapt. 6 July 1788 at 10 weeks.
John s/o James & Margaret GEDDIS bapt. 13 July 1788 at 16 days.
William s/o John & Margret WHEELER bapt. 13 July 1788 at 7 mo.
James WHEATLY s/o James & Mary WHEATLY bapt. 27 July 1788.{H-207}
Elisha s/o John & Jane HALL bapt. 10 August 1788 5 weeks.
Margaret RACE d/o George & Elizabeth bapt. 17 August 1788 at 5
    months, 13 days.
Jane d/o John & Elizabeth WOODWARD bapt. 17 August 1788 at 1 mo.
Ann d/o Richard & Elizabeth BELL bapt. 24 August 1788 at 2 years
    wanting 1 day.
Rebecca d/o John & Catherine TAYLOR bapt. 24 August 1788 at 2
    years, 6 months, wanting 4 days old.

BURIALS

Capt. PRATT bur. 14 February 1787.   {R-II-6} {H-208}
Mrs. BARLOW bur. 18 February 1787.
Mrs. SULLIVAN's child, At the Point, bur. 16 March 1787.
Mrs. John YOUNG, At the Point, bur. 21 March 1787.
Mr. Isaac BROWN's child, At the Point, bur. 23 March 1787.
Mr. CALVER's child, Old Town, buried 25 March 1787.
Mrs. NOEL bur. 2 April 1787.
Mr. Joseph SIMMON's child bur. 2 April 1787.
Mr. Samuel EVANS' child bur. 5 April 1787.
Mrs. SHEERS bur. 17 April 1787.
Dr. FALL's child bur. 18 April 1787.
Robert MORRIS, Sailor from the Point, buried 24 April 1787.
Mrs. CANNADEY bur. 1 May 1787.
Mr. ROSSEDAR bur. 1 May 1787.
Daniel LEARY's child bur. 11 May 1787.
Joseph BROTHERTON's child bur. 12 May 1787.
Dr. COLE's child bur. 13 May 1787.
Joseph BROTHERTON's child bur. 19 May 1787.
Dr. TROOP (no date given).
William HOLMES, clerk to Mr. HAMMOND, bur. 25 May 1787.
James SMITH bur. 26 May 1787.
Mr. BASHAW bur. 18 June 1787.

Mr. ROSS bur. 21 June 1787.
Mr. HUNT bur. 23 June 1787.
Mr. NICOLSON bur. 26 June 1787.
Mr. John HAMMOND's child bur. 13 July 1787.
Mrs. WEST bur. 15 July 1787.
Jn. YOUNG's child, At the Point, bur. in July 1787.
Mrs. SMYTH's child bur. 21 July 1787.
Mrs. DOWLEY bur. 23 July 1787.
William DANCER's child bur. 23 July 1787.
Mr. William HUGHES child bur. 24 July 1787.
Thomas RUSSEL, Esqr.'s child bur. 26 July 1787.
Mr. RAWLINGS bur. 27 July 1787.
Robert ALLEN's child bur. 3 August 1787.
John MOAL Esqr.'s child bur. 3 August 1787.
Robert MC CARTER's child bur. 4 August 1787.   {H-209}
Mr. MC LEAN's child bur. 7 August 1787.
Mr. VARHAM's child bur. 7 August 1787.
Mrs. Mary TRIMBLE bur. 8 August 1787.
Mrs. HUTSON's child bur. 10 August 1787.
Mrs. THOMAS' child bur. 17 August 1787.   {R-II-7}
Mr. MYERS' daughter bur. 17 August 1787.
Mr. Archibald CAMPBELL, Merchant, bur. 18 August 1787 (& child?)
Mr. Robert DUNMOODY's child, at Point, bur. in August 1787.
John HALL, Bricklayer, bur. 21 August 1787.
John WOODWARD, At Point, bur. in August 1787.
Sarah MARRYHAN bur. 31 July 1787.
William SAMPLE bur. 8 September 1787.
James CONNOLEY's child bur. 16 September 1787.
John WHEELER's child bur. 18 September 1787.
William GARNNES bur. 26 September 1787.
Ann HIGGINS bur. 27 September 1787.
Mr. POGE's child bur. 2 October 1787.
Mr. DROWN's child bur. 3 October 1787.
Mrs. KENNEDY bur. 7 October 1787.
Mr. LOANES' child bur. 19 October 1787.
Mr. SPENCER bur. 21 October 1787.
Mr. ROE's child bur. 26 October 1787.
Mr. JACKSON bur. 28 October 1787.
Mrs. DAVIS bur. 28 October 1787.
Mr. BELTON's child bur. 29 October 1787.
Mr. STRAWBERRY bur. 30 October 1787.
Elizabeth HICKS bur. 4 November 1787.
Mr. SLATON's daughter bur. 5 November 1787.
John MARTIN's child bur. November 1787.
Thomas CONSTABLE's child bur. 9 November 1787.
George GRANDY bur. 13 November 1787.
Capt. BRERETON bur. 14 November 1787.
Elizabeth SHEPHARD's child bur. 23 November 1787.
Mr. FINLAY bur. 24 November 1787.
Mrs. SIMMONS bur. November 1787.
Samuel CHASE, Esqr.'s child bur. 28 November 1787.
Mr. John LOYD bur. 2 December 1787.   {H-210}
Benjamin JARVIS bur. 3 December 1787.
Mrs. HUGHES' child, from the country, bur. 11 December 1787.
Mrs. DUFFEE bur. 24 December 1787.
Mrs. WRIGHT's child bur. 31 December 1787.
Mr. HOWEL's child bur. 5 January 1788.
John CRAIN, Ship Carpenter, bur. 15 January 1788.
John CROCKETT's child, At Point, bur. 21 January 1788.

John DRAIN, Watchman at Point, bur. 24 January 1788.
John YOUNG, At Point, bur. 27 January 1788.   {R-II-8}
John JONES' child (no date given).
Peggy GILES' child, at Mr. GOUGH's, (no date given).
Christopher HOLLINGSWORTH bur. 20 February 1788.
William WOOLHEAD bur. 21 February 1788.
William COLLINS bur. (no date given).
Daniel BOWLEY's daughter bur. 25 February 1788.
John JAMES, At Point, bur. 26 February 1788.
Dennis SULLIVAN bur. 27 February 1788.
Mr. GIBBONS' child bur. 3 March 1788.
Mary WOODS bur. 6 March 1788.
Patrick MILLION's child bur. 15 March 1788.
Mrs. HALE's son bur. 16 March 1788.
Mrs. DANCER bur. 20 March 1788.
Mrs. GRIFFY's child bur. 13 April 1788.
Daniel CARROLL's child bur. -- April 1788.
Mrs. HERMES bur. 17 April 1788.
Mrs. WILKES bur -- April 1788.
Mrs. HAMMOND bur. 24 April 1788.
Mr. HALL bur. 27 April 1788.
Mrs. ROSSES' child bur. 29 April 1788.
Mr. DEVITT's child bur. 8 May 1788.
Mr. HELLING's daughter bur. 17 May 1788.
Mrs. GILES' daughter bur. 23 May 1788.
Mr. CLARCK's child bur. 3 June 1788.
John COLEMAN's child bur. 13 June 1788.
William BUCHANAN's child bur. (no date given).
Robert JOHNSON's daughter bur. 29 May 1788.
Margret SMITH bur 20 June 1788.   {H-211}
James USHER bur. 29 June 1788.
Ann IRELAND bur. 1 July 1788.
Mr. WILLIAMSON bur. 10 July 1788.
Mr. William YOUNG bur. 23 July 1788.
Daniel DENNIS' child bur. 29 July 1788.
Mr. POTTS' child bur. 2 August 1788.
Daniel DENNIS' child bur. 6 August 1788.
Richard LEWIS bur. 7 August 1788.
A Sailor by order of Dr. HARRIS bur. (no date given).
Joseph CLARK's child bur. 13 August 1788.
Dr. WINECOOP's child bur. 15 August 1788.
Samuel SWAN's child bur. 19 August 1788.

Remaining burials in this section found in the back of the second
Register.

Mary FARRELL bur. 19 August 1788.   {R-II-R-1}
Daniel BROWNING bur. 19 August 1788.
Mrs. MILLS' child bur 21 August 1788.
Mr. JOYCE bur. 24 August 1788.
Isaiah DICK's child bur. 25 August 1788.
John MC CONEKY bur. 25 August 1788.
Ann BROWN bur. 26 August 1788.
Mrs. MC CONEKY bur. 8 September 1788.
Mr. HUGHES' child bur. 15 September 1788.
Thomas HOLLINGSWORTH child bur. 18 September 1788.
Martin WATERS' wife bur. 18 September 1788.
Mr. RICHMOND's child bur. 25 September 1788.
Mr. THORP's child bur. 27 September 1788.

BURIALS

John WHITE bur. 11 October 1788.
Mr. CURTAIN's child bur. 11 October 1788.
Mr. STARR's daughter bur. 12 October 1788.
Mr. AMOS bur. 12 October 1788.
Mrs. ASHMAN bur. 19 October 1788.
Mr. WORKMAN bur. 21 October 1788.
William JOHNSTON bur. 28 October 1788.
Mr. CLARK's child bur. 2 November 1788.
Kingston GODDARD bur. 14 November 1788.
Philip WALTERS' child bur. 15 November 1788.
Mr. PROCTOR's child bur. 23 November 1788.
I. M. BOWEN's child bur. 23 November 1788.
John MC CURDY bur. 2 December 1788.
Thomas JONES bur. 4 December 1788.
Mr. DIVINS' child bur. 11 December 1788.
John ARMITAGE bur. 15 December 1788.
Mr. TOWNSEND's child bur. 17 December 1788.
Mrs. SHULER bur. 19 December 1788.
Mrs. D. CARROLL bur. 21 December 1788.
A sailor by William WILLSON bur. 21 December 1788.
William WILLIAMS bur. 26 December 1788.
Mrs. FALLS bur. 16 January 1789.
Mrs. SHANKS bur. 23 January 1789.
Mr. GILES' child bur. 24 January 1789.   {H-335}
Mr. BARNARD's child bur. 23 January 1789.
Mr. ROSSES' child bur. 26 January 1789.   {R-II-R-2}
Mr. CARLSON's child bur. 6 February 1789.
Elizabeth WATSON's child, from Mr. COULT, bur. 13 Feb. 1789.
George WELLS bur. 22 February 1789.
Thomas BIDWELL bur. 22 February 1789.
Mrs. ARMITAGE bur. 6 March 1789.
Isaac WHEELER's child bur. 9 March 1789.
John HUGHES bur. 11 March 1789.
John REDMAN's wife bur. 14 March 1789.
Rachael L'ARGEAN bur. 25 March 1789.
Nicholas HINNER's child bur. 30 March 1789.
Mrs. CURSON bur. 2 April 1789.
Mrs. STEWARD's child bur. 12 April 1789.
Capt. JONES' child bur. 14 April 1789.
Mr. YOUNG's child bur. 19 April 1789.
Charles WILLIAMS' child bur. 20 April 1789.
Mrs. STEWART bur. 10 May 1789.
Mrs. FENDALL bur. 11 May 1789.
James WATKINS' child bur. 17 Mary 1789.
Francis GILBERTHORP's child bur. 23 May 1789.
William NOON bur. 27 May 1789.
Thomas RUSSEL, Esq., bur 7 July 1789.
Mr. NEWCOMER's child bur. 19 July 1789.
John WILLIAM's child bur. 24 July 1789.
Elizabeth RICHARDS' child bur. 26 July 1789.
George GRUNDIE's child bur. 27 July 1789.
Mary REACH's child bur. 28 July 1789.
Mrs. BIDDLE bur. 11 August 1789.
Rebecca TUTTIN's child bur. 13 August 1789.
John EDWARDS bur. 13 August 1789.
A seaman bur. 14 August 1789.
John HEAD's child bur. 26 August 1789.
William HAIMES' child bur. 30 August 1789.
Adam JAMESON's child bur. 3 September 1789.

47

Mr. WORTHINGTON's child bur. 4 September 1789.   {H-336}
Doctor JOINER's child bur. 5 September 1789.
Ann USHER bur. 9 September 1789.
Francis SMITH bur. 13 September 1789.
Mrs. DESILVER bur. 15 September 1789.
Mr. GUITER's child bur. 16 September 1789.
Mrs. EDWARDS bur. 20 September 1789.
Mrs. GRANT bur. 22 September 1789.
Mrs. HELMS bur. 23 September 1789.
Mrs. CURTAIN's child bur. 28 September 1789.   {R-II-R-3}
Luther MARTIN's child bur. 29 September 1789.
William DANCER's child bur. 5 October 1789.
A stranger from Fells Point bur. 7 October 1789.
Mrs. MC CARTER bur. 18 October 1789.
William CELLARS' child bur. 22 October 1789.
Mr. STEVENS' child bur. 22 October 1789.
John WILLIAMS' child bur. 26 October 1789.
Samuel GOTT's child bur. 26 October 1789.
Priscilla BANNING bur. 29 October 1789.
William GODDART's child bur. 30 October 1789.
John MAY bur. 1 November 1789.
Mr. ATCHINSON bur. 5 November 1789.
Matthew RIDLEY bur. 14 November 1789.
Amos LOONEY's child bur. 14 November 1789.
Samuel SADLER's child bur. 29 November 1789.
A stranger from Mr. Jn. GUEST's bur. 29 November 1789.
Mr. S. HOLLINGSWORTH's child bur 2 December 1789.
Miss GIBSON bur. 3 December 1789.
Mrs. PROCTOR bur. 5 December 1789.
Benjamin MC KENZIES bur. 9 November 1789.
Thomas GRIFFEN's child bur. 30 December 1789.
Mr. Thomas USHER, Jr.'s child named MARY bur. 4 January 1790.
Capt. JONES' child bur. 4 January 1790.
Matthew SHAW's child bur. 6 January 1790.
Capt. JONES' child bur. 13 January 1790.
Henry NELSON, a Sailor bur. 15 January 1790.
Capt. WHITE's child bur. 17 January 1790.   {H-337}
Mrs. LAMB's child bur. 19 January 1790.
Miles NUTBROWN bur. 20 January 1790.
William CLARKE bur. 20 January 1790.
A sailor from Capt. TURNER's vessel bur. 20 January 1790.
A young man, stranger at Mr. MC KENSY's bur. 20 January 1790.
Mr. TRAVER's child bur. 20 January 1790.
John CURTIS' child bur. 28 January 1790.
Thomas HAMMOND bur. 29 January 1790.
Joseph M. BOWEN bur. 6 February 1790.
Mrs. FLEETWOOD bur. 7 February 1790.
Mrs. LUX bur. 14 February 1790.
Elias BOLTON's child bur. 25 February 1790.
Mr. KETTLEMAN's child bur. (no date given).
Mrs. BURNS bur. 9 March 1790.
William RUSSEL's child bur. 9 March 1790.   {R-II-R-4}
William KING bur. 10 March 1790.
Isaac WHEELER's child bur. 20 March 1790.
John CROCKETT bur. 23 March 1790.
William BUCHANAN's child bur. 27 March 1790.
Doctor HARRISON bur. 23 April 1790.
Mr. RUSSEL's child bur. 26 April 1790.
Mr. STEVENS' child bur. (no date given).

Mrs. CHALMERS' child bur. (no date given).
Leaven COVENTRY's child bur. 13 May 1790.
Mrs. ROGERS bur. 27 May 1790.
Mrs. TUNSTILL bur. 13 June 1790.
Daniel PRICE's child bur. 1 July 1790.
William STATIA's child bur. 1 July 1790.
Mr. KELLY bur. (no date given).
Mrs. FINLAY bur. 16 June 1790.
Mary BENNETT's child bur. (no date given).
Fanny SWINGLE bur. (no date given).
John CHAMBERLAINE bur. 7 July 1790.
Mr. CRACROFT's child bur. 17 July 1790.
Jane MORRISS' child bur. (no date given).
John WEAVER's child bur. 20 July 1790.   {H-338}
James LONG's child bur. 26 July 1790.
Doctor WYNCOOP's child bur. 28 July 1790.
Patrick MILLEN's child bur. 29 July 1790.
Mrs. TULL's child bur. 29 July 1790.
Henry YOUNG's child bur. 31 July 1790.
Thomas MORROW's child bur. 2 August 1790.
Benjamin SPENCER's child bur. 5 August 1790.
Phebe MARSHAL bur. 7 August 1790.
Mary CONSTABLE bur. 9 August 1790.
John CONNELLY's child bur. 9 August 1790.
Daniel LEARY bur. 11 August 1790.
James LONG's child bur. 13 August 1790.
Mrs. LEWIS' child bur. 15 August 1790.
John MC QUIRE bur. 15 August 1790.
Daniel PRICE's child bur. 16 August 1790.
John BATES' child bur. 7 August 1790.
John BURNS bur. 7 August 1790.
Mr. JACKSON's child bur. 19 August 1790.   {R-II-R-5}
William EVANS' child bur. 20 August 1790.
Mrs. PAYNE bur. 23 August 1790.
Samuel FRENCHES child bur. 28 August 1790.
John ORES' child bur. 31 August 1790.
Robert WARD bur. 3 September 1790.
Mr. CONNERS' child bur. 3 September 1790.
John YATES bur. 5 September 1790.
Joshua ENNIS's child bur. 10 September 1790.
Mr. CONNOR's child bur. 11 September 1790.
Mr. BARKER's child bur. 15 September 1790.
Joseph CLARK's child bur. 24 September 1790.
Capt. FLEETWOOD's daughter bur. 28 September 1790.
Mr. HOLMER child bur. 28 September 1790.
Daniel LEARY's child bur. 4 October 1790.
James EDWARDS' daughter but. 14 October 1790.
Mrs. LEWIS bur. 17 October 1790.
Thomas DROWNE's child bur. 19 October 1790.
Lewis DENROCHE's child bur. 21 October 1790.   {H-339}
Joseph KNIGHT's child bur. 25 October 1790.
John RICHMOND's child bur. 27 October 1790.
John GORT bur. 30 October 1790.
Joseph KNIGHT's wife bur. 31 October 1790.
James PATTERSON's child bur. 31 October 1790.
Joseph MONROE's wife bur. 2 November 1790.
Mrs. EWALL bur. 16 November 1790.
Mr. SELLMAN's child bur. 21 November 1790.
Henry TUNSTALL bur. 24 November 1790.

BURIALS

Mrs. MURRY bur. 26 November 1790.
John LARNING (LAMING?) bur. 11 December 1790.
David CASSEN bur. 15 December 1790.
Joseph WHITE bur. 19 December 1790.
William HEARNS bur. 20 December 1790.
Jacob SAMPSON's nephew bur. 24 December 1790.
A woman from LEWIS' (at the point) bur. 29 December 1790.
Saunders MOOR bur. 30 December 1790.
William DIXON bur. 30 December 1790.
John NUTBROWN bur. 31 December 1790.
John PROCTOR bur. (no date given).
William BROWNING bur. (no date given).
Peter LAVING's child bur. 10 January 1791.   {R-II-R-6}
Jane ALLEN bur. 14 January 1791.
Adam JAMESON bur. 24 January 1791.
Henry CALEB's child bur. 11 February 1791.
Thomas ROWE bur. (no date given).
John FORRESTER's Mother in law bur. (no date given).
Mr. GRIFFITH's child bur. 19 February 1791.
Mrs. WYNCOOP bur. 10 March 1791.
Rev. Dr. William WEST, Rector of St. Pauls, Baltimore, bur. 30
   March 1791.
Mr. PRICE's child bur. 2 April 1791.
Mr. GILBERTHROP's child bur. 20 April 1791.
Phillips & Dummone, belonging to Mr. STERRETT bur. 13 April 1791.
Hugh BENNETT's child bur. 29 April 1791.   {H-340}
Caroline GLEED's Mother bur. 2 May 1791.
Mrs. WEBSTER bur. 15 May 1791.
Mrs. PERKINS son bur. 25 May 1791.
Mr. WEAVER's child bur. 28 May 1791.
Mrs. TAYLOR's child bur. 28 May 1791.
Benjamin SPENCER's child bur. 5 June 1791.
John WOODWARD's child bur. 7 June 1791.
Ann PARSONS bur. 9 June 1791.
Solomon SHIELDS cousin's child bur. 12 June 1791.
Thomas CONNOLY's child bur. 13 June 1791.
John HILL bur. 16 June 1791.
Mr. NICHOLS (ommitted) bur. (no date given).
Larn WRIGHT - Registrar
{End of that section found in the back of the second Register.}

MARRIAGES
                                                            {R-II-9}
John BARRETT m. Margery BRAITHWAITE 31 August 1788. Marriage
   witnessed by Thomas DINAN, Eleanor RICHEY, Mary WILLSON.
Edward PALMER m. Mary NOWLAN 4 September 1788. Witnesses: Robert
   EDMONSTON, Mary BROWN, Larn WRIGHT.
William BRADFORD m. Sarah SNIDER 5 August 1786.
John HAMMOND m. Elizabeth MC CONNELL 27 November 1783.
John BRIAN m. Mary DREEVES 7 October 1788.
Daniel MILES m. Mary GORMAN 20 November 1788.   {H-212}
Henry MITCHESON m. Mary HINGDON 21 September 1788.

CHRISTENINGS
                                                           {R-II-10}
Ezekiel RITTER s/o John & Elizabeth bapt. 24 August 1788 at 9
   months, 24 days.
Elizabeth d/o John & Eleanor TAYLOR, b. 18 November 1787; bapt.
   24 August 1788.

50

CHRISTENINGS

Thomas s/o Joseph & Mary SUTHERLAND b. 24 June 1788; bapt. 24 August 1788.

Sarah Rogers b. 22 March 1784; Elizabeth b. 4 March 1786; Nicholas Rogers b. 26 April 1788; children of John, Baltimore Town merchant & Sarah MERRYMAN.

Elizabeth b. 21 April 1781; William b. 9 August 1782; George Agustus [sic] b. 27 January 1784; Eleanor b. 8 February 1875; Christopher & Peggy, twins, b. 11 February 1876; Louisa b. 4 November 1787; children of Christopher & Peggy HUGHES.

John Mc Connell b. 23 July 1786; John Barnett b. 12 April 1788; s/o John & Elizabeth HAMMOND.   {H-213}

Jacob s/o John & Rachel LEEF b. 25 April 1788; bapt. 14 September 1788.

MARRIAGES

John Winfield WILLIS m. Ann BAKER 2 November 1788; witness, James BATESON.   {R-II-11}

Lawrence FANNON m. Ann HENSELLER 29 October 1788.

John LOWE m. Elizabeth DEBLEGY 24 July 1784.

Samuel CRAWFORD m. Ann SOUTHALL 30 October 1788.

Christopher HUGHES m. Peggy ----- 20 January 1779.

John COLEMAN m. Leah SPRINGFIELD 5 December 1787.

Aquila JARVIS m. Elizabeth ROWLES 9 December 1787.   {H-214}

Jonathan HAYWORTH m. Rebbecca RANDALL 11 December 1787.

Samuel NORWOOD m. Rebecca BROWN 11 December 1787.

CHRISTENINGS

Jesse William s/o John & Catherine BELL b. 11 August 1788; bapt. 14 September 1788.   {R-II-12}

Conrad s/o Jacob & Elizabeth HOOD b. 25 March 1788; bapt. 14 September 1788.

John s/o Benjamin & Mary SELLMAN b. 1 September 1788; bapt. 14 September 1788.

Rebbecca? d/o John & Mary PRIMER b. 10 May 1788; bapt. 14 September 1788.

John b. 8 April 1788, bapt. 12 October 1788; James b. 30 May 1786; s/o William & Eleanor SOLLARS.

Henrietta HUDSON d/o John & Frances b. 10 September 1788; bapt. 12 October 1788.

David Andrew s/o Michael & Mary BARRY b. 23 December 1787; bapt. 12 October 1788.   {H-215}

James s/o John & Ellen WILLIAMS b. 1 September 1788; bapt. 12 October 1788.

Jacob s/o Jacob & Ann MADEIRA bapt. 20 October 1788 at 3 years.

Rebbecca? d/o Isaac & Elizabeth WHEELER bapt. 2 November 1788 at 17 months.

James s/o John & Elizabeth TRIPLETT bapt. 2 November 1788 at 15 months.   {R-II-13}

Francis [sic] d/o James & Mary FISHWICK bapt. 2 November 1788 at 2 months.

Thomas s/o John & Catherine GILL b. 27 September 1788; bapt. 30 November 1788.

Margret d/o Francis & Catherine BLUNDELL b. 2 October 1788; bapt. 11 December 1788.

John b. 5 November 1785, bapt. 8 January 1786; Joseph b. 11 October 1787; bapt. 14 October 1787; s/o John & Ann WILLIAMS.

CHRISTENINGS

Lydia d/o Isaac & Margaret TURNER bapt. 21 December 1788 at 3
  weeks, 2 days.   {H-216}
Samuel s/o Joseph & Barbary GRANGER bapt. 21 December 1788 at 6
  weeks, 2 days.

MARRIAGES

James FISHWICK m. Mary CRAIG 11 December 1787.   {R-II-14}
Frederick PARKS m. Rachel PARKS 13 December 1787.
Phillip DORSEY m. Elizabeth JOYCE 13 December 1787.
Michael KING m. Mary GORDON 16 December 1787.
Christopher BLACK m. Elizabeth BARLOW 20 December 1787.
John HACKETT m. Jane GRANT 1 January 1788.
John WILMOT m. Hannah WHEELER 3 January 1788.
Jacob BARNETT m. Catherine HISSEY 12 February 1788.
Joseph RICE m. Ann GRAY 16 February 1788.
Frederick BROWN m. Sarah WILLSON 19 February 1788.   {H-217}
John BRANCH m. Rebecca STRAWBLE 29 February 1788.
Elias BARNABY m. Rachel RIFFETT 8 March 1788.   {R-II-15}
James CROXALL m. Eleanor GITTINGS 11 March 1788.
Daniel HOOFMAN m. Biddy O'BRIEN 11 April 1788.
Alexander SANDS m. Delilah BURK 13 April 1788.
John SCOTT, Jr. m. Elizabeth Goodwin DORSEY 15 May 1788.
James WATKINS m. Rebecca MILLER 17 May 1788.
John CAMPBELL m. Marion MAXWELL 18 May 1788.
William HARVEY m. Eleanor JACKSON 7 June 1788.
Elisha HALL m. Mary TODD 1 July 1788.
Matt. FORBES m. Polly BEVANS 14 July 1788.
John PARKS m. Ruth HENDRICKSON 4 September 1788.   {H-218}
Robert HICKS m. Elizabeth HENRY 7 September 1788.   {R-II-16}
Eleazer CURTIS m. Bridget HARNES 8 September 1788.
John WILLIAMS m. Jane MORRISON 8 September 1788.
Michael DARLEY m. Caroline MILLER 17 September 1788.
Joseph WATSON m. Fanny MOODY 25 September 1788.
Samuel ARMER m. Susanna SWAN 2 October 1788.
Standish BARRY m. Nancy THOMPSON 11 October 1788.
Daniel MILES m. Mary GORMAN 28 October 1788.
Burrage SCOTT m. Ann DAVIES 6 November 1788.
Greenbury COOK m. Ann BASEMAN 20 November 1788.
John POCOCK m. Temperance ISGRIG 6 November 1788.
Benjamin HIPSLEY m. Elizabeth BISHOP 20 November 1788. {H-219}
Andrew ROADS m. Sussana JONES 27 November 1788.
Peter DITZENBACK m. Sussanna MERCIN 15 April 1788. {R-II-17}
Adam DITZENBACK m. Elizabeth HOULEMAN 15 April 1788.
Ralph GAITER m. Sarah ROWLES 30 November 1788.
Zebulon WEATHERS m. Ann COATES 16 November 1786.
John WILLIAMS m. Ann WELLS 17 March 1785.
Joseph READ m. Agnes SMITH 24 February 1789.
Thomas MORROW m. Catherine MC CURDY 22 February 178?; by Rev.
  Lewis RICHARDS, Minister of Baptist Church, Baltimore.
Daniel HOOFMAN m. Bridget O'BRIAN 11 April 1788.
Moses STEVENSON m. Eleanor SHAW 21 April 1789.
John WILLSON m. Margaret DERRY 9 August 1787.   {H-220}

CHRISTENINGS

Eleanor b. 12 February 1766; Moses b. 17 August 1767; Meshack b.
  28 June 1768; John b. 28 January 1770; William b. 31 July 1771;
  Samuel b. 5 April 1776; Shedrack b. 18 February 1781; Jacob b.

CHRISTENINGS

1 March 1783; Jesse b. 1 March 1785; Charlotte b. 28 January 1789; children of Moses & Eleanor STEVENSON (Malotto Man Father.) {R-II-18}
Harry Dorsey Gough s/o James & Sophia CARROLL b. 3 October 1788; bapt. 11 January 1789.
Henrietta d/o Timothy & Molly MC NEMARA b. 18 October 1787; bapt. 9 November 1787.
Mary Ann d/o James & Mary CURTAIN b. 6 November 1788; bapt. 1 January 1789.
Louisa d/o Lewis & Sarah RUSSEL b. 2 September 1788; bapt. 15 March 1789.
James s/o James & Eleanor STEWART b. 10 December 1788; bapt. 22 March 1789.

MARRIAGES

James CARROLL of City of Annapolis m. Sophia GOUGH d/o Harry Dorsey GOUGH 20 December 1787. {R-II-19} {H-221}
Samuel HEATH m. Eleanor JOYCE 12 February 1789.
James PATTERSON m. Jane HEATH 13 May 1789 by Rev. Patrick ALLISON, Minister of the Presbyterian Congregation Baltimore.
William BALDRY m. Mary GREEN 25 June 1789.
George FUSBURY m. Eleanor GEANY 13 Spetember 1789.
James WILLCOCKS m. Sarah GRAY 29 October 1789.
Jacob READ m. Elizabeth RUSSEL 20 October 1789.
Hilliare DELISLLE m. Marie Rose POIRICE 19 February 1785.
John ALLEN m. Catherine Elizabeth HAWKINS 1 February 1789.
Philip WATERS m. Nelly HINCKS 9 September 1789.

CHRISTENINGS
{R-II-20} {H-222}
John s/o John & Hannah WILLIAMS bapt. 5 April 178? at 8 weeks.
Nancy d/o George & Eliza. ALLEY b. 25 January 1787; bapt. 9 April 1789.
Robert s/o John & Isabella WILLSON b. 6 December 1788; bapt. 17 May 1789.
Fanny d/o John & Fanny TUNE b. 16 March 1787; bapt. 17 May 1789.
Mary Ann Murry d/o William & Sarah SHILLING b. 12 December 1788; bapt. 31 May 1789.
George s/o Henry & Sarah SHERING b. 27 December 1789; bapt. 31 May 1789.
John COLE s/o John & Margret b. 24 April 1789; bapt. 7 June 1789.
George s/o Joseph & Ann JENKINS b. 7 June 1789; bapt. 24 April 1789.
Mary d/o William & Catherine LEMON b. 18 February 1784; bapt. 7 June 1789.
David Gosegh s/o Charles & Mary JESSAP b. 17 November 1788; bapt. 14 June 1789.
Johnathan Hanson s/o John & Eliza. RUTTER b. 19 November 1787; bapt. 14 June 1789. {H-223}
John s/o John & Mary MILLER b. 8 May & bapt. 14 June 1789.
Rachel d/o William & Elizabeth CROSS b. 12 October 1788; bapt. 14 June 1789.
William Westfield s/o Henry & Mary HENDON b. 11 February & bapt. 21 June 1789. {R-II-21}
Elizabeth d/o Nicholas & Priscilla RUMAGE b. 13 February & bapt. 28 June 1789.
Eleanor d/o John & Eliza. BURN b. 1 August & bapt. 11 September 1788.

Frances b. 12 June ----; bapt. 12 July 1789; Elizabeth b. 6
February ----; bapt. 6 March 1787; d/o Peter & Catherine
SWINDLE.
Jane b. May & bapt. 26 July 1789, d/o Alexander & Rachel RUSSEL.
John s/o Daniel & Elizabeth EVERTON b. 17 October 1788; bapt. 2
August 1789.
Robert s/o Robert & Elizabeth LANGLEY b. 5 March & bapt. 9
August 1789.   {H-224}
Jesse s/o Nicholas & Elizabeth LEWIS b. 15 March & bapt. 16
August 1789.
Josias s/o Henry & Mary HENDON b. 11 March 1787; bapt. 21 June
1789.
Thomas s/o Paul & Ann RUST b. 21 Jan. 1789; bapt. 21 June 1789.
Harriot d/o Major SWAN bapt. 21 June 1789.   {R-II-22}
Catura d/o Charles & Ann HISS b. 17 April & bapt. 23 August 1789.
Jacob Frederick s/o Thomas & Elizabeth RICHARDSON b. 14 December
1788; bapt. 23 August 1789.
Elizabeth d/o Isaac & Elizabeth DICK b. 19 July & bapt. 30
August 1789.
Joshua s/o Christopher & Elizabeth BLACK b. 3 September & bapt.
30 August 1789.
Mary d/o James & Sarah WARD b. 1 March & bapt. 6 September 1789.
William s/o William & Catherine MARTIN b. 3 February & bapt. 6
September 1789.
Margaret d/o William & Elizabeth FIELDS b. 22 April & bapt. 13
September 1789.   {H-225}
Patience d/o Ezekiel & Hesia STANSBURY b. 24 March & bapt. 20
September 1789.
Hannah d/o John & Sarah HOLLAND b. 10 August & bapt. 20 September
1789.   {R-II-32}
John s/o John & Nancy FANE b. 14 May & bapt. 8 November 1789.
Mary d/o William BERRIGE b. 1 November & bapt. 16 Dec. 1789.
Mary d/o Matthew & Jane STATIA b. 22 February & bapt. 27
September 1789.
Samuel s/o John & Eisch CALELF b. 27 June & bapt. 27 September
1789.
Ann b. 22 June 1788, bapt. 11 October 1789; Eliza b. 10 August
1789, bapt. 11 October 1789; d/o Jacob & Sarah KNIGHT.
Rebecca b. 30 September 1789, bapt. 18 October 1789; Elizabeth b.
11 March 1786, bapt. 18 October 1789; d/o John & Ann FARMER.
Thomas s/o John & Elizabeth BURNS b. 2 October & bapt. 1 November
1789.
William b. 10 September 1778; Charles b. 28 October 1780; Joshua
b. 8 May 1783; John & James, twins, b. 4 November 1785; Ann b.
19 June 1788; children of Charles & Sarah MEREKIN.
Jemima Barton d/o Joshua & Ann POCOCK b. 2 January & bapt. 21
February 1790.
Mary d/o James & Sarah MASON b. January 1789; bapt. 7 March 1790.
George s/o George & Mary GILES b. 20 December 1789; bapt. 17
January 1790.   {R-II-24}
Sarah d/o Joseph & Mary CROWDER b. 24 May & bapt. 20 December
1789.
Peregrine s/o Thomas & Elizabeth SPICER b. 27 November 1788;
bapt. 27 December 1789.
Thomas s/o Thomas & Elizabeth TAYLOR b. 10 January 1773; bapt. 27
December 1789.
John s/o John & Ann BARKITT b. 1 October 1789; bapt. 1 Jan. 1790.
Abraham s/o Levin & Mary COWIN b. 18 February & bapt. 7 March
1790.

CHRISTENINGS

John s/o George & Ann TAYLOR b. 25 February & bapt. 14 March 1790.
George s/o Griffith & Sarah WHITE b. 25 December 1789; bapt. 4 April 1790.
James s/o Benjamn & Elizabeth SELLMAN b. 31 December 1785; bapt. {H-227} 4 April 1790.
Elizabeth SELLMAN d/o above b. 5 January & bapt. 4 April 1790.
John s/o John & Ann HEAD b. 22 December 1789; bapt. 4 April 1790.
Betsy d/o Henry & Casia DUNN b. 11 May 1789; bapt. 11 April 1790.

MARRIAGES

Thomas CORVALL m. Elizabeth DAVIDSON 12 November 1786. {R-II-25}
John MALCOLM m. Elizabeth DOUGLAS 30 July 1789.
Lewis THOMAS m. Mary LASQUE 10 August 1789.
William MAYHEW m. Eleanor MC KENSIE 7 January 1790.
Samuel GOOD m. Eleanor WHITE 4 February 1790.
Samuel OSBURN m. Sussanna AKELS 21 March 1790.
Thomas BROWN m. Elizabeth SMITH 28 April 1790. {H-228}
John ALLEN m. Christiana PENNY 23 March 1790.
Richard PERRY m. Sophia THOMAS 8 October 1789.
John LEAGUE m. Sarah FOWLER 6 May 1790.
Matthias SUNDAY m. Elizabeth LEWIS 19 May 1790.
Thomas ROBSON m. Hannah DENNY 16 August 1790.
Martin FIELD m. Jane HOGAN 2 September 1790. {R-II-26}
Michael BALLARD m. Elizabeth PAGE 11 August 1787.
John CURTIS m. Peggy EDWILLS 5 January 1784.
John BENTLY m. Ann THOMPSON 2 October 1790(?).
Moses STEPHENSON m. Margret MC CARTHY 2 October 1790(?).
Thomas POWELL m. Margret DOYLE 10 October 1790.
Peter HAMMER m. Ann CAPOST in 1790. {H-229}
James MC MAHON m. Jane LILLY 16 December 17--.
Michael DARLEY m. Caroline MILLER in 1788.
William ALLEN m. Sarah DEAN 7 March 1791.
Thomas ABRAHAM m. Sarah NUMEN (no date given).
Samuel MEALE m. Kessia CROSS 25 April 17--.

CHRISTENINGS

{R-II-27}
Ann b. 19 March & bapt. 11 April 1790; Margret b. 28 February 1786; d/o Edward & Kitty DAVIES.
Margaret d/o Daniel & Mary SAP b. 10 March & bapt. 11 April 1790.
John Williams SMEWING s/o John & Drewey b. 29 December 1788.
William s/o Charles & Mary ALDIN bapt. 31 January 1790 at 16 mos.
Elizabeth d/o Isaac & Pleasant WHEELER b. 20 October 1789; bapt. 7 February 1790.
George s/o Cutlip'd & Elizabeth TEEDS b. 31 August 1790. {H-230}
Nancy d/o Charles & Fanny HARBONG b. 27 February & bapt. 25 April 1790.
Mary d/o Robert & Mary ALLEN b. 21 November 1787; bapt. 25 April 1790.
Jane d/o John & Susanna MASE bapt. 25 April 1790 at 6 weeks.
Michael bapt. 25 April 1790 at 9 months; Charlotte bapt. 25 April 1790 at 3 years; s/o & d/o Michael & Racheal RUSSELL.
Sarah d/o Samuel & Eleanor MADDEN b. 14 June 1781.
Mary d/o Charles & Nancy STEWART b. February 1790.
Samuel s/o Michael & Flora HORN b. January 1790.

Rachel d/o Charles & Eliza. THOMPSON b. 11 November 1789; bapt. 4 July 1790.

Mary d/o Patrick & Margaret PENDERGRASS b. 2 March & bapt. 13 June 1790. {R-II-28}

Henry s/o Henry & Mary MITCHESON b. 8 December 1789; bapt. 10 January 1790.

Livinia d/o John & Mary KETTLEMAN b. 12 June 1789; bapt. 10 January 1790.

Sarah d/o Jacob & Mary CLARK bapt. 25 July 1790 at 11 weeks.

Ann d/o Larkin & Deborah YOUNG b. 12 May & bapt. 1 August 1790.

Frances d/o Caleb & Bridget HALL b. 5 April & bapt. 1 August 1790. {H-231}

Rachael d/o Charles & Elizabeth THOMPSON b. 11 November 1789; bapt. 4 July 1790.

Kessiah d/o Moses & Eleanor STEPHENSON b. 17 August 1790.

Rachael d/o Alexaner & Kessiah GALE b. 12 January 1777.

Samuel s/o John & Catherine HILSDEN "10 years old January 1791."

Conrad s/o Adam & Peggy MILLER b. 17 February 1790; bapt. 13 July ----.

Thomas s/o Thomas & Mary PILKINGTON b. 6 January & bapt. 1 May 1791.

William s/o Thomas & Jane BURROWS b. 15 February & bapt. 1 May 1791. {R-II-29}

John s/o John & Nancy CANNON b. 9 August 1777.

Swan s/o Joseph & Ann JUSTICE b. 28 September 1786. {H-232}

John b. 16 April 1788, bapt. 31 October 1790; Deborah b. 29 June & bapt. 31 October 1790; s/o & d/o Dennis & Airey LOWREY.

Benedict s/o James & Rebecca POCOCK b. 2 October & bapt. 7 November 1790.

Mary d/o Henry & Patty TREACLE b. 5 August & bapt. 12 December 1790.

Sarah d/o John & Sarah TYSE b. 15 July & bapt. 30 Dec. 1790.

John s/o Edward & Delilah KELLY b. 25 October 1790; bapt. 13 February 1791.

James s/o Job & Elizabeth DAVISON b. 1 December 1790; bapt. 13 March 1791.

Luke s/o John & Catherine GILL b. 6 February & bapt. 10 April 1791.

Mary d/o John & Elizabeth WOODWARD b. 28 August & bapt. 3 October 1790.

Cecilius Cowden s/o Adam & Mary JAMESON b. 18 July & bapt. 17 October 1790.

Thomas Byrom s/o George & Mary GRUNDY b. 24 August & bapt. 17 October 1790. {R-II-30}

John s/o Francis & Margret GILVERTHROP b. 28 August & bapt. 17 October 1790. {H-233}

Thomas s/o Elias & Margreet KING b. 17 September & bapt. 24 October 1790.

Elizabeth d/o John & Hannah HILL 15 May & bapt. 24 Oct. 1790.

Mary d/o John & Rachel LEEF b. 6 July & bapt. 24 Oct. 1790.

Ann d/o John & Ann WILLIAMS b. 1 October & bapt. 31 October 1790.

William s/o Thomas & Margaret GRIFFIN b. 3 October & bapt. 31 October 1790.

Harriet d/o James & Elizabeth FLYN b. 29 December 1787; bapt. 31 October 1790.

William Newton s/o Benjamin James & Anna MERCER b. 10 April & bapt. 15 May 1791.

Maria d/o William & Margret STRAUGHAN b. 4 June & bapt. 19 June 791.

CHRISTENINGS

James s/o Robert & Mary TAYLOR b. 19 April & bapt. 27 March
  1791. [sic]
John s/o John & Martha LEE b. 4 July 1790; bapt. 27 March 1791.
Samuel s/o Samuel & Susanna OSBURN b. 3 February & bapt. 24
  April 1791.   {H-234}

MARRIAGES
                                                          {R-II-31}
William BRANSON m. Margaret SMITH 2 January 1791.
John BATSON m. Rachel KIRTH 16 January 1791.
George TRYER m. Ann READ 3 March 1791.
George HAZZARD m. Eleanor BURGHES 3 May 1791 by. Rev. Lewis
  RICHARDS, Minister of the Baptist Congregation.
Isaac DUNWICK m. Jane RAY 24 September 1789.
John WARDEN m. Ann FISHER 3 June 1791.
Joshua HOLMES m. Arit SELLMAN 25 December 1783.
Henry FELLERS m. Rachel MILLER 10 April 1791.
Frederick FIGHTMASTER m. Sarah KENEDY 15 May 1791.
Aquila MILDEW m. Zena GERMAN 7 July 1791.
Henry LUNT m. Sarah STEWART 29 December 1790.   {H-235}
Darby CARMADY m. Sussana GORDON 14 August 1791.
David ELPHINSTON m. Lydia HAMBLETON 19 April 1791.   {R-II-32}
John THOMPSON m. Ann ENGLISH (Formerly MC FEE) 22 August 1791.
Adam LONGHEAD m. Sarah CONNELLY 15 July 1790.

CHRISTENINGS
                                                    {R-II-33}
Elizabeth d/o Alexander & Delilah ------- b. 12 November 1790;
  bapt. 12 June 1791.
Mary d/o Richard & Elizabeth BELL b. 14 October 1790; bapt. 12
  June 1791.
Charlotte Caroline d/o Thomas & Elizabeth RICHARDSON b. 2 October
  1790; bapt. 12 June 1791.
Mary d/o Richard & Elizabeth ROBBNET b. 9 March; bapt. 3 June
  1791.
Juliana Catherine b. 13 March, bapt. 14 April 1785; Rossanna b.
  21 February, bapt. 17 April 1787; Sarah b. 9 July 1789, bapt.
  27 June 1791; Solomon b. 29 April, bapt. 26 June 1791;
  children of Jacob & Mary BALLEBRAGA.
Sarah CROSS 11 years old, baptized in care of Samuel & Kessia
  LIETH, christened July 10, 1791.
Polly d/o William & Elizabeth FIELDS b. 1 February, bapt. 17
  July 1791.
Mary HUTSON d/o John & Elizabeth b. December 1789; bapt. 17 July
  1791.
Mary d/o Elijah & Mary WEST b. 15 February, bapt. 24 July 1791.
Sally James d/o William & Hannah SLATER b. 19 June, bapt. 24
  July 1791.
Samuel s/o Samuel & Mary SENEY b. 14 June 1790; bapt. 31 July
  1791.   {R-II-34}
William s/o Matthew & Jane STACEY b. 2 June, bapt. 31 July
  1791.
Rachael d/o George & Eleanor RIGBY b. 13 January, bapt. 31
  July 1791.
Eleanor d/o John & Ann PALMER b. 19 June, bapt. 7 August 1791.
Elizabeth d/o Joseph & Mary CROWDER b. 2 July, bapt. 7 August
  1791.   {H-237}
Ann Newton d/o Jacob & Ann MULL b. 17 February, bapt. 14 August
  1791.

CHRISTENINGS

Kiturah d/o Jacob & Elizabeth COOK b. 3 February, bapt. 14
    August 1791.
Edward s/o Roger & Jane MC GINNISS b. 28 August, bapt. 25
    September 1791.
Henry s/o Thomas & Mary CHAMBERS b. 5 June, bapt. 25 Sept. 1791.
Thomas Bodley s/o John & Elizabeth RITTER b. 9 November 1790;
    bapt. 25 September 1791.
Richard Isaacs s/o Richard JONES & Mary DONALDSON b. 24 March,
    christened September 28, 1791.
Rachael Isaacs d/o Richard JONES & Mary DONALDSON b. 30 January
    1790, christened 28 September 1791.
John s/o Benjamin & Elizabeth JONES b. 29 October 1788; bapt. 28
    August 1791.   {R-II-35} {H-238}
Hanah d/o John & Mary ROSS b. 17 January, bapt. 28 August 1791.
Catherine b. 6 May, bapt. 28 August 1791; Ann (no dates given);
    Mary b. 16 November 1783; Samuel b. 6 July 1787; children of
    John & Ann JOICE.
John s/o John & Eleanor WILLIAMS b. 5 March, bapt. 16 Oct. 1791.
Mary Ann d/o Henry & Elizabeth GROEFF (GROESS?) b. 6 September,
    bapt. 16 October 1791.
Francis [sic] Arabella d/o Amos & Mary Ann LOONEY b. 24 April,
    bapt. 6 October 1791.
Mary Ann d/o Benjamin & Jane CROCKETT b. 10 September 1789; bapt.
    5 October 1791.
Eliza Sophia d/o Luther & Maria MARTIN b. 10 July, bapt. 2
    October 1791.   {R-II-36}
Matthew s/o Thomas & Hanah ROBSON b. 31 May, bapt. 23 Oct. 1791.
Fanny d/o Zephania & Ruth CHANEY b. 1 September, bapt. 30 October
    1791.
Mary d/o William & Eliza. SELLERS b. 21 July, bap. 30 Oct. 1791.
Deborah d/o Peter & Elizabeth PITTRING b. 4 April, bapt. 30
    October 1791.   {H-239}
Sarah b. 7 February, bapt. 30 October 1791; Conrad & Bettsy b. 10
    March 1788; Eliza b. 5 July 1789; children of Joseph & Amelia
    BARKER.
William Kid s/o Abraham & Rebecca LYNCH b. 1 July, bapt. 6
    November 1791.
Moreton s/o Joseph & Ann JUSTICE b. 2 Sept., bapt. 6 Nov. 1791.
Eliza. d/o James & Mary CURTAIN b. 14 Feb., bapt. 23 Nov. 1791.
Eleanor d/o Benjamin & Mary SULLIVAN b. 14 November, bapt. 27
    November 1791.
Hanah d/o Peter & Catherine SWINDLE b. 29 October, bapt. 27
    November 1791.   {R-II-37}
Andrew s/o John & Elizabeth LEAKIN b. 11 August, bapt. 27
    November 1791.
James s/o John & Charlotte KELLY b. 16 October, bapt. 27
    November 1791.   {H-240}
Jane Stuart d/o Richard & Elizabeth FRANCIS b. 25 October, bapt.
    4 December 1791.
James s/o George & Ann ALDERSON b. 17 January, bapt. 30 November
    1791.
Robert s/o Thomas & Jane DARLING b. 13 November, bapt. 11
    December 1791.
John s/o Isaac & Plesant WHEELER b. 11 November, bapt. 25
    December 1791.
James s/o Joseph & Ann JENKINS b. 24 October, bapt. 25 Dec. 1791.
Sarah d/o Alexander & Elizabeth FURNIVAL b. 20 October, bapt. 27
    December 1791.

CHRISTENINGS

Elizabeth d/o Phillip & Elizabeth DORSEY b. 11 July, bapt. 27 December 1791. {R-II-38}

Frances d/o Paul & Mary PUELY b. 26 August, bapt. 28 Dec. 1791.

James s/o Charles & Fanny HERBERT b. 6 May 1786; bapt. 21 August 1791.

Mary d/o John & Christiana ALLEN bapt. 12 October 1791. {H-241}

Turbot s/o William & Hester WRIGHT b. 16 October, bapt. 14 December 1791.

William s/o Robert & Sarah BROWN b. February 1789; bapt. 21 August 1791.

Sarah GODFREY d/o Robert GODFREY & Mary ALLEN b. 1 August 1790; bapt. 21 August 1791. (She professes herself his wife, but desires to be called by the above name.)

John b. 11 January 1779; Jonathan b. 8 May 1780; Henry b. 29 September 1781; Jesse b. 7 May 1783; Joseph b. 9 March 1785; Josias b. 21 February 1787; Elizabeth b. 15 July 1789; children of Rudolph & Catherine HOOK.

Elizabeth d/o James & Susan BUCHANAN b. 24 June, bapt. 10 July 1791. {R-II-40} {H-242}

Cumberland s/o Cumberland & Margret DUGAN b. 22 December 1790; bapt. 28 July 1791.

Keturah d/o James & Pricilla PENNINGTON b. 26 August 1790; bapt. 6 August 1791.

George Washington b. 15 March 1791; bapt. 12 August 1791 s/o Charles & Ruth RIDGELY.

Elizabeth d/o William & Mary STOCKETT b. 14 September 1790; bapt. 12 August 1791.

John Heathcote s/o James & Charlotte DALL b. 6 June, bapt. 25 August 1791.

George s/o John Eager & Margaret HOWARD b. 21 November 1789; bapt. 28 August 1791.

John Butler s/o Jesse & Catherine HOLLINGS b. 16 November 1790; bapt. 28 September 1791.

Nathaniel Cooper s/o Thomas & Sarah JOHNSON b. 11 January, bapt. 7 September 1791.

Mary d/o John & Mary COCKEY b. 23 May 1790; bapt. 20 Sept. 1791.

Elizabeth d/o John & Mary FISHPAW b. 11 April, bapt. 20 September 1791.

Jemima d/o John & Sarah PARISH b. 17 February 1790; bapt. 20 September 1791.

Thomas s/o Henry & Christiana RUTTER b. 10 April 1790; bapt. 20 September 1791.

Francis Smith s/o William & Margaret BELTON b. 7 August, bapt. 20 November 1791. {R-II-41} {H-243}

Elenor b. 17 September 1785, bapt. 20 September 1791; Ann Tully b. 18 April 1787, bapt. 20 September 1791; Elizabeth b. 4 January 1789, bapt. 20 September 1791; Ruth b. 18 December 1790, bapt. 20 September 1791; children of William & Rebecca TOWSON.

Mary d/o Edward (deceased) & Cornelia YOUNG b. 20 April 1789; bapt. 20 September 1791.

Margaret Lente YOUNG d/o above b. 9 August 1791; bapt. 20 September 1791.

Henry b. 11 March 1789, bapt. 25 September 1791; Charles b. 11 Jan. 1791, bapt. 25 Sept. 1791; s/o Joseph & Sarah SLATOR.

Rebecca Waldgrave d/o Francis & Elizabeth CRACROFT b. 8 February, bapt. 30 September 1791.

Susanna d/o George & Letitia BUCHANAN b. 10 April 1790; bapt. 6 October 1791.

Mary Ann d/o John & Catherine WEATHERBOURN b. 31 March 1791; bapt. 23 October 1791.

George James s/o Joseph & Sarah DAVIS b. 27 September, bapt. 29 October 1791.

Margret d/o Joseph & Clara FARRELL b. 22 October, bapt. 2 November 1791.

Edward s/o Thomas & Rebecca PAMPHILION b. 12 July, bapt. 2 November 1791.

Mary d/o Richard & Mary PERKINS b. 4 May, bapt. 13 November 1791.

Harriot d/o Thomas & Mary YATES b. 8 August, bapt. 26 Nov. 1791.

James s/o Richard & Polly GITTINGS b. 25 June, bapt. 25 December 1791.

Boyd McKirdy s/o William & Elizabeth HUGHES b. 28 February, bapt. 16 November 1791.

Juliana d/o Joshua & Sarah ENNIS b. 13 October 1791; bapt. 1 January 1792.

John s/o Thomas & Rebecca COOPER b. 28 October 1791; bapt. 4 January 1792.

Patty d/o Charles & Ann STEWART b. 29 November 1791; bapt. 8 January 1792. {R-II-42} {H-244}

Sarah d/o Joseph & Elizabeth BRADY b. 27 November 1791; bapt. 8 January 1792.

Margret d/o Andrew & Mary GARRETT b. 14 January, bapt. 29 January 1792.

Edward s/o Edward & Catherine DAVIES b. 22 December 1791; bapt. 1 February 1792.

John Holly s/o Henry & Sarah NEWMAN b. 23 June 1791; bapt. 8 February 1792.

Edward s/o Edward & Ann JOHNSON b. 29 December 1791; bapt. 5 February 1792.

Thomas Jacob b. 3 May 1790; bapt. 29 February 1792 s/o Thomas & Ann HOLLINGSWORTH.

Jacob b. 6 August 1790; bapt. 29 February 1792 s/o Samuel & Sarah HOLLINGSWORTH.

Theophilus s/o Theophilus & Ann SIMCOCK b. 31 August 1791; bapt. 29 February 1792.

Elizabeth PERRY d/o John & Margaret b. 3 February, bapt. 29 February 1792.

Joseph Chick s/o Thomas & Catherine NASH b. 2 January, bapt. 11 March 1792.

Elizabeth d/o Levin & Sussana COLEMAN, both free blacks, b. in August 1791, bapt. 11 March 1792.

Mary d/o John & Mary (deceased) SLAMEKER b. February 1792; bapt. 11 March 1792.

Esther d/o William & Judious KIRBY b. 18 March, bapt. 28 March 1792.

James s/o James & Sophia CARROLL b. 2 December 1791; bapt. 15 March 1792. (R-II-43} {H-245}

James s/o William Rilpin & Mary OATES b. 15 November 1791; bapt. 1 April 1792.

Lydia d/o Nathaniel & Lydia PECK, both free negroes, b. 1 August 1791; bapt. 1 April 1792.

John s/o John & Mary TRAVERS b. 30 Oct. 1791; bapt. 4 April 1792.

William Osburn s/o William & Eleanor JOHNS b. 21 January, bapt. 4 April 1792.

Charles s/o John & Mary ROSS b. 13 February, bapt. 8 April 1792.

William s/o Henry & Rachel FELLERS b. 13 Feb.,bapt. 8 April 1792.

Elizabeth d/o Charles & Sarah MEREKIN b. 9 March, bapt. 22 April 1792.

James Hervey s/o Joseph & Margaret HOOK b. 19 June 1791; bapt. 22 April 1792.

Ann Boyd d/o Hercules & Mary COURTENAY b. 17 February, bapt. 23 April 1792.

John Charles s/o William & Elizabeth VANWYCK b. 27 January, bapt. 18 April 1792.

Elizabeth d/o Daniel & Martha DENNIS b. 6 December 1792??; bapt. 29 April 1792.

William s/o Thomas & Blanche BROTHERTON b. 17 February; bapt. 29 April 1792.

Peggy d/o John & Catherine NOBLE b. 7 February, bapt. 29 April 1792.   {R-II-44} {H-246}

Rufus s/o Thomas & Margaret GRIFFIN b. 23 February, bapt. 29 April 1792.

Charles s/o Charles & Rebecca GRIFFIN b. 29 December 1790; bapt. 29 April 1792.

Mary d/o Daniel & Elizabeth EVERTON b. 1 October 1791; bapt. 8 April 1792.

William s/o William (deceased) & Sarah ROBINSON b. 7 April & bapt. 25 April 1792.

Mary STAHL d/o Andrew STAHL & Mary YOUNG b. 20 March & bapt. 13 May 1792.

John s/o John & Achsah CALF b. 14 March & bapt. 20 May 1792.

Charles s/o Walter & Sarah ROE b. 5 January & bapt. 23 May 1792.

Elizabeth d/o James & Mary STAR b. 22 July 1791; bapt. 25 May 1792.

Elizabeth d/o William & Margaret BRANSON b. 23 March & bapt. 27 May 1792.

John b. 25 April 1789, bapt. 27 May 1792; James b. 19 March 1792, bapt. 27 May 1792; s/o Joseph & Hanah WILLSON.

John b. 29 January 1787, bapt. 27 May 1792; Richard b. 29 December 1785, bapt. 27 May 1792; William b. 26 November & bapt. 27 May 1792; s/o John & Mary BEVINS.   {R-II-45} {H-247}

George s/o John & Ann HEAD b. 29 October 1791;bapt. 13 June 1792.

Rebecca d/o William & Mary EVANS b. 22 September 1791; bapt. 17 June 1792.

Martha d/o William & Elizabeth GODDART b. 15 March & bapt. 17 June 1792.

Eleanor & Sarah, twins, d/o John & Margaret WHEELER b. 9 January 1792; bapt. 17 June 1792.

Sophia d/o Isaac & Margaret TURNER b. 31 December 1791; bapt. 17 June 1792.

Jane d/o Richard & Margaret REEVES b. 21 November 1791; bapt. 24 June 1792.

Patty d/o Samuel & Mary CHAMBERLAYNE b. 5 February 1792; bapt. 24 June 1792.

Julia d/o Charles & Ruth RIDGELY b. 11 December 1782; bapt. 27 June 1792.

Elizabeth d/o Daniel & Ann BOWLEY b. 17 October 1791; bapt. 20 May 1792.

James s/o William & Sarah STRAN b. 22 February 1790; bapt. 25 July 1792.

Sussanna Wharton d/o James & Sarah STRAN b. 25 April & bapt. 25 July 1792.

Mary d/o Nicholas Sluby & Margaret MC CARTHY b. 14 June & bapt. 1 August 1792.

William s/o James & Mary FISHWICK b. 25 June & bapt. 1 August 1792.

61

CHRISTENINGS

John Reuben s/o John & Eleanor TAYLOR b. 16 February & bapt. 1 August 1792.

Hannah Sophia d/o George & Mary GRUNDY b. 21 June & bapt. 12 August 1792.

Margaret d/o John & Rachel BATSON b. 28 July & bapt. 19 August 1792. {R-II-46} {H-248}

Hannah d/o William & Rebecca STRIKE b. 12 August & bapt. 19 August 1792.

Jemima d/o Nicholas & Rachel HALE b. 7 March 1777; bapt. 26 August 1792.

Edward Francis Gill HUGHES b. 2 January 1790, bapt. 2 September 1792; Mary HUGHES b. 24 December 1791, bapt. 2 September 1792; children of Christopher & Peggy HUGHES.

David b. 15 November 1780, bapt. 2 September 1792; Mary b. 12 November 1786, bapt. 2 September; s/o & d/o Joseph & Letitia JOHNSON.

Sarah Susanna d/o Henry & Mary HENDON b. 18 July & bapt. 29 August 1792.

Ann d/o Rudolph & Catharine HOOK b. 20 December 1791; bapt. 2 September 1792.

James s/o Henry & Elenor WEBB b. 20 September & bapt. 30 September 1792.

John s/o John & Elenor FLOOD b. 17 February & bapt. 23 September 1792.

Thomas s/o Jacob & Elizabeth HOOK b. 12 April 1791; bapt. 9 September 1792.

John s/o Thomas & Elizabeth RUTTER b. 25 September 1791.

Polly d/o Joseph & Anna TAYLOR b. 15 January 1791. {H-249}

William s/o William & Elizabeth FIELDS b. 22 July & bapt. 3 October 1792. {R-II-47}

Sarah d/o John & Rebecca STRAN b. 16 April & bapt. 3 Oct. 1792.

Abraham s/o Levin & Mary JONES b. 27 February & bapt. 17 October 1792.

Sarah Ann d/o John Zee & Sarah SELLMAN b. 8 April & bapt. 28 October 1792.

Abraham, Isaac & Jacob BOOVEY (triplets?) s/o Thomas & Rachel BOOVEY b. 20 June & bapt. 4 November 1792.

John s/o John & Elenor BUSH b. 10 Sept. & bapt. 7 November 1792.

Sarah d/o James & Ann DONALDSON b. 22 September 1792.

Sarah s/o Samuel & Elenor HURST b. 4 April & bapt. 7 Nov. 1792.

Ann b. 5 March 178-, bapt. 7 November 1792; George b. 15 July 1792, bapt. 7 November 1792; d/o & s/o John & Rebecca VANDERVOORT.

Daniel s/o Johnathan & Margaret HARRISSON b. 18 February 1792; bapt. 18 Novmber 1792.

Joseph Berry s/o William & Cloe GRAY b. 9 September 1792; bapt. 14 November 1792.

Sussanna Margaret MC KENZIE s/o Benjamin & Sussana b. 24 October 1790; bapt. 14 November 1792.

Tench Tilghman s/o Jacob & Martha SAMPSON b. 15 April 1792; bapt. 21 November 1792.

Margaret d/o William & Jane POLLOCK b. 3 September 1792; bapt. 25 November 1792.

William Bradford s/o Joseph G.J. & Mary B. BEND b. 30 September & bapt. 11 November 1792.

Mary b. 24 September 1789; William b. 27 August 1792; d/o & s/o James & Mary HARDY.

Elizabeth wife of Michael BALLARD bapt. 13 June 1792, 27 years old. {R-II-48} {H-250}

Mary Ann d/o George & Letitia BUCHANAN b. 14 October & bapt. 30 November 1792.

Elizabeth d/o Benjamin & Dorothy LOUNDER b. 2 July & bapt. 30 November 1792.

George Slater s/o Archibald & Elizabeth CAMPBELL b. 24 March & bapt. 16 June 1792.

Louisa d/o Thomas & Martha COULSON b. 3 July 1791; bapt. 11 July 1792.

Catherine d/o Adam & Mary JAMISON b. 12 March & bapt. 11 July 1792.

Mary b. 21 February 1788, bapt. 11 July 1792; Herman b. 21 November 1791, bapt. 11 July 1792; children of John & Hannah STUMP.

Richard s/o James & Elenor CROXALL b. 11 November 1791; bapt. 16 August 1792.

Benjamin Chew s/o John Eager & Margaret HOWARD b. 5 November 1791; bapt. 12 August 1792.

Sydney d/o Caleb & Bridget HALL b. 15 November 1787; bapt. 30 August 1792.

Elizabeth b. 12 March 1790, bapt. 11 October 1792; Rebecca b. 6 March & bapt. 11 October 1792; d/o William & Susanna HYATT.

Joshua b. 5 October 1789, Job Garretson b. 8 June 1792, both bapt. 11 October 1792, s/o Daniel & Eliza. STANSBURY.

Samuel s/o Robert & Sarah THOMPSON b. 3 July & bapt. 17 October 1792.

Elizabeth d/o John & Charlotte PECK b. 20 June 1791; bapt. 19 October 1792.

David s/o Thomas & Christiana ROLLS b. 13 July & bapt. 19 October 1792.   {H-251}

George s/o Charles & Mary RUST b. 29 January & bapt. 19 October 1792.

Thomas s/o Thomas William & Mary STOCKETT b. 29 August 1791; bapt. 19 October 1792.

Daniel s/o Johnathan & Margery HARRISSON b. 18 February & bapt. 18 November 1792.

Thomas s/o Thomas & Mary HAYNAM b. 7 August 1790; bapt. 11 October 1792.   {R-II-49}

Benjamin Kirby b. 2 February 1788, bapt. 31 October 1792; Alexander Bradford b. 27 September 1789, bapt. 31 October 1792; Daniel b. 18 February & bapt. 18 November 1792; s/o Jonathan & Margery HARRISSON.

Ann NEWMAN or Ann Newman ABRAHAMS d/o Sarah ABRAHAMS b. 16 June 1774; bapt. 11 November 1792.

Peter s/o Conrod & Eleanor HUSH b. 10 December 1791; bapt. 2 December 1792.

William Jacob b. 19 October 1785; Anna b. 16 July 1787; Maria b. 12 August 1789, all bapt. 12 December 1792; children of Thorndyke & Mary CHASE.

James s/o James & Rebecca POCOCK b. 14 November & bapt. 16 December 1792.

James b. 13/23(?) March 1783, Catharine b. 10 April 1789, both bapt. 16 December 1792, children of James & Elenor ASKIN.

John s/o David & Elizabeth GREGORY b. 25 October & bapt. 23 December 1792.   {H-252}

Hellen d/o Benjamin & Fanny HYTHE (free negroes) b. April 1792 & bapt. 23 December 1792.

Benjamin s/o Benjamin & Sarah SPENCER b. 6 November 1791; bapt. 9 January 1793.

CHRISTENINGS

Hezekiah JACKSON, a free mulatto, an adult near 17 years old, s/o Dorcas JACKSON, bapt. 23 December 1792.

Isaac CONNAWAY s/o Samuel & Mary CONNAWAY b. 23 August & bapt. 28 December 1792.

John Sank s/o Thomas & Elizabeth FENTON b. 11 December 1791; bapt. 28 December 1792.

Ann d/o Benjamin & Agnes WALTERS b. 25 April 1792; bapt. 13 January 1793.   {R-II-50}

Mary d/o Benjamin & Mary SELLMAN b. 26 December 1792; bapt. 13 January 1793.

Nancy d/o Joseph (deceased) & Rebecca SILBY b. 1 January 1789; bapt. 13 January 1793.

Elizabeth d/o Alexander & Mary HALL b. 20 October 1792; bapt. 20 January 1793.

Margaret Ann d/o Samuel & Catharine MUNRO b. 18 December 1792; bapt. 27 January 1793.

Mary d/o Samuel & Susanna ARMOR b. 25 November 1792; bapt. 13 January 1793.

Margaret d/o Hugh & Margaret LONG b. 15 January & bapt. 3 February 1793.

Rebecca d/o Nathaniel & Lydia PECK, free negroes, b. 1 September 1792; bapt. 3 February 1793.

Clarissa d/o Giles COALE & Sarah JONES b. 4 June 1791; bapt. 3 February 1793.   {H-253}

Sally d/o Richard & Mary JONES b. 5 August 1792; bapt. 8 February 1793.

Betsy d/o Solomon & Margaret TAYLOR b. 25 October 1791; bapt. 8 February 1793.

Richard s/o James & Jemima STANSBURY b. 10 January & bapt. 22 February 1793.

William b. 25 January & bapt. 24 February 1793; John b. 5 February 1789, bapt. 20 Nov. 1791; s/o John & Rebecca RUSSAEL.

John s/o Matthew & Frances SHAW b. 31 Jan. & bapt. 3 March 1793.

Mary d/o John & Susanna MARSHAL, free negroes, b. 31 December 1792; bapt. 3 March 1793.

MARRIAGES
{R-II-52} {H-254}

John Cockey Robert Burley BOON m. Elizabeth HALE 16 June 1791.

George WATERS m. Abigail WILLIAMS 9 July 1791, free negroes.

Benjamin SHIPLEY m. Amelia WEBSTER 16 August 1791.

Simon BULLEN m. Jane WILLSON 27 August 1791.

Isaac HOLMES m. Christiana JOHNSTON 28 August 1791.

Dennis HOGAN m. Elizabeth LUCAS 1 September 1791.

Michael HENESY m. Elizabeth WARRINGTON 18 September 1791.

Robert LITTLE m. Lucy CONNOLLY 13 September 1791.

Thomas SCAGS m. Lydia HILLEN 7 September 1791.

William RILEY m. Barbara HODGKIN 28 September 1791.

Benjamin RICKETTS m. Cassandra FORRESTER 29 September 1791.

Nicholas JOYCE m. Deborah Sanders LANSDALE 8 October 1791.

James FISH m. Nancy HUNTER 11 October 1791.

Samuel SMYTHE m. Elizabeth WIGNELL 15 October 1791.

Levin SHIPLEY m. Mary LOYD 20 October 1791.

Richard LAWSON m. Diana PARKINSON 29 October 1791.

Joseph WHIFFIN m. Susanna KNIGHT 30 October 1791.

Valentine PERRETT m. Elizabeth EAREE 6 November 1791.   {R-II-53}

William Briscoe TRAVERS m. Sarah FLANTEROY 9 November 1791.

William COX m. Dorcas EDWARDS 23 November 1791.

Joshua Merrican JONES m. Helen BAKER 26 November 1791.

MARRIAGES

William SKEEL m. Ann STAPLE 26 November 1791.
John GOODWIN m. Elizabeth BLINIO 25 December 1791.
Robert DEAN m. Margret YOUNG 10 December 1791.
William MINCHER m. Elizabeth HANEY 25 December 1791.   {H-255}
John ROBB m. Susanna DUNKIN 25 December 1791.
John LINHAM m. Elizabeth BAXTER 1 January 1792.
George LEE m. Rosanna PETERKIN 1 January 1792.
Christian APPLE m. Margret HERNS 3 January 1792.
David DUTTON m. Leah HEALY 1 February 1792.
Alexander BELL, a free black, m. Eleanor PINE, a slave of William
    PATERSON, 8 January 1792.
Edward MORRIS, a free black, m. Frances FERREL, a slave of John
    HAMMONDS 8 January 1792.
Robert FITZGERALD m. Catharine COOK 19 February 1792.
Abraham HARRISON m. Lilly MADKINS 22 January 1792.   {R-II-54}
John HEDRICK m. Margaret GALF 22 January 1792.
Nathan ROBERTS m. Mary SAUNDERS 1 March 1792.
Edward NAGLE m. Margaret MILLER 7 March 1792.
John ROYAL m. Mary SHEELS (SKEELS?) 15 March 1792.
Christian DETLIFF (DETLISS?) m. Mary KENLY 18 March 1792.
William Bell MEAKS m. Lydia JAMES 21 March 1792.
Thomas MAC CREERY m. Susannah NELSON 21 April 1792.   {H-256}
Samuel CONWAY m. Sarah HENRY 19 May 1792.
William WATKIN m. Susanna MINSKIE 3 May 1792.
Joseph FARLANA m. Mary FRAZIER 15 May 1792.
John PAYNE m. Mary GLENN 29 May 1792.
John BURN m. Mary Ann Dorsey MC DONALD 29 May 1792.
Walter WALLER m. Ealy PARKS 6 June 1792.
Christopher MINNER m. Frances BRYAN 11 June 1792.
Joseph BARNSLEY m. Elizabeth HALL 14 June 1792.
William JUB m. Avis HAMMOND 17 June 1792.   {R-II-55}
Richard LUMBERT (LIMBERT?) m. Elizabeth DAVISON 19 June 1792.
Bartholomew VINARD m. Susanna ROBERTS 24 June 1792.
William BOOTH m. Jane KAYL 14 July 1792.
John TOWERS m. Elizabeth HANNAN 18 August 1792.
William CURRAM m. Elizabeth BUCKINGHAM 16 July 1792.
William CONWAY m. Sarah ATKINSON 25 August 1792.
John WOODARD m. Rachael JOHNSON 31 July 1792.   {H-257}
Thomas GIBBERTHROP m. Rachael JOY 6 August 1792.
James JORDAN m. Sarah SMITH 29 August 1792.
John MC LARAN m. Ann TAYLOR 26 August 1792.
John WHITE m. Elizabeth ROBERTS 9 August 1792.
Robert DOWNES m. Allafar WITZEEL 29 September 1792.
John SAUNDERS m. Dorcas ALLEN 3 October 1792.
Laurant LEDUE m. Sussanna MIFFORD 9 October 1792.
James TAYLOR m. Margaret MURRY 13 October 1792.   {R-II-56}
Robert MC KINLIE m. Elizabeth MC LAUGHLIN 18 October 1792.
John BURLAND m. Mary NEIL 11 November 1792.
Edward FAIRS m. Margaret MATTHEWS 18 November 1792.
Richard BENFIELD m. Ann SMITH 8 April 1792.
John MURRAY m. Elizabeth AYRES 10 April 1792.
Benjamin HOWARD m. Susanna KNIGHT 17 April 1792.
John WILLSON m. Milcah TAYLOR 26 April 1792.   {H-258}
Hill MADKINS m. Priscilla DICKESON 27 April 1792.
Samuel SHEPHERD m. Sarah ORRICK, free blacks, 28 April 1792.
John GRAY m. Lucy FOSTER 26 April 1792.
John Frederick FISHER m. Elizabeth BIRSHALL 29 May 1792.
John BURLAND m. Mary NEIL 10 November 1792.
Patrick MALLOY m. Gressey NICKELL 11 November 1792.

MARRIAGES

Reuben WRIGHT m. Elizabeth GRIFFITHS 22 November 1792.
Frederick Raymond LALANNE m. Rachel CANNON 28 November 1792.
James KELSO m. Mary WALKER 3 January 1793.   {R-II-57}
Michael DUBOURG m. Elizabeth GRAINGER 6 January 1793.
William Thomas ROSS m. Mary PRICE 8 January 1793.
Rezin HAMMOND m. Nancy JOYCE 10 January 1793.
Henry HOLLINGSWORTH m. Levinah CROSS 13 January 1793.
William MARGAR m. Mary ANDERSON 17 January 1793.
Joseph COLEMAN m. Mary MC MECHAN 30 January 1793.
Joshua KNIGHT m. Sarah ANDERSON 31 January 1793.
Thomas HEATHRINGTON m. Sarah POLLOCK 7 February 1793.
Roger MC BRIDE m. Mary PHILE 11 February 1793.
James HOLLAND m. Sarah WEEKS 17 February 1793.
William POOL m. Rachel DERBIN 21 February 1793.
Omitted through mistake: {H-259}
Joshua GUTTRY m. Elizabeth KEENER 2 December 1792.
Solomon ARMSTRONG m. Margaret GRIFFIN 6 December 1792.
John THOMPSON m. Catherine COTTER 9 December 1792.
Ralph HAWKINS m. Susanna JACOBS m. 20 December 1792.
Christopher TREAKLE m. Mary WILSON 23 December 1792.
George DURTO m. Elizabeth STANSBURY 23 December 1792.
Robert MORRISON m. Margery MORRISON 30 December 1792.

BURIALS

William MAUCABY's child bur. 8 July 1791.   {R-II-58}
Mr. CHILD's child bur. 9 July 1791.
Mr. LOVE's child bur. 23 July 1791.
William HODGES daughter Ann bur. 5 August 1791.
Lucas DYSES bur. 6 August 1792.
John DALRYMPLE's child bur. 6 August 1791.
Thomas DROWN's child bur. 6 August 1791.
Robert BROWN's child bur. 26 August 1791.
Arthur HAGUE bur. 28 August 1791.
John GOODWIN's child bur. 31 August 1791.
George CHILD bur. 5 September 1791.
Charlotte DALL wife of Jams DALL bur. 7 September 1791.
Elizabeth MITCHELL wife of William MITCHELL bur. 9 Sept. 1791.
Daniel COOK child of Rebecca COOK bur. 19 September 1791.
Widow ALDRIDGE's child bur. 21 September 1791.
William WIGNAL bur. 23 September 1791.
Walter Donaldson ROE child to Walter ROE bur. 24 September 1791.
James CHILGORE bur. 28 September 1791.
Elizabeth BAILEY bur. 30 September 1791.   {R-II-59} {H-260}
William TRAVERSE s/o John TRAVERSE bur. 9 October 1791.
Francis HOBDY (stranger) (by Edward TOMPKINS) bur. 19 Oct. 1791.
William MARTIN's child bur. 24 October 1791.
William HUGHES bur. 26 October 1791.
Richard BARNANCE bur. 28 October 1791.
Catherine wife of John WEATHERBOURN bur. 29 October 1791.
John ALLEN bur. 31 October 1791.
Sarah wife of Roger ARMITAGE bur. 31 October 1791.
James LAWS' son bur. 1 November 1791.
Ann d/o William ROBINSON bur. 1 November 1791.
James DALL's son bur. 3 November 1791.
Joseph CLARK's son bur. 5 November 1791.
Francis CRAYCROFT's daughter bur. 17 November 1791.
Sarah CLARK d/o Jacob CLARK bur. 18 November 1791.
Rev. Joseph G.J. BEND's son bur. 25 November 1791.

Frances, sister of Samuel JOHNSTON, Esqr. bur. 27 November 1791.
Elizabeth DAVIS' child stillborn, bur. 27 November 1791.
Daniel RAY child of George RAY bur. 30 November 1791.
Luther MARTIN's daughter bur. 28 December 1791.   {R-II-60}
Ann LYEN d/o Benjamin LYEN bur. 27 December 1791.
Matthew ROBINSON s/o Mrs. ROBINSON bur. 29 December 1791.
William GALLION from Harford bur. 9 January 1792.
Mary IRELAND bur. 12 January 1792.
Benjamin SELLMAN's daughter bur. 13 January 1792.
William QUIG bur. 25 January 1792.
Capt. Joseph MOORE's son bur. 25 January 1792.
Ann PHILPOT bur. 27 January 1792.
Thomas NASH's wife bur. 28 January 1792.
Patty ARMSTRONG's child bur. 29 January 1792.
Mrs. LUCAS' husband bur. (no date given).
Magaret? d/o Andrew JARRETT bur. 1 February 1792.   {H-261}
Mr. JOHNSON's son bur. 14 February 1792.
William ROBERTSON bur. 16 February 1792.
Sally d/o Robert ALLEN bur. 20 February 1792.
Thomas s/o John COLEMAN bur. 26 February 1792.
Mary d/o John YOUNG of Fell's Point bur. 9 March 1792. {R-II-61}
Sally James d/o William SLATOR bur. 12 March 1792.
James s/o Col. James SILBY of the Eastern Shore bur. 15 March
     1792.
Margaret HILL d/o Asa HILL bur. 18 March 1792.
George TREGAIL bur. 25 March 1792.
Samuel HOLLINGSWORTH, stillborn child, bur. 1 April 1792.
Sarah wife of William POOL bur. 6 April 1792.
John VANDEVORT, formerly of New York, bur. 12 April 1792.
Henry GIBSON s/o William bur. 22 April 1792.
Benjamin CROCKETT, merchant, bur. 23 April 1792.
William POTTER, from Norwich in Great Britain, bur. 25 April
     1792.
John MC DONALD's stillborn child bur. 25 April 1792.
Benjamin LARNING bur. 20 May 1792.
Isaac TURNER bur. 25 May 1792.
Thomas HEPBURN bur. 1 June 1792.
Robert HEDRICK s/o John bur. 1 May 1792.
Mary d/o Richard WELLS bur. 23 June 1792.
Elizabeth wife of Joseph RAWLINGS bur. 23 June 1792.
Ann d/o Daniel HARRIS bur. 3 July 1792.
George HUGH s/o Conrad bur. 5 July 1792.
Mary d/o Charles GRIFFIN bur. 9 July 1792.
Mary d/o John PAGE bur. 11 July 1792.
David WOODYEAR s/o Edward b. 12 July 1792.
Elizabeth Ann d/o James HICKLEY bur. 17 July 1792.   {H-262}
Thomas RUSK bur. 18 July 1792.
Deborah d/o George JACKSON bur. 19 July 1792.
Samuel NASH s/o Thomas bur. 25 July 1792.   {R-II-62}
A child of Henry LEGGETT bur. 25 July 1792.
James GEOGHEGHAN s/o George bur. 29 July 1792.
Nathaniel Cooper s/o Thomas JOHNSTON bur. 30 July 1792.
Arabella d/o Daniel LEARY deceased bur. 1 August 1792.
Frances d/o Paul PUELY bur. 5 August 1792.
Susanna EVANS wife of William, laborer, bur. 7 August 1792.
Sarah d/o James ASKIN bur. 8 August 1792.
Thorndick CHASE's daughter, Caroline, bur. 13 August 1792.
John HURST s/o John bur. 18 August 1792.
James LAWRENCE bur. 18 August 1792.

BURIALS

Philip Zacharie s/o Philip WATERS bur. 20 August 1792.
Ann d/o Walter BELT bur. 21 August 1792.
Sarah d/o Joseph GRAINGER bur. 24 August 1792.
James or Samuel s/o Robert DAVIDSON bur. 1 September 1792.
Deborah wife of Obed GARDINER bur. 3 September 1792.
George s/o John HEAD bur. 8 September 1792.
Mary BARDLEY's child, a mulatto bur. 15 September 1792.
Rufus s/o Thomas GRIFFIN bur. 16 September 1792.
Sarah d/o Joseph CROWDER bur. 18 September 1792.
Thomas s/o Thomas DILLON bur. 19 September 1792.
Mary d/o William SELLERS bur. 22 September 1792.
Mary RIBBON bur. 29 September 1792.
Elizabeth wife of Elkin SOLOMON bur. 5 October 1792.
Christina d/o Providence LANE bur. 7 October 1792.
Ann wife of Frederick TRAVERS bur. 7 October 1792.
Elizabeth d/o Philip DORSEY bur. 8 October 1792.
John brother of Daniel DENNIS bur. 10 October 1792.
Isaac STANSBURY, son of widow STANSBURY bur. 11 October 1792.
Isaac WILSON bur. 16 October 1792.   {H-263}
Mary d/o Frederick PULLENGER bur. 17 October 1792.
Elizabeth d/o Zachariah SMITH bur. 21 October 1792.   {R-II-63}
Susanna YANTZ d/o George bur. 25 October 1792.
Elizabeth d/o Joseph SILVY bur. 16 November 1792.
Elenor d/o Joseph STANSBURY of Back River Neck bur. 24 Nov. 1792.
John HOLMES bur. 2 December 1792.
Thomas s/o William BERRIDGE bur. 13 December 1792.
Elizabeth wife of John MC KIRDY bur. 25 December 1792.
John WILLIAMS bur. 26 December 1792.
---- wife of Vincent GREEN of Back River Neck bur. 27 Dec. 1792.
---- s/o William HAMMOND (Iron Works) bur. 29 December 1792.
Joseph SILVY bur. 4 January 1793.
William MC COY, stepson to William CROW bur. 9 January 1793.
Joseph FOSTER bur. 10 January 1793.
Elizabeth BOWLY, mother & Ann wife of Daniel BOWLY bur. 10
    January 1793.
Sarah d/o Elizabeth TRUMBO bur. 31 January 1793.
John brother of Thomas CONSTABLE bur. 10 February 1793.
Maria d/o James NICOLS bur. 12 February 1793.
Ruth wife of John Dixon STANSBURY of Back River Neck bur. 22
    February 1793.
Josias BOWEN of Patapsco Neck bur. 26 February 1793.

CHRISTENINGS

                                                        {R-II-64}
Sarah d/o Jehu & Susanna BOWEN of Patapsco b. 20 March 1791;
    bapt. 5 March 1793.   {H-264}
Elizabeth KELSO (ASKEW?) d/o William ASKEW & Hannah KELSO b. 5
    April 1778; bapt. 6 March 1793.
Adelina Alice d/o John & Ruth SARGENT b. 14 January & bapt. 6
    March 1793.
Jane d/o John & Mary GRAY b. 13 Jan. 1774; bapt. 12 March 1793.
Margaret d/o Elias & Margaret KING b. 28 January & bapt. 17 March
    1793.
Mary d/o John & Elizabeth WILSON b. 11 November 1790; bapt. 17
    March 1793.
Susan d/o James & Susanna BUCHANAN b. 20 February & bapt. 18
    March 1793.
Elizabeth Mary Trippe d/o Seth & Sarah Emerson BARTON b. 22
    February & bapt. 19 March 1793.

CHRISTENINGS

Elizabeth d/o Thomas & Rebecca PAMPHILION b. 25 November 1792; bapt. 20 March 1793.
William s/o Thomas & Sarah JOHNSON b. 21 January & bapt. 20 March 1793.

MARRIAGES

John TROTTEN m. Sarah SOLLERS 5 March 1793.
Peter PEOT m. Louisa AVELIN 11 March 1793.
William SINGLETON m. Elizabeth SLATER 20 March 1793.
William LAWRENCE m. Mary SHIELDS 23 March 1793.

BURIALS

Charles ROE s/o Walter ROE bur. 9 March 1793.
Mary LEWIS wife of John LEWIS bur. 15 March 1793.
Ann AGIN (EGAN?) from Ireland bur. 18 March 1793.
Thomas GASH in Patapsco Neck bur. 26 March 1793.{R-II-65} {H-265}
Elizabeth LOWREY bur. 12 April 1793.
Thomas MITCHESON bur. 12 April 1793.

CHRISTENINGS

Thomas s/o Walter & Ann BELT b. 6 January & bapt. 27 March 1793.
Jacob s/o Nicholas & Esther HEINER, blacks, b. 12 February & bapt. 31 March 1793.
Martha d/o Henry & Hanah NANTZ b. 29 March & bapt. 31 March 1793.
Sarah RICHARDS (DAY?) d/o John DAY & Kitty RICHARDS b. 11 June 1792; bapt. 7 April 1793.
James Chapman s/o Benjamin & Sarah BAKER b. 28 January 1792; bapt. 10 April 1793.
Ann COLE wife of Joshua b. 1771; bapt. 14 April 1793.

MARRIAGES

Charles Caple COALE m. Sarah RHOADES 24 March 1793.
Butler KELLY m. Ann KITELY 24 March 1793.
Henry BULGER m. Mary KETTLEMAN 28 March 1793.
Philip EDWARDS m. Ann RAWINGS 28 March 1793.
Gerard GOVEN m. Sarah GILES 2 April 1793.
Jeremiah POWELL m. Sarah NICOLSON 14 April 1793.

CHRISTENINGS

{R-II-66}
Elizabeth d/o Joshua & Ann COLE b. 1 September 1791; bapt. 14 April 1793.
{H-266}
Rose d/o John & Catharine TRUMBO b. September 1789; bapt. 14 April 1793.
Sarah d/o George & Mary ROBERTS b. 1 December 1792; bapt. 16 April 1793.
Eliza d/o William & Eliza TWINAM b. 7 May & bapt. 16 April 1793.
Pollard Edmondson b. 1 May 1790 & Ann Wright b. 18 April 1792, both bapt. 17 April 1793; children of Christopher & Ann BIRCKHEAD.
Joseph s/o Philip & Elenor WATERS b. 3 March 1793 & bapt. 18 April 1793.
Philip s/o James & Eliza WATERS b. 2 February 1793 & bapt. 18 April 1793.

69

CHRISTENINGS

Catherine d/o Thomas & Elizabeth DEWITT b. 3 January & bapt. 24 April 1793.
Anna d/o John & Jane HALL b. 26 February & bapt. 24 April 1793.
William s/o Edward Jr. & Ann JOHNSON b. 4 February & bapt. 4 May 1793.
William s/o Henry & Elizabeth CABLE b. 15 April 1792; bapt. 5 May 1793.

MARRIAGES

Anthony REEVES m. Elizabeth MC KENZIE 2 May 1793.
Thomas BUCKINGHAM m. Mary STOPHEL 3 May 1793.
John CLARK m. Mary WHALEY 5 May 1793.

BURIALS

William BURROWS bur. 18 April 1793.
Isabella ARMSTRONG bur. 23 April 1793.

CHRISTENINGS

{R-II-67} {H-267}
James s/o William & Sarah GIBSON b. 8 February; bapt. 5 May 1793.
Sarah d/o Silas & Margaret ENGLE b. 19 May 1792; bapt. 8 May 1793.
James s/o James & Sarah MASON b. 18 Nov. 1792; bapt. 12 May 1793.
Jane d/o James & Patience LONG b. 18 Feb. & bapt. 15 May 1793.
Peggy & Betsey, twins, d/o George & Elizabeth SHELHAMER b. 29 March & bapt. 19 May 1793.
Betsey d/o John & Mary WATKINS b. 1 January 1792; bapt. 19 May 1793.

MARRIAGES

Jacob EVENSON m. Sophia PARKS 5 May 1793.
Daniel LASWORT m. Catherine ROBINSON 9 May 1793.
Thomas NELSON m. Mathilda JOHNSON 9 May 1793.
Robert MOORE m. Jane GALLOWAY 13 May 1793.
Anthoney KIRBY m. Drusilla ROBERTS 14 May 1793.
James REYNOLDS m. Sarah JOHNSON 17 May 1793.
Samuel PERRY m. Rebecca PENNINGTON 19 May 1793.

BURIALS

John ELLIS bur. 21 May 1793.
Pamela MINTZ bur. 21 May 1793.
John HINDMARSH bur. 22 May 1793.   {R-II-68} {H-268}
Elizabeth LEWIN bur. 23 Mary 1793.
Jane GRAY bur. 27 May 1793.
Anne MULL bur. 31 May 1793.
Solomon ARMSTRONG bur. 5 June 1793.
Jacob Frederick RICHARDSON bur. 9 June 1793.

CHRISTENINGS

Mary JAMESON wife of Adam b. October 1764; bapt. 7 June 1793.
Thomas JOHNSON, adult, b. 24 February 1766; bapt. 7 June 1793.
Catharine LE GROSS, adult, b. 23 January 1769; bapt. 7 June 1793.
John s/o Andrew & Martha BAHLER b. 22 December 1792; bapt. 9 June 1793.

CHRISTENINGS

Eliza. d/o Thomas & Rebecca PETERS b. 23 January & bapt. 9 June 1793.

Harry Dorsey Gough s/o James & Sophia CARROLL b. 4 April & bapt. 9 June 1793.

Elijah s/o Elijah & Mary WEST b. 13 April 1792; bapt. 9 June 1793.

Robert s/o Robert Allen & Mary GODFREY b. 15 April & bapt. 9 June 1793.

MARRIAGES

Frederick LINHART m. Mary ISLER 6 June 1793.
William CRANE m. Nancy HENSHAW 8 June 1793.
William COLEMAN m. Sinah ALLEN 12 June 1793.   {R-II-69} {H-269}
George LONGFIELD m. Ann CRAWFORD 13 June 1793.
Samuel FLOYD m. Fanny SOMELIN 15 June 1793.
Demas WALLINGTON m. Elizabeth MC GEE 20 June 1793.
William Jones BOWEN m. Margarte MURPHY 23 June 1793.
Jacob PEACOCK m. Mary GARDINER 27 June 1793.
Henry MORGAN m. Ann COLLINS 30 June 1793.
George REDDEN m. Elenor THOMPSON 1 July 1793.

CHRISTENINGS

Mary d/o Richard & Elizabeth FELLERS b. 2 May & bapt. 9 June 1793.

James s/o John & Ann WILLIAMS b. 9 May & bapt. 16 June 1793.

Elizabeth d/o Joseph & Letitia JOHNSON b. 28 February & bapt. 27 June 1793.

BURIALS

Mary CHASE bur. 20 June 1793.
Thomas CHATTLE bur. 22 June 1793.
Catherine JAMESON bur. 27 June 1793.
Jane Stuart FRANCIS bur. 2 July 1793.
Daniel BOWLEY, Jr. bur. 9 July 1793.   {R-II-70} {H-270}
Ann Wright BIRCKHEAD bur. 11 July 1793.
Sarah KEARNY bur. 15 July 1793.
James Loyd ROGERS bur. 17 July 1793.
Sarah STRAN bur. 18 July 1793.
John WOODARD's child. bur. 19 July 1793.
William STRONG bur. 20 July 1793.
Susanna ELLIS bur. 28 July 1793.
Joseph WARD, Jr. bur. 4 August 1793.
David GREY bur. 5 August 1793.
William HARVEY bur. 5 August 1793.
James Gifford YOULE bur. 7 August 1793.
Ann GREY bur. 7 August 1793.
Robert BALLARD bur. 9 August 1793.

MARRIAGES

Michael HEDDINGER (Michael Heddinger INLEY?) m. Catharine HERMAN 11 July 1793.

Philip LEONARD m. Mary Ann GRAY 18 July 1793.

CHRISTENINGS

William s/o John & Mary ENSOR b. 3 Aug. 1792; bapt. 7 July 1793.
Nancy d/o John & Sarah HOLLAND b. 28 December 1791; bapt. 4 August 1793.
Rebecca d/o Henry & Ruth FISHPAW b. 28 March & bapt. 11 August 1793.   {R-II-71} {H-271}
Mary d/o John & Mary FISHPAW b. 19 December 1792; bapt. 11 August 1793.
Elizabeth d/o Joshua & Catherine CLARK b. 2 October 1792; bapt. 11 August 1793.
Anne d/o Thomas & Elenor BURTON b. 14 December 1792; bapt. 16 August 1793.
Jemima d/o Patrick & Elizabeth LYNCH b. 29 April & bapt. 16 August 1793.
Richard s/o Herman & Frances TRICE b. 14 January & bapt. 18 August 1793.
Jesse s/o Jesse & Hannah FEARSON b. 30 August 1792; bapt. 19 August 1793.
John s/o John & Margaret YOUNG b. 3 January 1792; bapt. 19 August 1793.
Joseph s/o Samuel & Susanna OSBURN b. 20 February & bapt. 25 August 1793.

MARRIAGES

David WATSON m. Mary Magdalen ROORBACH 11 August 1793.
John LOYD m. Catherine REAR 23 August 1793.
Stephen BULL m. Hannah SULPH 24 August 1793.

BURIALS

John DIBLEY bur. 10 August 1793.
Mary BENNETT bur. 14 August 1793.
Mary CLIFTON bur. 15 August 1793.
A daughter of Thomas BURTON bur. 16 August 1793.
Henry WALTER bur. 17 August 1793.
David MOORHEAD bur. 19 August 1793.
Sally Fay MOORE bur. 24 August 1793.
David SLATER bur. 28 August 1793.   {R-II-72} {H-272}
George VANDERVOORT bur. 28 August 1793.
Mary North MOALE bur. 29 August 1793.

CHRISTENINGS

John & Ann, twins, children of Matthew & Jane STACEY b. 26 July & bapt. 25 August 1793.

MARRIAGE

John RAWLINGS m. Margaret SMITH 29 August 1793.   {H-273 is blank}

CHRISTENINGS
                                                      {R-II-73} {H-274}
Hannah d/o Peter & Phebe MILLER b. 28 July & bapt. 1 Sept. 1793.
John Conorod SMITH s/o John Jacob SMITH & Jane PARRAN his wife b. -- February & bapt. 21 September 1793.
Charlotte d/o Stephen & Mary WHEELER b. 17 May 1789; bapt. 22 September 1793.
Harriot d/o Job & Elizabeth DAVIDSON b. 1 March & bapt. 22 September 1793.

72

CHRISTENINGS

George s/o George & Elenor REDDEN b. 4 July & bapt. 22 September 1793.

Sydney d/o James (deceased) & Elenor THOMPSON b. 11 October 1782; bapt. 22 September 1793.

Charlotte d/o William & Elizabeth SELLER b. 20 August & bapt. 22 September 1793.

William Pickett b. 29 December 1791, bapt. 25 September 1793; Elizabeth b. 16 June & bapt. 25 September 1793; s/o & d/o John & Mary DALRYMPLE.

Anna Maria d/o Richard & Polly GITTINGS b. 4 March & bapt. 26 September 1793.

James s/o Joseph & Margaret GREY b. 17 September 1790; bapt. 29 September 1793.

Sarah of "Robert MC KINLEY & Elizabeth MC LAUGHLIN" b. 10 January 1791; bapt. 6 October 1793.

Cecilius s/o John & Catharine BELL b. 2 March 1792; bapt. 20 October 1793.

Mary d/o John & Dorcas SAUNDERS b. 13 August & bapt. 20 October 1793.

Anna d/o John & Margaret EVERHART b. 30 June & bapt. 20 October 1793.

MARRIAGES

{R-II-74}
{H-275}

William ANNIS m. Marggaret THOMPSON 3 September 1793.
Alexander LANDIN m. Sarah BEACHGOOD 19 September 1793.
Francis HANWAY m. Belinda CANE 21 September 1793.
John Hurle CHANDLESS m. Sarah ANDERSON 1 September 1793.
Edward HIGGINS m. Anne ELLERTON 24 September 1793.
John HODGES m. Mary BRYAN 26 September 1793.
Andrew PERRY m. Martha MURRAY 28 September 1793.
Levin CORNISH m. Milly GOVARE 28 September 1793.
Elijah TOWNSEND m. Nancy COGLIAN 29 September 1793.
John HELMS m. Catharine CLARK 2 October 1793.
Titus IMPFORD m. Elizabeth THOMAS 9 October 1793.
Thomas FOWLER m. Sarah BARTON 10 October 1793.
Robert MC LANE m. Elizabeth WHEELER 11 October 1793.
Joseph MORIE m. Josephine SCROTE 14 October 1793.
Dennis BURN m. Sarah CORD 18 October 1793.
Edward THOMPSON m. Mary DUNN 20 October 1793.
William MC DOE m. Elizabeth RIDDLE 21 October 1793.
Joseph PUMPHREY m. Sarah STEWART 22 October 1793.
Michael HURLEY m. Joanna GWINN 29 October 1793.

BURIALS

{R-II-75}
{H-276}

Eliza. d/o Daniel DENNIS bur. 1 September 1793.
Nancy d/o James PATERSON bur. 2 September 1793.
John s/o John PERRY bur. 8 September 1793.
William s/o Isaac DICKS bur. 13 September 1793.
Elizabeth WOOD bur. 13 September 1793.
William LONEY of Harford County bur. 15 September 1793.
Abraham s/o Levin JONES bur. 16 September 1793.
Catharine ORRICK of Anne Arundel County bur. 23 September 1793.
James FORBES bur. 24 September 1793.
John s/o Peter MC DONNELL bur. 25 September 1793.
James s/o of Samuel O'DONNEL bur. 26 September 1793.
Sarah wife of William NORRIS bur. 29 September 1793.
John Jacob s/o Parker PHELPS bur. 29 September 1793.

BURIALS

Jane d/o Jane MAGGS bur. 30 September 1793.
Rebecca wife of Robert BALLARD bur. 8 October 1793.
Rebecca WELLS d/o Hannah FEARSON bur. 9 October 1793.
John WILLIAMS bur. 9 October 1793.
Frances wife of William RUSSELL bur. 13 October 1793.
Luke s/o John GILL bur. 21 October 1793.
William s/o William CROW bur. 22 October 1793.
Margaret d/o Hugh LONG bur. 24 October 1793.
Thomas KNAB bur. 26 October 1793.
John s/o Henry WEBB bur. 10 November 1793.   {R-II-76} {H-277}
Margaret wife of Robert TOWNSEND bur. 14 November 1793.
Rosanna d/o James LOVE bur. 15 November 1793.
Richard s/o James STANSBURY bur. 15 November 1793.
William JONES bur. 27 November 1793.
Margaret WINNING bur. 1 December 1793.
John QUAY bur. 8 December 1793.
John CLARK bur. 10 December 1793.
James Warner THOMAS bur. 11 December 1793.
Mary Hill HOPKINS bur. 12 December 1793.
John s/o John HUDLER bur. 15 December 1793.
A child of Henry FELLERS bur. 15 December 1793.
Priscilla BOOKER bur. 24 December 1793.
Mary APPLE (or APPLEMAN) bur. 27 December 1793.
Elizabeth PECKARD bur. 28 December 1793.
John CUMMINS bur. 29 December 1793.
John s/o William TOWNSLEY bur. 30 December 1793.

CHRISTENINGS

Kelso Cumberland s/o Cumberland & Margaret DUGAN b. 31 October   {R-II-77} {H-278}
1792; bur. 2 November 1793.
Henrietta JAMES, an adult, bapt. 10 November 1793.
Molly JAMES d/o Henrietta, widow, b. 11 March 1785; bapt. 10
November 1793.
Martha & Anne, twins, d/o Joshua & Frances PRICE b. 1 July 1792;
bapt. 10 November 1793.
William Veazey s/o William & Hester WRIGHT b. 16 August & bapt.
13 November 1793.
Richard Revel s/o Patience ARMSTRONG b. 23 August & bapt. 17
November 1793.
Sarah d/o William & Sarah CROW b. 18 August & bapt. 27 November
1793.
Elizabeth d/o Edward & Teressa HANNAH b. 19 January 1790; bapt. 1
December 1793.
James Etbridge of James Warner THOMAS & Rebecca HUTCHINSON his
wife b. 15 July & bapt. 5 December 1793.
Elenor d/o John & Anne HEAD b. 2 October & bapt. 11 Dec. 1793.
William s/o Thomas & Anne CARBACK b. 15 October & bapt. 20
December 1793.
Mary Anne d/o Thomas & Margaret GRIFFIN b. 27 September & bapt.
22 December 1793.
Joseph s/o George & Martha TAYLOR b. 11 August & bapt. 26
December 1793.
Sarah d/o Joshua & Anne COLE b. 24 Nov. & bapt. 29 Dec. 1793.
Sarah d/o John & Bennet PAGE b. 27 Nov. & bapt. 29 Dec. 1793.
Mary d/o Hammond & Mary ROSS, free Mulattoes, b. -- October &
bapt. 29 December 1793.

MARRIAGES

Solomon TIPTON m. Mary RANDALL 1 November 1793. {R-II-78} {H-279}
John JENNINGS m. Elizabeth KOUGH 2 November 1793.
Francis LEESON m. Elizabeth MACKANERNEY 10 November 1793.
Robert THORNBURGH m. Elizabeth KITTLEMAN or GIDERMAN 10 November 1793.
John BROW m. Catharine PERKINS 10 November 1793.
John HAGEN m. Mary BRYAN 4 December 1793.
Henry NICOLS m. Rebecca SMITH 5 December 1793.
Patrick LYON m. Jane BAILEY 8 December 1793.
Jonathan ASKEW m. Mary PORTER 14 December 1793.
John ROBERTSON m. Maria WILLSON 16 December 1793.
Robert PORTER m. Susanna BUCK 17 December 1793.
John CARPENTER m. Helen GWINN 24 December 1793.
Edward JARVIS m. Nancy ORAM 25 December 1793.
George WILEY m. Jane SMITH 26 December 1793.
Peter DUGAR m. Elizabeth TULLY 30 December 1793.
Henry HOWARD m. Mary BROWN 31 December 1793.

CHRISTENINGS

{R-II-79}

Charlotte d/o Joseph & Amelia BARKER b. 15 June 1793; bapt. 5 January 1794.

{H-280}

Elizabeth d/o Lewis & Sarah JEWEL b. 11 October 1793; bapt. 5 January 1794.
John Lloyd Holsey & Rust Morgan, twins, s/o Thomas & Sally FOWLER b. 19 December 1783; bapt. 5 January 1794.
Thomas s/o Thomas & Susanna LAMETIN b. 27 October 1793; bapt. 9 January 1794.
Elizabeth d/o William & Elenor MAYO b. 7 September 1793; bapt. 9 January 1794.
Robert s/o Philip & Anne SHERWOOD b. 8 October 1793; bapt. 9 January 1794.
Isabella d/o Basil & Anne SMITH b. 26 November 1793; bapt. 9 January 1794.
Louisa Georgina & Washington children Alexander & Elizabeth FURNIVAL b. 9 October 1793(?); bapt. 10 January 1794.
Jane d/o Joseph & Sarah LANGDON b. 17 September 1793; bapt. 17 January 1794.
James s/o John & Mary BURLAND b. 31 October 1793; bapt. 19 January 1794.
Lydia Agness Monkhouse(?) d/o Seth & Sarah Emerson BARTON b. 11 January & bapt. 6 February 1794.
Frances Georges s/o Joseph Jr. & Frances Anne RAWLINS b. 23 December 1793; bapt. 7 February 1794.
William s/o William & Rebecca TOWSON b. 15 October 1793; bapt. 8 February 1794.
Charlotte Elizabeth d/o Charles & Elizabeth BUTLER b. 10 January & bapt. 9 February 1794.
Francis s/o Leonard & Elizabeth WOOD b. 20 February 1793; bapt. 12 February 1794.
Rebecca Harriet d/o James & Mary Charlotte DARRINGTON b. 25 July 1788; bapt. 13 February 1794.
John b. 21 August 1785; Mary b. 10 July 1789; Sarah b. 24 April 1793, chilren of John & Frances TUNE, all bapt. 19 Feb. 1794.
John s/o Jacob & Jane CRONMILL b. 13 Feb. & bapt. 26 Feb. 1794.
Joseph Edwards s/o Edward & Catherine DAVIS b. 24 January & bapt. 26 February 1794.

CHRISTENINGS

Robert b. 17 December 1780; Charles Carnan b. 25 March 1785;
William Augustus b. 2 February 1787; John b. 31 March 1789;
Thomas Pirken b. 5 February 1793; all bapt. 28 February 1794;
s/o Charles RIDGELY of William & Ruth his wife.

MARRIAGES

Pearl DIRGA m. Joanna GAILE 5 January 1794.   {R-II-80} {H-281}
James PIKE m. Alice BUTLER 9 January 1794.
Charles WARD m. Sophia DELAHAYE 9 January 1794.
Robert TOWNSEND m. Juliet FREELAND 19 January 1794.
Robins CHAMBERLAYNE m. Mary CROOKSHANKS 30 January 1794.
William THOMAS m. Janet Anne FAURE 30 January 1794.
Hugh WILSON m. Hannah HILL 3 February 1794.
Alexander Peter BURNOR m. Margaret LUSHROW 3 February 1794.
Abraham TOWSON m. Jane GATES 12 February 1794.
William DOWNES m. Margaret BURNS 13 February 1794.
Augustine LAVIGNE m. Cassandra ANDREW 13 February 1794.
William BAYZAND m. Susanna Aisquith MOORE 19 February 1794.
William GARNONS m. Jane TUNE 19 February 1794.
Samuel CRANFORTH m. Anne PARKER 22 February 1794.
                                             {R-II-81} {H-282}
Maryland to wit: William EDWARDS, master of the Brig Hero,
   maketh Oath and saith, that Jane FOX, wife of John Hopkins FOX,
   died on board the said Brig on 24 May last on Her passage from
   Liverpool to the Town of Baltimore. Signed, William EDWARDS
   Sworn at Baltimore this 30th day of June 1794 before me, Samuel
   CHASE.

BURIALS

William s/o Christopher HUGHES bur. 2 January 1794.
Anne d/o Matthew STACEY bur. 3 January 1794.
William s/o William LEE bur. 5 January 1794.
William Tinker s/o William PELTON bur. 6 January 1794.
Thomas ROSSITER bur. 9 January 1794.
Robert s/o Robert Allen GODFREY(?) bur. 14 January 1794.
Sophia STEVENS bur. 19 January 1794.
Sarah USHER bur. 19 January 1794.
Henry MITCHESON s/o Mary bur. 20 January 1794.
Margaret YATES bur. 21 January 1794.
William s/o Thomas JOHNSON bur. 6 February 1794.
Sarah wife of Charles MERRIKEN bur. 8 February 1794.
Catharine BARNETT bur. 9 February 1794.
Harriot d/o William JOHNSON bur. 16 February 1794.
Alexander PAYAN bur. 18 February 1794.
Margaret wife of Hugh LONG bur. 23 February 1794.
Anna Maria d/o Richard GITTINGS bur. 1 March 1794.   {H-283}
Joshua s/o Daniel STANSBURY bur. 5 March 1794.   {R-II-82}
John s/o Charles STANSBURY bur. 5 March 1794.
William STEVENS bur. 5 March 1794.
William CONSTABLE bur. 7 March 1794.
John s/o David (?) GREGORY bur. 13 March 1794.
Richard CARTER bur. 17 March 1794.
Thomas TODD at Samuel NORWOOD's bur. 17 March 1794.
Elenor d/o John BURN bur. 23 March 1794.
Elizabeth d/o Frederick PRATT bur. 27 March 1794.
Eliza d/o William TWINAM bur. 28 March 1794.
Elizabeth BRISCOE bur. 5 April 1794.

BURIALS

Thomas s/o Thomas DEWITT bur. 8 April 1794.
Roanna? d/o Frances WHITE bur. 9 April 1794.
Catharine wife of William MARTIN bur. 10 April 1794.
Robert s/o Frances WHITE bur. 11 April 1794.
Charles VASHON bur. 11 April 1794.
William MOORE allias WILMER bur. 15 April 1794.
Frances MOALE d/o Rebecca RUSSELL, widow, bur. 16 April 1794.
Anne d/o James HOLMES bur. 17 April 1794.
George s/o Griffith WHITE bur. 19 April 1794.
Mary JOHNSON d/o Benjamin MC KENZIE bur. 20 April 1794.
Antun, baptized child of John RAWLINGS bur. 21 April 1794.

CHRISTENINGS

Joanna d/o Robert & Sarah BROWN b. 5 September 1793; bapt. 3
   March 1794.   {R-II-83} {H-284}
Thomas s/o Daniel & Elizabeth STANSBURY b. 31 December 1793;
   bapt. 3 March 1794.
Mary Fowler d/o David & Henrietta Maria STANSBURY b. 27 March
   1793; bapt. 3 March 1794.
Sarah LAZIRE, adult, wife of John LAZIRE b. -- September 1770;
   bapt. 15 March 1794.
Henry Howcroft s/o John & Catharine GILL b. 24 January & bapt. 9
   March 1794.
Mary d/o Samuel & Phebe DEAN b. 15 July 1788; bapt. 17 March
   1794.
Samuel b. 23 November 1792; Margaret b. -- November 1790, both
   bapt. 17 March 1794, children of Samuel, deceased, & Margaret
   MILES.
John s/o Samuel & Mary NORWOOD b. 25 November 1791; bapt. 17
   March 1794.
Rachel d/o Thomas & Anne BERGEN b. 28 December 1793; bapt. 21
   March 1794.
Reuben s/o George & Elizabeth DUTRO b. 1 October 1793; bapt. 26
   March 1794.
John s/o Charles & Fanny HERBERT b. 7 August 1793; bapt. 26 March
   1794.
Anna d/o John & Mary O'NEIL b. 23 March 1793; bapt. 30 March
   1794.
Joseph s/o Thomas William & Mary STOCKETT b. 18 August 1793;
   bapt. 4 April 1794.
John s/o Jacob & Rebecca BREWER b. 17 October 1793; bapt. 6 April
   1794.
James s/o John & Achsah CALEF b. 1 February & bapt. 6 April 1794.
William HULL s/o Richard HULL & Susanna POTTER b. 16 February &
   bapt. 11 April 1794.
Elizabeth b. -- August 1783, Hanna b. 3 December 1784, Ruth b. 9
   April 1793, all bapt. 17 April 1794; children of Richard &
   Rebecca COLE.
Solomon Scindall s/o Solomon & Elizabeth CARTER b. 15 January &
   bapt. 17 April 1794.
John s/o William & Hannah SCINDALL b. 16 February 1793; bapt. 17
   April 1794.
Thomas s/o Thomas & Mary BUCKINGHAM b. 19 March & bapt. 18 April
   1794.
Thomas Woodley s/o Thomas & Blanche BROTHERTON b. 6 January &
   bapt. 20 April 1794.
Mary d/o John & Mary Anne Dorsey BURN b. 10 March & bapt. 20
   April 1794.

CHRISTENINGS

Honor d/o Patrick & Prudence ROSE b. 31 August 1793; bapt. 30
April 1794.
Isaac Henry s/o Henry & Elizabeth GROEFF (GROESS?) b. 22 November
1793; bapt. 23 April 1794.
James s/o Thomas & Rachel GILBERTHORPE b. 4 November 1793; bapt.
23 April 1794.
Rebecca Worthley d/o William Kilpin & Mary OATES b. 26 May 1793;
bapt. 23 April 1794.
Benjamin s/o Anthony & Elizabeth REEVES b. -- August 1793; bapt.
23 April 1794.
Sarah d/o William & Anne ARMSTRONG b. 15 February 1793; bapt. 27
April 1794.   {H-285}

MARRIAGES

George WRIGHT m. Sophia WRIGHT 1 March 1794.   {R-II-84}
James INLOES m. Barsheba HACKET 5 March 1794.
William Stephen MOORE m. Catharine LEYPOLD 6 March 1794.
James GIBBINS m. Hannah BUSH (BUSHER?) 8 March 1794.
Andrew WELLER m. Mary RHODE 9 March 1794.
Richard CURSON, Jr. m. Elizabeth MOALE 13 March 1794.
Luke WILLS m. Elenor REED 15 March 1794.
Thomas MORGAN m. Sarah MULLEN 20 March 1794.
Bartholomew HABLISTEN m. Harriote MACHAUX 20 March 1794.
John COOPER m. Susanna BEACH 24 March 1794.
James LEMANE m. Mary TAYLOR 31 March 1794.
William NEWEL m. Susanna MOREHEAD 1 April 1794.
William LORMAN m. Mary FULFORD 3 April 1794.
Richard HULL m. Susanna POTTER 6 April 1794.
John STUBBS m. Sarah QUAY 7 April 1794.
Michael LAKE m. Sarah MC LAUGHLIN 10 April 1794.
Samuel LEE m. Mary JACKSON 10 April 1794.
Alexander MACKEE m. Margaret MURRAY 17 April 1794.
James MOORE m. Elizabeth PLUNKETT 20 April 1794.
Meshach STEVENSON m. Esther JONES 21 April 1794, free negroes or
mulattoes.
James Elvin KEY m. Elizabeth SMITH 24 April 1794.
Colin CRAIG m. Sarah HILL 24 April 1794.
Richard ROBERTS m. Daphne JOHNSON 27 April 1794.
Christopher LIMES m. Mary LITTON 29 April 1794.

CHRISTENINGS
                                                              {R-II-85}
Walter Pomphrey s/o Benjamin & Rachel HALL b. 21 October 1793;
bapt. 2 May 1794.   {H-286}
Barbara d/o Valentine & Elizabeth PERET b. 10 January 1793; bapt.
2 May 1794.
John "of Edward MORRIS & Elizabeth EARCE now PERET" b. 14
December 1793; bapt. 2 May 1794.
Sarah d/o Lynch & Catharine GRAY b. 21 March 1793; bapt. 4 May
1794.
Elizabeth d/o Samuel & Margaret TAYLOR b. 8 March 1790; bapt. 4
May 1794.
Edward s/o Edward & Margaret HARRISON b. 10 February & bapt. 7
May 1794.
Winifred d/o John & Elizabeth MURRAY b. 31 May 1793; bapt. 7 May
1794.
Rebecca d/o William, deceased, & Sarah ALWELL b. 25 November 1794
[sic]; bapt. 11 May 1794.

CHRISTENINGS

Jane d/o John & Anne SCOTT b. 20 March & bapt. 11 May 1794.
William s/o Thomas & Mary YATES b. 23 July 1793; bapt. 20 May 1794.
Sarah Anne b. 30 January 1791, bapt. 21 May 1794; Charles Wentworth b. 5 September 1793 bapt. 21 May 1794; children of Samuel & Mary FREEMAN.
Walter s/o William & Mary PRICE b. 10 April & bapt. 21 May 1794.
Clarissa d/o Joseph & Anne JUSTIS b. 8 April & bapt. 21 May 1794.
Margaret Kanna COURTNEY, widow, b. 29 December 1772; bapt. 22 May 1794.
Alexander s/o James & Elizabeth CLARK b. 19 March & bapt. 25 May 1794.
Mary d/o Isaac & Elizabeth JOHNS b. 20 October 1774; bapt. 30 May 1794.
Harry s/o Conrod & Elenor HUSH b. 20 January & bapt. 1 June 1794.
Harriet d/o Isaac & Pleasant WHEELER b. 29 August 1793; bapt. 5 June 1794.
Edward Waldegrave s/o Francis & Elizabeth CRACROFT b. 23 September 1792; bapt. 6 June 1794.
John s/o Edward & Elisabeth BURNS b. 18 September 1793; bapt. 7 June 1794.
Mary d/o William & Elizabeth PELL b. 11 April & bapt. 10 June 1794.
William s/o William & Margaret BRANSON b. 10 January & bapt. 18 June 1794.
Emily Jane Pearson d/o George & Mary GRUNDY b. 21 April & bapt. 22 June 1794.
Joseph s/o Joseph & "Irene or Urania, his wife" WARD b. 7 April & bapt. 22 June 1794.
David Harris s/o Joseph & Sarah SLATER b. 9 May & bapt. 28 June 1794.
Matthew s/o Thomas & Anne HAMMOND b. -- September 1793; bapt. 29 June 1794.

MARRIAGES

{R-II-86}
{H-287}

Joseph STANSBURY m. Frances Philips GOUGH 1 May 1794.
William B. DORMAN m. Julian GORSUCH 10 May 1794.
Nicholas GILL m. Elizabeth GILL 13 May 1794.
William JONES m. Elenor HARP 13 May 1794.
Elihu DAVIS m. Hannah STANSBURY 13 May 1794.
James PASSEY m. Anariah MC GUIRE 17 May 1794.
Philemon DAWSON m. Jane HENDERSON 22 May 1794.
James THOMPSON m. Elizabeth CLEAVES 22 May 1794.
Abraham HILTON m. Catharine THOMPSON 22 May 1794, free blacks.
William SMITH m. Mary BRYAN 24 May 1794.
James SMITH m. Elizabeth TUCKER 24 May 1794.
Robert AVERY m. Mary MC BRIDE 25 May 1794.
Michael DEAL m. Nancy AGNEW 26 May 1794.
Jeremiah COSDEN m. Elenor BUCHANAN 5 June 1794.
Robert CROSS m. Charlotte LEWIS 12 June 1794.
John RICHARDSON m. Mary V. HAYES 18 June 1794.
Nehemiah DONNELLAN m. Mary MULL 19 June 1794.
William HOOK m. Sarah DUNKIN 28 June 1794.
James SARGENT m. Mary YOUNG 29 June 1794.

BURIALS

Septimus NOEL bur. 11 May 1794.   {R-II-87} {H-288}
John PERRY bur. 14 May 1794.
Thomas B. USHER bur. 16 May 1794.
David s/o William JOHNS bur. 18 May 1794.
Thomas SWEENY bur. 3 July 1794.
Jacob BALABREGA bur. 4 July 1794.
Thomas FARNSWORTH bur. 5 July 1794.
Samuel BELLFRAGE bur. 8 July 1794.
Susanna wife of Thomas MC CREERY bur. 12 July 1794.
Elizabeth d/o Nancy WALTON bur. 13 July 1794.
Rebecca d/o John SHAHANASSYE bur. 14 July 1794.
Mary d/o Mary HAYES bur. 14 July 1794.
Sarah d/o Rebecca SILVY bur. 21 July 1794.
Antun, bapt. child John DILLON bur. 21 July 1794.
Sally d/o Hannah WILLIAMS 24 bur. July 1794.
William EAGLESTON bur. 26 July 1794.
Edward BOOTH bur. 27 July 1794.
Hugh GANER bur. 30 July 1794.
Elizabeth d/o Joseph JOHNSON or JOHNSTON bur. 30 July 1794.
Anne wife of Philip SISSLER bur. 4 June 1794.   {R-II-88} {H-289}
Margaret wife of Robert THOMPSON bur. 12 June 1794.
Antun, baptized child of George EASTON bur. 17 June 1794.
Jane d/o John CARPENTER bur. 20 June 1794.
Thomas GORDON bur. 23 June 1794.
Joseph Warren THOMPSON bur. 3 August 1794.
Charles CROOKSHANKS bur. 4 August 1794.
Thomas HIPKINS bur. 7 August 1794.
Francis MURPHY bur. 13 August 1794.
Edward s/o Edward HARRISON bur. 14 August 1794.
William HOULDSHIP bur. 17 August 1794.
John HEAD bur. 17 August 1794.
Anne d/o William HOPKINS bur. 18 August 1794.
Malcolm ACHESON bur. 20 August 1794.
George GEOGHEGAN bur. 24 August 1794.
Alexander CUMMINS bur. 28 August 1794.
Lydia wife of William Bell MEEKS bur. 29 August 1794.
Mary Anne d/o Henry GROEFF (GROESS?) bur. 29 August 1794.
Mary wife of John GIDERMAN, commonly called KITTLEMAN bur. 30
    August 1794.

CHRISTENINGS

{R-II-89} {H-290}
Thomas s/o Thomas & Mary USHER b. 22 March & bapt. 4 July 1794.
Elenor d/o John & Mary CONNER b. 14 August 1792; bapt. 13 July
    1794.
William s/o Thomas & Sally CHAMBERS b. 30 November 1793; bapt. 13
    July 1794.
Margaret d/o Robert & Lucy LITTLE b. 13 July 1793; bapt. 13 July
    1794.
Thomas s/o John & Helen BUSK b. 21 January & bapt. 20 July 1794.
Nancy d/o Samuel & Rebecca PERRY b. 25 May & bapt. 20 July 1794.
Lydia MEEKS, adult, William Bell MEEKS her husband, b. 7
    September 1775; bapt. 23 July 1794.
John s/o John & Mary MC DONNELL b. 11 July & bapt. 24 July 1794.
Nancy d/o John & Deborah HILL b. 15 January 1792; bapt. 24 July
    1794.
Mary d/o William & Anne PHILIPS b. 5 March & bapt. 10 Aug. 1794.
James s/o John & Susanna ROBB b. 8 March & bapt. 13 August 1794.

CHRISTENINGS

Elizabeth d/o John & Charlotte KELLY b. 23 February & bapt. 20
August 1794.

Margaret b. 1 April 1792, Sarah b. 1 June 1794, both bapt. 31
August 1794; d/o Samuel & Anne MC DONNELL.

MARRIAGES

James HEDRICKS m. Anne FISH 2 July 1794.   {R-II-91}
Jacob KLEIN m. Mary DIFFENDERFFER 8 July 1794.   {H-291}
William B. SMITH m. Frances STEELE 10 July 1794.
Amos SMITH m. on 13 July 1794.
Benjamin WATTS m. Susanna GRIFFIN 13 July 1794.
Robert HENLEY m. Elenor FLOOD 15 July 1794.
James REW m. Nancy ASHMORE 15 July 1794.
Patrick MYERS m. Anne HALEY 15 July 1794.
Jacob ROWLES m. Elizabeth DUNGAN 20 July 1794.
James WHITE m. Catharine MERRICK 10 August 1794.
Joseph ROBERTSON m. Nancy GRAY 12 August 1794.
Thomas ENGLE m. Margaret HURST 16 August 1794.
John DOYNE m. Mary MEYERS 20 August 1794.
Beal DUVALL m. Anne DEAN 21 August 1794.
Anthony BOYE m. Sarah BROWN 27 August 1794.
Benjamin MYERS m. Susanna KELLY 28 August 1794.

CHRISTENINGS

Esther d/o Thomas, deceased, & Sarah KNAB b. 31 January & bapt. 7
September 1794.

William s/o John & Margaret HEDRICK b. 18 August & bapt. 21   {H-292}
September 1794.

John s/o William & Susanna BANKS b. 18 May & bapt. 25 Sept. 1794.

Perry s/o John & Jane HUTCHINS of Anne Arundel County b. 20
September 1793; bapt. 29 September 1794.

Mary d/o Isaac & Elizbeth DICKES b. 8 September bapt. 5 October
1794.

James s/o Jacob & Sophia EVENSON b. 19 Feb. bapt. 5 Oct. 1794.

John s/o George & Jemima GARVEY b. 2 September & bapt. 5 October
1794.

John b. 27 December 1785; Anne b. 12 October 1787; Elizabeth b. 7
January 1790; Maria b. 16 August 1794, all bapt. 5 October
1794; children of Daniel & Elizabeth STREET.

Mary Hanson d/o John & Elizabeth RUTTER b. 3 March & bapt. 9
October 1794.

Charles s/o Walter & Mary CROOK b. 5 May & bapt. 9 October 1794.

Charles s/o William & Elizabeth SINGLETON b. 20 August & bapt. 18
October 1794.

George Hutchson s/o Hugh & Elizabeth BENNETT b. 23 July & bapt.
19 October 1794.

William s/o Thomas & Catharine MORROW b. 17 September & bapt. 19
October 1794.

Hugh s/o Edward & Mary THOMPSON b. 8 September & bapt. 19 October
1794.

Mary Essig, an adult, wife of John MASS, b. 28 May 1772; bapt.
29 October 1794.

MARRIAGES

Patrick FREEMAN m. Catharine FARMER 2 September 1794.   {H-293}
James CLOONEY m. Mary LANDRAKEN 3 September 1794.   {R-II-93}

MARRIAGES

Cornelius SHEEHAN m. Catharine THOMPSON 8 September 1794.
James MARTIN m. Sarah ROUSE 8 September 1794.
Joseph YOUNG m. Elizabeth RIDGLY 11 September 1794.
John HOLLINS m. Charlotte MAHONEY 24 September 1794.
William PENN m. Deborah CONNOWAY 25 September 1794.
Humphrey KEEBLE m. Lucy BERRY 1 October 1794.
George COAL m. Sarah BIDDISON 9 October 1794.
Daniel RACINE m. Harriot Perry GENTILLE 9 October 1794.
Henry STEVENSON m. Anne CAULK 9 October 1794.
Edward WEST m. Nancy JOHNSTON 13 October 1794.
Thomas ELWOOD m. Elizabeth DEVINE 20 October 1794.
Thomas RATLIEF m. Elizabeth CANNON 23 October 1794.
James SIMPSON m. Anne YATES 27 October 1794.
John RINEY m. Nancy DUNNAWAY 28 October 1794.
Thomas BROWN m. Jane CAMEL 31 October 1794.

BURIALS
{R-II-93}

John GILDERMAN, alias KITTLEMAN bur. 1 September 1794.
Robert SLATER bur. 1 September 1794.
Loeuis? s/o Joseph BANKSON bur. 1 September 1794.
An unbaptized child of Daniel STREET bur. 4 September 1794.
Wife of Daniel RUSH bur. 4 September 1794.
Elizabeth wife of Thomas BARRETT bur. 5 September 1794.
John ORR bur. 6 September 1794.
Mones DORLING bur. 8 September 1794.
Mary d/o John SAUNDERS bur. 9 September 1794.
Samuel ASHBURNER bur. 10 September 1794.
Anne d/o John ORR, deceased, bur. 10 September 1794.
Thomas COULSON bur. 12 September 1794.
James s/o Thomas MOORE bur. 14 September 1794.
Massy d/o Silas ENGLE bur. 15 September 1794.   {H-294}
Mary CROOKSHANKS bur. 15 September 1794.
Mary d/o John FACKNEY bur. 17 September 1794.
Mary MURPHY bur. 18 September 1794.
Elizabeth KELLY bur. 21 September 1794.
Robert MOORE bur. 21 September 1794.
Helen wife of John CARPENTER bur. 23 September 1794.
Larn WRIGHT bur. 24 September 1794.
John HARPER bur. 26 September 1794.
John SHAW bur. 26 September 1794.
Anne d/o Lydia STEVENS bur. 26 September 1794.
William s/o Hugh LONG bur. 28 September 1794.
John KAY bur. 28 September 1794.
Margaret d/o Fredrick DIGNELL bur. 28 September 1794.
Sarah KINGS bur. 30 September 1794.
Susanna d/o Robert DAVIDSON bur. 30 September 1794.
Unbaptized child of Robert ROSS bur. 30 September 1794.
James s/o James HOLMES bur. 1 October 1794.   {R-II-94}
Jonna wife of Michael HURLEY bur. 6 October 1794.
Maria MOORE, a native of Ireland, bur. 8 October 1794.
Mary HANSON, at Hanson's Mills, the widow of the late Jonathan
  HANSON bur. 9 October 1794.
Joseph MOORE, a native of Ireland, bur. 13 October 1794.
Anne Davey d/o Henrietta JAMES bur. 16 October 1794.
James s/o James PATTERSON bur. 17 October 1794.
Elizabeth THOMPSON, mother of Mrs. LATOUCHE bur. 22 October 1794.
Edward EVES bur. 24 October 1794.
John s/o Ann HEAD bur. 25 October 1794.

CHRISTENINGS

Agnes d/o William & Mary MORGAN b. 5 July 1793; bapt. 2 November 1794. {R-II-95} {H-295}

Joseph s/o Benjamin & Sarah SPENSER b. 19 October & bapt. 2 November 1794.

William s/o Thomas & Matilda NELSON b. 7 May & bapt. 2 Nov. 1794.

Henry & Hariot, twins, children of William & Sarah BLUFORD b. 26 August & bapt. 6 November 1794.

William s/o James & Mary DUNSTABLE b. 27 March & bapt. 9 November 1794.

Charles s/o Patrick & Margaret BENDERGRASS b. 22 March 1792; bapt. 9 November 1794.

William s/o John Eager & Margaret HOWARD b. 15 December 1793; bapt. 15 November 1794.

Maria Cecilia d/o William & Sarah CONWAY b. 9 September 1793; bapt. 19 November 1794.

Anne d/o James & Elizabeth CONWAY b. 5 July & bapt. 19 November 1794.

John s/o Michael & Patty COYL b. 14 October & bapt. 27 Nov. 1794.

Benedict s/o George & Mary LEE b. 22 October & bapt. 27 November 1794.

Louisa d/o William & Margaret COOK b. 2nd & bapt. 30 Nov. 1794.

Isaac David s/o William & Elenor JOHNS b. 11 October & bapt. 30 November 1794.

Mary Margaret d/o Charles & Hannah ADDERLEY b. 25 May & bapt. 1 December 1794.

Susann Porter d/o Jonathan & Mary ASKEW b. 5 September & bapt. 3 December 1794.

Job s/o Joseph & Anne JENKINS b. 6 November & bapt. 7 Dec. 1794.

John b. 26 January 1788; Harriot b. 13 September 1789; William b. 18 January 1792; Elizabeth b. 19 December 1793, all bapt. 7 December 1794; children of Richard & Margaret BERTON.

Samuel, Sollers & Acworth, children of John & Mary MILLER b. 31 July & bapt. 14 December 1794.

Anna Maria d/o Joseph Grove John & Mary Boudinot BEND b. 17 October & bapt. 27 December 1794.

A child of Rezin & Ruth PENN bapt. 29 December 1794.

MARRIAGES

{R-II-96} {H-296}

Baptista CHICARD m. Rachel EYRES 8 November 1794.

Lazarus MITCHELL m. Adeleaide ROBERTS 17 November 1794.

John STEVENS m. Achsah OWINGS 20 November 1794.

Barnet POWERS m. Rachel BENNETT 24 November 1794.

Samuel FOWLER m. Mary REESE 26 November 1794.

Stephen WEST m. Ann PUE 26 November 1794.

James COLLINGS m. Sarah MOONSHOT 27 November 1794.

Matthew SOULSBY (or SALISBURY) m. Prudence TRAVIS 30 Nov. 1794.

John WEARER m. Mary MC FEEL 6 December 1794.

William LEMMON m. Susanna PENN 7 December 1794.

John SIMPSON m. Elizabeth HOBBS 9 December 1794.

Christian MILLER m. Mary CROMLY 9 December 1794.

John CUNNINGHAM m. Catharine LEARY 10 December 1794.

Henry HARWOOD m. Jane BUCKLER 11 December 1794.

Jacob SMALL m. Nancy FLEETWOOD 11 December 1794.

William CHAMBERS m. Rebecca EVANS 14 December 1794.

Louis BARBARIN m. Maria CORBET 16 December 1794.

Michael LINDSAY m. Catharine PORTER 16 December 1794.

George Wythe CLAIBORNE m. Mary King HELLEN 20 December 1794.

Robert THOMPSON m. Catharine ASKEW 20 December 1794.

MARRIAGES

Francis COATES m. Charlotte LINTON 25 December 1794.
John ORRICK m. Mary GARVEY 25 December 1794.
Patrick MC GROGGEN m. Charlotte OWINGS 27 December 1794.

BURIALS

William ANDERSON bur. 1 November 1794.   {R-II-97} {H-297}
Anne LAWRENCE bur. 8 November 1794.
Jane d/o Samuel CASKEY bur. 8 November 1794.
Henry s/o Patrick MERRICK bur. 10 November 1794.
Charlotte Elizabeth d/o Charles Henry BUTLER bur. 12 Nov. 1794.
Mary d/o William MARSH bur. 13 November 1794.
Catharine d/o Lem GODDARD bur. 22 November 1794.
Rachel wife of Benjamin LEVY bur. 12 November 1794.
Mary wife of James DUNSTABLE bur. 28 November 1794.
John ANDERSON bur. 1 December 1794.
William LAVENDER, a native of Virginia, bur. 3 December 1794.
Mary d/o Michael JOHNS bur. 4 December 1794.
Archibald s/o Robert AVERY bur. 14 December 1794.
Mary wife of William PEALE bur. 15 December 1794.
"Peter or Adam" TRUMBO bur. 17 December 1794.
Elizabeth ROGERS bur. 20 December 1794.
Emily Jane Pearson d/o George GRUNDY bur. 21 December 1794.
Elizabeth Ann d/o William PEALE bur. 24 December 1794.
Matthew GALE bur. 26 December 1794.
Anne wife of Samuel GAIKES bur. 28 December 1794.
Elizabeth d/o William BRANSON bur. 1 January 1795.   {R-II-98}
Robert DUDLEY bur. 1 January 1795.
Thomas s/o Elizabeth CUMMINS bur. 4 January 1795.
Susanna wife of Joseph GOSHOE bur. 7 January 1795.
Thomas PINSTON bur. 11 January 1795.
William JOHNSON bur. 13 January 1795.
Harriot d/o Samuel CASKEY bur. 13 January 1795.
Martha Curtain d/o Ann PALMER bur. 16 January 1795.
Stuart JOHNSON or JOHNSTON bur. 18 January 1795.
Marianne wife of Pierre BARTRAN bur. 21 January 1795.
Anna Maria d/o Joseph G. J. BEND bur. 22 January 1795.
James s/o --- ROBB bur. 23 January 1795.
A child of Henry PURDY bur. 24 January 1795.   {H-298}
Dolly Anne ROBBINET bur. 30 January 1795.
Joseph RAWLINGS from St. Christophers bur. 1 February 1795.
John s/o George GARVEY bur. 4. February 1795.
John s/o John RIDGLY bur. 4 February 1795.
William MC LAUGHLIN bur. 10 February 1795.
Harriot wife of William CALBERSON bur. 11 February 1795.
Rebecca wife of John PERRIGO bur. 13 February 1795.
Elizabeth d/o Joseph CROWDER bur. 15 February 1795.
Patience ARMSTRONG bur. 17 February 1795.
George TROTMAN bur. 22 February 1795.

CHRISTENINGS

Stedman s/o William & Elizabeth VAN WYCK b. 8 September 1794;
    bapt. 1 January 1795.   {R-II-99}
Mary d/o Walter & Anne BELT b. 6 September 1795; bapt. 1 January
    1795.
Mary d/o James & Charlotte NICOLS b. 29 July 1794; bapt. 11
    January 1795.

CHRISTENINGS

Anne d/o James & Susanna BUCHANAN b. 20 September 1794; bapt. 11 January 1795.

Elizabeth b. 4 April 1788; Catharine b. 17 May 1790; Frances b. 22 October 1792; all bapt. 11 January 1795; d/o Charles & Mary WILLIAMS.

Henrietta Maria d/o Philip & Anne EDWARDS b. 2 October 1794; bapt. 4 February 1795.

Edward s/o John & Mary RIDGLY b. 15 October 1791; bapt. 4 February 1795.

Zany s/o(?) Vincent & Mary CORBIN b. January 1777 or 1778; bapt. 8 February 1795.

Betsy d/o Henry & Rachel FELLERS b. 7 December 1794; bapt. 8 February 1795.

Vincent b. 12 March 1792; Samuel b. 28 December 1794, both bapt. 11 February 1795; children of James & Dalilah HOLMES.

Henrietta Perigo d/o Benjamin & Deborah CURTIS b. 28 October 1794; bapt. 13 February 1795.

Elenor d/o Nicholas & Sarah BAXTER b. 6 January & bapt. 13 February 1795.

Edmund Burke s/o Charles & Ann CAVALIER b. 27 September 1794; bapt. 15 February 1795.

Maria d/o William & Susanna WATKIN b. 7 December 1794; bapt. 15 February 1795.

William b. 9 December 1771; Sally b. 17 February 1775, both bapt. 18 February 1795; children of John MINCHER.

Susanna d/o John ESSIG of Philadelphia b. 19 January 1775; bapt. 18 February 1795.

Margaret d/o Elijah & Mary WEST b. 3 January & bapt. 22 February 1795.

Mary Anne d/o William & Priscilla LEE b. 21 December 1794; bapt. 22 February 1795.   {H-299}

William s/o Thomas & Anne DEEN b. 12 & bapt. 22 February 1795.

Edward Hall s/o Seth & Sarah Emerson BARTON b. 12 December 1794; bapt. 24 February 1795.

MARRIAGES

Arthur MITCHELL m. Elizabeth CANNON 1 January 1795.   {R-II-100}
George ST. CLAIR m. Celia Anne CONNOLLY 4 January 1795.
Robert ANDREW m. Elenor TOBY 5 January 1795.
George LINDENBERGER m. Anne Henry STEVENSON 8 January 1795.
William STEARNES m. Catharine ASTERMAN 11 January 1795.
Pearce Lacey TANNER m. Pamela PEPPER 13 January 1795.
Reine Guillaume BUTTON m. Jane MATTHEWS 15 January 1795.
Lewis PORTER m. Catharine BROWN 18 January 1795.
William RUSSELL m. Elizabeth WILLIAMSON 22 January 1795.
James LEWIS m. Bridget CHRISTIE 24 January 1795.
Levin BAILEY m. Margaret LOWDER 27 January 1795.
James HARRIS m. Elenor MOORE 28 January 1795.
James DONOVAN m. Mary MEHAN 1 February 1795.
Thomas MATTHEWS m. Anne GILL 2 February 1795.
William WARREN m. Bethia HOWARD 5 February 1795.
Livin LAVENDER m. Mary BEATTY 12 February 1795.
William GRANT m. Caroline GLEDE 12 February 1795.
John KNOPWOOD m. Mary LAGONS 15 February 1795.
Samuel HAYDN m. Elizabeth MAHONEY 15 February 1795.
Richard BRYAN m. Sarah TIMBRELL 23 February 1795.
John A. SCORS m. Elizabeth SUMMERS 24 February 1795.

CHRISTENINGS

Jane d/o William & Catharine MONDELL b. 4 January & bapt. 1 March 1795. {R-II-101} {H-300}

James s/o Humphrey & Sarah HIPWELL b. 7 February & bapt. 11 March 1795.

Elizabeth d/o Alexander & Lily HARRISON b. 14 September 1794; bapt. 15 March 1795.

Joseph s/o Joseph & Frances Anne RAWLINS b. 30 January & bapt. 21 March 1795.

John Anderson s/o Joshua & Sarah KNIGHT b. 9 September 1794; bapt. 22 March 1795.

Elizabeth d/o Peter & Mary NOGLE b. -- February 1794; bapt. 25 March 1795.

Elizabeth d/o Thomas & Elizabeth FOXALL b. -- September 1794; bapt. 25 March 1795.

Thomas s/o Thomas & Catharine MONTGOMERY b. 17 January & bapt. 3 April 1795.

Johnzie s/o Edward & Nancy JARVIS b. 2 October 1794; bapt. 4 April 1795.

Samuel s/o Richard Jr. & Elizabeth CURSON b. 9 January & bapt. 5 April 1795.

Joshua s/o Philip & Elizabeth SCINDALL b. 20 June 1794; bapt. 6 April 1795.

John Smith s/o George & Jane WILY b. 1 Feb. & bapt. 8 April 1795.

Cassandra d/o James & Susanna CANNON b. 27 December 1793; bapt. 11 April 1795.

Daniel b. 26 September 1790, Isabella b. 22 December 1792, both bapt. 12 April 1795; children of Daniel, deceased, & Sarah VARDON.

Mary d/o Edward Jr. & Anne JOHNSON b. 17 January & bapt. 16 April 1795.

Elizabeth d/o James & Rebecca LOVE b. 28 January & bapt. 19 April 1795.

William Brown s/o William & Elizabeth FIELD b. 10 September 1794; bapt. 22 April 1795.

Stephen s/o Richard & Diana LAWSON b. 2 January bapt. 29 April 1795.

Susanna & Sidney b. 16 November 1794; bapt. 29 April 1795; children of William & Susanna Aisquith BAYZAND.

William s/o Benjamin & Agnes WALTERS b. 15 October 1794; bapt. 30 April 1795.

Milcah d/o James & Elizabeth FLINN b. 20 February 1791; bapt. 30 April 1795.

MARRIAGES

John HAMMOND m. Elizabeth ANDERSON 5 March 1795.{R-II-102}{H-301}
Thomas WHITNEY m. Susanna NEWEL 5 March 1795.
Edward Hanson RUTTER m. Margaret MC CLURE 5 March 1795.
Thomas WATSON m. Anne OGDEN 7 March 1795.
Hugh MC NAMARA m. Anne WILLIAMS 14 March 1795.
Nicholas LEMON m. Ruth MILLS 12 April 1795.
William CONNOWAY m. Hanna STEWART 12 April 1795.
Alexander ADAMS m. Elizabeth MC LURE 14 April 1795.
Nicholas HOPKINS m. Rebecca DUKE 16 April 1795.
John VOLMAR m. Elizabeth REED 16 April 1795.
Thomas CASWELL m. Jane LEARY 18 April 1795.
William JACKSON m. Margaret BUTLER 19 April 1795.
Richard WILMEN m. Mary MORRIS 20 April 1795.
James FOWLER m. Elizabeth MOORE 20 April 1795.

MARRIAGES

Thomas PEARCE m. Elizabeth CUMMINS 20 April 1795.
John SHANEY m. Elizabeth CHESTER 20 April 1795.

BURIALS

Richard RANDALL bur. 1 March 1795.   {R-II-103} {H-302}
Henry s/o Richard COWARD bur. 3 March 1795.
Elizabeth d/o John DALRYMPLE bur. 9 March 1795.
John PULLING bur. 12 March 1795.
Elizabeth wife of John FRENCH bur. 12 March 1795.
Daniel GASH bur. 13 March 1795.
Adam JAMISON bur. 18 March 1795.
William s/o Thomas DEEN bur. 19 March 1795.
John HOWARD bur. 19 March 1795.
Thomas COLEGATE bur. 20 March 1795.
Charlotte wife of George DAVEY bur. 22 March 1795.
A child of Thomas WYATT bur. 31 March 1795.
Augusta d/o Andrew VAN BIBBER bur. 3 April 1795.
Ebenezer PRATT bur. 8 April 1795.
Robert HILL bur. 12 April 1795.
Darby LUX bur. 12 April 1795.
John WILLIAMS bur. 17 April 1795.
Maria d/o William WATKINS bur. 20 April 1795.
George James L'ARGEAN bur. 20 April 1795.
James s/o James HICKLEY bur. 20 April 1795.
Rowland LAWSON bur. 24 April 1795.
John STRAUGHN bur. 27 April 1795.
Mary wife of William CHATTEL bur. 29 April 1795.
---- STOCKETT brother of Thomas William STOCKETT bur. 30 April
    1795.
Mary d/o Edward JOHNSON, Jr. bur. 1 May 1795.   {R-II-104} {H-303}
Joanna wife of Benjamin LYEN bur. 4 May 1795.
Williamson WEBB of Virginia bur. 7 May 1795.
Peter BERRY bur. 8 May 1795.
James POLLOCK bur. 9 May 1795.
Thomas JOHNSON bur. 19 May 1795.
Ferdinand s/o Philip WALTER bur. 20 May 1795.
Dorothy FULHAM bur. 30 May 1795.
Mary d/o George ALDERSON bur. 1 June 1795.
Cornelius FENTON bur. 1 June 1795.
Henry FRINCHAM bur. 8 June 1795.
Mary WILSON mother of Joseph bur. 10 June 1795.
Isabella wife of John WILSON bur. 12 June 1795.
George CARR bur. 18 June 1795.
Benjamin s/o Anthony REEVES bur. 30 June 1795.

CHRISTENINGS

Peggy CARPENTER d/o Allen CARPENTER & Nancy SKEWSE b. 20 April &
    bapt. 3 May 1795.   {R-II-105} {H-304}
Hannah d/o Joseph & Hannah WILSON b. 10 March & bapt. 3 May 1795.
Elizabeth d/o Benjamin & Catharine ASHLEY b. 31 December 1794;
    bapt. 6 May 1795.
Anne d/o Stuart, deceased, & Mary JOHNSON b. 26 February & bapt.
    6 May 1795.
Elizabeth d/o David & Elizabeth GREGORY b. 7 February & bapt. 10
    May 1795.
Kitty d/o Dongal & Elizabeth CARMICHAEL b. 24 September 1794;
    bapt. 20 May 1795.

CHRISTENINGS

John s/o Matthew & Prudence SOULSBY b. 21 February & bapt. 20 May 1795.

Nelly d/o Samuel & Elenor HURST b. 17 & bapt. 20 May 1795.

George s/o Joseph & Margart GRAY b. 28 Jan. & bapt. 24 May 1795.

Margaret d/o Larkin & Deboro YOUNG b. 10 February & bapt 24 May 1795.

William s/o Abraham & Mary HARDING, free blacks, b. 6 April & bapt. 24 May 1795.

Mary Anne b. 1 November 1794, Eliza (no birth date) both bapt. 24 May 1795; children of Samuel & Fanny DONOVAN.

Samuel s/o John & Mary MASS b. 19 April & bapt. 31 May 1795.

William s/o Robert & Susanna HERRON b. 17 May & bapt. 31 May 1795.

Priscilla d/o Thomas & Mary LETTER b. 1 May & bapt. 3 June 1795.

James s/o Thomas & Sarah HILL b. 26 May & bapt. 3 June 1795.

Harriet NEWMAN d/o Sarah ABRAHAM b. 31 October 1773; bapt. 4 June 1795.

John Skinner s/o Hercules & Mary COURTENAY b. 24 November 1793; bapt. 7 June 1795.

William s/o James & Mary CRANGLE b. 1 May & bapt. 7 June 1795.

Angelina d/o Y--- & Mary BYRON b. 2 May 1794; bapt. 17 June 1795.

Hugh Davy s/o Joseph & Elizabeth EVANS b. 26 April 1792; bapt. 10 June 1795.

Henry b. 8 August 1792; Elizabeth b. 22 November 1794; both bapt. 24 June 1795. Children of Simon & Jane BULLEN.

Mary d/o James & Patience LONG b. 2 May & bapt. 24 June 1795.

Sarah d/o Patrick & Elizabeth MC INTYRE b. 15 February 1794; bapt. 29 June 1795.

Sophia WALL (MOODY?) d/o William MOODY & Betsy WALL, free colored, b. -- April & bapt. 29 June 1795.

MARRIAGES

Hezekiah JACKSON m. Frances HEINER 7 May 1795. {R-II-106} {H-305}

Thomas PURSE m. Mary PILKINGTON 9 May 1795.

John JAMES m. Mary JOHNS 9 May 1795.

Allen CARPENTER m. Anne SKUSE 9 May 1795.

John GIBSON m. Elizabeth JOICE 10 May 1795.

William S. DAVIS m. Sarah STUBBS 11 May 1795.

William WEATHERBY m. Urith SCINDALL 14 May 1795.

Hugh Charles MC LEAN m. Mary FRENCH 17 May 1795.

Levin COVENTON m. Mary GREEN 18 May 1795.

James CONNOR m. Elizabeth GRAHAM 24 May 1795.

George CROOK m. Jane MORROW 28 May 1795.

Thomas CUSHION m. Catharine SMITH 30 May 1795.

John CANN m. Margaret HELMES 1 June 1795.

John FITZGERALD m. Mary DRAKE 2 June 1795.

Felix CARR m. Catharine FIGGANCE of Queen Caroline Parish 4 June 1795.

James BLACK m. Mary CARROLL 6 June 1795.

Gabriel MENSON m. Margaret DEITER 15 June 1795.

William MARTIN m. Nancy MAHONEY 17 June 1795.

Matthew SHIRRID m. Elizabeth HALL 23 June 1795.

Louis SELLERNE (SELLERUE?) m. Margaret DAILY 23 June 1795.

Joshua GORSUCH m. Anne SMITH 25 June 1795.

Isaac ELZEY, slave of George HALL, m. Rachel CORNISH, free black, 28 June 1795.

Alexander COWAN m. Rhoda HUBBERT 29 June 1795.

CHRISTENINGS

Isaiah s/o William & Blanche DOWNS b. 21 August 1793; bapt. 12 July 1795.

Elizabeth Anne d/o James & Alice PIKE b. 16 June & bapt. 12 July 1795. {R-II-107} {H-306}

Sally s/o Parick [sic] & his deceased wife Rebecca KELLY b. 15 July 1794; bapt. 14 July 1795.

Elizabeth d/o John & Margaret COLE b. 25 August 1794; bapt. 16 July 1795.

James s/o Douglass James & Isabella MILLHOLLAND b. 12 June 1795 or 1793; bapt. 18 July 1795.

Samuel s/o Hezekiah & Frances CLAGETT b. 14 July 1794; bapt. 22 July 1795.

Margaret d/o James & Rebecca STEUART b. 9 & bapt. 26 July 1795.

Joseph s/o Thomas & Sarah KEARNY b. 12 June & bapt. 26 July 1795.

James s/o John & Elenor FLOOD b. 24 April 1794; bapt. 26 July 1795.

William s/o Charles & Grace NASH b. 21 June & bapt. 26 July 1795.

John s/o Benjamin & Fanny HITHE, free blacks, bapt. 26 July 1795, 16 months old.

Mary d/o Thomas & Sarah MORGAN b. 18 January & bapt. 5 July 1795.

Daniel s/o Jupiter a slave & Rachel a free woman bapt. 28 July 1795, 10 months old.

Soloman s/o George & Anne FROST b. 10 February 1790; bapt. 28 July 1795.

William s/o Alexander & Dalilah SANDS b. 1 May & bapt. 2 August 1795.

Sarah d/o John & Mary HODGES b. 11 July & bapt. 2 August 1795.

John s/o Charles & Rebecca GRIFFIN b. 18 February 1794; bapt. 2 August 1795.

William s/o William & Mary CUTFIELD b. 11 July & bapt. 9 August 1795.

Mary d/o Alexander & Margaret MACKIE b. 16 January 1794; bapt. 9 August 1795.

Joseph s/o William & Sinah COLEMAN b. 13 February & bapt. 9 August 1795.

Kitty d/o George, deceased, & Ann FROST b. 10 August 1793; bapt. 12 August 1795.

William s/o William & Rebecca EVANS b. 2 March & bapt. 19 August 1795.

Ruth d/o James Dent & Mary SUMMERS b. 7 April 1793; bapt. 31 August 1795.

John s/o John & Rebecca STRAN b. 5 May 1795; bapt. 31 August 1795.

William Henry s/o Thomas, deceased, & Sarah JOHNSON b. 13 June 1795?; bapt. 21 August 1795.

MARRIAGES

William PATERSON m. Nancy CRAIG 2 July 1795. L {R-II-108} {H-307}

Samuel STEVENSON m. Elizabeth PEATHERS 5 July 1795. L

James LAW m. Elizabeth DAVIES 9 July 1795. L

William GRIFFIN m. Jane CHAMBERS 10 July 1795. L

James PAYNE m. Letitia MILWARD 11 July 1795. L

Samuel GAIKES m. Elizabeth FLOOD 12 July 1795. L

David HISER m. Charlotte SWEETING 16 July 1795. L

John INGLE m. Anne WITCOMB 18 July 1795. L

Richard SISSON m. Mary INGRAM 18 July 1795. L

L = License

MARRIAGES

Patrick CLANSEY m. Hanna HOGAN 18 July 1795. L
John ARMITAGE m. Elenor JONES 28 July 1795. B
Colin C. WILLS m. Susanna ROBBERDS 30 July 1795. L
George Adwell POCOCK m. Anne LISTON 2 August 1795. L
Nathaniel EVERSON m. Elsbeth NASH 2 August 1795. L
Joseph FOLEY m. Mary BURNET 3 August 1795. L
George L. STORY m. Christy DASHIELL 4 August 1795. L
Jacob WEAVER m. Elizabeth NICHOLSON 11 August 1795. L
James BEEMAN m. Amelia JOHNSON 16 August 1795. L
William PURDON m. Susanna ESSECK 23 August 1795. L
William HALL m. Mary FLITCHER 27 August 1795. L

BURIALS

John s/o Theops. SIMCOCK bur. 3 July 1795.   {R-II-109} {H-308}
James READ of Nevis bur. 3 July 1795.
John s/o Benjamin KING bur. 5 July 1795.
Anne wife of Richard BURLAND bur. 8 July 1795.
Elizabeth wife of John WINCHESTER bur. 10 July 1795.
Mary Agnes d/o John Gee SELMAN bur. 13 July 1795.
George POULSTON from Eastern Shore bur. 13 July 1795.
John COMMINS bur. 13 July 1795.
John s/o Henry REES bur. 14 July 1795.
Anne d/o Hugh BOYLE bur. 16 July 1795.
Mary d/o Jarnes NICOLS bur. 18 July 1795.
Isabella d/o Thomas WHITE bur. 20 July 1795.
James s/o Thomas HILL bur. 22 July 1795.
Thomas s/o Sarah MILLS bur. 22 July 1795.
William ADAMS bur. 23 July 1795.
Thomas Kennedy MC DOWELL bur. 23 July 1795.
John WOODARD bur. 24 July 1795.
James EVERETT bur. 24 July 1795.
William s/o William KIRBY bur. 24 July 1795.
William SMITH bur. 25 July 1795.
Catharine d/o Henry REESE bur. 26 July 1795.
Samuel s/o John MILLER bur. 26 July 1795.
Margaret wife of William STRAUGHAN bur. 27 July 1795.
Harriet d/o Isaac WHEELER bur. 27 July 1795.
Anne d/o James CONWAY bur. 28 July 1795.
Thomas s/o John MEYERS bur. 28 July 1795.
Perry BROWN bur. 29 July 1795.
Martha d/o Martha COULSON bur. 29 July 1795.
William GRAHAM, a child, bur. 29 July 1795.
Sarah wife of Robert EDWARDS bur. 29 July 1795.
Nancy d/o Peres NOWLAND bur. 29 July 1795.
Harry s/o Henry HOLLINGSWORTH bur. 1 August 1795.   {H-309}
George William WEST bur. 2 August 1795.   {R-II-110}
Polly d/o John DOWLING, unbaptized, bur. 2 August 1795.
Mrs. BAILEY, mother of Elam BAILEY bur. 2 August 1795.
George DAVY, native of Old England, bur. 4 August 1795.
Susanna d/o Mary BALABREGA bur. 4 August 1795.
William CHINN of Virginia bur. 5 August 1795.
Elizabeth wife of William HAYES bur. 6 August 1795.
James JAMES bur. 7 August 1795.
Richard ARTHINGTON of Old England bur. 7 August 1795.
Thomas GILBERTHORPE bur. 10 August 1795.
Jane wife of John HALL bur. 11 August 1795.

B = Banns L = License

BURIALS

William HARRISON of Silas ENGLE bur. 11 August 1795.
William MC CARTER bur. 13 August 1795.
Elizabeth d/o William WHITE bur. 15 August 1795.
Elizabeth wife of Robert DUNWYDDIE bur. 15 August 1795.
Catharine ADAMS bur. 20 August 1795.
Thomas s/o Thomas BUCKINGHAM bur. 20 August 1795.
William s/o William BRANSON bur. 25 August 1795.
Susanna d/o George BUCHANAN bur. 26 August 1795.
Anne d/o William ALEXANDER bur. 26 August 1795.
Urith YOUNG bur. 27 August 1795.
Jane d/o James WIGNELL bur. 30 August 1795.
Anne d/o James BUCHANAN bur. 30 August 1795.
Jane d/o William WHITE bur. 30 August 1795.
Henrietta Perigo d/o Benjamin CURTIS bur. 31 August 1795.

CHRISTENINGS

Mary Anne d/o Herman & Frances TRICE b. 7 February & bapt. 2
  September 1795.
Sarah, adult, widow of Henry NEWMAN b. 11 April 1770; bapt. 2   {R-II-111} {H-310}
  September 1795.
Francis s/o John & Catharine BROWN b. 31 March & bapt. 6
  September 1795.
Adam William s/o Henry Philip & Mary UHLER b. 18 February & bapt.
  6 September 1795.
Benjamin Mickael s/o Peter & Pheebe MILLER b. 3 August & bapt. 6
  September 1795.
Elenor d/o John & Mary EVERHART b. 21 March & bapt. 6 Sept. 1795.
Matilda d/o Francis (MC DONOUGH's) & Mary (free) b. 4 July 1794;
  bapt. 6 September 1795.
James s/o Robert & Elizabeth MC KINLEY b. 4 August & bapt. 20
  September 1795.
Josiah s/o Frederick & Fanny PRATT b. 15 August & bapt. 27
  September 1795.
Mary d/o Christian & Mary DAVIS b. 31 December 1792; bapt. 1
  October 1795.
William s/o James & Margaret COOK b. 10 February & bapt. 7
  October 1795.
Nancy d/o James Dent & Mary SUMMERS b. 21 September 1795 & bapt.
  7 October 1795.
Anne d/o Joseph, deceased, & Mary Anne EDES b. 20 July & bapt. 10
  October 1795.
Susanna b. 18 August 1791, Sarah b. 26 April 1794, both bapt. 11
  October 1795; children of William & Susanna MILLER.
Rebecca b. 16 August 1785, George b. 1 October 1787, David b. 19
  July 1789, Charles b. 23 May 1791, Lycurgus b. 5 September
  1795, all bapt. 12 October 1795; children of William & Mary
  WINCHESTER.
Nancy d/o Matthew & Mary MC NAMARA b. 30 August & bapt. 13
  October 1795.
Walter s/o Thomas & Blanch BROTHERTON b. 4 July & bapt. 14
  October 1795.
William s/o Robert & Mary RICHARDSON b. 14 August 1794; bapt. 24
  October 1795.
Mary d/o Jonathan & Mary ENSOR b. 16 March & bapt. 24 Oct. 1795.
William WARD s/o William (E. IRELAND) & Betsy WARD (free) b.
  -- December 1794; bapt. 27 October 1795.
Matilda Eleonora Anne d/o James & Elizabeth WATERS b. 18 June &
  bapt. 29 October 1795.

MARRIAGES

Samuel MC ADUE m. Anne SPENCER 1 September 1795. L   {H-311}
Joseph GRAY m. Elizabeth WILSON 3 September 1795. L   {R-II-112}
John WALLACE m. Nancy BUCKINGHAM 3 September 1795. L
Joseph SHANE m. Mary CUTFIELD 6 September 1795. L
Alexander LAYING m. Henrietta DAWSON 25 September 1795. L
John PICKESGILL m. Maria YOUNG 2 October 1795. L
Daniel CHEVES m. Mary CARNES 3 October 1795. L
John MC CRAY m. Mary ELLIS 6 October 1795. L
Nathaniel WILLSON m. Elizabeth SHIPWAY 15 October 1795. L
Henry SHUTE m. Mary HISLET 19 October 1795. L
Timothy CASHMAN m. Maria BELL 21 October 1795. L
William PRITCHARD m. Eliza FLINN 21 October 1795. L
James WINTKLE m. Elizabeth JENKINS 22 October 1795. L
John LATOUR m. Grace SMITH 23 October 1795. L
John ALEXANDER m. Elizabeth BAGFORT 25 October 1795. L
Thomas GAMBLE m. Mary MC PILLON 29 October 1795. L
Thomas WRIGHT m. Mary PECKER (BOCKER?) 31 October 1795. L

                    L = License

CHRISTENINGS

Henry s/o Edward & Margaret HARRISON b. 13 May & bapt. 1 November
   1795.   {R-II-113} {H-312}
Prudence Gough d/o James & Sophia CARROLL b. 15 October & bapt. 3
   November 1795.
Sarah d/o Richard & Sarah RYLAND b. 7 October & bapt. 5 November
   1795.
James s/o Valentine & Elizabeth PERET b. 16 April & bapt. 7
   November 1795.
Anne Stuart d/o Richard & Elizabeth FRANCIS bapt. 8 November
   1795. (No birth date.)
Henry s/o Henry & Hannah NANTZE b. 18 October & bapt. 15 November
   1795.
Samuel s/o Henry & Ruth FISHPAW b. 27 July & bpa.t 15 Nov. 1795.
Aquila s/o Orman & Hannah JARVIS b. 19 March & bapt. 18 November
   1795.
Elenor Addison & Eliza Bradford, twins, b. 5 November & bapt. 22
   November 1795, d/o James & Sarah Brook DALL.
Eliza Harwood d/o Daniel Jr. & Isabella GRANT b. 14 August &
   bapt. 25 November 1795.
Thomas s/o Thomas & Ariana POULTON b. 4 January 1793; bapt. 6
   December 1795.
Maria d/o Samuel & Mary NORWOOD b. 11 April & bapt. 6 December
   1795.
Susanna d/o Samuel & Rebecca PERRY b. 16 October & bapt. 8
   December 1795.
John s/o Frederick & Sarah FEIDMASTER b. 28 March 1794; bapt. 13
   December 1795.
Mary Helen d/o John Hooper & Mary STEWART b. 20 February & bapt.
   20 December 1795.
John s/o James & Mary FISHWICK b. 29 October & bapt. 25 December
   1795.
Jane d/o Joshua & Elenor WRIGHT b. 31 May & bapt. 26 Dec. 1795.
William s/o John & Sarah MEYERS b. 25 October & bapt. 27 December
   1795.
William John s/o William & Elizabeth SELLERS b. 13 September &
   bapt. 27 December 1795.

MARRIAGES

Hugh MC MECHEN m. Amelia HEWETT 1 November 1795. L   {H-313}
Thomas PENRICE m. Mary WEBB 5 November 1795. L   {R-II-114}
John KILMAN m. Alice RILEY 7 November 1795. L
Samuel O. HARO m. Juliana ROLORS 9 November 1795. L
John EVANS m. Elizabeth SHAFFER 12 November 1795.
Roger KESSUCK m. Milcah THOMAS 16 November 1795.
John OBER m. Elizabeth WOODWARD 18 November 1795.
James CHAOER m. Sarah JOURDAN 19 November 1795.
James BRYSEN m. Elizabeth STEVENSON 22 November 1795.
Philip GORDON m. Silby WILLIAMS 27 November 1795.
Robert PRIMROSE m. Sidney CLEMENT 28 November 1795.
John WILSON m. Darcus TOON 2 December 1795. L
John Wilks HOWLAND m. Mary GUDGEON 3 December 1795. L
Abraham ALDRIDGE m. Mary HALEY 3 December 1795. L
William GREEN m. Chloe LEAGUE 21 December 1795. L
John CUNNINGHAM m. Mary PUELY 25 December 1795. L

L = License

BURIALS

{R-II-115} {H-314}

Hannah wife of Elihu DAVIS bur. 5 September 1795.
William EASTON s/o George bur. 13 September 1795.
William s/o James DUNSTABLE bur. 7 September 1795.
Thomas PILKINGTON bur. 14 September 1795.
James s/o Thomas CHATTEL bur. 14 September 1795.
Sarah d/o John SHAHANNESIC bur. 14 September 1795.
Adam s/o Henry CABLE bur. 20 September 1795.
Alice wife of Robert SLATER bur. 25 September 1795.
George BRADSHAW bur. 25 September 1795.
Hannah wife of William PITT bur. 27 September 1795.
William s/o Susanna DAWSON bur. 28 September 1795.
Kitty d/o Mathew STACY bur. 29 September 1795.
Howard GRIFFITH of Barbados bur. 30 September 1795.
Mrs. SMITH, widow of William SMITH bur. 30 September 1795.
----- STEVENSON bur. 30 September 1795.
Sarah of Richard REEVES bur. 2 November 1795.
Harry s/o Conrad HUSH bur. 8 November 1795.
Mary Margaret d/o Charles ADDERLEY bur. 9 November 1795.
At Springfield, the seat of Thomas YATES, Harriot, his daughter
   bur. 9 November 1795.
Mary d/o Michael BOGGY bur. 13 November 1795.
Abraham s/o Thomas DONOVAN bur. 15 November 1795.
Anne wife of Edward JOHNSON, Jr. bur. 15 November 1795.
Henry MANSPEAKER bur. 27 November 1795.
Margaret CARMICHAEL bur. 29 November 1795.
Charles s/o John HAMMOND bur. 29 November 1795.
Old Mrs. TROTTEN, in Patapsco Neck, bur. 1 October 1795. {H-315}
Abram USHER bur. 2 October 1795.   {R-II-116}
John Washington DENNIS s/o Daniel bur. 4 October 1795.
James DUNWYDDIE bur. 5 October 1795.
John WOOD bur. 6 October 1795.
Alice JOHNSON bur. 8 October 1795.
Nancy d/o James D. SUMMERS bur. 11 October 1795.
Cullen POLLOCK bur. 11 October 1795.
Margaret d/o Elias BARNABY bur. 12 October 1795.
George s/o Joseph GREY bur. 13 October 1795.
Elisabeth wife of Henry PENNY bur. 19 October 1795.
William s/o Thomas PAMPHILION bur. 20 October 1795.
George EASTON bur. 22 October 1795.

BURIALS

Benjamin PARROTT bur. 29 October 1795.
The widow of Mones DORLING bur. 30 October 1795.
Elizabeth d/o William MARSH bur. 31 October 1795.
Hannah d/o Elizabeth EASTON, widow of George EASTON bur. 7 December 1795.
Sarah wife of Hill SAVAGE bur. 8 December 1795.
Lambert s/o Lambert SMITH bur. 9 December 1795.
James s/o John MC CONNELL bur. 10 December 1795.
Thomas CHATTEL bur. 13 December 1795.
Sarah, or Sally, d/o Silas ENGLE bur. 25 December 1795.
Mary Helen d/o Mary STEWART bur. 31 December 1795.

CHRISTENINGS

Seth s/o Seth & Sarah Emerson BARTON b. 8 December 1795; bapt. 5 January 1796. {R-II-117} {H-316}
Mary d/o John & Elizabeth AMONSCOARS b. 14 December 1795; bapt. 10 January 1796.
Mary d/o John & Mary GREEN b. 23 December 1795; bapt. 10 January 1796.
Mary Anne d/o David & Ann HAMILTON b. 30 October 1795; bapt. 10 January 1796.
Edward Merchant s/o John & Catharine BELL b. 14 April 1794; bapt. 16 January 1796.
Mary d/o Hugh & Hannah WILSON b. 17 March 1795; bapt. 17 January 1796.
Anne d/o John & Rachel BARLETT b. 8 January 1795; bapt. 24 January 1796.
Eliza d/o George & Mary ROBERTS b. 23 September 1795; bapt. 28 January 1796.
Hannah CONOWAY, adult, wife of William bapt. 3 February 1796.
Sarah STEWART, adult, sister of Hannah CONAWAY b. May 1779; bapt. 3 February 1796.
Rebecca d/o William & Mary HAMMOND b. 6 December 1793; bapt. 3 February 1796.
Mary Hammond b. 4 May 1794; bapt. 3 February 1796; Gerard b. 29 August 1795; bapt. 3 February 1796, children of Gerard & Sarah GOVER.
Susanng d/o Edward & Catharine DAVIS b. 5 January & bapt. 14 February 1796.
Sidney Hellen d/o Samuel & Anne WHITE b. 11 March 1795; bapt. 14 February 1796.
William s/o Dillon Benjamin & Susanna MC KENZIE b. 13 January & bapt. 16 February 1796.
John s/o Anthony & Elizabeth REEVES b. 11 January & bapt. 16 February 1796.
Mary Ann d/o John & Charlotte HOLLINS b. 6 & bapt. 16 Feb. 1796.

MARRIAGES
{R-II-118} {H-317}
John DILLEHUNT m. Harriet NEWMAN 2 January 1796. L
Jabez ANDERSON m. Elizabeth GOCOGHEGAN 2 January 1796. L
Peter LARYON m. Jane POE 2 January 1796. L
Reuben ALLEN m. Anne WINGAT 3 January 1796. L
William PEMBERTON m. Mary MAXWELL 11 January 1796. L
Barney JOHNSTON m. Catharine SMITH 14 January 1796. L
Alexander CRAFORD m. Sara RYAN 14 January 1796. L
William WILSON m. Elenor RIDDLE 17 January 1796. L
Samuel LEWIS m. Rachel REEMS 30 January 1796. B (free Mulattoes)

MARRIAGES

Edward CATO m. Sinah MARTON 30 January 1796. L
John IVORY m. Anne GRAVES 1 February 1796. L
Thomas JACKSON m. Elizabeth ALLENDER 2 February 1796. L
Amos BAILY m. Anne REAMS 10 February 1796. L
John BOWLIN m. Ally HOBBS 10 February 1796. L
Maurice READING m. Prudence ROLLS 14 February 1796. B
Thomas WELLS m. Thompsa DEVALL 15 February 1796. L
Clark BABCOCK m. Margaret FLINN 23 February 1796. L
John CLARK m. Charlotte BOBBIN 23 February 1796. L
William SMITH m. Elizabeth ROWLAND 25 February 1796. L
William DONALDSON m. Priscilla CHAMBERLAND 25 February 1796. L
Edmund CURTIS m. Elizabeth KIRBY 27 February 1796. L

B = Banns   L = License

BURIALS

John MAGGS bur. 3 January 1796.   {R-II-119} {H-318}
Sarah Emerson wife of Seth BARTON bur. 5 January 1796.
Frances wife of Edward STONE bur. 10 January 1796.
Sarah widow of the late Henry NEWMAN bur. 12 January 1796.
An upbaptized child of Jesper DELANAP bur. 26 January 1796.
An unbaptized child of William CONNOWAY bur. 28 January 1796.
Richard WATKINS from Old England bur. 14 February 1796.
James YOULE formerly of New York bur. 14 February 1796.
Jeremiah COSDEN, Jr. from Cecil County bur. 17 February 1796.
William LEONARD formerly of Massachusetts, late of Halifax Nova
    Scotia bur. 18 February 1796.
William LEE, plasterer, husband of Priscilla bur. 20 Feb. 1796.
John s/o John YOUNG bur. 21 February 1796.
An unbaptized child of Betty RAMAGE b. 22 February 1796.
William s/o John MEYERS bur. 23 February 1796.
William SPURRIER, Jr. at Elkridge Landing bur. 23 February 1796.
John PERIGO of & in Patapsco Neck bur. 1 March 1796.   {H-319}
An unbaptized child of John FACKNEY bur. 2 March 1796. {R-II-120}
Anne d/o Thomas LAMDIN bur. 3 March 1796.
Thomas s/o William JOHNS bur. 8 March 1796.
James MANWARING, a native of England, bur. 19 March 1796.
Sarah FOSTER, widow of the late Joseph FOSTER bur. 26 March 1796.
Eliza d/o John KELLY bur. 31 March 1796.
Sarah wife of James MARTIN & native of England bur. 4 April 1796.
James DAY, hair dresser & a native of England bur. 8 April 1796.
Thomas s/o John BAXLEY living at the second mill on Jones's Falls
    bur. 12 April 1796.
Margaret d/o Hugh HAGE bur. 15 April 1796.
John s/o John CALDWELL bur. 17 April 1796.
Thomas PHENIX of Charles County bur. 24 April 1796.

CHRISTENINGS

Sally d/o Philip & Nancy BROWN, free, b. 16 January & bapt. 5
    March 1796.   {R-II-121} {H-320}
Sarah d/o Samuel & Anne CRANFORTH b. 6 Feb. & bapt. 6 March 1796.
Elizabeth d/o William & Isabella REED, natural, b. 10 September
    1795; bapt. 6 March 1796.
William s/o William & Susanna WATKIN b. 5 February & bapt. 9
    March 1796.
George s/o John & Dorcas SAUNDERS b. 13 January & bapt. 20 March
    1796.

CHRISTENINGS

Barbara d/o Thomas & Ann MACKIE b. 25 January & bapt. 23 March 1796.

Anne d/o Francis & Mary SIEGERS b. 2 October 1795; bapt. 28 March 1796.

Mary d/o William & Elizabeth PAINE b. 5 October 1784; bapt. 30 March 1796.

Elizabeth, no surname or parents listed, perhaps another d/o William & Elizabeth PAINE, b. 5 Oct. 1787; bapt. 30 March 1796.

Mima d/o John & Lydia HILTON b. 24 August 1795; bapt. 3 April 1796.

Elizabeth b. June 1794, William b. 1 October 1795, both bapt. 3 April 1796; children of William T. & Pamela PEACHEY.

Richard Pickett s/o John & Mary DALRYMPLE b. June 1796 [sic], bapt. 4 April 1796.

Thomas s/o John & Susanna Maria BAXLEY b. 25 February & bapt. 11 April 1796.

Harriet d/o Peregrine & Rebecca NOWLAND b. 4 December 1795; bapt. 12 April 1796.

Elenor d/o Richard & Margaret BERTON b. 24 December 1795; bapt. 13 April 1796.

Louisa d/o John & Elenor SMITH b. 19 Feb. & bapt. 13 April 1796.

George s/o Thomas & Elenor WINTERSCALE b. 2 March & bapt. 14 April 1796.

George s/o Manly Benjamin & Jane FORTESCUE b. 23 March & bapt. 17 April 1796.

William s/o Thomas & Elizabeth PEARCE b. 1 January & bapt. 17 April 1796.

Mary Anne d/o Geffroy & Phoebe MEAD, free, b. 1 April & bapt. 17 April 1796.

James s/o James & Elenor CROXALL b. 10 bapt. 22 April 1796.

James s/o Thomas & Mary USHER b. 5 March & bapt. 24 April 1796.

Anne d/o George & Elizabeth SMITH b. 8 November 1795; bapt. 24 April 1796.

William s/o Philip & Elenor WATERS b. 28 May 1795; bapt. 28 April 1796.

James s/o Thomas & Sarah Nevett BAILEY b. October 1795; bapt. 29 April 1796.

MARRIAGES

Daniel HARRISON m. Elizabeth TILLINGSWORTH 3 March 1796. L {R-II-122} {H-321}
Edward CLEMENTS m. Charlott WADE 4 March 1796. L
William SHARP m. Susanna COWAN 10 March 1796. L
John GOULD m. Margaret WHEELER 13 March 1796. L
William STOVALL m. Mary ENSOR 13 March 1796. L
John MC FALL m. Margaret HAYES 15 March 1796. L
Peter PRYAN m. Margaret COLE 19 March 1796. L
Samuel TOMLINSON m. Hannah FAX 21 March 1796. L
Francis EVANS m. Anne PORTER 23 March 1796. L
William ADAMS m. Hannah HALLAN 26 March 1796. L
Robert THEOBALD m. Nancy Frances WOOD 27 March 1796. B
Robert RICHARDSON m. Elizabeth RIDGLY 27 March 1796. L
Joseph MYRICK m. Lilly REESE 27 March 1796. L
Thomas LITTLEJOHN m. Sarah MC CARTER 28 March 1796. L
John MERCHANT m. Elizabeth HARRISON 31 March 1796. L
Ephraim BAKER m. Sacey REIMY 31 March 1796. L
James MC MAHON m. Bridet MAHONEY 3 April 1796. B

B = Banns   L = License

96

MARRIAGES

Thomas SHEPBURN m. Mary WOOLHOUSE 7 April 1796. L
John BOTNER m. Eliza SHERWOOD 7 April 1796. L
Walter GRIFFIN m. Elizabeth PEARSON 10 April 1796. L
George HAMILTON m. Rachel WILLIAMS 14 April 1796. L
Joseph ROGERS m. Sarah SHEPERD 14 April 1796. L
Joseph HALL m. Sarah DAY 24 April 1796. L

B = Banns   L = License

CHRISTENINGS

Emily Anne d/o George & Mary GRUNDY b. December 1795; bapt. 1 May
1796.   {R-II-123} {H-322}
Keturah d/o George & Sarah Biddeson COAL b. December 1795; bapt.
1 May 1796.
James s/o William & Eliza TWINAM b. Feb. 1796; bapt. 4 May 1796.
John b. July 1793, bapt. 5 May 1796; Mary Anne b. June 1795,
bapt. 5 May 1796; children of Amos & Mary Anne LONEY.
Benjamin b. 29 July 1795, bapt. 5 May 1796, s/o Benjamin & Jane
CROCKETT.
Elizabeth Anne b. 23 April, bapt. 8 May 1796 d/o William & Mary
HAMMOND.
Jacob b. 7 August 1793, bapt. 8 May 1796; Catharine b. 29 June
1795, bapt. 8 May 1796; children of Michael & Catharine MASON.
Caleb b. 14 Jan. 1796, bapt. 8 May 1796 s/o John & Mary FISHPAW.
Johnzee b. 20 Dec. 1795, bapt. 8 May 1796 s/o John & Rachel LEAF.
Rufus b. 10 Feb., bapt. 8 May 1796 s/o Thomas & Margaret GRIFFIN.
Hezekiah b. 26 Jan., bapt. 8 May 1796 s/o Andrew & Martha BAHLER.
Margaret b. 26 April, bapt. 8 May 1796 d/o John & Catharine
CUNNINGHAM.
Juliana Elizabeth b. in May & bapt. 8 May 1796 d/o John Eager &
Margaret HOWARD.
Thorowgood b. 10 Feb., bapt. 14 May 1796 s/o Isaac & Mary SMITH.
William b. 25 March, bapt. 15 May 1796 s/o James & Sarah (dec'd.)
MARTIN.
Joseph b. 6 March, bapt. 16 May 1796 s/o William & Margaret
BRANSON.
Elizabeth b. 25 March, bapt. 22 May 1796 d/o Henry & Levina
HOLLINGSWORTH.
Rebecca b. 10 April, bapt. 22 May 1796 d/o Daniel & Margaret
METZLER.
Levi b. 10 April, bapt. 22 May 1796 s/o George & Elizabeth DUTRO.
Sarah b. 6 February, bapt. 26 May 1796 d/o Frederick & Sarah
FIGHTMASTER.
Joseph Hutchin b. 18 February, bapt. 26 May 1796 s/o Joseph
Grove John & Mary Bondinot BEND.
Thomas b. 12 November 1795, bapt. 5 June 1796 s/o Samuel &
Elizabeth FULLER.
James b. 31 July 1794, bapt. 12 June 1796; Robert b. 26 May,
bapt. 12 June 1796, s/o Lyde & Abby GOODWIN.
James & Charlott NICOLS bapt. 19 June 1796.
Sarah b. 29 May, bapt. 26 June 1796 d/o Nicholas (dec'd.) & Mary
GORSUCH, his widow.

MARRIAGES

John PARKS m. Mary STEWART 1 May 1796.   L   {R-II-124} {H-323}
Samuel SHANAN m. Jane BURN 5 May 1796.   L
David PIKE m. Ketty NIXON 15 May 1796.   L
James KILNER m. Catharine BURGOYNE 15 May 1796.   L

97

MARRIAGES

Joseph DOUGHERTY m. Joyce HOLMES 23 May 1796. L
Josias RUTTER m. Mary PENNINGTON 24 May 1796. L
Patrick SAVAGE m. Elizabeth CORRIE 26 May 1796.
Andrew PEARSON m. Patty SMITH 31 May 1796. L
Thomas GENT m. Judith LANDERS 1 June 1796. L
Samuel HUTCHINS m. Mary JUSTIS 9 June 1796. L
Philip KEY of St. Marys m. Sophia HALL 9 June 1796. L
Joseph JAY m. Anne WILLIAMS 19 June 1796. L
Elisha ALLISON m. Ann SHEPPERD 19 June 1796. L
David JOHNSON m. Bridget LANON 21 June 1796. L
Israel RANDALL m. Dalilah LEE 23 June 1796. L
Mayberry PARKS m. Mary COLLINS 26 June 1796. L
John RIELY m. Lucy SCANTLAN 27 June 1796. L

L = License

BURIALS

{R-II-125} {H-324}

An upbaptized child of Georg BUCHANAN bur. 1 May 1796.
Eliza d/o Robert OSBORN bur. 5 May 1796.
Nicholas GORSUCH bur. 4 May 1796.
William s/o Jonas CLAPHAM 9 May 1796.
Samuel HURST of Fells Point bur. 9 May 1796.
Elizabeth wife of James WATERS bur. 13 May 1796.
Anne wife of Isaac VANBIBBER bur. 19 May 1796.
John SMITH bur. 28 May 1796.
John s/o John DALRYMPLE bur. 19 May 1796.
An unbaptized child of William BURK bur. 30 May 1796.
Isaac s/o James HAYES bur. 1 August 1796.
A child of William CRANE bur. 3 August 1796.
Thomas GILL from Old England bur. 4 August 1796.
Frances wife of Mark PRINGLE bur. 5 August 1796.
Mary d/o James LONG bur. 6 August 1796.
Robert LUX bur. 10 August 1796.
William BONUS, a native of Old England bur. 11 August 1796.
Kitty d/o Dongal CARMICHAEL bur. 14 August 1796.
William s/o Charles NASH bur. 15 August 1796.
Samuel s/o Hezekiah CLAGETT bur. 19 August 1796.
William s/o James GOWDY bur. 21 August 1796.
Mary wife of John MITCHELL bur. 24 August 1796.
Margaret wife of Francis GILBERTHORPE bur. 25 August 1796.
John Manly FORTESCUE bur. 30 August 1796.
Joseph s/o Thomas HILL bur. 2 June 1796.   {R-II-126} {H-325}
Joseph s/o Catharine YOULE bur. 5 June 1796.
An unbaptized child of William WARREN bur. 11 June 1796.
A child of Joh [sic] WOODARD, dec'd. bur. 18 Junhe 1796.
Charlotte wife of William RIDDELL bur. 19 June 1796.
William s/o Thomas PEARSE bur. 26 June 1796.
Jane d/o James LONG bur. 27 June 1796.
Peter s/o Peter O'DONNAL bur. 29 June 1796.
Joseph s/o Joseph GREY bur. 29 June 1796.
Mary d/o Alexander MACKY bur. 31 June 1796.
Levin COVENTON & Morris bur. 4 July 1796.
John s/o Robert MOORE dec'd. bur 2 July 1796.
Anne Stuart d/o Rd.[sic] FRANCIS bur. 3 July 1796.
Anne HOPKINS of the Eastern Shore bur. 4 July 1796.
Matilda d/o Thomas KETTLE bur. 4 July 1796.
Sarah wife of Philip WALKER bur. 4 July 1796.
Alice d/o William SINGLETON bur. 5 July 1796.
Rose ?? bur. 7 July 1796.

BURIALS

Lydia wife of Francis NEWMAN bur. 8 July 1796.
Harriet d/o John Joseph ABERCROMBIE bur. 9 July 1796.
Andrew KELLY bur. 10 July 1796.
George s/o Thomas WINTERSCALE bur. 10 July 1796.
Edward Francis Gill s/o Chrr. HUGHES bur. 14 Juy 1796.
Thomas s/o Thomas USHER bur. 17 June 1796.
George WEST bur. 17 July 1796.
Sarah wife of John MEYERS bur. 19 July 1796.
Michael BOGGETT bur. 20 July 1796.
An unbaptized child of Charles TINGES bur. 21 July 1796.
Prisilla d/o Thomas LETTER bur. 21 July 1796.
Anne wife of Jeremiah DRISCOLL bur. 23 July 1796.
Jonas OSBORN bur. 24 July 1796.
An unbaptized child of Jona. ENSOR bur. 24 July 1796.
Clarissa d/o Joseph JUSTIS bur. 26 July 1796.
William s/o Benjamin MC KENZIE bur. 27 July 1796.
Ralph s/o Ralph SHAW bur. 28 July 1796.
Daniel DENNIS bur. 29 July 1796.
Thomas s/o John BUSH bur. 29 July 1796.
Sarah d/o Richard TURNER bur. 29 July 1796.

CHRISTENINGS

Sally b. 4 February 1794; bapt. 3 July 1796 d/o Benjamin &
Elizabeth KELLY free Micbs.[sic]   {R-II-127} {H-326}
George b. 10 December 1794, bapt. 3 July 1796 s/o Joseph & Mary
FRANCE.
John b. 26 November 1795, bapt. 3 July 1796 s/o John & Elizabeth
PATERSON.
James b. May 1795, bapt. 8 July 1796 s/o James WILLIAMS, a white
man & Kitty WILLIAMS, a free black.
Leonora b. 14 December 1794, bapt. 9 July 1796 d/o Martha [sic]
Charles & Sophia Elizabeth WARD.
Eliza bapt. 10 July 1796 d/o Samuel & Mary (dec'd.) GREEN.
Samuel Vanbooskirk (Note: This name bracketed with Eliza above.
It is not clear if he is also a child of the GREENS. No birth
or baptism date given.)
William Henry b. 10 September 1793, bapt. 10 July 1796; John
Hawkins b. 15 October 1795, bapt. 10 July 1796, s/o Christopher
& Peggy HUGHES.
Linda b. 2 August 1791, bapt. 10 July 1796 d/o George, a slave &
Mary (free) [no last name given].
Sarah b. 6 June 1794, bapt. 13 July 1796 d/o Richard & Elizabeth
TURNER.
Mary Anne b. 12 September 1795, bapt. 17 July 1796 d/o Thomas &
Sarah CHAMBERS.
Delia b. 4 February 1794, bapt. 17 July 1796 d/o Thomas &
Elizabeth QUAY.
Sophia Bankson b. 21 April, bapt. 17 July 1796 d/o Charles Henry
& Elizabeth Grant WILMANS.
Ebenezer b. 8 March & bapt. 17 July 1796 s/o Joseph & Irene WARD.
Eliza b. 31 May 1793, bapt. 24 July 1796 d/o John & Susanna Maria
BAXLEY.
Thomas b. 3 October 1795, bapt. 24 July 1796 s/o William &
Elizabeth WARD.
Simon b. 13 August 1795, bapt. 27 July 1796 s/o Simon & Jane
BULLEN.
Diana b. 28 December 1795, bapt. 29 July 1796 d/o William &
Hannah SLATER.

CHRISTENINGS

Mary Ireland b. January 1796, bapt. 4 August 1796; Edward Ireland b. 30 December 1791, bapt. 4 August 1796, children of Zebulon & Elizabeth HOLLINGSWORTH.

John Benjamin b. 29 June & bapt. & August 1796 s/o Joseph & Anne FRIETZ.

Martha b. 9 July & bapt. 10 August 1796 d/o Samuel & Susanna OSBORN.

William b. 16 May 1781, bapt. 24 August 1796 s/o William Welsh & Elizabeth COLLINS. (WELSH?)

Jane b. 23 June & bapt. 24 August 1796 d/o Henry & Elizabeth GROEFF.

Nancy b. July or August 1795, bapt. 28 August 1796 d/o Sharper & Catharine WHITE.

MARRIAGES

{R-II-128} {H-327}

James BARNET m. Polly FITZGERALD 2 July 1796. L
John BOUTE m. Louise GUERSOIS 2 July 1796. L
Thomas ASHMAN m. Margaret LEATHORN 2 July 1796. L
James FLINN m. Elizabeth COONEY 5 July 1796. L
Larkin SMITH m. Rachel NICHOLSON 6 July 1796. L
Edward EVANS m. Jane COALE 10 July 1796. L
London m. Beckey (slaves of Christopher HUGHES - by consent) 10 July 1796.
Richard MC COY m. Catharine HOGAN 18 July 1796. L
Lawrence KELLY m. Margaret CHAMBERLAIN 20 July 1796. L
Peter REED m. Jane CATON 23 July 1796. L
Samuel GREEN m. Hannah NAILOR 23 July 1796. L
Thomas BUCKLEY m. Rachel GARRISON 25 July 1796. L
Lambert m. Daphne (belonging to the Balto. Company, by consent) 31 July 1796.
Robert PURTEL m. Catharine SITLER 4 August 1796. L
Greenbury BUSH m. Rhoda DAVIS 17 August 1796. L
Joseph CLAYTON m. Sarah WELLS 18 August 1796. L
Robert SMALLWOOD m. Margaret KEITHOLTZ 25 August 1796. L
Abraham LEWIS m. Emilia TWOGOOD 28 August 1796. B
Thomas GREENWOOD m. Kezia STANSBURY 28 August 1796. L
Barney DAVIS m. Mary MITCHELL 28 August 1796. L

B = Banns L = License

CHRISTENINGS

Juliana b. 29 June, bapt. 4 September 1796 d/o John & Achsah CALEF.

{R-II-129} {H-328}

George Anderson b. 18 August, bapt. 11 September 1796 s/o James & Susanna BUCHANAN.

John b. 22 July & bapt. 11 September 1796 s/o Patrick & Sarah HALFPENNY.

John b. 12 August & bapt. 18 Sept. 1796 s/o Joshua & Mary COCKEY.

Belinda b. December 1795, bapt. 18 September 1796 d/o Benjamin & Frances HYTHE.

Joshua b. 5 December 1784; Ezekiel b. 18 January 1787, both bapt. 23 September 1796, s/o Edward & Sarah BELL (DELL?).

Mary b. 22 June & bapt. 23 Sept. d/o George & Margaret TAYLOR.

Elizabeth b. 28 March & bapt. 25 September 1796 d/o Thomas & Mary PURSE.

Simon b. 13 August & bapt. in September of 1796 s/o Simon & Jane BULLEN.

Edward b. 28 June & bapt. 5 October 1796 s/o George & Jane COOK.

CHRISTENINGS

George Washington b. 25 September 1795, bapt. 6 October 1796 s/o
Rev. John IRELAND & Joanna GILES, his wife.

Sarah b. 11 September & bapt. 9 October 1796 d/o John & Margaret
CANN.

Elenor b. 9 June & bapt. 9 October 1796 d/o John & Elenor BUSK.

Harriot Robert b. 11 January & bapt. 16 October 1796 s/o William
& Jane BUTTON.

Harriot Mangin b. 6 August & bapt. 19 October 1796 s/o? Aquila &
Maria Charlotte Sophia BROWN.

Mary b. 11 September & bapt. 23 October 1796 d/o Amos & Anne
BAILEY.

Susanna b. 29 June & bapt. 26 Oct. 1796 d/o John & Sarah TROTTEN.

Thomas b. 17 January & bapt. 26 October 1796 s/o Robert JOINER, a
free white & Charlotte KENNEDY, a free black.

Anne BROADSHAW (Adult) b. 25 December 1778, bapt. 28 October
1796 (since married to John PATERSON).

John b. 23 March & bapt. 30 Oct. 1796 s/o Felix & Catharine CARR.

Rezin b. 7 March & bapt. 30 October 1796 s/o Benjamin &
Cassandra RICKETTS.

Alfred b. 29 March 1788, bapt. 30 October 1796 s/o John & Achsah
CLARK.

Juliana b. 22 April & bapt. 30 October 1796 d/o George &
Elizabeth SHELHAMMER.

MARRIAGES

{R-II-130} {H-329}

Daniel DASHIELL m. Polly DASHIELL 4 September 1796. L
David GEDDES m. Elizabeth COURTNEY 4 September 1796. L
Joshua LEE m. Priscilla MALKINS 7 September 1796. L
Richard MILLER m. Elenor FIELAS 8 September 1796. L
Peter DICTERLY m. Elizabeth REESE 12 September 1796. L
Adam BOYD m. Violet BOYD 13 September 1796. L
Manning BAKER m. Rebecca CLAIR 13 September 1796. L
John CAMPBELL m. Biddy O'DONNELL 17 September 1796. L
John RANDALL m. Ann WILLESS 20 September 1796. L
Thomas ETHERTON m. Mary BRYAN 22 September 1796. L
John BITTERS m. Elizabeth DONOVAN 22 September 1796. L
John Baptiste BELA m. Winy BRADY 25 September 1796. L
Samuel MEDLICAT m. Anne CARTER 26 September 1796. L
John APPLEBY m. Elenor Fair JACOB 26 September 1796. L
Alfred DRESSER m. Rachel POWERS 2 October 1796. L
John BARRET m. Mary HAGERTY 3 October 1796. L
Francis HOWARD m. Margaret FITZGERALD 7 October 1796. L
Thomas HAWK m. Sara BROWN 8 October 1796. L
John DUFFEY m. Hannah GRIMES 18 October 1796. L
Edward PARKINSON m. Mary WARD 20 October 1796. L
William PEALE m. Elizabeth BERRY 20 October 1796. L
Edward FITZGERALD m. Mary DONOVAN 27 October 1796. L
John PATTERSON m. Nancy BRADSHAW 29 October 1796. L
William WATERS m. Anne FALLOWS 30 October 1796. L

L = License

BURIALS

{R-II-131} {H-330}

A brother of John HAMMOND bur. 1 September 1796.
William HENRY of Ireland bur. 4 September 1796.
Henry s/o John EVANS bur. 4 September 1796.
Mary d/o Eliza. HOWCROFT bur. 7 September 1796.
William s/o John WHEELER bur. 7 September 1796.

BURIALS

An unbaptized child of Isaac DICKES bur. 7 September 1796.
John s/o William STRAUGHAN bur. 8 September 1796.
Harriet d/o John HARPER bur. 9 September 1796.
Eliza EDGAR, step-daughter of T. STOBRIDGE bur. 11 Sept. 1796.
James s/o Henry WEBB bur. 11 September 1796.
Robert s/o James THOMPSON bur. 12 September 1796.
William Henry s/o Christopher HUGHES bur. 14 September 1796.
George Hutcheson BENNET bur. 18 September 1796.
William BIERS's child bur. 21 September 1796; also another child
   of his buried the next day, 22 September 1796.
John Hawkins s/o Christopher HUGHES bur. 22 September 1796.
Richard FELLERS bur. 22 September 1796.
Mary wife of Thomas William STOCKET bur. 23 September 1796.
Hugh MC BRIDE bur. 24 September 1796.
John BICKHAM bur. 27 September 1796.
Barbara d/o Hum. HIPWELL bur. 28 September 1796.
Matilda Elenora Anne d/o James WATERS bur. 28 September 1796.
James NICOLS bur. 2 November 1796.
*John SHAHANNESYE, Hannah d/o William STRIKE, Unbaptized child of
   Walter BELT, William s/o Philip WATERS, Susanna d/o William
   BAYZAND, Daniel GRANT, Jr., Sarah d/o John FACKNEY, Susanna d/o
   Nilhel CHAPMAN. * No dates given, presumed buried during the
   month of November 1796.
Hannah HOLMES bur. 1 October 1796.   {R-II-132} {H-331}
**John Benjamin s/o Joseph FRIETZ, Mary HOWARD, Louisa d/o
   Henary? PRIEST, Rachel MILLS, Harriet d/o William BOBLET,
   Thomas s/o Ed. MARTIN, John s/o John LATOUR, John SMITH,
   Isabella wife of William GRUMES, Joseph s/o Benjamin SPENSER,
   Philip HAUFMAN, Nehemiah DONNELLAN, Rebecca d/o William EVANS,
   A child of James JOHNSON, Maria wife of Luther MARTIN, A child
   of Adam MC LANE, Charles s/o Thomas THARPE, An unbaptized child
   of William MONDELL, Mary d/o Thoma[sic] THARPE, Thorowgood s/o
   Isaac SMITH, Joseph DEAKINS, An unbaptized child of Thomas MC
   CONKEY. ** No dates given, presumed buried during the month of
   October 1796.
Nancy sister of James JOHNSON bur. 2 December 1796.
***Joshua GRAY, Thomas s/o Caleb HALL, Isaac MC CORD, Mary d/o
   John SEARS, Rebecca SEWARD, William DAWSON, A child of Joseph
   NEWTON, Prudence MARSH, Mary wife of Thomas YATES at Spring-
   field, Elizabeth widow of late Thomas GILL, A child of
   Frederick William CALLAHAN, William s/o William WHITE. Joseph
   s/o William STARR.
   *** No dates given, presumed buried December 1796.
Thomas s/o William CROW bur. 20 December 1796.   {H-332}
Thomas WHITNEY's unbaptized child bur. 22 December 1796.
John MC DONALD bur. in December 1796.
Richard s/o Jonn. DALRYMPLE bur. 24 December 1796.
Walter s/o Thomas BROTHERTON bur. 26 December 1796.
Jeremiah PICKETT bur. 27 December 1796.
James s/o Joseph DIXON bur. 31 December 1796.

CHRISTENINGS

                                                     {R-II-133}
Anne b. 20 August & bapt 6 Nov. 1796 d/o Samuel & Anne ROBINSON.
Mary b. 30 June & bapt. 6 Nov. 1796 d/o Joshua & Sarah KNIGHT.
William b. 13 July 179-, bapt. 6 November 1796 s/o William &
   Hannah WHITE.
George b. 15 August & bapt. 9 Nov. 1796 s/o Walter & Sarah ROE.

CHRISTENINGS

Anne b. 6 July & bapt. 13 November 1796 d/o Joseph & Anne ROBINSON.

Elizabeth b. 28 November 1795, bapt. 16 November 1796 d/o William & Sarah JACKSON.

Elizabeth b. 16 June 179-, bapt. 20 November 1796 d/o Francis & Mary RUNDLET.

Rebecca b. 11 September & bapt. 16 November 1796 d/o William & Mary Anne PATERSON.

Thomas b. 8 September & bapt. 26 November 1796 s/o Thomas & Mary SOUTHWOOD.

William b. 29 July & bapt. 27 November 1796 s/o John & Elenor TAYLOR.

Anne b. 20 & bapt. 28 November 1796 d/o John & Elizabeth HAMMOND.

Elizabeth Rebecca Baker b. 6 May & bapt. 11 December 1796 d/o Richard & Elizabeth CURSON.

Samuel b. 22 February 1794, bapt. 13 December 1796 s/o Samuel & Sarah HOLLINGSWORTH.

Thomas b. 4 August 1789; Joseph b. 11 November 1792; Benjamin b. 30 August 1795; all bapt. 17 December 1796, s/o William & Dorcas STARR.

William b. 26 November & bapt. 25 December 1796 s/o John & Harriet DILLEHUNT.

Susanna b. 28 September & bapt. 19 December 1796 d/o George Fraser & Rebecca WARFIELD.

Jonathan b. 7 November & bapt. 21 December 1796 s/o William & Sarah BLUFORD.

James s/o Oxford, dec'd., & Honor, late his wife (no surname) b. 13 December & bapt. 31 December 1796.

MARRIAGES

Francis DAVIS, free black m. Milly, slave of John KER (by consent) 4 November 1796. L   {R-II-134} {H-333}

Robert OZARD m. Anne JOHNSTON 5 November 1796. L

Joseph HOPKINS m. Mary HUGHES 7 November 1796. L

Thomas TENANT m. Mary WATERS 8 November 1796. L

Edward SNEAD m. Jane WEBB 10 November 1796. L

John BROW m. Mary KELLY 15 November 1796. L

Joseph HOPKINS m. Sarah DOWNEY 17 November 1796. L

Joseph JOHNSON m. Maria AGNEW 18 November 1796. L

Soloman BETTS m. Araminta ALEXANDER 24 November 1796. L

Joseph HARVEY m. Mary THOMPSON 1 December 1796. L

John Yates CHINN of Virginia m. Sarah Farfax CARTER 8 December 1796. L

John E. STANSBURY m. Mary PROCTER 8 December 1796. L

James COX m. Catharine FULFORD 8 December 1796. L

Georg CARRICK m. Carey BAKER 12 December 1796. L

Mathew PHELT m. Margaret MC BLAHERTY 15 December 1796. L

John CARTY m. Elizabeth FELLERS 18 December 1796. B

John THOMPSON m. Hannah NEFTLAND 21 December 1796. L

George LEWIS m. Henrietta BEEMS 24 December 1796. B

John Joseph MOROSSA m. Mary PAYNE 25 December 1796. L

David MISHAW m. Achsah MESHAW 31 December 1796. L {End of ORII}

B = Banns L = License

CHRISTENINGS

John Alexander s/o John & Jane HACKET b. 26 September 1796 &
    bapt. 1 January 1797.   {R-III-1} {H-341}
Joseph s/o James & Patience LONG b. 11 December 1796, bapt. 1
    January 1797.
Sarah d/o Adam & Mary DENMEAD b. 10 December 1796, bapt. 4
    January 1797.
James s/o Samuel & Elisabeth GAIKES b. 7 October 1796, bapt. 8
    January 1797.
Mary Anne d/o Michael & Elisabeth BOGGERT b. 22 May 1795, bapt. 8
    January 1797.
Mary d/o Edward & Elizabeth BURNS b. 6 September 1796, bapt. 8
    January 1797.
Margart d/o Alexander & Elizabeth ADAMS b. 27 August 1796, bapt.
    15 January 1797.
_____ child of Thomas & Susanna LAMDIN bapt. 17 January 1797.
Elizabeth d/o Lambert & Elizabeth SMITH b. 11 January & bapt. 22
    January 1797.
Daniel s/o Roger & Rebecca ROBINS b. 22 December 1795, bapt. 27
    January 1797.
Mary b. 30 August 1793; Eliza b. 31 March 1795; Sarah b. 8
    November 1796; all bapt. 28 January 1797, children of John &
    Mary ROSS.
William Gregory s/o William & Margaret COOK b. 5 January & bapt.
    28 January 1797.

MARRIAGES

Nicholas STRIKE m. Margaret PHENIX 1 January 1797.
Jonathan HARVEY m. Lucy ARMSTEAD 3 January 1797.
Michael PURDEN m. Alice KINSLEY 7 January 1797.
John CONWAY m. Sarah STEELE 8 January 1797.
John WALSH m. Ann JAMES 12 January 1797.
Burch DIMMITT m. Catharine LEGROSS 14 January 1797.
Thomas STARKINS m. Catharine COSSETT 18 Januaryr 1797.

BURIALS

William, s/o Robert RICHARDSON bur. 4 January 1797.
Sarah d/o Adam DENMEAD bur. 5 January 1797.
Mary d/o Joshua KNIGHT bur. 5 January 1797.
Jennet STEVENS bur. 6 January 1797.
John M. STEVENS s/o Jennet bur. 6 January 1797.
Mary d/o Amos BAILEY bur. 9 January 1797.
Matthew GRAVES from Connecticut bur. 11 January 1797.
James HICKLEY, a native of England, bur. 12 January 1797.
Mary d/o Richard FELLOWS, dec'd., bur. 12 January 1797.
Margaret d/o John CUNNINGHAM bur. 14 January 1797.
Abraham SHEKELS bur. 19 January 1797.
Sarah wife of Godfrey NEWBY bur. 28 January 1797.

CHRISTENINGS

                                                       {H-342}
William s/o Robert & Elizabeth HICKES b. 28 November 1796; bapt.
    5 February 1797.   {R-III-2}
Mary Louisa d/o William & Elisabeth VAN WYCK b. 21 April 179-;
    bapt. 5 February 1797.
Anna MILLS, an adult near 16 years old, bapt. 5 February 1797.
Mary Anne d/o Joseph & Sarah ANTHONY b. 1 January & bapt. 5
    February 1797.

CHRISTENINGS

William George s/o William & Jane MARSH b. 25 December 1796, bapt. 8 February 1797.

Mary of John DENMEAD & Sarah DAVIDSON b. 19 December 1796; bapt. 19 February 1797.

Joel s/o William & Hannah CONNAWAY b. 1 January & bapt. 20 February 1797.

William s/o William & Margaret WATKINS b. 29 January & bapt. 23 February 1797.

Andrew s/o Thomas & Mary LETTER b. 27 Jan. & bapt. 5 March 1797.

Sarah d/o John & Charlotte KELLY b. 14 July 1796; bapt. 5 March 1797.

John s/o William & Chloe GRAY b. 25 September 1796; bapt. 5 March 1797.

John William s/o John & Mary RIDGLEY b. 21 September 1795; bapt. 13 March 1797.

Mary Anne d/o Hugh & Catharine HAZE b. 5 February & bapt. 13 March 1797.

Anna d/o Joseph & Elisabeth MASSY b. 26 September 1793; bapt. 15 March 1797.

MARRIAGES

William BALL m. Anna Pamela GREEN 12 February 1797.
George SMITH (free) m. Nancy GRANT (a slave) 19 February 1797.
William MORGAN m. Catharine SCANLAN 20 February 1797.
James JOHNSON m. Mary COLE 24 February 1797.
George GARLAND m. Mary MESSER 28 February 1797.
Michael MC LINSEY m. Mary HACKEY 28 February 1797.
John MASON m. Sarah REDING 5 March 1797.
William JOHNSON m. Grace PIPER 8 March 1797.
John DENMEAD m. Sarah DAVIDSON 11 March 1797.
Anthony FOCKE m. Biddy SULLIVAN 12 March 1797.
Edmond RIGGEN m. Elisabeth COLEMAN 12 March 1797.
Pearl DURKEE m. Mary HANKEY 16 March 1797.   {R-III-3}
Andrew BERRY m. Mary GILBERTHORPE 18 March 1797.
(The entries in this portion appear on pages 2 and 3 in Register III.)

BURIALS

An unbaptized child of Mary HANKEY bur. 1 February 1797.{R-III-2}
Rachel wife of John BARTLETT bur. 1 February 1797.
Mary reputed wife of Jonas OSBORNE bur. 4 February 1797.
An unbaptized child of Thomas BROTHERTON bur. 21 February 1797.
William s/o William WATKINS bur. 26 February 1797.
A child of John BAXLEY at the Second Mills bur. 10 March 1797.
William RIDGELY bur. 13 March 1797.
Mary wife of John R. FORRESTER bur. 13 March 1797.
Elizabeth d/o Joseph BARKER bur. 13 March 1797.

CHRISTENINGS

Alice d/o John & Anne PALMER b. 14 April 1793; bapt. 19 March 1797.

                                          {R-III-3} {H-341}

Margaret d/o John & Elizabeth SMITH b. 21 February 1796; bapt. 19 March 1797.

Joseph s/o Joseph & Sarah DAVIS b. 28 May 1796; bapt. 21 March 1797.

Catharine d/o Samuel & Catharine MUNRO b. 7 January 1796; bapt. 22 March 1797.

CHRISTENINGS

Benjamin s/o Moses & Ruth HARRIS (free blacks) b. 17 January & bapt. 25 March 1797.

Charlotte Jane d/o Nathaniel & Charlotte RAMSAY b. 3 January & bapt. 27 March 1797.

Margaret d/o Thomas & Margaret WAGER b. 5 March & bapt. 2 April 1797.

Charlotte d/o John & Rebecca SHAHANASYC b. 5 February & bapt. 5 April 1797.

Priscilla d/o Solomon & Clarissa CLAYTON (free blacks) b. 28 March & bapt. 8 April 1797.

Thomas Galloway & James Gittings, twin s/o Thomas & Mary RINGGOLD b. 11 November 1795; bapt. 9 April 1797.

Anne Maria d/o John & Mary BOSLER b. 26 January & bapt. 11 April 1797.

Elizabeth Dorsey d/o George & Alisana OGLE b. 26 February & bapt. 17 April 1797.

William Henry s/o James & Sarah Brook DALL b. 23 March & bapt. 17 April 1797.

William s/o Henry & Sarah HODGES b. 24 August 1796; bapt. 17 April 1797.

MARRIAGES

Abraham DODD m. Elisabeth SMITH 21 March 1797.   {R-III-3}
Eli HEWITT m. Martha DENNIS 25 March 1797.
John STEELL m. Nancy PAYSON 28 March 1797.
Lucas ALLEN m. Catharine EMMERT 9 April 1797.
John LEWIS m. Elizabeth GARDINER 11 April 1797.
Robert LING m. Anne CHAPMAN 12 April 1797.
John CARNEY m. Esther HUDD 13 April 1797.
John Burke RYLAND m. Sarah JONES 15 April 1797.
Daniel LEAR (TEAR/FEAR?) m. Charlotte MC COY 17 April 1797.

BURIALS

Daniel DULANY bur. 21 March 1797.
Joseph s/o Joseph DAVIS bur. 23 March 1797.
Hannah wife of Edward WILLIAMS bur. 31 March 1797.
Martha HAGE, widow, bur. 6 April 1797.
Jame HOBBS bur. 6 April 1797.

After this point records of events no longer appear under specific headings.

Simeon WEST m. Polly CLASBY April 18, 1797.   {R-III-4} {H-344}
Thomas SMITH bur. 20 April 1797.
George Griffith s/o Griffith & Sarah WHITE b. November 179-; bapt. 23 April 1797; bur. 24 April 1797.
Elizabeth d/o Joel & Joyce DOUGHERTY b. 16 February & bapt. 23 April 1797.
Abraham GROVER bur. 23 April 1797.
George Griffith s/o Griffith WHITE bur. 24 April 1797.
Thomas SOLLERS m. Sarah PENNINGTON 25 April 1797.
James HAY m. Mary COMICAL 27 April 1797.
Hannah, widow of Thomas SMITH, bur. 29 April 1797.
Elisha TURNER m. Mary Anne ROWE 29 April 1797.
Jane Stuart d/o William & Priscilla DONALDSON b. 31 January 1977; bapt. 30 April 1797.

Emma Broughton d/o Henry & Mary PRIEST b. 21 September 1796; bapt. 30 April 1797.

John COOPER m. Elisabeth MC LANE 30 April 1797.

Thomas LEAKINS m. Mary SMITH 1 May 1797. (Error vide May 1, 1798)

Maria d/o Isaac & Pleasant WHEELER, b. 29 August 1795; bapt. 2 May 1797.

An unbaptised child of James WINCHESTER bur. 3 May 1797.

Thomas SHEPPERD m. Anne WEARY 4 May 1797.

Jenny Wignell d/o Samuel & Elisabeth SMYTHE b. 15 March 1797; bapt. 6 May 1797.

John Godart DELISLE m. Elizabeth LAROCHE 6 May 1797.

Thomas Hayley s/o William & Elisabeth PELL b. 4 February & bapt. 7 May 1797.

John Charles s/o James & Sophia CARROLL b. 7 March & bapt. 7 May 1797.

Susanna Mary Margaret d/o Roger & Milcah KESSUCH b. 4 January 1797; bapt. 7 May 1797.

Sarah Sophia d/o Archibald & Elisabeth CAMPBELL b. 15 November 1793; bapt. 7 May 1797.

John ROBERTS m. Elisabeth HOLMES 7 May 1797.

John MC CLASKEY m. Mary WHEELER 7 May 1797.

William b. 1 September 1795; James b. 3 April 1797; both bapt. 7 May 1797, s/o Archibald & Elisabeth CAMPBELL.

Sarah d/o Elijah & Mary WEST b. 28 April & bapt. 7 May 1797.

William Y. LEWIS m. Rachel STEWART 8 May 1797. (Error vide May 8, 1798)
{R-III-5}

Anna Maria d/o William & Elizabeth FIELDS b. 13 November 1796; bapt. 9 May 1797.

Anne d/o William PURDEN bur. 14 May 1797.

Mary d/o Andrew & Elisabeth WILSON b. 18 October 1793; bapt. 14 May 1797.

John Henry s/o Samuel & Sarah CONAWAY b. 11 November 1796; bapt. 14 May 1797.

John s/o Andrew & Elisabeth WILSON b. 1 March & bapt. 14 May 1797.

Ernestine d/o John Joseph & Sarah ABERCROMBIE b. 16 September 1792; bapt. 14 May 1797.
{H-345}

Elisabeth d/o John & Susanna NICHOLSON b. 23 August 1796; bapt. 14 May 1797.

Thomas Griffin s/o William Traverse & Amelia PEACHY b. 27 October 1796; bapt. 14 May 1797.

Emily d/o William & Mary GREEN b. 23 April & bapt. 14 May 1797.

Mary wife of George GRUNDY bur. 15 May 1797.

A child of Samuel GATSKILL or GATCHELL bur. 15 May 1797.

Francis Hopkinson s/o Isaac & Mary SMITH b. 14 March & bapt. 15 May 1797.

Anne d/o William & Susanna PURDON b. 10 May & bapt. 15 May 1797.

William s/o Thomas & Rebecca JOYCE b. 13 March & bapt. 16 May 1797.

Emma B. d/o Henry PRIEST bur. 17 May 1797.

William s/o Thomas & Anne CARBACK b. 20 November 1796; bapt. 17 May 1797.

Elisabeth wife of Thomas MC DOWELL bur. 21 May 1797.

Maria Deliverance d/o William & Margaret BELTON b. 16 September 1795; bapt. 21 May 1797.

Sophia d/o William & Margaret BELTON b. 19 March & bapt. 21 May 1797.

Edward FELLERS m. Jane HIGDON 23 May 1797.

Maria Frances b. 28 November 1797 [sic]; bapt. 23 May 1797.
Anne b. 30 March 1790; Hebe Holland b. 4 January 1793; Evelina
  b. 22 April 1797, all bapt. 23 May 1797; children of John
  Holland & Charity BARNEY.
Francis BLOT m. Patty MEYER 25 May 1797.
A child of Thomas WYATT bur. 25 May 1797.   {R-III-6}
George s/o Richard & Diana LAWSON b. 25 May & bapt. 26 May 1797.
Jane d/o Henry GROEFF bur. 27 May 1797.
John CONNINGHAM m. Anne CARTER 28 May 1797. (Error vide May 28,
  1798) (Banns)
Philip s/o Philip & Mary UHLER b. 28 October 1796; bapt. 28 May
  1797.
George COX m. Biddy LEWIS 29 May 1797.
Pamela d/o Barnet & Ruth BOND b. 25 Nov. 1796; bapt. 29 May 1797.
Sarah d/o Thomas & Elisabeth BOND b. 2 Jan. & bapt. 29 May 1797.
Anne d/o Conrad & Anne MILLER b. 12 April 1796; bapt. 29 May
  1797.
Eleanor d/o Daniel & Elizabeth STREET b. 2 October 1796; bapt. 29
  May 1797.
Edward JOHNSON m. Elisabeth MC CUBBIN 31 May 1797. (Error vide
  May 31, 1798).
Isaac s/o Isaac Gardiner & Diana STEWART b. 27 February & bapt. 4
  June 1797.   {H-346}
Peter ROUR m Anne MC COY 4 June 1797. (Error vide June 3, 1798).
Mary Jane d/o Joseph Grove John & Mary Boudinot BEND b. 13 April
  1797; bapt. 5 June 1797, celebrated by Revd. Legh MASTER.
Philip s/o William & Margaret HUTTON b. 28 January & bapt. 6 June
  1797.
John s/o Daniel & Molly BOUGHTON b. 5 April & bapt. 8 June 1797.
Amelia d/o James & Maria THOMPSON b. 11 April & bapt. 11 June
  1797.
Sarah d/o Solomon & Jane BIRCKHEAD b. 20 August 1796; bapt. 13
  June 1797. Celebrated by Revd. Mr. KEMP of Dorchester County.
James WILLIAMS m. Rachel MAID 15 June 1797.
Anne d/o Joseph ROBINSON bur. 15 June 1797.
Sophia d/o Benjamin KING bur. 15 June 1797.
Daniel PAGE m. Polly HUGHES 18 June 1797.
Sarah d/o Elijah & Mary WEST b. 27 April & bapt. 18 June 1797.
Mary d/o Thomas & Mary WELLS b. 22 May & bapt. 18 June 1797.
Nancy d/o John & Rachel BATSON b. 2 March & bapt. 18 June 1797.
Mary Anne Catharine d/o Francis & Eliza Maria CURTIS b. 8
  November 1768; bapt. 18 June 1797.
George s/o Richard LAWSON bur. 19 June 1797.
Alexander MC DONALD m. Polly DAVIS 19 June 1797.   {R-III-7}
Harriot d/o James & Harriot GITTINGS b. 18 May & bapt. 21 June
  1797.
John s/o James & Alice BLACKBURN b. 4 May & bapt. 21 May 1797.
William s/o John TAYLOR bur. 22 June 1797.
Joseph James NEWTON bur. 22 June 1797.
Joseph & Lurnley (Lumley?) Warner, children of Edward & Mary
  WOODYEAR bapt. 22 June 1797. Joseph b. 4 January 1793; Lurnley
  Warner b. 22 May 179-.
Thomas s/o Thomas & Nancy FITZGERALD b. 18 December 1796; bapt.
  22 June 1797.
Henry s/o Charles Beford & Elisabeth YOUNG b. 22 April 1797;
  bapt. 25 June 1797.
David s/o Philip & Elisabeth SCINDALL b. 11 January 1797; bapt.
  25 June 1797.
Elisabeth wife of John FRY of Connecticut bur. 25 June 1797.

Peter REO m. Maria DE BOYSENE 26 June 1797.
Joseph WATKINS m. Polly SHANEY 26 May 1797.
Thomas TILLEN m. Elizabeth JOYCE 27 May 1797.
Samuel LONG m. Mary CUMMINS 28 May 1797.
John s/o Joseph & Anne JUSTIS b. 28 Feb. & bapt. 28 June 1797.
Thomas HENDER m. Nancy TOWNSEND 29 June 1797.
William BIECH m. Elisabeth PRICE 29 June 1797.
John ROBERTS bur. 30 June 1797.
Elisabeth wife of Alexander ADAMS bur. 30 June 1797.   {H-347}
John WILLIAMS m. Martha HOGGINS 1 July 1797.
Daniel s/o William & Hannah SCINDALL b. 21 February & bapt. 2 July 1797.
Eleanor d/o John BUSK bur. 5 July 1797.
James s/o James & Hannah PETRINGLE b. 5 June & bapt. 5 July 1797.
William JOHNS bur. 5 July 1797.
Abraham ENSOR or INSOR bur. 8 July 1797.
James YOUNG m. Martha COULSON (Error vide 8 July 1798).
Elisabeth d/o Patrick & Joanna CLANSEY b. -- July 1796; bapt. 9 July 1797.
Anne d/o Charles & Grace NASH b. 15 May & bapt. 9 July 1797.
William Clayton BORDLEY m. Margaret KEENER 10 July 1797.{R-III-8} (Error vide July 10, 1798).
Mary d/o Thomas & Rachel FITZGERALD b. -- July 1796; bapt. 11 July 1797.
Mary d/o James & Elisabeth WINTKLE b. 27 May & bapt. 11 July 1797.
John LANSFIELD m. Mary KELLY 11 July 1797.
Eliza d/o William & Elisabeth HUGHES b. 18 November 1796; bapt. 11 July 1797.
Mary Anne Fitt d/o Christian & Jane POE b. 28 January 1794; bapt. 11 July 1797.
George s/o James & Ruth WHAN b. 9 Aug. 1796; bapt. 11 July 1797.
Mary Anne d/o John & Mary EVERHARD b. 22 May & bapt. 11 July 1797.
Mary d/o James WINTKLE bur. 17 July 1797.
John WEIR m. Sarah MADDEN 18 July 1797.
Joseph s/o James & Sarah CHADER b. 23 August 1796; bapt. 19 July 1797.
William s/o John & Eleanor TAYLOR b. 29 July 1796; bapt. 22 July 1797.
Joseph s/o James CHADER bur. 22 July 1797.
Elisabeth d/o George & Elizabeth GORDON b. 9 February & bapt. 23 July 1797.
William s/o Thomas & Elisabeth BAXLEY b. 16 April & bapt. 23 July 1797.
Emmy wife of Samuel GOLDTHWAITE bur. 24 July 1797.
Lemuel TAYLOR's child bur. 25 July 1797.
John s/o William & Nancy MARTIN b. 8 June & bapt. 26 July 1797.
Maria wife of Louis BARBARIN bur. 27 July 1797.
Jane Stewart d/o William DONALDSON bur. 27 July 1797.
Elisabeth Dashiel d/o George & Christy STORY b. 19 April & bapt. 27 July 1797.
Mrs. LOWES, formerly of England, bur. 28 July 1797.
Martha LOWES d/o above bur. 28 July 1797.
Elisabeth d/o Robert & Mary RICHARDSON b. 10 February & bapt. 28 July 1797.
John s/o John & Mary Anne Dorsey BURN b. 26 November 1796; bapt. 29 July 1797.
Andrew s/o John & Mary SMITH b. 23 July & bapt. 29 July 1797.

Robert RUSSEL m. Elisabeth HOBBS 30 July 1797. (Error vide 30 July 1798).

Nancy d/o Moses & Nancy TAYLOR b. 4 April 1795; bapt. 30 July 1797.

John s/o John BURN bur. 31 July 1797.

Elisabeth d/o John BURLAND bur. 31 July 1797.

James SMITH m. Mary MAGHER 2 August 1797. (Error vide 2 August 1798). {R-III-9}

George LUX bur. 2 August 1797.

Joseph WEARY m. Rebecca PERRIGO 2 August 1797. (Error vide 2 August 1798).

William MANSON m. Catharine DAUGHERTY 3 August 1797.

Eleanor BROWN bur. 3 August 1797.

John s/o Joseph JUSTIS bur. 4 August 1797.

Samuel CLASKEY's wife bur. 4 August 1797.

Joseph CROWDER & Judith CLASSAY (by Banns) m. 5 August 1797. (Error vide 5 August 1798)

Mary PHILPOT bur. 6 August 1797.

Elisabeth d/o Arthur MURRAY bur. 6 August 1797.

John TRIMBLE m. Lydia BRICK 6 August 1797.

Eleanor d/o William ALCOCK bur. 7 August 1797.

Raphael CLARCK m. Martha PETERSON 8 August 1797.

William STRANGHAN bur. 8 August 1797.

William MC KEAG m. Peggy NALEY 8 August 1797.

Elisabeth d/o Jesse FEARSON bur. 9 August 1797.

Isaac COHEN m. Peggy MOORE 9 August 1797.

Peter LAMBERT bur. 10 August 1797.

Thomas Johnson s/o John & Rebecca STRAN b. 23 June & bapt. 10 August 1797.

William LESTER m. Elisabeth JOHNSON 10 August 1797.

William THOMPSON m. Elisabeth ANDERSON 10 August 1797.

James JOHN m. Mary Anne ALEXANDRIA 10 August 1797.

James s/o Francis GILBERTHORPE bur. 13 August 1797.

John CARR m. Eleanor HERRON 15 August 1797.

John s/o William MARTIN bur. 18 August 1797.

Joseph HYNER m. Elisabeth SHERARD (by Banns) 19 August 1797. (Error vide 19 August 1798)

Juliana d/o William & Margaret BAILEY b. 21 December 1793; bapt. 20 August 1797.

Peter s/o Peter & Phebe MILLER b. 29 June & bapt. 20 July 1797.

Mary d/o Richard & Anne LOAN b. 1 August & bapt. 21 August 1797.

A child of George LEE bur. 21 August 1797.

Lucy GIBBS bur. 23 August 1797.

John CASTILLO & Anne JONES m. 23 August 1797. {R-III-10}

Carvel Bell s/o John & Martha MC GILL b. 17 August & bapt. 24 August 1797.

A child of John MC GILL or GILL bur. 25 August 1797. {H-349}

Juliana d/o William BAILEY bur. 27 August 1797.

Edward s/o Larkin & Deborah YOUNG b. 28 May & bapt. 27 Aug. 1797.

Dennis MC HENRY m. Joyce WHILTON 28 August 1797.

Michael HAGERTY m. Eleanor CAREY 28 August 1797.

Thomas LAWRENCE & _____ MITCHELL m. 29 August 1797.

James COLLINS m. Mary DONELLAN 30 August 1797. (Error vide 30 August 1798)

Humphrey CABEL bur. 30 August 1797.

William s/o William WATKINS bur. 30 August 1797.

Robert s/o Joseph WOOLEY bur. 30 August 1797.

Thomas FIGG bur. 31 August 1797.

Henry SHEEHAN m. Martha PERRY 31 August 1797.

William s/o Joseph & Drusilla CHENEY b. 27 August & bapt. 1 September 1797.
Thomas Easleyson KIMBLE bur. 2 September 1797.
Joseph s/o William GRAY bur. 3 September 1797.
John JACKSON m. Rebecca HILL 4 September 1797.
John LOWE m. Mary JONES 7 September 1797.
Sarah wife of Thomas WEARY bur. 8 September 1797.
John DYKEN of Jamaica bur. 8 September 1797.
Melissa d/o Levin LAVENDER bur. 8 September 1797.
William BENNETT bur. 8 September 1797.
Thomas JACKSON m. Anne RILEY 8 September 1797.
Elisabeth d/o Stephen & Prudence WATERS b. 29 August 1791; bapt. 8 September 1797.
Juliana d/o John & Letitia WALTER b. 28 April & bapt. 10 September 1797.
Anne d/o Henry & Elizabeth GROFF b. 4 August & bapt. 10 September 1797.
Josias s/o Josias & Jemima PENNINGTON b. 2 June & bapt. 11 September 1797.
Sarah d/o John & Elisabeth RUTTER b. 29 October 1796; bapt. 11 September 1797.
George ROBERTS bur. 11 September 1797.   {R-III-11}
William BAYLEY bur. 11 September 1797.
Sarah HANSON bur. 11 September 1797.
Catharine d/o Jacob MULL bur. 12 September 1797.
Thomas GOLDSMITH bur. 12 September 1797.
Jane d/o Stephen & Ann GUNBY b. 21 March & bapt. 13 Sept. 1797.
Mary Young d/o Walter & Elizabeth D. ADDISON b. 5 March & bapt. 13 September 1797.
John RYE m. Mary BARBARY 13 September 1797.
Elisabeth wife of William SMITH bur. 13 September 1797.
George EASTON bur. 13 September 1797.
Sarah wife of Joseph ANTHONY bur. 15 September 1797.
Robert RICHARDSON's child bur. 15 September 1797.
William CONNAWAY bur. 16 September 1797.
James s/o Philip & Elisabeth WATERS b. 12 June & bapt. 16 September 1797.
Basil Baily s/o Daniel & Priscilla ELLISON b. 10 June & bapt. 17 September 1797.
William s/o John & Anne PATERSON b. 22 August & bapt. 17 September 1797.
William & George s/o John & Elisabeth MADAN (free Mulattoes); William b. 24 July 1791 & George b. 5 February 1797; both bapt. 17 September 1797.
Arthur s/o William GREEN bur. 17 September 1797.
Hannah, Widow of William CONNAWAY, bur. 19 September 1797.
John MILLER bur. 20 September 1797.
A child of John CARTY bur. 20 September 1797.
Biddy d/o Thomas & Jane MONTGOMERY b. 24 April & bapt. 20 September 1797.
Herman WILMANS, a German, bur. 21 September 1797.
Elisabeth wife of John CARTY bur. 21 September 1797.
Sophia d/o Charles WILMANS, bur. 22 September 1797.
Benjamin MASON bur. 22 September 1797.
Harriot d/o George GARVEY bur. 23 September 1797.
Hannah DUKES bur. 23 September 1797.
Eleanor wife of Francis GILBERTHORPE bur. 23 September 1797.
Louis BARBARIN m. Elisabeth MOORE 23 September 1797.

Mary Anne d/o Robert & Elisabeth RIGBEY b. 25 August & bapt. 24
   September 1797.
Thomas s/o John EVANS bur. 24 September 1797.   {R-III-12}
Nancy wife of James LYONS bur. 24 September 1797.
Benjamin LYEN bur. 24 September 1797.
James KELLY bur. 24 September 1797.
Jane DORING bur. 24 September 1797.
James s/o _____ RAY bur. 24 September 1797.
Dr. Edward JOHNSON bur. 25 September 1797.
Susanna MASON, Widow of Benjamin, bur. 25 September 1797.
Robert s/o John RUSK bur. 26 September 1797.
John RUSK bur. 26 September 1797.
Mary d/o William BEVRIDGE bur. 26 September 1797.
Nancy d/o Jane DORING bur. 26 September 1797.   {H-351}
Cecilius JOHNSON bur. 26 September 1797.
Margaret d/o Richard & Margaret BERTON b. 21 & bapt. 27 September
   1797.
James JENNINGS m. Eleanor MC GOWAN 28 September 1797.
Thomas DUNGAN m. Mary GRAY 28 September 1797.
Margaret d/o Richard BERTON bur. 28 September 1797.
James MARSHALL bur. 29 September 1797.
Richardson Stewart s/o Richard & Elisabeth FRANCIS b. -- August &
   bapt. 1 October 1797.
Shadrack s/o Resin & Ruth PENN b. 4 May & bapt. 2 October 1797.
Richard GRAY bur. 2 October 1797.
James CRAGGS bur. 2 October 1797.
Charles s/o Charles MERRIKEN bur. 5 October 1797.
John s/o Richard FELLOWS bur. 5 October 1797.
Thomas Stubbs TAYLOR m. Anne Fox LINDSAY 5 October 1797.
Elisabeth Sullivan d/o James & Elisabeth TAYLOR b. 2 December
   1796; bapt. 5 October 1797.
John THOMPSON bur. 6 October 1797.
John s/o Henry & Mary BROOME b. 4 July & bapt. 8 October 1797.
William HARVEY m. Margaret BURNS 11 October/Sept.? 1797.
Thomas PINE m. Susanna CREMAR 11 October 1797.
Hugh BOYCE m. Eleanor MOONEY 11 October 1797.
Sarah wife of James JOHNSON bur. 12 October 1797.
Thomas OSBURN bur. 12 October 1797.   {R-III-13}
The wife of William GROVE bur. 12 October 1797.
Elisabeth wife of John ROBINSON bur. 15 October 1797.
William s/o John CALDWELL bur. 15 October 1797.
Urith d/o Conrad & Eleanor HUSK b. 26 December 1795; bapt. 15
   October 1797.
Sarah d/o Walter & Elisabeth GRIFFIN b. 24 July & bapt. 15
   October 1797.
Thomas s/o Thomas & Rebecca PETERS b. 13 August & bapt. 19
   October 1797.
James SMITH bur. 19 October 1797.
Hannah wife of James PETRINGEL bur. 20 October 1797.
Frances WHITE bur. 20 October 1797.
John s/o Joshua KNIGHT bur. 21 October 1797.
Bridget wife of Patrick STAFFORD bur. 22 October 1797.
Nicholas HOPKINS bur. 22 Oct. 1797.
Elizabeth d/o Thomas & Mary WHITE b. 12 & bapt. 22 October 1797.
Francis CADERMAN m. Biddy BRYAN 22 October 1797.
Hugh CONNOLLY bur. 24 October 1797.   {H-352}
Thomas Slater s/o William & Elisabeth SINGLETON b. 16 September
   1797 & bapt. 25 October 1797.
Peter HICKEY m. Margaret AIRES 25 October 1797.

Thomas KELL m. Mary Anne GOLDSMITH 25 October 1797.
William LEWIS m. Catharine PORTER 28 October 1797.
Catharine wife of James MORGAN bur. 31 October 1797.
John s/o Humphry & Sarah HIPWELL b. 18 September & bapt. 1
   November 1797.
David CLOSE m. Mary BENTLY 1 November 1797.
Peter JOHNSON m. Priscilla WHITE 1 November 1797.
Jesse s/o Jesse FEARSON bur. 2 November 1797.
Patrick MUHALL m. Barbara SCULL 2 November 1797.
Andrew ALEXANDER bur. 2 November 1797.
Isaac HOOPER m. Jane KIRKWOOD 2 November 1797.
Elisabeth d/o William & Eliza TWINAM bapt. 4 November 1797.
John BURCH m. Fanny MILLER 7 November 1797.
Thompson s/o William & Sarah MILLER b. 29 September & bapt. 8
   November 1797.   {R-III-14}
Susanna wife of Robert DOWNS bur. 8 November 1797.
Elisabeth d/o William TWINAM bur. 8 November 1797.
Juliana Thompson d/o John & Juliana HOLMES b. 17 April 1797;
   bapt. 10 November 1797.
Gunning Bedford s/o George & Mary READ b. 30 June & bapt. 10
   November 1797.
Morrs (Mons?) FLORENCE m. Barbara BROWN 11 November 1797.
Joseph s/o Joseph & Hannah WILSON b. 2 September & bapt. 12
   November 1797.
Samuel HENRY m. Bridget CROSS 15 November 1797.
James RICHARDSON m. Eleanor SULLIVAN 16 November 1797.
Henry BUCKLERS m. Rachel GILBERTHORPE 17 November 1797.
Isabella d/o Hope & Elisabeth BEAN b. 12 September 1796 & bapt.
   19 November 1797.
Anne Susanna d/o Joseph & Anne FRIETS b. 4 October & bapt. 19
   November 1797.
Thomas WATTS m. Elisabeth GARNONS 21 Nov. 1797.
Eleanor d/o James & Elisabeth ROBERTS b. 10 & bapt. 22 Nov. 1797.
Joseph FRIETS bur. 22 November 1797.
Mary Eleanor d/o Robert & Sarah WINN b. 22 October & bapt. 23
   November 1797.
Michael BRIAN m. Mary MILLER 25 November 1797.
Joseph Hutchins s/o Joseph G. J. BEND bur. 25 November 1797.
George Allison s/o William & Elisabeth PEALE b. 24 July & bapt.
   26 November 1797.
Armonella Catharine d/o Levin P. & Mary LAVENDER b. 8 July &
   bapt. 26 November 1797.
John FREER m. Chloe LEAGUE 27 November 1797.
Charles s/o Sarah HICKLEY bur. 27 November 1797.   {H-353}
John Long s/o Zachariah ALLEN bur. 29 November 1797.
Louisa d/o Charles MYERS bur. 29 November 1797.
William Corbin s/o George & Anne ALDERSON b. 1 November & bapt. 3
   December 1797.
Henry HAYWARD m. Harriot BARNEY 7 December 1797.
James WILCOCKS m. Mary or Polly MC KENSIE 7 December 1797.
Andrew RHODES m. Anne PINFIELD 7 December 1797.
Benjamin MASON m. Sarah COOPER 7 December 1797.
John SMITH m. Rosanna JACKSON 10 December 1797.
Jacob William s/o Nicholas & Catharine KONECKE b. 4 September &
   bapt. 10 December 1797.
Samuel s/o Revel & Sarah JOHNSON b. 3 December 1796; bapt. 10
   December 1797.
Anna Maria d/o Samuel & Hannah CHURCH b. 15 February & bapt. 10
   December 1797.   {R-III-15}

Mary Anne d/o Cornelius & Sarah MC CARTHY b. 22 June 1796; bapt. 10 December 1797.
A child of William BAER bur. 11 December 1797.
Joseph s/o Joseph CHENEY bur. 15 December 1797.
Anna d/o John & Mary Essek MASS b. 5 November & bapt. 17 December 1797.
John s/o John & Susanna WINN b. 22 November & bapt. 17 Dec. 1797.
William DICK bur. 17 December 1797.
Daniel TWINE m. Anne WEST 19 December 1797.
Thomas HOLLAND m. Margaret O'CONNOR 21 December 1797.
John CURTIS bur. 22 December 1797.
James BANKSON's child bur. 23 December 1797.
Thomas KELLY m. Honor CAPEN 23 December 1797.
Like CRACROFT m. Alice HALL 23 December 1797.
John ROBINSON m. Tamar WILLIAMS 24 December 1797.
William s/o John DILLEHUNT bur. 24 December 1797.
Anna Maria d/o Richard & Elisabeth CURSON b. 1 September & bapt. 25 December 1797.
Priscilla wife of Joseph CHENEY bur. 26 December 1797.
Alexander Whitesides s/o Hugh & Elizabeth BENNET b. 20 & bapt. 26 December 1797.
Samuel Owings s/o Thomas & Eleanor MOALE b. 3 October 1796; bapt. 26 December 1797.
John Courtnay s/o John & Mary THORNTON b. 23 January 1796; bapt. 26 December 1797.
Mary wife of Joseph CROWDER bur. 27 December 1797.
Joseph WILSON bur. 29 December 1797.
William s/o Francis & Eleanor GILBERTHORPE b. 9 September & bapt. 31 December 1797.
Jane d/o of Benjamin, Slave of Dr. WEISENTHAL & Mary, a free black b. 9 September & bapt 31 December 1797.   {H-354}
James s/o John & Margaret COAL b. 4 & bapt. 31 December 1797.
Henry s/o Henry & Hannah NANTZE b. 26 & bapt. 31 December 1797.
John WHITE m. Patty WILSON 31 December 1797.

1798

A child of ____ ALLEN bur. 2 January 1798.
Peter DESHAW m. Mary DAILY 3 January 1798.
Lawrence WENDLAKE m. Margaret CONLEY 3 January 1798.
James BELT m. Eleanor MOORE 3 January 1798.
John OGEIR m. Margaret REESE 4 January 1798.   {R-III-16}
Peter CASSAT m. Susan STANSBURY 4 January 1798.
Benjamin s/o John & Mary SEARS b. 29 September 1797; bapt. 10 January 1798.
A child of Adam DENMEAD bur. 11 January 1798.
Susanna b. 9 September 1794; Samuel b. 14 November 1797; children of John & Rachel JENNINGS, both bapt. 13 January 1798.
George s/o Michael & Catharine SHRYOCK b. 19 May 1786; bapt. 13 January 1798.
Thomas ACRES m. Elisabeth BERRY 13 January 1798.
Louisa d/o Burch & Catharine DEMMIT b. 3 December 1797; bapt. 14 January 1798.
Eleanor wife of John FLOOD bur. 14 January 1798.
James ROBINSON bur. 15 January 1798.
Eleanora d/o Daniel STREET bur. 15 January 1798.
William THOMAS m. Catharine BRADSHAW 15 January 1798.
A child of William HOLLINS bur. 17 January 1798.

John Green s/o James & Jemima TAYLOR b. 12 September 1797; bapt. 18 January 1798.

Averell s/o Thomas & Sarah MORGAN b. 29 December 1797; bapt. 19 January 1798.

Anne Demillion BROWN bur. 21 January 1798.

James s/o William & Catharine MORGAN b. 5 January 1795; bapt. 21 January 1798.

John C. LUTTIG m. Sally PRATT 21 January 1798.

John Simon s/o Simon & Margaret PERINE b. 22 December 1796?; bapt. 24 January 1798.

John s/o Joseph & Mary FRANCE b. 14 April 1797; bapt. 24 January 1798.

Bamber WHITESIDES m. Martha WEEKINS 24 January 1798.

Eleanor d/o John EVERHART bur. 26 January 1798.

A child of Richard GITTINGS bur. 28 January 1798.

Sarah Hadden d/o Philip & Mary HOWARD b. 11 & bapt. 29 Jan. 1798.

Above named Sarah HOWARD bur. 29 January 1798.

Jonathan LEVER bur. 29 January 1798.

John DALEY m. Ally KEEFE 31 January 1798.

Leonard SADLER bur. 31 January 1798.   {H-355}

Rebecca Elisa, Philemon, Mary Anne & Isabella, children of Stephen & Sarah WINCHESTER, the first born 26 November 1793; the second 11 February 1794; the third 4 April 1796; & the last 22 January 1798; all bapt. 31 January 1798.

Elisabeth d/o Joseph & Elisabeth MASSEY b. 12 June 1797; bapt. 31 January 1798.   {R-III-17}

John b. 23 September 1793; William b. 26 October 1795; & Lloyd b. 4 August 1797; children of _____ BANKSON; all bapt. 31 January 1798.

John NANVORRUCK or NAUBONUCK m. Mary NOBS 2 February 1798.

Esther d/o Edward & Margaret RICHARDS b. 17 January & bapt. 4 February 1798.

Hezekiah s/o Thomas & Mary TENANT b. 3 November 1797; bapt. 5 February 1798.

Joseph s/o Christopher & Peggy HUGHES b. 8 October 1797; bapt. 5 February 1798.

Maria d/o John & Mary DALRYMPLE b. 29 April 1797; bapt. 5 February 1798.

Eliza d/o John & Hannah BINGLEY b. 8 August 1797; bapt. 7 February 1798.

Eliza. d/o John & Elisabeth BICKHAM b. 27 September 1788; bapt. 7 February 1798.

Rebecca d/o Abraham & Mary HARDING (free blacks) b. 21 September 1797; bapt. 7 February 1798.

Peter STEEL bur. 11 February 1798.

James s/o James & Catharine NINDE b. 14 December 1797; bapt. 11 February 1798.

James s/o George & Elizabeth SMITH b. 12 October 1797; bapt. 11 February 1798.

Joseph s/o Christopher HUGHES bur. 12 February 1798.

Sophia d/o James & Sarah ELLIOTT b. 16 January & bapt. 13 February 1798.

James ELLIOTT's wife bur. 13 February 1798.

Walter BELT bur. 13 February 1798.

Samuel GOODALE bur. 16 February 1798.

A child of Capt. PEAKE bur. 16 February 1798.

Peggy d/o Alexander & Jane COULTER b. 29 January & bapt. 20 February 1798.

Michael WHITE m. Julian LARY 20 February 1798.

Maria d/o Daniel STREET bur. 21 February 1798.
Abraham b. 29 January 1793; Catharine b. 11 September 1795; both bapt. 21 February 1798; children of Abraham & Sarah FALCONAR.
James Charles s/o James & Harriot GITTINGS b. 3 September 1795; bapt. 23 February 1798.
Abraham ALDRIDGE's child bur. 28 February 1798.
Juliana wife of John HOLMES bur. 1 March 1798.
Maria Cecilia d/o William CONWAY bur. 1 March 1798.
Judith Maria d/o William & Sarah CONWAY b. 25 August 1795; bapt. 1 March 1798.
Robert b. 11 June 1796; Nicholas b. 27 August 1797; both bapt. 1 March 1798, s/o Samuel & Mary NORWOOD.   {R-III-18} {H-358}
Eleanor Clemaretta d/o Thomas & Elisabeth CROUCH b. 23 July 1797; bapt. 3 March 1798.
Keturah d/o Zachariah & Catharine KEENE b. 6 May 1797; bapt. 4 March 1798.
Joseph RATCLIFF m. Mary LLOYD 6 March 1798.
Philip CRAMER m. Peggy MC KEAN 7 March 1798.
Elijah s/o John BEATTY bur. 11 March 1798.
James s/o John Eager & Margaret HOWARD b. 17 December 1797; bapt. 14 March 1798.
Mary Anne d/o Silas & Margaret ENGLE b. 17 October 1797; bapt. 18 March 1798.
Edward s/o Edward & Margaret HARRISON b. 20 July 1797; bapt. 18 March 1798.
Catharine ROE bur. 20 March 1798.
Thomas HAILE m. Sarah Edmondson NEIGHBORS 20 March 1798.
Peter GRAY m. Mary BRADBURN 20 March 1798.
Rebecca HOGNER b. 13 April 1770; bapt. 21 March 1798.
Mary Anne HANKEY b. 4 May 1778; bapt. 21 March 1798.
Jemima TAYLOR b. 14 July 1780; bapt. 21 March 1798.
Dalilah b. 20 June 1793; William Mass b. 21 December 1794; Ruth b. 2 December 1796; children of John & Rebecca HOGNER all bapt. 21 March 1798.
Margaret d/o Henry & Eleanor WEBB b. 5 & bapt. 24 March 1798.
William Boyce s/o John & Elisabeth SMITH b. 20 December 1797; bapt. 24 March 1798.
Elisabeth d/o Thomas & Sarah CHISHOLM b. 21 March 1797; bapt. 24 March 1798.
Andrew Moore SULLIVAN m. Araminta BURNHAM 24 March 1797.
David Sterret s/o Richard & Mary GITTINGS b. 17 August 1797; bapt. 25 March 1798.
Joanna d/o John & Joanna Giles IRELAND b. 9 February & bapt. 25 March 1798.
Sarah d/o John Amon SCOARCE & Elisabeth his wife, born 25 November 1797; bapt. 25 March 1798.
Charles John Stricker s/o Charles Henry & Elisabeth Grant WILMANS b. 22 September 1797; bapt. 25 March 1798.
Mary Anne d/o John & Elisabeth WARD b. 13 September 1797; bapt. 25 March 1798.
Elisa d/o James & Sarah MASON b. 28 March 1796; bapt. 25 March 1798.
Anne d/o James & Mary FISHWICK b. 12 Jan. & bapt. 26 March 1798.
Charles Louis SIEGFRIED m. Charlotte FRAZER 26 March 1798.
Sarah d/o Lambert & Elisabeth SMITH b. 10 March 1798; bapt. 26 March 1798.   {R-III-19}
William STAINES m. Susanna HUGHES 29 March 1798.   {H-357}
Henry THOMPSON m. Anne Lux BOWLEY 29 March 1798.
John CARVILL m. Anne PERRY 31 March 1798.

John s/o Adam & Violet BOYD b. 19 Nov. 1797; bapt. 1 April 1798.
Thomas s/o John & Margaret GOULARD b. 5 January & bapt. 1 April 1798.
Mary Johnson d/o Edward & Jane FELLERS b. 11 March & bapt. 1 April 1798.
Fanny Pinion d/o Harry, a slave of Humphrey PEIRCE & Maria a free Mulatto, born 22 February & bapt. 1 April 1798.
Anne d/o Matthew & Frances SHAW b. 29 November 1796; bapt. 1 April 1798.
Hannah wife of Philip ABEL bur. 3 April 1798.
Mary HINCKES bur. 3 April 1798.
James DONALLY m. Mary MC KENSIE 3 April 1798.
Vachel DORSEY m. Elizabeth DORSEY 5 April 1798.
James SHRADER m. Jemima JOHNSON 7 April 1798.
Alexander MELONE m. Mary JENNINGS 8 April 1798.
James s/o John & Hannah HARRIS b. - May 1796; bapt. 8 April 1798.
Lucretia d/o Robert & Mary EVERY b. 9 March & bapt. 8 April 1798.
Anne d/o Mary BERRY bur. 10 April 1798.
Lydia d/o Edward & Anne HALL b. 3 Nov. 1797; bapt. 10 April 1798.
James Field s/o Eleanor & Richard MILLER b. 10 June 1797; bapt. 10 April 1798.
Elisa Crane d/o George & Martha TAYLOR b. 22 October 1797; bapt. 13 April 1798.
John BURTLES bur. 14 April 1798.
Henry MARSHALL m. Eve ROTHROCK 14 April 1798.
John GROVE m. Anne CARROLL 14 April 1798.
Eliza Vaughn d/o Thomas & Sarah HEATHRINGTON b. 29 November 1797; bapt. 15 April 1798.
John QUESANG m. Elisa WHIPPLE 15 April 1798.
Gilbert JACKSON bur. 16 April 1798.
William s/o Greenbury & Rhoda BUSK b. 1 February & bapt. 16 April 1798.
James COLE m. Anne CHRISTOPHER 16 April 1798.
Louisa wife of David MIERKEN bur. 17 April 1798.
William s/o Greenbury BUSK bur. 18 April 1798.
William Slater s/o Joseph & Sarah DAVIS b. 15 February & bapt. 18 April 1898.   {R-III-20}
James s/o Greenbury BUSK bur. 19 April 1798.
Francis GILBERTHORPE m. Sarah PRATT 19 April 1798.
Joanna Giles d/o Rev. John IRELAND bur. 20 April 1798.
Matilda d/o John & Catharine BROWN b. 4 October 1796; bapt. 22 April 1798.
Anne d/o Joseph & Barbara HOOK b. 2 July 1797; bapt. 22 April 1798.
Sarah d/o William & Elisabeth SELLER b. 12 February & bapt. 22 April 1798.   {H-358}
James LYON bur. 23 April 1798.
Isaac s/o Hannah (no last name) bur. 23 April 1798.
Josias s/o John & Sarah CRIMSON b. 18 January & bapt. 25 April 1798.
Joseph CLARKE bur. 27 April 1798.
Eliza Caroline d/o Frederick John Magnus & Sophia Louisa AMELUNG born 18 February & bapt. 27 April 1798.
Kitty d/o Robert TAYLOR bur. 28 April 1798.
John ROSS bur. 28 April 1798.
John s/o James & Mary CRANGLE b. 9 Feb. & bapt. 29 April 1798.
Peter s/o John & Chloe FREER b. 1 & bapt. 29 April 1798.
Mary d/o William & Margaret BRANSON b. 4 March 1798; bapt. 29 April 1798.

Alexander s/o Robert JOINER & Charlotte, a free Mulatto b. 6
February & bapt. 29 April 1798.
John Falconar s/o John & Anne STEELL b. 2 March 1798; bapt. 29
April 1798.
Martha wife of Jesse HEATH bur. 30 April 1798.
A child of James THOMPSON, dec'd., bur. 1 May 1798.
Thomas LEAKINS m. Sarah SMITH 1 May 1798.
John BALDEN m. Elizabeth JONES 3 May 1798.
William s/o Thomas & Anne SHEPPARD b. 19 February & bapt. 3 May
1798.
Dennis CAREY m. Judy MOORE 6 May 1798.
William Y. LEWIS m. Rachel STEWART 8 May 1798.
A child of John FLOOD bur. 8 May 1798.
Thomasin d/o(?) Hanson & Catharine GLENN b. 17 September 1798;
bapt. 9 May 1798.
Robert s/o Henry & Elizabeth CABLE b. 19 November 1796; bapt. 9
May 1798.
Martha d/o Hugh & Hannah WILSON b. 23 January & bapt. 9 May 1798.
William s/o Thomas SHEPPARD bur. 10 May 1798.   {R-III-21}
James s/o John & Nancy DOUGLASS b. 15 September 1797; bapt. 20
May 1798.
John s/o Louis & Elizabeth GIFFORD b. 23 April & bapt. 20 May
1798.
William Robert s/o John & Mary ROGERS b. 27 January & bapt. 20
May 1798.
Thomas s/o John & Sarah TROTTEN b. 19 March & bapt. 22 May 1798.
William s/o Jesse & Rachel PORTER b. 19 November 1794; bapt. 22
May 1798.
John s/o Joseph & Frances Philips STANSBURY b. 16 January 1796;
bapt. 22 May 1798.
Rachel PORTER m. William MILBY 22 May 1798.
Jane d/o Stephen GUNBY bur. 22 May 1798.   {H-359}
Lucretia d/o Robert AVERY bur. 23 May 1798.
Archibald MC KENZIE m. Elizabeth DOYLE 24 May 1798.
Elisabeth d/o Patrick & Mary HALFPENNY b. 18 February & bapt. 27
May 1798.
Cassandra d/o John & Betsy CULLEN b. 5 November 1797; bapt. 27
May 1798.
Thomas MOOREHEAD m. Eleanor BROADBURN 28 May 1798.
Jane d/o William & Jane POLLOCK b. 20 July 1797; bapt. 28 May
1798.
John CONNINGHAM m. Anne CARTER 28 May 1798. (By Banns)
Robert Alexander s/o Solomon & Araminta BETTS b. 3 September
1797; bapt. 31 May 1798.
Araminta d/o William & Margaret ALEXANDER b. 15 September 1797;
bapt. 31 May 1798.
Edward JOHNSON m. Elizabeth MC CUBBIN 31 May 1798.
Edward Pennington s/o Thomas & Sarah SOLLERS b. 20 February &
bapt. 1 June 1798.
Anne d/o George & Sarah COLE b. 6 Nov. 1797; bapt. 1 June 1798.
Jacob WEAVER m. Sarah LAUDERMAN 3 June 1798.
Peter ROUX or ROUSE m. Anne MC COY 3 June 1798.
Sally d/o Mayberry & Mary PARKS b. 24 April & bapt. 3 June 1798.
John Joseph s/o John Joseph & Sarah ABERCROMBIE b. 4 March &
bapt. 3 June 1798.
Maria d/o Edward & Catharine DAVIS b. 3 March & bapt. 3 June
1798.
Charles Stowards CARTER m. Sarah BERRY 4 June 1798.
Thomas GLEVES m. Elizabeth DOYLE 4 June 1798.

John Addison Steel of William Baxter SMITH & Frances his wife b.
16 November 1797; bapt. 6 June 1798.
Thomas s/o Edward GANTIER bur. 6 June 1798.
Rebecca d/o Joseph & Rebecca HOPKINS b. 31 December 1797; bapt.
12 June 1798.
John ZIMMERMAN m. Mary HISSEY 16 June 1798.
Anthony CHRISTIAN m. Elisabeth WELSH 16 June 1798.   {R-III-22}
James s/o Stephen & Fanny HORSEFORD b. 8 May 1792; bapt. 17 June
1798.
Mary d/o John & Catharine BELL b. 31 October 1796; bapt. 17 June
1798.
William s/o John & Fanny COLEMAN b. 6 May & bapt. 17 June 1798.
Jeremiah URIE m. Sarah MATTHEWS 19 June 1798.
Harriot d/o Samuel & Jane COPPER b. 23 October 1797; bapt. 19
June 1798.
John s/o Richard H. & Judith C. MOALE b. 8 January & bapt. 24
June 1798.
Archibald BARNETT bur. 27 June 1798.
William THOMPSON m. Jane SUMMERS 28 June 1798.
William JOHNSON m. Elizabeth FITZPATRICK 29 June 1798.
Zachariah SHIELDS m. Anne BAILEY 30 June 1798.
John ROBERTSON m. Margaret LASHLEY 1 July 1798.
Sarah d/o Joseph POOLE bur. 2 July 1798.
James s/o John DOUGLASS Bur. 3 July 1798.
Joan MOALE bur. 6 July 1798.
Anne d/o Joseph & Mary SHANE b. 8 Oct. 1797; bapt. 8 July 1798.
James YOUNG m. Martha COULSON 8 July 1798.
Rachel d/o John & Mary PARKS b. 1 March 1797; bapt. 8 July 1798.
Nicholas FORNEY m. Charlotte POTEE 8 July 1798.
William RIMMER m. Mary STONE 8 July 1798.
Nancy d/o Richard & Martha CLARKE b. 24 October 1797; bapt. 9
July 1798.
William Clayton BORDLEY m. Margaret KEENER 10 July 1798.
Joseph s/o Joseph & Hannah PILGRIM b. 1 June 1797; bapt. 12 July
1798.
John Abbott s/o Benjamin & Sarah DISNEY b. 17 March 1797; bapt.
12 July 1798.
John ABBOTT m. Anne LITTLE 11 July 1798.
William WHITTERFIELD m. Margaret WARFIELD 13 July 1798.
Daniel KEIGHLER m. Mary ASHBURNER 14 July 1798.
James CURTAIN's child bur. 14 July 1798.
Henry Ashpaw s/o Thomas & Margaret BUSSY b. 22 December 1797;
bapt. 15 July 1798.
Samuel CASLOW m. Catharine MARR 16 July 1798.
James Edwards s/o William & Blanche DOWNS b. 25 January 1797;
bapt. 17 July 1798.
Dorothy d/o William & Mary EDGEBURY b. 26 February & bapt. 18
July 1798.
James Bandel s/o William & Sarah RIDDELL b. 26 January & bapt. 18
July 1798.
John s/o John & Mary DILLON b. 20 May 1793; bapt. 18 July 1798.
Thomas & Mary Anne of James & Elisabeth CONWAY; Thomas b. 13
March 1796; Elisabeth [sic] b. 17 December 1797, both bapt. 18
July 1798.
Robert s/o John & Anne MAITLAND b. 9 October 1796; bapt. 19 July
1798.   {R-III-23}
Joel WEST m. Juliana Francisca REPP 19 July 1798.
Amelia d/o Hosea JOHNS bur. 20 July 1798.
John PAYNE's child bur. 20 July 1798.

Susanna d/o Isaac & Elisabeth DIXON b. 1 December 1797; bapt. 21 July 1798.

Sarah d/o Andrew & Martha BAHLER b. 13 March & bapt. 22 July 1798.

Charles Kilbern s/o James & Allyfair DASHIELL b. 8 March 1797; bapt. 22 July 1798.

Elisabeth wife of James PATTERSON bur. 23 July 1798.

Thompson s/o William MILLER bur. 23 July 1798.

James ELLIOTT's child bur. 23 July 1798.

Richard Wilson s/o John & Mary ORRICK b. 9 June & bapt. 23 July 1798.

William ADAMS m. Patty STEWART 24 July 1798.

John B. MC NAIR m. Mary PUMPHRY 26 July 1798.

William s/o William & Rachel MC NAIR b. 14 September 1797; bapt. 26 July 1798.

Rachel d/o of John PARKS bur. 26 July 1798.

George (no surname given) m. Hannah WILSON 27 July 1798.

Mary Andlestone d/o John & Anne CLARKE b. 22 January & bapt. 28 July 1798.

Robert ROBERTSON m. Abigail FONDER 28 July 1798.

Nancy d/o Conrad MILLER bur. 28 July 1798.

James s/o James & Elisabeth WINTKLE b. 17 & bapt. 28 July 1798.

Henrietta Maria d/o Walter & Anne BELT b. 15 & bapt. 28 July 1798.

Susanna Somers d/o George & Anne POCOCK b. 10 June 1797; bapt. 29 July 1798.

Matilda d/o William WARDEN b. 16 Sept. 1797; bapt. 29 July 1798.

James Dent s/o James Dent SUMMERS & Mary his wife b. 21 August 1797; bapt. 29 July 1798.

John s/o John & Mary BARRETT b. 25 & bapt. 29 July 1798.

Robert RUSSELL m. Elisabeth HOBBS 30 July 1798.

Averell d/o Thomas MORGAN bur. 1 August 1798.

John s/o Samuel & Mary READY b. 4 June & bapt. 1 August 1798.

Mary d/o Clarke & Mary INGRAHM b. 28 June & bapt. 1 August 1798.

James SMITH m. Mary MAGHER 2 August 1798.

Joseph WEARY m. Rebecca PERRIGO 2 August 1798.

Richard Stiles s/o John & Sarah CONWAY b. 15 December 1797; bapt. 2 August 1798.

George s/o Abraham SELLERS bur. 2 August 1798.

John BORDLEY m. Catharine STARCK 2 August 1798.

Rebecca Perrigo d/o Hayes & Eleanor BOSS b. 5 June & bapt. 2 August 1798.

Elizabeth wife of Mansel ALCOCK bur. 3 August 1798.

Anne d/o John RAWLINS bur. 3 August 1798.

Esther d/o Edward RICHARDS bur. 3 August 1798.   {R-III-24}

Lawrence s/o Lawrence & Mary KENNEDY b. 23 October 1796; bapt. 4 August 1798.

Joseph CROWDER m. Judith CLASSAY 5 August 1798 (By Banns).

Catharine USHER bur. 6 August 1798.

Robert Alexander s/o Solomon BETTS bur. 8 August 1798.

Elisabeth d/o Thomas & Martha WELSH b. 11 January 1797; bapt. 10 August 1798.

John s/o William & Mary SHIDLE b. 1 June 1797; bapt. 10 August 1798.

William s/o Gerard & Sarah GOVER b. 25 April 1797; bapt. 10 August 1798.

Susan d/o John & Susan MARSHALL, free blacks, b. 6 May 1796; bapt. 11 August 1798.

Emilia d/o William GREEN bur. 11 August 1798.
John s/o William & Jane ALEXANDER b. 6 May & bapt. 12 Aug. 1798.
John RUSK or RUST bur. 12 August 1798.
William MONDELL's child bur. 13 August 1798.
Margaret d/o Henry WEBB bur. 13 August 1798.
John MC CORMICK m. Jane GRAYDY 13 August 1798.
Christopher SAUL m. Sarah DAVIS 14 August 1798.
Sally REYNOLDS bur. 15 August 1798.
Elizabeth wife of Charles GOLDSBOROUGH bur. 15 August 1798.
Esther d/o Robert TAYLOR bur. 17 August 1798.
Thomas s/o John ELLIS bur. 18 August 1798.
Joseph HYNER m. Elizabeth SHERARD 19 August 1798.
John Jordan or Gordon TATE bur. 20 August 1798.
Richard s/o Harman TRICE bur. 20 August 1798.
Robert s/o Robert ELLIOTT bur. 21 August 1798.
Mary Anne d/o Elisha & Mary Anne TURNER b. 3 June & bapt. 22 August 1798.
John s/o George & Jane CROOK b. 9 March & bapt. 22 August 1798.
Margaret d/o Henry & Martha SHEHAN b. 4 & bapt. 26 August 1798.
William s/o Samuel & Elizabeth SPARKS b. 6 April & bapt. 26 August 1798.
Patrick CLARKE m. Margaret READING 27 August 1798.
James ALCOCK bur. 27 August 1798.
Susanna BUCHANAN, Widow, bur. 28 August 1798.
William EAKIN bur. 28 August 1798.
Anne d/o Hannah RINGOOSE or PRINGOOSE bur. 28 August 1798.
Harriot d/o Robert ELLIOTT bur. 29 August 1798.
James s/o Alexander & Jane GWIN b. 13 June 1797; bapt. 29 August 1798.
John FREELOCK m. Sidney WALKER 30 August 1798.
James COLLINS m. Mary DONELLAN 30 August 1798.   {R-III-25}
James s/o Thomas & Mary DURNER b. 11 May 1797; bapt. 31 August 1798.
Rebecca Maria d/o William & Anne PITT b. 7 June & bapt. 31 August 1798.
Juliana d/o John WALTON bur. 31 August 1798.
Thomas TODD bur. 1 September 1798.
Jane d/o William & Elizabeth ELVINS b. 18 July & bapt. 1 September 1798.
Matthew WILLING bur. 3 September 1798.   {H-363}
Eleanor SCHIVELY bur. 4 September 1798.
Anna Maria d/o Richard CURSON, Jr., bur. 4 September 1798.
Conrad s/o Conrad & Anne MILLER b. 21 March & bapt. 9 Sept. 1798.
John s/o Bartholomew & Sarah JACOBS b. 26 February & bapt. 9 September 1798.
Alexander LAWSON bur. 11 September 1798.
Nicholas LATIMER or LATERMAN m. Mary MILLWATERS 11 Sept. 1798.
Christian APPLE m. Anne FOWLER 11 September 1798.
Sarah HAMILTON bur. 13 September 1798.
Benjamin s/o John SEARS bur. 13 September 1798.
Susan d/o Robert KEENER bur. 14 September 1798.
James s/o Alexander GWIN bur. 14 September 1798.
Thomas CLARKE m. Priscilla BEVINS 14 September 1798.
Francis s/o Richard & Mary ARNOLD b. 20 March & bapt. 14 September 1798.
Mary d/o Joseph ANTONIE bur. 16 September 1798.
Sarah d/o William & Elizabeth BEACH b. 12 July & bapt. 16 September 1798.
Henry JENKS m. Jane WEBB 16 September 1798.

James s/o John HARRIS or John HERRIS bur. 18 September 1798.
Anthony PEPPERMAN m. Mary CLAYTON 18 September 1798.
James s/o Richard MILLER bur. 19 September 1798.
Philip WATERS bur. 21 September 1798.
Mary wife of John SLY bur. 21 September 1798.
Anne wife of William WATERS bur. 21 September 1798.
George s/o Archibald CAMPBELL bur. 21 September 1798.
Rodolph s/o Rodolph & Catharine HOOK b. 1 February & bapt. 23 September 1798.
Valentine s/o Frederic & Sarah HOOK b. 14 February & bapt. 23 September 1798.
James s/o James PETRINGEL bur. 23 September 1798.
Sarah b. 22 November 1796; Eade Rebecca b. 3 November 1798; d/o Nicholas & Sophia HISCA both bapt. 23 September 1798.
Mary wife of Henry WINERMAN bur. 24 September 1798.   {R-III-26}
Benedictus MORSE m. Elizabeth FERREN 27 September 1798.
Catharine d/o Robert & Anne LING b. 22 August & bapt. 30 September 1798.
Mary wife of Richard OWINGS bur. 30 September 1798.
Joseph BEAVENS m. Elizabeth THOMPSON 30 September 1798.
Theodore HANSON m. Nancy CLAY 30 September 1798.
William Rogers SMITH m. Margaret DUGAN 2 October 1798.   {H-364}
Emilia d/o Simon & Jane BULLEN b. 8 July & bapt. 3 October 1798.
Margaret ARMITAGE bur. 4 October 1798.
John GRIFFITH m. Sarah JEFFERS 4 October 1798.
John ELLIOTT's child bur. 5 October 1798.
John DODD m. Margaret DINSMORE 6 October 1798.
Polly d/o Pritchard & Elizabeth WINGATE b. 9 May & bapt. 6 October 1798.
John s/o Elizabeth DOWSON bur. 7 October 1798.
Isaac ISAACS m. Henrietta MULAKIN 7 October 1798.
Obed s/o Samuel ROBINSON bur. 8 October 1798.
Elizabeth d/o Thomas & Elizabeth GLEVES b. 6 October & bapt. 8 October 1798.
Elizabeth d/o Thomas GLEVES bur. 10 October 1798.
Eleanor wife of William MAYO bur. 10 October 1798.
Henrietta Maria d/o Anne BELT bur. 14 October 1798.
Valentine FORMAN m. Rebecca LUCAS 14 October 1798.
John s/o David & Rachel GUISCHARD b. 24 March & bapt. 14 October 1798.
Benjamin s/o William & Eleanor TAYLOR b. 14 June & bapt. 15 October 1798.
Mannel GUMS m. Sarah KREBS 16 October 1798.
William MILLER s/o William & Elisabeth THOMPSON b. 21 August 1798; bapt. 17 October 1798.
Matilda Mass d/o John & Rebecca HOGNER b. 8 June & bapt. 17 October 1798.
John KINGAN m. Martha ALLCRAFT 18 October 1798.
John Paul JACQUETT m. Rebecca STRAN 18 October 1798.
John BROWN m. Elisabeth MORRIS 18 October 1798.
John TAYLOR bur. 21 October 1798.
A child of the Widow YOULE bur. 21 October 1798.
Sarah d/o John & Mary BURLAND b. 23 September & bapt. 21 October 1798.
Edward HAYES m. Maria O'BRIEN 23 October 1798.
John SHERLOCK m. Eliza GILMOR 25 October 1798.
William s/o John & Mary FIBBLES b. 18 August & bapt. 26 October 1798.
Mary d/o Benjamin & Mary FLOWERS b. 11 May & bapt. 26 Oct. 1798.

Mary d/o Thomas & Elizabeth BAXLEY b. 18 August & bapt. 28 October 1798.

Anne d/o Thomas & Elisabeth POWELL b. 5 May & bapt. 28 Oct. 1798. {R-III-27}

Jacob s/o Eli & Martha HEWITT b. 8 January & bapt. 28 Oct. 1798.

George Adams s/o Hope & Elisabeth BEAIN b. 6 July & bapt. 29 October 1798.

John s/o Thomas & Ann MC CONKEY b. 22 August & bapt. 29 October 1798.

Thomas BENNETT m. Comfort KING 29 October 1798. {H-365}

Susanna Frost d/o Charles & Kitty ROSS (free blacks) b. 19 October 1795; bapt. 31 October 1798.

Sarah b. 15 January 1795; James Anderson b. 22 February 1798; children of James & Martha MATTHEWS, both bapt. 1 Nov. 1798.

A child of James WHAN bur. 1 November 1798.

A child of Thomas MC CONKEY bur. 2 November 1798.

Richard SMITH m. Sinah TRUMAN 4 November 1798.

John HUNLEY m. Anne PERRY 4 November 1798.

Moses MACE m. Chloe JONES 4 November 1798.

Maria d/o Edmund Channel & Jenny KAIN or KEAN b. 9 February & bapt. 4 November 1798.

Joseph Columbus s/o William & Eleanor JOHNSON b. 4 July & bapt. 6 November 1798.

Maria Fragleton b. 26 December 1795; James b. 27 October 1797, children of James & Anne SIMPSON, both bapt. 7 November 1798.

A child of James WINCHESTER bur. 9 November 1798.

David Hellen s/o Samuel & Anne WHITE b. 18 October & bapt. 10 November 1798.

Susanna Aisquith & Anne King both b. 5 September 1798 & bapt. 10 November 1798, children of Peter Young & Arcajah HELLEN.

George WILSON bur. 14 November 1798.

Adelaide d/o Mark & Lucy PRINGLE b. 17 June & bapt. 16 Nov. 1798.

Anne Christianna d/o John & Catharine SABEL b. 21 September & bapt. 16 November 1798.

James s/o John & Ruth WOOLFOOT b. 19 January & bapt. 16 November 1798.

Jane Lowes d/o Philemon & Jane DAWSON b. 17 July & bapt. 16 November 1798.

Catharine MATTHEWS bur. 19 November 1798.

Alexander THOMPSON m. Margaret ARNEST 20 November 1798.

George MC KENZIE m. Mary JACKSON 22 November 1798.

Jane wife of James SHAW bur. 23 November 1798.

Elizabeth d/o Joseph & Irene WARD b. 24 October & bapt. 25 November 1798.

Charles DOWD m. Margaret MOORE 26 November 1798.

Matthew TAYLOR m. Mary TOPHAM 26 November 1798.

Margaret GREEDY bur. 29 November 1798.

Susanna MC KENSIE bur. 2 December 1798. {R-III-28}

James s/o Humphrey HIPWELL bur. 5 December 1798.

Eleanor d/o William & Bethia WARREN b. 25 September & bapt. 6 December 1798.

William WHIPPLE m. Elizabeth PATE 6 December 1798. {H-366}

John Robert s/o James & Sarah Brook DALL b. 1 November & bapt. 6 December 1798.

Eleanor d/o William WARREN bur. 7 December 1798.

Nancy wife of Thomas MC CONKEY bur. 7 December 1798.

John EAGERTON m. Fanny BURCH 9 December 1798.

Joseph s/o Joseph & Anne FRIETZ b. 11 November & bapt. 9 December 1798.

Elisabeth d/o Abraham & Mary KERSHAW b. 12 September & bapt. 10
  December 1798.
Joseph BURTON m. Rebecca RITTER 10 December 1798.
Joseph STANSBURY bur. 11 December 1798.
William GORDON bur. 12 December 1798.
Harriot d/o Joshua & Sarah KNIGHT b. 8 November & bapt. 13
  December 1798.
Thomas s/o Thomas & Rebecca PAMPHILION b. 5 September & bapt. 13
  December 1798.
John YOUNG m. Martha ALL 13 December 1798.
George WOELPER m. Mary WEARY 13 December 1798.
Sibyl d/o Levi & Margaret TWIST b. 10 November & bapt. 16
  December 1798.
Anna Maria d/o Jonathan & Mary ASKEW b. 12 August & bapt. 16
  December 1798.
John Philips s/o Thomas & Mary LETTER b. 12 November & bapt. 16
  December 1798.
Francis WILSON bur. 18 December 1798.
Elisabeth d/o James & Elizabeth GIBBONS b. 30 November & bapt. 20
  December 1798.
William s/o John SEARS bur. 22 December 1798.
Hannah d/o J. Dixon STANSBURY bur. 22 December 1798.
Elisabeth b. 20 February 1797; Daniel b. 6 December 1798,
  children of Daniel & Elisabeth STANSBURY both bapt. 22 December
  1798.
Hammond s/o Cumberland & Mary DUGAN b. 5 January 1797? & bapt. 22
  December 1798.
Juliana Lindenberger d/o Jacob & Barbara LEGG b. 8 September &
  bapt. 23 December 1798.
William s/o William ELLIOTT bur. 24 December 1798.
Mary Anne Elisa d/o Walter & Elizabeth GRIFFEN b. 17 Octoboer &
  bapt. 25 December 1798.
James s/o John & Susanna JOHNSON b. 18 November & bapt. 25
  December 1798.
Robert MERRY bur. 26 December 1798.
Daniel DALEY m. Elisabeth KILLEN 27 December 1798.
James b. 20 April 1797; Mary b. 19 August 1798, both bapt. 28
  December 1798; children of James & Catharine SEARIGHT.
George s/o William & Prudence ELLIOTT b. 27 December & bapt. 28
  December 1798.   {R-III-29}
Thomas HARGROVE m. Margaret BUCKLEY 29 December 1798.
John s/o William & Mary Anne PATERSON b. 11 November & bapt. 29
  December 1798.
Elisa d/o William & Elizabeth GODDARD b. 24 April & bapt. 30
  December 1798.   {H-367}
George s/o George & Maria BEHER b. in 1798; bapt. 30 Dec. 1798.
Jane d/o Samuel & Mary LONG b. 4 May & bapt. 30 December 1798.

1799

James LOVE bur. 1 January 1799.
John EVANS m. Nancy WEBB 1 January 1799.
Columbus s/o William & Margaret COOK b. 5 December 1798; bapt. 1
  January 1799.
John TOBEN m. Jane LODGE 2 January 1799.
Richard GRICE m. Charlotte HOLLINS 3 January 1799.
Margaret wife of John WILSON bur. 3 January 1799.
John Stewart s/o John & Mary PARKS b. 23 December 1798; bapt. 3
  January 1799.

Anne d/o Robert C. & Sarah LONG b. 19 September 1798; bapt. 3 January 1799.
William EDWARDS m. Sophia LERONETT 6 January 1799.
Delia d/o James NORRIS bur. 7 January 1799.
Jacob DEATH m. Elizabeth MILLER 8 January 1799.
Joseph PIERCE m. Mary CABLES 9 January 1799.
Columbus Washington s/o Robert & Margaret KENT b. 16 November 1798; bapt. 13 January 1799.
James s/o Patrick & Catharine STAFFORD b. 3 December 1798; bapt. 15 January 1799.
Mary FLINN bur. 19 January 1799.
Joshua GILL m. Jemima GORSUCH 19 January 1799.
John POWERS m. Elizabeth SLAUN 19 January 1799.
Sibyl d/o Levi TWIST bur. 20 January 1799.
Hannah wife of Adam MC LEAN bur. 21 January 1799.
Henry DASHIELL m. Mary LEEKE 24 January 1799.
Bamber WHITESIDES's child bur. 25 January 1799.
Daniel PEARSON m. Sally Anastatia HOLDEN 27 January 1799.
John WOOLFORD m. Mary DUKE 27 January 1799.
Sarah d/o James & Julia MARTIN b. 28 February 1798; bapt. 28 January 1799.
John COLEMAN m. Fanny HORSEFOOT 29 January 1799.
Francis MC CORMICK m. Martha MOORE 31 January 1799.
Catharine wife of Samuel FALKNER bur. 1 February 1799.
John DAWSON m. Susanna HARBORD 2 February 1799.
A child of Lewis CAPHERD bur. 3 February 1799.   {R-III-30}
John REESE m. Elisabeth RUSK 3 February 1799.
Elizabeth d/o James NORRIS bur. 3 February 1799.   {H-368}
Mary wife of Robins CHAMBERLAYNE bur. 3 February 1799.
Charles JACOBS m. Mary MALONEY 4 February 1799.
Peter CAMPBELL m. Altha WILKINS 4 February 1799.
John GILLNAR m. Rachel DARLEY or DARBY 5 February 1799.
Thomas YATES m. Mary ATKINSON 7 February 1799.
A strange young Woman from the country bur. 9 February 1799.
Anne d/o Patrick MC GREGORY bur. 10 February 1799.
Andrew WOODS m. Mary TODD 10 February 1799.
Catharine wife of James COX bur. 11 February 1799.
Edward WATTS bur. 13 February 1799.
Rachel d/o Samuel & Elizabeth STEVENSON (free Mulatoes) b. 27 May 1798; bapt. 13 February 1799.
Elizabeth d/o David CHADDERS bur. 14 February 1799.
Richard BOSTON m. Keziah PEAKS, free blacks, 14 February 1799.
Thomas QUINN bur. 18 February 1799.
Henry Nicholas ANSPACH m. Elizabeth FURNIVAL 19 February 1799.
Mary d/o Benjamin BAKER bur. 20 February 1799.
James GOODWIN m. Jane HOGAN 23 February 1799.
William s/o Thomas & Christie CARTER b. 1 September 1797; bapt. 24 February 1799.
William s/o Patrick & Grace MALOY b. 29 November 1797; bapt. 24 February 1799.
Jonathan s/o Hezekiah Taylor & Hetty DOYLE b. 9 February & bapt. 25 February 1799.
James Williams s/o James & Anne JOHNSON b. 16 January & bapt. 26 February 1799.
David SHEARSTRAND m. Kitty FONBAKER 28 February 1799.
John MUNNICKHUYSEN m. Mary HOWARD 28 February 1799.
William Robert s/o John HODGES bur. 1 March 1799.
Margaret Carroll d/o Robins & Mary CHAMBERLANE b. 1 February & bapt. 1 March 1799; bur. 3 March 1799.

Adeline d/o Edward & Elisa WATTS b. 14 August 1798; bapt. 4 March
1799.
Charles LATIMER bur. 5 March 1799.
Elisabeth d/o Nathaniel & Elizabeth WILSON b. 6 & bapt. 7 March
1799.
Sarah Anderson Warfield d/o Dr. Warfield & Jane CLARKE b. 17
January & bapt. 8 March 1799.
Anthony SAWYER m. Sarah SPALDING 10 March 1799.   {R-III-31}
Joseph Ford HOWARD m. Mary WALDEN 11 March 1799.
Thomas b. 29 April 1797; Fanny Caroline b. 17 Jan. 1799; children
of Hezekiah & Frances CLAGETT, both bapt. 11 March 1799.{H-369}
Thomas WEASON m. Mary STANSBURY 14 March 1799.
Joseph Rawlins s/o William & Elisabeth VAN WYCK b. 14 June 1798;
bapt. 14 March 1799.
John MATHISON m. Mary GILBERTHORP 15 March 1799.
John C. HILL m. Judy FENNER 18 March 1799.
Elisabeth d/o William Burrell & Helen MAGRUDER b. 5 January &
bapt. 18 March 1799.
Anthony HADLEY's child bur. 18 March 1799.
Joseph DOUGHERTY's child bur. 19 March 1799.
Thomas BOWLING bur. 20 March 1799.
Anne wife of Nicholas DANIEL bur. 20 March 1799.
Samuel TOON m. Hetty TENNANT 20 March 1799.
Isaac CLOUD (slave) m. Rachel JOHNSON (free black) 20 March 1799.
Thomas WATKINS m. Elisabeth SPURRIER 21 March 1799.
George Washington MOALE bur. 21 March 1799.
William WILSON (slave) m. Leah SPARKSMAN (free Mulatto) 24 March
1799.
Harriot d/o Thomas & Margaret GIFFIN b. 5 November 1798; bapt.
24 March 1799.
Thomas Green s/o William & Sophia SPURRIER b. 23 January & bapt.
24 March 1799.
Elisabeth d/o John & Anne SPURRIER b. 28 August 1798; bapt. 24
March 1799.
Joseph Benjamin Christopher Hughes s/o Richard & Mary SISSON, b.
29 November 1797; bapt. 24 March 1799.
Henry DUGAN m. Charlotte PIERPOINT 25 March 1799.
Amos LONEY's child bur. 25 March 1799.
John MANLY m. Patty CREW 26 March 1799.
Sarah MACKUBIN bur. 29 March 1799.
Abraham POCOCK m. Lydia FOSTER 30 March 1799.
Daniel GALLAGHER m. Jane HIGGINBOTTOM 30 March 1799.
Mary MC LAUGHLIN bur. 1 April 1799.
John MC HARRY m. Margaret FITZGIBBON 1 April 1799 (also appears
under 1 June 1799)
James KELLY m. Sarah JORDAN 1 April 1799.
Thomas HARDING m. Polly MARCHANT 5 April 1799.
An unbaptized child of John STUMP bur. 6 April 1799.
Thomas BARNSWELL, a mulatto, native of Kingston, Jamaica, b. 26
January 1779; bapt. 7 April 1799.   {H-370} {R-III-32}
Rebecca d/o Daniel & Mary MC KENNY b. 7 May 1798; bapt. 7 April
1799.
Harriot d/o William & Priscilla DONALDSON b. 15 December 1798;
bapt. 8 April 1799.
Elisabeth Stewart d/o Thomas & Mary USHER b. 29 August 1799 [sic]
& bapt. 8 April 1799.
Matthew REDMOND m. Margaret Anne FLINN 8 April 1799.
John CRAWFORD m. Jane JOHNSON 8 April 1799.
William ANDERSON m. Mary ROE 11 April 1799.

Joseph SMITH m. Winifred MC CARTY 11 April 1799.
John ELLIS's child bur. 14 April 1799.
Mary b. 13 January 1797; William b. 23 October 1799; children of
Henry & Mary SHUTE; both bapt. 14 April 1799.
Irene wife of Joseph WARD bur. 16 April 1799.
Maria Charlotta Sophia d/o William & Ann EDWARDS b. 20 October
1798; bapt. 17 April 1799.
David BUTLER m. Susan Maria JOHNS 18 April 1799.
Eliza Emilia d/o Jasper & Elisabeth DE CARNAP b. 20 April 1799,
bapt. same day.
James s/o James & Sarah CHAYTOR b. 1 December 1798; bapt. 20
April 1799.
Jane d/o Peter & Phebe MILLER b. 9 March & bapt. 20 April 1799.
Louisa d/o Philip & Mary UHLER b. 12 December 1798; bapt. 20
April 1799.
Charles William Augustus s/o William & Sarah CONWAY b. 8 December
1798; bapt. 20 April 1799.
Thomas s/o William & Mary HAMMOND b. 13 January & bapt. 20 April
1799.
Daniel Bowly s/o Henry & Anne THOMPSON b. 20 December 1798; bapt.
21 April 1799.
Rebecca Letitia b. 7 November 1793; George b. 27 July 1796;
McKean b. 27 July 1798; children of George & Letitia BUCHANAN
all bapt. 21 April 1799.
Susanna d/o Andrew & Anne BUCHANAN b. 27 February 1798; bapt. 21
April 1799.
Michael GERMLEY m. Biddy FOCKES 22 April 1799.
Elisa Amelia d/o Jasper DE CARNAP bur. 22 April 1799.
John b. 11 January 1796; Alexander Hilman b. 26 October 1798; s/o
Anthony & Elisabeth REEVES bapt. 22 April 1799.
John GRAY bur. 23 April 1799.
Isabella d/o Solomon & Araminta BETTS b. 26 November 1798; bapt.
23 April 1799.
Alexander FINLEY m. Jane CARRUTHERS 27 April 1799.
Frances d/o Harman & Frances TRICE b. 4 August 1797; bapt. 28
April 1799.
Edmund s/o William & Sarah GIBSON b. 19 February & bapt. 28 April
1799.
Elisabeth b. 16 November 1797; Anne b. 8 January 1799; d/o
Samuel & Ann MC DOO bapt. 29 April 1799.
Samuel SHEPPERD bur. 29 April 1799.   {H-371, R-III-33}
William BARNEY m. Rebecca RIDGLEY 2 May 1799.
John S. HORNE m. Mary RIDGLEY 2 May 1799.
Sarah d/o John & Sarah DENMEAD b. 22 September 1798; bapt. 2 May
1799.
John LEWIS m. Nancy SILVERTHORN 2 May 1799.
John s/o John & Christiana HARNEL b. 14 March & bapt. 5 May 1799.
James s/o John & Anne PATTERSON b. 16 December 1798; bapt. 5 May
1799.
Mary d/o Samuel & Anne ROBINSON b. 5 Oct. 1798; bapt. 5 May 1799.
Thomas SIMNALS m. Anna KERNS 5 May 1799.
Hugh s/o William MORRISON bur. 9 May 1799.
Peter s/o Peter & Fanny JOHNSON b. 13 April & bapt. 9 May 1799.
Sophia Elisabeth b. 18 November 1796; Richard Sprigg b. 30
October 1797; children of James & Rebecca STEWART, both bapt.
12 May 1799.
Jane d/o William & Jane MARSH b. 1 April & bapt. 12 May 1799.
Elisa d/o James & Elisabeth BIRD b. 14 March & bapt. 12 May 1799.

Samuel Stringer Coale s/o William & Mary THOMAS b. 4 October 1799 [sic], bapt. 12 May 1799.
Elisabeth d/o Jesse & Catharine ALLEN b. 9 April & bapt. 12 May 1799.
Caroline d/o John & Letitia WALTON b. 29 March & bapt. 12 May 1799.
Philip ABEL m. Priscilla FREEMAN 13 May 1799.
Edward DORSEY bur. 16 May 1799.
Elisabeth d/o Thomas & Elisabeth SADLER b. 28 February & bapt. 16 May 1799.
Margaret wife of Daniel CARMICHAEL bur. 18 May 1799.
Samuel BALL m. Judith MAGACY 18 April 1799.
A child of Simon BULLEN bur. 19 May 1799.
William Phenix s/o Nicholas & Margaret STRIKE b. 20 April & bapt. 19 May 1799.
Richard s/o William & Nancy MARTIN b. 4 July 1798; bapt. 19 May 1799.
Rebecca d/o Jeremiah & Sarah URIE b. -- Feb. & bapt. 19 May 1799.
Thomas s/o John SMITH bur. 22 May 1799.
Benjamin CLARE m. Charlotte BEVINS 23 May 1799.
Mary d/o Samuel ROBINSON bur. 25 May 1799.
John SMITH m. Abby THOMAS, free Mulattoes, 25 May 1799.
William HAMILTON m. Maria SELMAN 25 May 1799.
Elisabeth d/o Hugh & Eleanor BOYCE b. 11 December 1798; bapt. 26 May 1799.
Amelia d/o Joseph & Amelia BARKER b. 20 March & bapt. 26 May 1799.
John JONES m. Eleanor TAYLOR 28 May 1799.   {H-372}
John MC HARRY m. Margaret FITZGIBBON 28 May 1799.
John HAGUE m. Elizabeth TRENCHAM 28 May 1799.
William s/o William & Kitty MORGAN b. 12 March & bapt. 28 May 1799.   {R-III-34}
Lydia Ball d/o William & Hannah SLATER b. 5 April & bapt. 2 June 1799.
Henry s/o Samuel & Becky HAWKINS, free persons of colour, b. 2 April & bapt. 2 June 1799.
John s/o Francis & Sarah GILBERTHORPE B. 4 May & bapt. 2 June 1799.
William DANCER bur. 3 June 1799.
George Washington s/o William & Elizabeth FIELDS b. 29 January & bapt. 4 June 1799.
James SIMMONS m. Lydia ARMSTRONG 4 June 1799.
William s/o Adam & Mary DENMEAD b. 9 May & bapt. 5 June 1799.
Henrietta wife of Isaac ISAACS bur. 6 June 1799.
Robert MOODY m. Christian BUTLER 6 June 1799.
Elizabeth d/o Joseph WARD bur. 8 June 1799.
William Parker BARNES m. Mary OSBURNE 9 June 1799.
Anne b. 19 October 1795; Charlotte b. 30 May 1798, d/o John Andrews & Mary MORETON, both bapt. 9 June 1799.
William GRANT m. Susanna DENNIS 10 June 1799.
Joseph DONALDSON bur. 11 June 1799.
John MERCER m. Elizabeth PIERPOINT 11 June 1799.
James URIE m. Elisabeth LONG 13 June 1799.
James PROBART m. Mary VEALE 13 June 1799.
John MC CONNELL m. Sarah LERET 16 June 1799.
George s/o Richard & Lilly THOMPSON b. 25 December 1797; bapt. 16 June 1799.
Rebecca Anne Ireland d/o Arthur & Rebecca Ireland MURRAY b. 19 February & bapt. 16 June 1799.

Rachel d/o Zachariah & Anne SHIELDS b. 15 January 1798; bapt. 16 June 1799.
William Dalrymple s/o John & Catharine BROWN b. 31 January & bapt. 16 June 1799.
Adam MC LEAN m. Demaris HARRY 16 June 1799.
John MARTIN m. Betsy LINDSAY 18 June 1799.
Thomas James s/o James & Sarah HICKLEY b. 12 August 1798; bapt. 19 June 1799.
Henry Nicholas ANSPACH bur. 20 June 1799.
Abner s/o Sarah PARROTT bur. 21 June 1799.
Edward ORN m. Rhoda BREWER 22 June 1799.
Thomas s/o Thomas & Catharine MORROW b. 5 May & bapt. 22 June 1799.
Elisabeth d/o William & Mary GREEN b. 3 & bapt. 22 June 1799.
Killison Bond child of Harry & Rittah (free Negroes) b. in March & bapt. 22 June 1799.   {H-373, R-III-35}
Frances Hellen d/o George Wythe Claiborne & Mary KEITH his wife b. 15 January & bapt. 22 June 1799.
Edward MC GAUGHY m. Jane WILSON 25 June 1799.
Sarah HALL bur. 25 June 1799.
Alexander Clarke s/o Nathan & Elizabeth PHILIPS b. 13 January & bapt. 29 June 1799.
Joseph GOLAN m. Anna PENN 29 June 1799.
George s/o George BOWYER bur. 30 June 1799.
William MC MASTERS m. Anne SADLER 30 June 1799.
Miles RAY m. Rachel HARDY 30 June 1799.
Benjamin MC KENZIE m. Rebecca BEETLE 30 June 1799.
Anna d/o Thomas & Anne SHEPPARD b. 5 April & bapt. 30 June 1799.
Joseph s/o Joseph & Sarah OSBORNE b. 30 May & bapt. 30 June 1799.
John HARDING bur. 1 July 1799.
William MORROW m. Ann HAZLETON 1 July 1799.
Maria b. 25 November 1795; Elisa b. 22 November 1798; d/o Abraham & Jane SELLERS, bapt. 1 July 1799.
John s/o William GRAY bur. 2 July 1799.
Patty wife of Francis BLOT bur. 4 July 1799.
Elisabeth wife of James CONNELL bur. 5 July 1799.
Francis QUIDAMAN m. Jane CROW 6 July 1799.
William Nevett s/o Thomas & Sarah BAILEY b. 24 March & bapt 7 July 1799.
Margaret d/o John & Elisabeth CARMICHAEL b. 24 July 1798; bapt. 7 July 1799.
John s/o Owen & Elisabeth WILLIAMS b. 18 January 1798; bapt. 7 July 1799.
George ROBINSON m. Elisabeth HOBBS 8 July 1799.
Elisa d/o James BIRD bur. 9 July 1799.
Judith wife of John C. HILL bur. 9 July 1799.
James Townley s/o Robert & Elisabeth RIGBY b. 12 October 1798; bapt. 10 July 1799.
William s/o Francis & Margaret GARISH b. 1 December 1798; bapt. 11 July 1799.
Lewis s/o George Fraser WARFIELD & Rebecca his wife b. October 23, 1799 [sic]; bapt. 12 July 1799.
Louis Francis Isidore LE FORT m. Frances DES CHAMPS 12 July 1799.
Mary d/o Henry & Rachel FELLERS b. 1 Jan. & bapt. 14 July 1799.
Rachael d/o James & Sarah COLLINS b. 15 November 1798; bapt. 14 July 1799.
Mary Anne d/o Lawrence & Mary KENNEDY b. 12 November 1798; bapt. 14 July 1799.   {R-III-36}
William s/o Francis GARISH bur. 17 July 1799.

Juliana d/o Christopher & Peggy HUGHES b. 21 December 1798; bapt. 17 July 1799.   {H-374}
William s/o Thomas & Sarah MORGAN b. 12 June & bapt. 18 July 1799.
Jenny d/o Joseph & Hannah RICHARDSON b. 26 June 1798; bapt. 19 July 1799.
Maria d/o Abraham SELLERS bur. 29 July 1799.
Thomas BURK m. Mary LEARY 20 July 1799.
Thomas MC MECHEN m. Sarah RAVEN 21 July 1799.
Thomas HUROGAN m. Ruth PATTY 21 July 1799.
William EDWARD's child bur. 21 July 1799.
Fanny d/o Jacob CREAFF bur. 21 July 1799.
Eliza d/o Richard & Eleanor MILLER b. 28 February & bapt. 21 July 1799.
John s/o William & Mary HALL b. 24 June 1798; bapt. 21 July 1799.
Mary d/o Zachariah & Kittura KEENE b. 6 February & bapt. 21 July 1799.
Eliza d/o Thomas GRIFFIN bur. 22 July 1799.
William HENDERSON's child bur. 22 July 1799.
James CAREY's child bur. 23 July 1799.
Joseph ROGERS m. Deborah STANSBURY 23 July 1799.
James s/o Robert RIGBY bur. 24 July 1799.
Joseph RANEY m. Rebecca FRINCHAM 25 July 1799.
Matilda d/o John HOGNER bur. 26 July 1799.
Dr. WARFIELD's child bur. 26 July 1799.
Graves ADAMS's child bur. 26 July 1799.
John ORRICK's child bur. 26 July 1799.
Samuel COPPER's child bur. 26 July 1799.
Eleanor wife of Joseph BIGNELL bur. 26 July 1799.
James s/o James & Sarah WOODLAND b. 4 May & bapt. 26 July 1799.
Jonathan REED m. Catharine HANDLEN 27 July 1799.
Thomas John s/o Thomas & Margaret BUSSEY b. 17 March (1797 or 1799?) & bapt. 28 July 1799.
Henry s/o Henry & Hannah NANTZE b. 1 & bapt. 28 July 1799.
James s/o Joseph & Mary FRANCE b. 1 April & bapt. 28 July 1799.
George s/o John & Margaret EVERHART b. 6 November 1798; bapt. 28 July 1799.
David CLINE m. Catharine SHAKES 28 July 1799.
Polly b. 2 July 1799; Elisabeth b. 28 July 1797, children of William & Sarah MORRIS, both bapt. 29 July 1799.   {R-III-37}
John RYAN m. Eleanor MURPHY 29 July 1799.
James M. WISHART m. Sarah CARTER 29 June 1799.
Charles WALTERS m. Elisabeth HEIDE 29 July 1799.
William b. 2 January 1797; John b. 19 April 1799, s/o Stephen & Susanna PRESHUR, both bapt. 29 July 1799.   {H-375}
Helena Maria d/o William GALLOWAY 30 July 1799.
John s/o John & Charlotte KELLY b. 29 April & bapt. 31 July 1799.
Francis s/o John & Frances BICHER b. 23 August 1798; bapt. 31 July 1799.
Burch DIMMITT bur. 1 August 1799.
John GOODMAN bur. 1 August 1799.
George Gardner s/o John & Elisabeth LEWIS b. 20 November 1798; bapt. 1 August 1799.
William s/o Stephen PRESHUR bur. 2 August 1799.
Ann King d/o Peter HELLEN bur. 2 August 1799.
Sarah NUTBROWN bur. 2 August 1799.
Louisa d/o Philip UHLER bur. 2 August 1799.
James s/o Partick & Margaret HARRISON b.2 February 1798; bapt. 2 August 1799.

Margaret d/o Henry SHEEHAN bur. 3 August 1799.
Gustavus s/o John RYE bur. 3 August 1799.
Rebecca d/o Rebecca HOPKINS bur. 3 August 1799.
George Gardner s/o John LEWIS bur. 3 August 1799.
Thomas s/o Charles & Elisabeth JOHNSON b. 26 September 1798;
   bapt. 3 August 1799.
Mary Anne d/o John & Susanna NICHOLSON b. 18 July & bapt. 3
   August 1799.
Eliza d/o William & Sophia BOWEN b. 16 June & bapt. 3 Aug. 1799.
Joseph HOOPER m. Susanna BENTON 4 August 1799.
Elizabeth d/o William MORRIS bur. 4 August 1799.
Joseph TALL bur. 6 August 1799.
Charles ATWORTH or ATTORTH bur. 7 August 1799.
William s/o James & Eleanor RICHARDSON b. 29 April & bapt. 7
   August 1799.
Thomas LYONS m. Mary SILVERTHORN 7 August 1799.
George MC KINLEY's child bur. 8 August 1799.
John KIRKWOOD m. Maria POWERS 9 August 1799.
William s/o William MORGAN bur. 10 August 1799.
John BARBER m. Margaret RICHARDS 10 August 1799.
Aquila s/o Edward & Nancy JARVIS b. 31 May 1798; bapt. 11 August
   1799.   {R-III-38}
Benjamin s/o William TAYLOR bur. 12 August 1799.
John ROBERTS m. Martha COLEMAN 12 August 1799.
Matilda d/o Jesse & Sarah WEATHERBY b. 26 November 1798; bapt. 12
   August 1799.
Olivia or Lavinia RIDLEY bur. 13 August 1799.
Patrick MC INTYRE's child bur. 15 August 1799.   {H-376}
William JONES bur. 15 August 1799.
A female child of James FISHWICK bur. 15 August 1799.
John WEAVER bur. 16 August 1799.
Mary d/o Zachariah KEENE bur. 16 August 1799.
Joshua s/o Joshua CLARKE bur. 16 August 1799.
Jesse s/o Daniel HARRISON bur. 16 August 1799.
John BRIGHTMAN m. Polly PITTAY 16 August 1799.
Henry DICE m. Elisabeth WINSTANLY 17 August 1799.
Thomas TIBBELS m. Mary BRADSHAW 17 August 1799.
Elisabeth Martha d/o John & Joanna Giles IRELAND b. 14 June
   1799; bapt. 18 August 1799.
David s/o David & Elizabeth WHITAKEY b. 1 July & bapt. 18 August
   1799.
Robert b. 24 August 1794; Josias b. 20 February 1799; s/o Joseph
   & Hannah ASKEW, both bapt. 18 August 1799.
Thomas MC DOWELL bur. 19 August 1799.
John KERNS m. Alice GREADY 19 August 1799.
Thomas s/o Thomas & Jane MONTGOMERY b. 19 August & bapt. 21
   August 1799.
Sarah c/o John KELLY bur. 22 August 1799.
Zachariah SMART m. Esther DUNN 22 August 1799.
William WOODWARD m. Margaret INGLES 22 August 1799.
Andrew s/o Samuel & Anne MC DONNEL b. 22 February 1797; bapt. 22
   August 1799.
A person, name unknown, bur. 23 August 1799.
Cornelius EVANS m. Rosanna SMITH 24 August 1799.
Robert s/o William & Elizabeth SINGLETON b. 20 July & bapt. 25
   August 1799.
Catharina d/o Christian & Anne KAUDERER b. 29 May & bapt. 25
   August 1799.
George SANK m. Hannah VANSANDT 25 August 1799.

John s/o Thomas & Susanna PINE b. 10 & bapt. 25 August 1799.
Levin William Probart s/o Levin William Probart LAVENDER & Mary
  his wife b. 20 March & bapt. 26 August 1799.
William & John, s/o John & Catharine FORSYTH b. 18 July & bapt.
  17 August 1799.   {R-III-39}
Florence DRISCOLL m. Elisabeth ASHBURNER 27 August 1799.
Susanna Aisquith d/o Peter Y. HELLEN bur. 28 August 1799.
Peirce DILLON bur. 29 August 1799.
Robert THOMAS m. Eve REESE 29 August 1799.
Eliza d/o James & Martha SUMMERS b. 17 & bapt. 30 August 1799.
George WILLIS bur. 31 August 1799.   {H-377}
Alexander s/o William & Catharine CLARKE b. 8 March & bapt. 1
  September 1799.
Mary d/o Thomas & Rachel DROWN b. 2 July & bapt. 1 Sept. 1799.
Henry s/o Zachariah & Mary PAUL b. 4 December 1798; bapt. 1
  September 1799.
Robert GALLOWAY m. Judy MC KAFFERTY 2 September 1799.
Joseph LYMAN m. Eleanor RIX 3 September 1799.
Alexander MC CANNON bur. 3 September 1799.
John HARKINS m. Peggy POWELL 3 September 1799.
Frances Pearsall d/o James & Susanna BUCHANAN b. 20 August &
  bapt. 4 September 1799.
A child of Thomas WEARY bur. 4 September 1799.
Thomas LANGTON bur. 5 September 1799.
Jacob WILLIAMS m. Nancy SMITH 5 September 1799.
James MANNELL m. Mary DOLY 5 September 1799.
Henry GREEN m. Anne WALKER 5 September 1799.
John THOMAS m. Nancy SPANSBY 5 September 1799.
Reynolds KNOX m. Grace COATS 5 September 1799.
Thomas BRYAN m. Kitty HUNT 7 September 1799.
Levin William Probart s/o Levin William Probart LAVENDER bur. 8
  September 1799.
Elisa d/o Roger & Milkah KESSUCK b. 9 October 1798; bapt. 8
  September 1799.
Thomas Keibard BEALE m. Isabella CLARKE 8 September 1799.
William s/o John & Margaret CROZIER b. 25 December 1798; bapt. 9
  September 1799.
John SCOTT m. Sally COLEBY 15 September 1799.
Henry WARREN m. Elisabeth SHIELDS 15 September 1799.
Rachel d/o John MOALE bur. 16 September 1799.
Mary d/o Joseph & Anne JUSTIS b. 4 April & bapt. 16 Sept. 1799.
Susanna d/o Samuel & Mary HUTCHINS b. 7 May 1798; bapt. 16
  September 1799.
George LYNHAM m. Mary DE PANG 16 September 1799.
William WALLS m. Euphemia JOHNS 18 September 1799.
James FOSTER m. Rebecca SHANACY 18 September 1799.
Rachel d/o Shadrach & Rebecca TOWSON b. 25 November 1798; bapt.
  18 September 1799.   {R-III-40}
Rachel d/o Shadrach TOWSON bur. 19 September 1799.
Zachariah s/o Sliter & Rebecca PAUL b. 27 October 1798; bapt. 19
  September 1799.
William WEARY m. Anne MERRIT 19 September 1799.
William CRABBIN bur. 19 September 1799.
John CORBY m. Jane GORDON 19 September 1799.
Frances Pearsall BUCHANAN bur. 19 September 1799.   {H-378}
Joseph LYMAN bur. 19 September 1799.
Sarah HICKLEY bur. 19 September 1799.
Child of Daniel BEACHUM bur. 19 September 1799.
Nicholas s/o Thomas KIRKMAN bur. 19 September 1799.

William s/o William THOMPSON bur. 19 September 1799.
Anna d/o William & Elizabeth PELL b. 30 March & bapt. 19
September 1799.
Matilda d/o Solomon & Jane BIRCKHEAD b. 3 August & bapt. 20
September 1799.
Sarah wife of William HODGES bur. 22 September 1799.
Edmund JONES m. Catharine ELMORE 22 September 1799.
William s/o William & Jane ARMSTRONG b. 2 & bapt. 22 Sept. 1799
Elisabeth wife of Thomas MOORE bur. 23 September 1799.
Henry SANSOM(?) m. Anna KINS 23 September 1799.
Jacob CLARKE bur. 24 September 1799.
William MOORE m. Ann JONES 24 September 1799.
Jane d/o Thomas & Catharine CHOATE b. 25 August & bapt. 25
September 1799.
Anne Fleming d/o Daniel TIMMINGS bur. 26 September 1799.
John HYMAN m. Nancy ORRICK 26 September 1799.
James MAY m. Sarah CORBETT 26 September 1799.
John HOLLAND m. Elisabeth ETHRINGTON 26 September 1799.
Mary FRAZIER bur. 27 September 1799.
William MUNRO m. Jane MC CONKEY 28 September 1799.
Mary d/o Joseph JUSTIS bur. 29 September 1799.
Robert b. 16 April 1798; John b. 26 April 1799, s/o Charles
Bedford & Elisabeth YOUNG, both bapt. 29 September 1799.
Benjamin DASHIELL bur. 30 September 1799.
Dennis CLIFFORD m. Eleanor JOHNSON 30 September 1799.
John Melchor Keener s/o William Clayton BORDLEY & Margaret Keener
BORDLEY b. 5 July & bapt. 30 September 1799.
Susanna & James b. 28 February 1793, children of Joshua &
Elisabeth GUTTRY, bapt. 30 September 1799.   {R-III-41}
William s/o James SPARKS bur. 1 October 1799.
Letilla b. 10 December 1793; Joshua Kirby b. 12 May 1796; Anne
Caroline b. 7 July 1798; children of Jonathan & Margery
HARRISON, all bapt. 1 October 1799.   {H-379}
Jane Maria b. 1 May 1797; Henry b. 20 July 1794; children of
Daniel & Eleanor HARRISON bapt. 1 October 1799.
Mary d/o Samuel & Elisabeth SMYTHE b. 6 July & bapt. 2 Oct. 1799.
Otho s/o Daniel HARRISON bur. 4 October 1799.
Matilda d/o John MOALE bur. 5 October 1799.
Samuel FAULKNER m. Mary BROWN 5 September 1799.
Henry s/o Elijah & Hannah LANE b. 28 July & bapt. 6 Oct. 1799.
John s/o Henry & Ruth FISHPAW b. 7 September 1798; bapt. 6
October 1799.
John TAYLOR m. Elisabeth CATLIN 8 October 1799.
Charles LEE m. Nancy BENTLY 8 October 1799.
Margaret d/o Francis & Catharine GLEESON b. 9 June & bapt. 9
October 1799.
George s/o Thomas KIRKMAN bur. 10 October 1799.
Sarah Harvey d/o Philip & Mary HOWARD b. 28 September & bapt. 10
October 1799.
Peter BENNET m. Sarah G. SELBY 10 October 1799.
Adam GLENDENNING m. Milcah GALE 10 October 1799.
James ARMITAGE bur. 11 October 1799.
Rachel d/o Zachariah SHIELDS bur. 12 October 1799.
Mary Anne d/o William Traverse & Amelia PEACHEY b. 12 September &
bapt. 12 October 1799.
David William s/o Jacob & Elisa MYERS b. 23 March & bapt. 12
October 1799.
Matilda d/o Jesse WEATHERBY bur. 13 October 1799.

John s/o William & Cassandra HUGHES b. 14 July & bapt. 13 October
1799.
Samuel MALE or MEALE bur. 14 October 1799.
James LERUE m. Elisabeth COUNNS(?) 15 October 1799.
William COX m. Mary CHAMBERS 15 October 1799.
Elisabeth EMORY bur. 17 October 1799.
Joseph GRAINGER bur. 17 October 1799.
William DUNHAM m. Polly CHANEY 17 October 1799.
Charles CHANEY m. Sarah DUNHAM 17 October 1799.
John BARRET m. Catharine RUKE 17 October 1799.
Alica SENNOR bur. 19 October 1799.
Francis CURTIS bur. 19 October 1799.
Catharine Isabella d/o Robert & Susanna HERONBORN b. 28 June &
bapt. 20 October 1799.   {R-III-42}
Jane d/o David & Elizabeth GREGORY b. (no date given) bapt. 20
October 1799.
Sarah wife of James TIBBET bur. 21 October 1799.
Susanna d/o James & Sarah WHEEDER b. 11 May & bapt. 26 Oct. 1799.
James s/o John Joseph & Sarah ABERCROMBIE b. 16 March & bapt. 27
October 1799.   {H-380}
Edward s/o Edward & Elisabeth JOHNSON b. 27 April & bapt. 27
October 1799.
John s/o James TAYLOR bur. 27 October 1799.
Thomas HALL bur. 29 October 1799.
Thomas HEWITT bur. 29 October 1799.
Samuel HAYLY m. Kitty ANDERSON 29 October 1799.
John HYLAND m. Nancy JOHNSON 31 October 1799.
Alexander RIGBY m. Esther MIMM 31 October 1799.
Anne d/o Nuthill CHAPMAN bur. 1 November 1799.
John BRENAN m. Elisabeth BLAKE 3 November 1799.
Thomas s/o James & Jemima TAYLOR b. 20 April & bapt. 6 Nov. 1799.
William s/o Alexander & Margaret THOMPSON b. 25 September & bapt.
6 November 1799.
George Weary s/o George & Mary WOELPER b. 24 September & bapt. 6
November 1799.
John CARTER m. Mary FORD 6 November 1799.
Thomas s/o James TAYLOR bur. 7 November 1799.
Lloyd NORRIS m. Jane PETERKIN 7 November 1799.
Mary Anne d/o George & Rosanna LEE b. 11 March & bapt. 7 November
1799.
William s/o John Amon SCOARS (?) & Elisabeth his wife b. 14
October 179?, bapt. 10 November 1799.
Elisabeth d/o William & Philadelphia BROWN b. 13 October & bapt.
10 November 1799.
Martha d/o Joseph & Mary SHANE b. 20 Oct. & bapt. 10 Nov. 1799.
Lawrence CONNOLLY m. Barbara COOK 12 November 1799.
Peter SPENCE m. Elisabeth JARVIS 12 November 1799.
Mary wife of George HOFFMAN bur. 13 November 1799.
Thomas COLE m. Elisabeth SMITH 13 November 1799.
Thomas FISHER m. Elisabeth YATES 14 November 1799.
Henry s/o Larkin & Deborah YOUNG b. 28 August & bapt. 16 November
1799.
Elisabeth d/o James & Sarah WILLCOX b. 22 October 1798; bapt. 16
November 1799.
Joseph ERMINE m. Nancy O'BRIAN 17 November 1799.
Eli s/o Eli & Martha HEWITT b. 15 August & bapt. 17 Nov. 1799.
John PETER m. Polly PORTER 18 November 1799.
Eliza d/o Thomas SADLER bur. 19 November 1799.
James s/o James & Anne CURTAIN b. 25 May & bapt. 21 Nov. 1799.

Christopher MOORE m. Priscilla LEE 21 November 1799.   {R-III-43}
John HART bur. 22 November 1799.
Eleanor Addison d/o William Rogers & Margaret SMITH b. 15 July &
    bapt. 24 November 1799.   {H-381}
Charles HARDING bur. 25 November 1799
Jane d/o Joseph L. & Sarah SALTONSTALL b. 11 December 1798; bapt.
    25 November 1799 by Rev. Mr. KEMP.
Richard BRIAN m. Elisabeth POTTER 30 November 1799.
John STEWART m. Catharine ENSOR 1 December 1799.
Joseph ADLINGTON m. Hannah GILBERTHORPE 1 December 1799.
David WILLIAMSON, a free person of color, or black, m. Lucy
    WILLIAMS, a slave of Hercules COURTENAY 1 December 1799.
Elisabeth d/o Solomon & Elisabeth CARTER b. 22 February 1797;
    bapt. 1 December 1799.
Louisa d/o Lewis & Elisabeth GEBHARD b. 17 October & bapt. 1
    December 1799.
Sarah wife of William JACKSON bur. 3 December 1799.
Sarah wife of William GIBSON bur. 3 December 1799.
Thomas s/o Anne WATSON bur. 4 December 1799.
Anne wife of Richard BENFIELD bur. 6 December 1799.
Thomas WAIT m. Rebecca BENTON 6 December 1799.
Margaret CUMMINGS bur. 8 December 1799.
Francis MATTHEWS m. Margaret O'DONNELL 13 December 1799.
John E. DORSEY m. Margaret HUDSON 14 December 1799.
Elisabeth d/o Joseph & Jemima FISH b. 18 August & bapt. 15
    December 1799.
James ELLIOTT m. Mary SLAUGHTER 17 December 1799.
John Ashburner s/o Daniel & Mary KEIGHLER b. 31 October & bapt.
    18 December 1799.
Ezekiel STEWART m. Elizabeth YIELDHALL 19 Dec. 1799.
Elisabeth ANSPACH bur. 20 December 1799.
John CHARTRESS m. Betsey LUCA 23 December 1799.
William EBDIDGE m. Anne DAVIS 26 December 1799.
Mary Pennington d/o Thomas & Sarah SOLLERS b. 27 October & bapt.
    26 December 1799.
Edward s/o John & Elisabeth RUTTER b. 9 January & bapt. 26
    December 1799.
Benjamin b. 28 June 1789; Anna Maria b. 11 July 1799; children
    of Benjamin & Hannah KING, both bapt. 28 December 1799.
George s/o John & Mary SEARS b. 11 October & bapt. 29 Dec. 1799.
Washington Thomas s/o John & Susanna WINN b. 25 November & bapt.
    29 December 1799.
James CHILDS m. Polly NEWCOMER 29 December 1799.
Charlotte WATERS, a free mulatto, 15 or 16 years old bapt. 30
    December 1799.
Daniel LAFFERTY m. Susanna BOWEN 30 December 1799.
John DOOLAN m. Mary JOANNA 30 December 1799.   {H-382, R-III-44}

1800

Henry STOFFELMAN m. Catharine BARTLEMAY 1 January 1800.
Richard Henry LEAKE m. Joanna LOEFFER 2 January 1800.
Louisa d/o John & Elisabeth SHERLOCK b. 15 October 1799; bapt. 2
    January 1800.
Mary d/o Andrew & Anne BUCHANAN b. 1 November 1799; bapt. 2
    January 1800.
Pamelia Joisa d/o John & Anne EVANS b. 13 November 1799; bapt. 2
    January 1800.

Anne d/o William E. SEWELL & Frances his wife b. 31 September 1798; bapt. 4 January 1800.

Susanna d/o Michael & Juliana WHITE b. 12 December 1799; bapt. 4 January 1800.

William s/o Thomas & Mary SHIRLEY b. 18 October 1799; bapt. 5 January 1800.

George Washington s/o James & ----- DASHIELL b. 17 July 1799; bapt. 5 January 1800.

Eliza d/o John & Margaret OGIER b. 26 September 1798; bapt. 7 January 1800.

Uriah ULVERSON m. Polly WATSON 8 January 1800.

Elisabeth d/o Nicholas & ------ ------ b. 25 June 1799; bapt. 12 January 1800.

George CEALIN m. Elisabeth GARNER 16 January 1800.

Reubin HILMAN bur. 17 January 1800.

John EDMONSON's child bur. 17 January 1800.

Maria b. 28 January 1797; Levina b. 14 January 1800, d/o Abraham & Belinda HUGHES, both bapt. 17 January 1800.

Jane COOK bur. 19 January 1800.

James SUMMERS m. Martha PERRY 20 January 1800.

Abraham HUGHES's child bur. 20 January 1800.

William s/o John MC GRATH bur. 20 January 1800.

Levina d/o Abraham & Belinda HUGHES bur. 20 January 1800.

Thomas HIGINBOTHOM m. Susanna BLUNDELL 21 January 1800.

Philip DORSEY's child bur. 22 January 1800.

Robert OGLE m. Polly FOSTER 23 January 1800.

Elisabeth wife of William THOMPSON bur. 26 January 1800.

Charles STEVENSON m. Mary BOYD 28 January 1800.

Ruth d/o Philip & Elisabeth DORSEY b. 25 & bapt. 28 Jan. 1800.

Elisabeth wife of Daniel ADLINGTON bur. 29 January 1800.

Catharine wife of Patrick MILLION bur. 1 February 1800.

George s/o George & Elisabeth SMITH b. November 8, 1799; bapt. 2 February 1800.

James s/o Stephen & Anne GUNBY b. 6 May 1799; bapt. 5 Feb. 1800.

William MERRYMAN m. Anne PRESBURY 6 February 1800.

William GILBERTHORP m. Elisabeth HART 9 February 1800.

Thomas DONALDSON bur. 11 February 1800.   {H-383, R-III-45}

Timothy RYAN m. Elisabeth B. PANNELL 11 February 1800.

Matthew s/o James & Elisabeth WINTKLE b. 2 & bapt. 12 Feb. 1800.

Sarah Jackson d/o John & Rosanna SMITH b. 24 September 1798; bapt. 13 February 1800.

William MURRAY m. Jane SIMPSON 13 February 1800.

Josias s/o Josias ASKEW bur. 18 February 1800.

Ira DRAPER m. Margaret LEARY 20 February 1800.

Calvin COOPER m. Margaret PALMER 20 February 1800.

William MC MECHEN m. Eleanor B. ARMISTEAD 20 February 1800.

Mary widow of Levin COVENTON bur. 23 February 1800.

George Washington s/o John & Rebecca HOGNER b. 23 January & bapt. 23 February 1800.

Henry s/o Josiah & Mary GREEN b. 8 January & bapt. 23 Feb. 1800.

Mary Anne d/o John & Anne MARTIN b. 11 October 1799; bapt. 23 February 1800.

Pamela Joyce d/o John EVANS bur. 24 February 1800.

Peter WILK m. Catharine MAGUIRE 24 February 1800.

Thomas FLETCHER m. Elizabeth DRANK 24 February 1800.

David or Daniel LOGAN's child bur. 28 February 1800.

Joseph s/o Joseph & Elisabeth MOULDER b. 14 February 1793; bapt. 28 February 1800.

Elisabeth d/o William & Elisabeth WARD b. 16 November 1798; bapt. 28 February 1800.
John b. 14 January 1798; Francis b. 16 February 1800, s/o Francis & Charlotte COATES both bapt. 2 March 1800.
Samuel MULLEN m. Rachel BOTNER 6 March 1800.
Charles HALL m. Mary Anne DUNSFORE 7 March 1800.
John Joseph s/o Daniel & Charlotte TEAR (TEAS?) b. 15 February & bapt. 7 March 1800.
Deborah d/o James & Elisabeth BARRANCE b. 12 June 1796; bapt. 7 March 1800.
John Washington s/o Benjamin & Sarah MASON b. 19 April 1799; bapt. 9 March 1800.
Joseph s/o William VAN WYCK bur. 12 March 1800.
Alice wife of Joshua WALKER bur. 13 March 1800.
Anthony HINKLE m. Kitty BOND 13 March 1800.
Zechariah s/o Philemon & Mary DAVIS 15 October 1799; bapt. 13 March 1800.
Sarah wife of William JOLLY bur. 15 March 1800.
Anne d/o Benjamin BAKER bur. 16 March 1800.
William Horatio s/o William & Margaret BELTON b. 4 December 1799; bapt. 16 March 1800.
Richard s/o Richard & Polly GITTINGS b. 9 December 1799; bapt. 16 March 1800.
Mary Bourdieu d/o Samuel & Rebecca STERRETT b. 28 January & bapt. 16 March 1800.
Hall HARRISON m. Elisabeth GAULT 17 March 1800.   {H-384}
William ATMORE m. Lilian MORROW 19 March 1800.
Humphrey Harding s/o Humphrey & Lucy KEEBLE b. 14 February 1800; bapt. 19 March 1800.
John s/o John & Elisabeth BROWN b. 24 October 1799; bapt. 23 March 1800.   {R-III-46}
John Donaldson of Alexander & -------- ALEXANDER [sic] b. 19 December 1799 & bapt. 23 March 1800.
Francis JOSEPH m. Elizabeth SHOCK 24 March 1800.
Josiah HASHAM m. Mary KNUPWOOD 26 March 1800.
Frances wife of John PATTEN bur. 27 March 1800.
James CONNELL m. Betsy CROMWELL 27 March 1800.
George Washington s/o James & Mary FISHWICK b. 26 January & bapt. 28 March 1800.
William s/o William & Rebecca BASDIL b. 7 December 1799; bapt. 29 March 1800.
David s/o John & Martha MANLY b. 12 & bapt. 29 March 1800.
John PETERS m. Hetty PIKE 30 March 1800.
Michael MC KINLEY m. Elisabeth ELBERT 30 March 1800.
Tabitha Rebecca d/o George & Elisabeth GORDON b. 17 December 1799; bapt. 30 March 1800.
John s/o Robert & Anne LING b. 23 January & bapt. 30 March 1800.
Anne Catharine d/o Jonas & Catharine CLAPHAM b. 4 March 1880 & bapt. 30 March 1800.
Henrietta d/o Benjamin & Anne Maria OGLE b. 16 February & bapt. 30 March 1800.
Joseph MILLER m. Susanna BELL 31 March 1800.
John Anthony s/o John & Mary MUNNIKHUYSEN b. 9 February & bapt. 31 March 1800.
William s/o William & Margaret DOWNIE b. 19 January & bapt. 1 April 1800.
John REYNOLDS m. Mary THOMAS 1 April 1800.
Anne d/o of Greenbury & Rhoda BUSK b. 27 January 1799; bapt. 2 April 1800.

Bathia d/o John & Elisabeth BROWN b. 8 July 1798; bapt. 2 April
1800.
Jane d/o John & Catharine MORROW b. 21 September 1799; bapt. 2
April 1800.
George s/o John SEARS bur. 3 April 1800.
Anne wife of Jacob MULL bur. 3 April 1800.
George STEVEN's child bur. 5 April 1800.
Daniel MURPHY m. Sarah RUTTER 5 April 1800.
Francis s/o William & Elisabeth BEERS b. 14 March & bapt. 6 April
1800.
Mary d/o Solomon & Araminta BETTS b. 7 January & bapt. 6 April
1800.
Louisa d/o John & Mary BARBARY b. 30 November 1799; bapt. 6 April
1800.
Susanna d/o John & Susanna BANNERMAN b. 6 November 1799; bapt. 6
April 1800.
Henry TULL m. Jane REED 6 April 1800.
Henry s/o Henry & Mary BROWN b. 21 Oct. 1799; bapt. 6 April 1800.
James s/o Philemon & Mary DAWSON b. 3 September 1799; bapt. 7
April 1800.   {H-385}
James WESTCOTE m. Mary WEST 9 April 1800.
Anne d/o Joseph & Anne JENKINS b. 28 Feb. & bapt. 11 April 1800.
David Stewart s/o Henry & Isabella COURTENAY b. 10 October 1799;
bapt. 12 April 1800.
Frances Anna d/o Joseph & Winefred SMITH b. in February 1800 &
bapt. 13 April 1800.
John s/o Richard & Charlotte GRICE b. 10 November 1799; bapt. 13
April 1800.
Thomas William Peregrine s/o Peregrine & Rebecca KNOWLAND b. 1
October 1799; bapt. 13 April 1800.   {R-III-47}
John s/o John & Christina PAYNE b. 1 December 1799; bapt. 16
April 1800.
Thomas s/o Valentine & Rebecca FOREMAN b. 9 November 1799; bapt.
16 April 1800.
George TRAUGHTEN m. Charlotte AIRY 16 April 1800.
Anthony TALL m. Nancy HARRINGTON 17 April 1800.
Margaret d/o Ralph HIGINBOTHOM Jur. & Isabella his wife b. 26
March & bapt. 18 April by Rev. Mr. HIGINBOTHOM.
Elisa Sarah d/o John & Elisabeth MOORE b. 27 August 1798; bapt.
19 April 1800.
Jane d/o Thomas & Mary WELLS b. 20 March & bapt. 20 April 1800.
James s/o James & Mary ADES b. 16 January & bapt. 20 April 1800.
Solomon s/o William & Elisabeth OWEN b. 21 September 1799; bapt.
20 April 1800.
William s/o Isaac & Pleasant WHEELER b. 17 December 1799; bapt.
20 April 1800.
Bartholomew s/o Bartholomew & Sarah JACOBS b. 22 October 1799;
bapt. 20 April 1800.
Eliza d/o Abraham SELLERS bur. 22 April 1800.
John Reason SELMON m. Kitty SOWERS 23 April 1800.
Lawrence s/o William & Sarah FURLONG b. 12 September 1799; bapt.
24 April 1800.
William s/o William & Eleanor SOLLERS b. 25 February & bapt. 24
April 1800.
Thomas REILEY m. Eleanor SCHAEFFER 25 April 1800.
John NICHOLAS m. Mary BEAR 26 April 1800.
Susanna d/o John & Mary HODGES b. 17 March & bapt. 27 April 1800.
Eleanor d/o Joseph & Anne GORSUCH b. 29 May 1800 [sic] & bapt. 27
April 1800.

Francis LUSHEY m. Anne CROMWELL 29 April 1800.
Ellen Moale d/o Richard CURSON Junr. & Elisabeth his wife b. 26
   October 1799; bapt. 30 April 1800.
John s/o Francis GILBERTHORPE bur. 1 May 1800.
Sophia Elisabeth Anspach d/o John Frederic Magnus AMELUNG &
   Sophia Louisa his wife b. 15 December 1799; bapt. 2 May 1800.
Joseph Lee MILLARD m. Anne Parren WHITE 3 May 1800.   {H-386}
Thomas RUSSEL m. Elisabeth TOWNSEND 3 May 1800.
Catharine d/o Edward & Catharine DAVIS b. 1 April & bapt. 4 May
   1800.
Henry s/o Henry & Elisabeth CABLE b. 16 September 1799; bapt. 4
   May 1800.
Eliza b. 1 December 1798; Harriot b. 18 December 1799, children
   of Michael & Sarah YOUNG both bapt. 4 May 1800.
William BOYD m. Sarah KEATLY 6 May 1800.
Patrick MILLION m. Hannah OWINGS 8 May 1800.
Mary d/o Samuel & Sarah CONNOWAY b. 6 May 1799; bapt. 11 May
   1800.
John s/o Gilbert GILBERTHORPE bur. 12 May 1800.
Edward s/o Edward HARRISON bur. 13 May 1800.
Mary FAIR bur. 14 May 1800.
James SELLERS m. Elisabeth JOICES 15 May 1800.
John HODGES's child bur. 16 May 1800.   {R-III-48}
James MARTIN m. Araminta HART 22 May 1800.
Samuel SCINDALL bur. 23 May 1800.
Joseph s/o William & Hannah SCINDALL b. 15 April 1799; bapt. 23
   May 1800.
Anne d/o Philip & Elisabeth SCINDALL b. 26 April & bapt. 23 May
   1800.
Mary Anne d/o Sylvester & Mary RYLAND b. 8 March & bapt. 23 May
   1800.
Sally d/o Solomon & Nancy SCINDALL b. 19 February & bapt. 23 May
   1800.
Catharine d/o James & Mary SPEAR b. 10 April 1795; bapt. 23 May
   1800.
Eleanor d/o Edward & Jane MC GAUGHY b. 11 April & bapt. 25 May
   1800.
Oliver s/o James & Juliana BOND b. 11 & bapt. 25 May 1800.
John s/o William MORGAN bur. 28 May 1800.
Sarah wife of Thomas CHADICK bur. 30 May 1800.
Maria d/o James & Patience LONG b. 17 March & bapt. 1 June 1800.
Rosanna d/o Hugh & Mary BONER b. 12 April 1799; bapt. 1 June
   1800.
James BEST m. Elisabeth ADAMS 1 June 1800.
John s/o Daniel & Rosanna LAFFERTY b. 25 February & bapt. 2 June
   1800.
Wilson ADLINGTON bur. 5 June 1800.
Jacob SMALL's child bur. 6 June 1800.
William DRAKE m. Catharine LECKLER 7 June 1800.
John HILL m. Jane BOWLAND m. 8 June 1800.
William PLOOM m. Rachel MC GARVEY 8 June 1800.
Anne d/o John & Hannah HARRIS b. 26 Oct. 1799; bapt. 8 June 1800.
Elisa d/o John & Elisabeth WARD b. 2 September 1799; bapt. 8 June
   1800.   {H-387}
John AUGHENBAUGH m. Susanna LITTLE 16 June 1800.
Thomas SPICER m. Anne CADLE 10 June 1800.
Joseph s/o Samuel & Mary ROBERTSON b. 12 October 1798; bapt. 11
   June 1800.

John Edward s/o John & Hannah DORSEY b. 18 February & bapt. 11 June 1800.
John Skinner WEBSTER m. Elisabeth THOMBURG 12 June 1800.
Joseph s/o Samuel ROBERTSON bur. 13 June 1800.
Joshua s/o William Bedford & Rebecca BARNEY b. 23 March & bapt. 14 June 1800.
Charles Ridgley s/o John Stedman & Dorothy Mary HORNE b. 28 March & bapt. 15 June 1800.
Polly b. 12 March 1788; Dolly Williams b. 9 February 1791; William Jova b. 8 June 1800; children of William & Elisabeth WHIPPLE. The last by a second wife; both wives named Elisabeth.
Theresa d/o Louis & Elisabeth BARBARIN b. 22 August 1798; bapt. 16 June 1800.
James WATERSON m. Grace CAMPBELL 17 June 1800.
John BURGESS m. Elizabeth MERCHANT 19 June 1800.
Hosea Bailey s/o Charles Dent SUMMERS & his wife Mary b. 25 May & bapt. 20 June 1800.   {R-III-49}
Polly Collins d/o John HITCH bur. 22 June 1800.
Carolina d/o William & Sophia EDWARDS b. 28 December 1799; bapt. 22 June 1800.
Louisa Pitt d/o Robert & Christiana MOODY b. 15 March & bapt. 22 June 1800.
Charles Ridgely s/o James & Sophia CARROLL b. 4 May & bapt. 22 June 1800.
John s/o Charles & Sarah DOWD b. 3 June 1800.
William SOUTHWORD m. Mary SPECK 24 June 1800.
Richard HILL m. Anna WILLIS 26 June 1800.
James WILSON m. Mary DAVIS 26 June 1800.
Thomas SLAUGHTER m. Susanna JONES 27 June 1800.
Maria Stith d/o Mark & Lucy PRINGLE b. 8 January & bapt. 27 June 1800.
Thomas Charles HOWE m. Martha ENSOR 28 June 1800.
Samuel SISSLER m. Kitty SMITH 29 June 1800.
Sophia d/o William & Anne ------ b. 24 May & bapt. 29 June 1800. (No surname given.)
Anne d/o John & Eleanor ARMITAGE b. 17 January 1799; bapt. 30 June 1800.
James MC EVOY m. Mary Anne HICKLEY 3 July 1800.
Jacob CARPENTER m. Polly HORN 3 July 1800.
Peter s/o Charles & Fanny HERBERT b. 29 October 1799; bapt. 6 July 1800.
Reuben LINCOLN m. Rachael OLIVER 8 July 1800.   {H-388}
William s/o Adam DENMEAD bur 8 July 1800.
Sophia Catharine d/o John Eager HOWARD & Margaret his wife b. 6 March & bapt. 10 July 1800.
William ALEXANDER bur. 10 July 1800.
David TIPTON s/o of Mary TIPTON b. 10 May & bapt. 10 July 1800, a free black.
Kitty d/o James & Rebecca HOOKER b. 25 June & bapt. 11 July 1800.
George SIMPSON m. Nancy EDWARDS 14 July 1800.
Jacob COUHNS m. Polly SALWAY (TALWAY?) 15 July 1800.
Elisabeth BROWN, an infant, bur 17 July 1800.
William s/o Henry SHUTE bur.18 July 1800.
Kitty d/o John & Sidney TRULOCK b. 12 June & bapt. 18 July 1800.
John s/o Thomas & Elisabeth TILLEN b. 23 June & bapt. 20 July 1800.
Anna Catharine d/o Joseph G. J. BEND bur. 20 July 1800.
Daniel HARRISON's child bur. 20 July 1800.
Jesse CULLEE m. Rachel RICKETTS 20 July 1800.

William OGLE m. Eleanor CLARKE 20 July 1800.
Alexander KNOX bur. 21 July 1800.
Catharine d/o Edward & Margaret MC GREGORY b. 27 December 1789;
 bapt. 21 July 1800.   {R-III-50}
George JOHNSON m. Elisabeth BURNHAM 22 July 1800.
Elisabeth wife of Alexander KNOX bur. 23 July 1800.
John ASHBURNER m. Anna GIBSON 25 July 1800.
Mary d/o James & Margaret MANAHAN b. 25 July 1800 & bapt. same
 day.
William s/o William & Sarah MILLS b. 20 November 1799; bapt. 25
 July 1700.
Elisabeth d/o John & Jane CORBITT b. 9 June & bapt. 27 July 1800.
John Amie s/o John & Mary Anne DOUGLAY b. 1 November 1799; bapt.
 27 July 1800.
Catharine d/o George & Margaret TAYLOR b. 27 March & bapt. 27
 July 1800.
Elias s/o Thomas & Margaret GRIFFIN b. 7 May & bapt. 27 July
 1800.
Jacob DEADEN m. Eleanor BONE 27 July 1800.
George FRAUGHTEN bur. 28 July 1800.
Joseph s/o Alexander & Elisabeth KNOX bur. 28 July 1800.
Alexander HILMAN m. Elisabeth WHIPPLE 30 July 1800.
Charlotte wife of Thomas ROSSITER bur. 30 July 1800.
Catharine d/o William & Mary BEARD b. 16 March & bapt. 31 July
 1800.
George GUNNET m. Nelly HUTCHELL 31 July 1800.
Thomas SPIERS m. Elisabeth KEMP 31 July 1800.   {H-389}
William s/o James HOOPER bur. 31 July 1800.
Samuel s/o Samuel & Anne ROBINSON b. 4 March & bapt. 1 August
 1800.
Edward s/o Edward BROWN bur. 1 August 1800.
John SIMPSON m. Anne ROBINSON 2 August 1800.
John s/o John & Anne PATERSON b. 28 July & bapt. 2 August 1800.
John Richard s/o Robert & Anne Margaret SMALLWOOD b. 29 June &
 bapt. 3 August 1800.
John Amie s/o John DOUGLAY bur. 3 August 1800.
John s/o John PATERSON bur. 3 August 1800.
Edward RUTTER m. Mary Anne RIPPER 3 August 1800.
Elisabeth d/o Walter & Elisabeth GRIFFIN b. 7 March & bapt. 3
 August 1800.
William GODFRITH m. Elisabeth SCHUNK 7 August 1800.
Thomas DAY m. Sarah BAKER 8 August 1800.
Isabella wife of William HENDERSON bur. 8 August 1800.
Amelia d/o George CALDWELL bur. 8 August 1800.
Anne, reputed wife of William READ bur. 8 August 1800.
William PRUE bur. 8 August 1800.
John s/o Nicholas & Mary LATERMAN b. 20 November 1799; bapt. 9
 August 1800.
William HENDERSON's child bur. 9 August 1800.
Henrietta d/o Thomas & Mary YATES b. 10 April & bapt. 9 August
 1800.
Margaret d/o William & Margaret BRANSON b. 2 April & bapt. 10
 August 1800.
Samuel s/o Richard CURSON Jur. bur. 11 August 1800.   {R-III-51}
William HENDERSON's child bur. 11 August 1800.
Johnsee DOUGHADIE bur. 12 August 1800.
Caleb Johnsee s/o Johnsee & Susanna DOUGHADIE b. 4 October 1799;
 bapt. 12 August 1800.

Elisabeth Hall d/o Vachel & Elisabeth DORSEY b. 26 June 1799;
   bapt. 12 August 1800.
Mary Anne d/o Thomas & Anne Eleanor LANGLEY b. 10 March & bapt.
   12 August 1800.
Hannah of Abraham & Phebe WYATT, free blacks, b. 10 August 1799;
   bapt. 12 August 1800.
Anne d/o William & Anne READ b. 4 & bapt. 10 August 1800.
Edward s/o Edward JOHNSON bur. 12 August 1800.
Hannah d/o Valentine & Sarah SPICER b. 1 August 1799; bapt. 13
   August 1800.
William s/o William Gibbons & Sarah MILLS bur. 14 August 1800.
Juliana d/o Robert ELLIOTT bur. 14 August.
Sidney wife of Richard FREEMAN bur. 14 August 1800.
Thomas WILLIAMS m. Nancy HUMPHRIES 15 August 1800.
Anne d/o Stoughton & Mary ADAMS b. 23 June & bapt. 15 Aug. 1800.
Elizabeth d/o John & Joanna BROWN b. 4 July & bapt. 15 Aug. 1800.
Joseph BANKSON Junr. bur. 16 August 1800.   {H-390}
Michael s/o Frederick & Rebecca ROW b. 13 October 1799; bapt. 17
   August 1800.
John HOWARD bur. 17 August 1800.
Joseph ENGLE bur. 18 August 1800.
Rebecca FARRIS bur. 19 August 1800.
Thomas USHER bur. 20 August 1800.
Anne d/o William READ bur. 20 August 1800.
William GROOM m. Rebecca HOPKINS 21 August 1800.
William CREIGHTON m. Lenora WEARY 21 August 1800.
Eleanor d/o George GARDNER bur. 21 August 1800.
Frances d/o Christopher & Peggy HUGHES b. 22 July & bapt. 21
   August 1800.
Hezekiah s/o Thomas TENANT bur. 21 August 1800.
Jane d/o William & Jane MARSH bur. 23 August 1800.
Edward Pennington s/o Josias & Mary RUTTER b. 16 July & bapt. 23
   August 1800.
William HUGHES m. Patience RUSH 24 August 1800 (by Banns).
Edward HARRISON bur. 25 August 1800.
William JONES bur. 25 August 1800.
Mary WEAVER bur. 26 August 1800.
Sarah d/o William RIDDELL bur. 27 August 1800.
Rebecca MURRAY bur. 28 August 1800.
Joseph, alledged s/o Joseph OSBORNE bur. 29 August 1800.
William s/o Amos & Mary Anne LONEY b. 14 December 1796; bapt. 29
   August 1800.
Elisa d/o Hugh BOYES bur. 29 August 1800.
Nicholas LATTERMAN bur. 30 August 1800.
George IRELAND bur. 30 August 1800.
Georgiana d/o Benjamin & Sarah SPENCER b. 24 February & bapt. 30
   August 1800.
Arthur MURRAY bur. 16 August 1800.
John NORRIS bur. 16 August 1800.
Elisa b. 18 February 1798; Nelly b. 6 February 1800, d/o Barnet &
   Ruth BOND, both bapt. 31 August 1800.   {R-III-52}
Henrietta d/o Thomas & Lucy BOSTON b. 21 May & bapt. 31 August
   1800.
John s/o William & Sarah RIDDELL b. 29 July 1799; bapt. 31 August
   1800.
John Goldsmith b. 17 August 1797; Lewis b. 19 July 1800, s/o
   Charles & Rebecca TINGES both bapt. 31 August 1800.
Alexander KEAN's or CAIN's child bur. 1 September 1800.
Patrick MILLION bur. 1 September 1800.

Mary Anne d/o Silas ENGLE bur. 1 September 1800.   {H-391}
Georgiana d/o Benjamin SPENCER bur. 1 September 1800.
Emilia d/o Joseph BARKER bur. 1 September 1800.
Joseph s/o Silas ENGLE bur. 2 September 1800.
John s/o John WARD bur. 3 September 1800.
Thomas CRAWFORD bur. 3 September 1800.
Harriot d/o David & Elisabeth STIDGER b. 18 March 1799; bapt. 3
    September 1800.
Charles WELLS bur. 4 September 1800.
Sarah wife of Robert LING bur. 4 Sept. 1800.
Eleanor MC LEAN bur. 5 September 1800.
Pamela d/o Barton WHETFORD bur. 5 September 1800.
Elisabeth wife of Simon HOWARD bur. 5 September 1800.
James DASHIELL bur. 5 September 1800.
Alexander SMITH m. Mary LEAGUE 6 September 1800.
Barbara LEGG bur. 6 September 1800.
Louis GEBHARD bur. 7 September 1800.
Mary Anne Davis d/o Richard & Mary SISSON b. 12 September 1799;
    bapt. 7 September 1800.
Frances Allanby d/o John & Nancy STEEL b. 20 June & bapt. 7
    September 1800.
Jesse HEATH bur. 8 September 1800.
Michael YOUNG bur. 8 September 1800.
John H. SCHREIBER m. Maria F. YEISER 7 September 1800.
Simon HOWARD bur. 9 September 1800.
Rebecca ARNOLD bur. 10 September 1800.
Mary d/o Clarke INGRAHAM bur. 10 September 1800.
John s/o Bartholomew JACOBS bur. 11 September 1800.
Anne wife of James HARVEY bur. 12 September 1800.
Thomas B. COLE bur. 12 September 1800.
Elisabeth GILBERTHORPE bur. 12 September 1800.
Charlotte BRICKS bur. 13 September 1800.
William WILSON m. Susanna WOLFE 14 September 1800.
Rosanna d/o Hugh & Hannah WILSON b. 17 May & bapt. 14 Sept. 1800.
John HALL m. Elisabeth RANDALL 14 September 1800.   {R-II-53}
John s/o Thomas PINE bur. 16 September 1800.
Sarah wife of John KELLEY bur. 16 September 1800.
James FISHWICK bur. 17 September 1800.
John Weaver Samuel s/o James HOLMES bur. 17 September 1800.
Sarah wife of ----- MITCHELL bur. 17 September 1800.   {H-392}
Margaret d/o Simon HOWARD bur. 17 September 1800.
Peter s/o Michael & Catharine FREDERICK b. 12 & bapt. 17
    September 1800.
Anne DONNELLAN bur. 17 September 1800.
Hugh HAGE bur. 17 September 1800.
Thomas WILSON bur. 17 September 1800.
James HISSEY m. Mary MILLER 18 September 1800.
Samuel SMITH of Virginia bur. 18 September 1800.
Daniel HARRISON bur. 18 September 1800.
Edward s/o Larkin YOUNG bur. 19 September 1800.
Margaret d/o Richard & Margaret BERTON b. 2 April 1799; bapt. 19
    September 1800.
John HARDY m. Sarah EVANS 19 September 1800.
Anne d/o Stoughton ADAMS bur. 19 September 1800.
Samuel STUBBLES m. Jane REANSER 20 September 1800.
Azor BATTIS m. Fanny STRANGER 20 September 1800, free negroes.
Joseph CHAPMAN bur. 21 September 1800.
Margaret d/o Richard BERTON bur. 22 September 1800.
Mary GREEVES bur. 22 September 1800.

A German, a Drayman bur. 23 September 1800.
James BENSON bur. 23 September 1800.
Juliana d/o Thomas PINE bur. 23 September 1800.
John STARR bur. 23 September 1800.
Elisabeth WOLMER bur. 24 September 1800.
Phineas WILLIAMS bur. 24 September 1800.
Archibald BUCHANAN bur. 25 September 1800.
George HOWARD bur. 25 September 1800.
Sarah RIDDELL bur. 26 September 1800.
Mary wife of Samuel BENGES bur. 27 September 1800.
Sarah COLLINS bur. 28 September 1800.
Bartholomew s/o Bartholomew JACOBS bur. 28 September 1800.
William s/o William DOWNEY bur. 28 September 1800.
Joseph CARNALL bur. 29 September 1800.
Mellaby CANNON bur. 29 September 1800.
A child of Capt. STAFFORD bur. 29 September 1800.
John HAGE bur. 30 September 1800.
Joel PASSMORE bur. 30 September 1800.   {H-393}
Joseph POOL bur. 30 September 1800.
Joseph WOOLEY's wife bur 30 September 1800.   {R-III-54}
Mr. FICKE bur. 1 October 1800.
Elisabeth d/o Thomas & Jane DERMOTT b. 18 March 1799; bapt. 1
   October 1800.
Nancy d/o Thomas & Christiana CARTER b. 31 October 1799; bapt. 2
   October 1800.
Thomas s/o Patrick & Grace MALOY b. 2 September 1799; bapt. 2
   October 1800.
Mary RYAN bur. 2 October 1800.
Elisabeth CHANDLER bur. 3 October 1800.
John s/o John & Patty YOUNG b. 4 October 1800, bapt. same day.
Mrs. BADCOCK bur. 4 October 1800.
John KIBEARD bur. 5 October 1800.
A s/o William SMITH bur. 5 October 1800.
A s/o Edward HARRISON bur. 6 October 1800.
Joshua LILLYWHITE bur. 8 October 1800.
John MELCHIOR bur. 9 October 1800.
Elisabeth wife of Florence DRISCOLL bur. 10 October 1800.
Sarah CHANDLER bur. 11 October 1800.
Mrs. JONES bur. 11 October 1800.
Ellen d/o Elisa CROUCH bur. 12 October 1800.
Betsey FALTON bur. 12 October 1800.
Benjamin s/o Caleb SMITH & Elizabeth his wife both bur. 13
   October 1800.
Francis GALLAHER m. Margaret DOLAN 13 October 1800.
Nathaniel WILSON bur. 14 October 1800.
Samuel s/o William & Margaret MOSGROVE b. 19 March & bapt. 14
   October 1800.
Joseph STERRETT m. Mary HARRIS 16 October 1800.
Azel ALWARD m. Sally MC CAMMON 16 October 1800.
John WILSON m. Hannah DUFFY 16 October 1800.
Elisabeth LEWIS bur. 17 October 1800.
Mary GREY bur. 17 October 1800.
Elisabeth b. 14 September 1793; Sarah b. 12 November 1796; Mary
   b. 9 September 1799, children of Thomas & Mary DUNCAN, all
   bapt. 18 October 1800.
Mrs. BUSH bur. 18 October 1800.   {H-394}
The d/o Samuel BENGES bur. 19 October 1800.
Catharine wife of Zachariah KEENE bur. 20 October 1800.
An unbaptized child of Zachariah KEENE bur. 20 October 1800.

Catharine KEENE, entered above bur. 20 October 1800.
William LEWIS bur. 21 October 1800.
Thomas s/o John MURPHY bur. 21 October 1800.
Charles Ridgely PINDALL m. Mary LANDERMAN 21 October 1800.
A child of a Mrs. CASSADY bur. 22 October 1800.
James PINKERTON m. Mary SHORT 22 October 1800.
William DYE m. Mary HAMMETT 23 October 1800.   {R-III-55}
Samuel THURSTON m. Maria NORRIS 23 October 1800.
Frederick PRATT bur. 24 October 1800.
Charles BAKER m. Mary CREBS 25 October 1800.
Zacharia ALLEN bur. 25 October 1800.
Margaret d/o Margaret & Silas ENGLE b. 31 August & bapt. 26
    October 1800.
Andrew FICKE's wife bur. 27 Oct 1800.
John GOUGH m. Martha LOWRY 28 October 1800.
John FOWNES bur. 30 October 1800.
Mr. NEALE bur. 30 October 1800.
Mrs. ALCOCK bur. 30 October 1800.
James ARMSTRONG m. Elisabeth DOUGLAS 30 October 1800.
John SEMPLE m. Mary LAMB 30 October 1800.
Francis DONOGHY m. Elisabeth DONNOLLY 30 October 1800.
Hugh s/o William & Barbara BIGLEY b. 15 September & bapt. 30
    October 1800.
Mary b. 10 March 1798; Sarah b. 2 January 1800, d/o Thomas & Anne
    GRIFFIN, both bapt. 31 October 1800.
A d/o Charles MERRIKEN bur. 31 October 1800.
Henry WALTER bur. 1 November 1800.
John s/o John Kelly & Sarah CURTAIN bur. 2 November 1800.
Michael RILEY m. Mary WATERS 3 November 1800.
Antoine CANNE m. Elisa CROSGROVE 4 November 1800.
John Addison SMITH m. Elisabeth GARDNER 4 Novembre 1800.
Eleanor KINNARD bur. 4 November 1800.
Sarah d/o John & Anne HUNLEY b. 4 November 1800 & bapt. same day.
Robert SMALLWOOD bur. 6 November 1800.   {H-395}
Christopher HARDING m. Anne LEE 6 November 1800.
Sarah wife of Jacob WEAVER bur. 7 November 1800.
George Burke b. 9 October 1796; Joseph b. 15 February 1797, s/o
    Joseph & Sarah MC CANNON both bapt. 7 November 1800.
Mary Anne d/o James & Mary PARKER b. 9 June 1799; bapt. 7
    November 1800.
William s/o James & Polly WILCOCKS b. 23 September & bapt. 9
    November 1800.
John NEEDHAM m. Nancy COLE 9 November 1800.
John RANDALL m. Nancy SIMMS (by Banns) 10 November 1800.
Eliza Mullen d/o Philip & Mary UHLER b. 20 February & bapt. 12
    November 1800.
Anne Maria d/o Bazil Lowman SMITH & Anne his wife b. 22 June &
    bapt. 12 November 1800.
Elisabeth Sarah d/o Thomas & Elisabeth WATTS b. 26 October &
    bapt. 12 November 1800.
John W. RAYMOND m. Sarah GARNONS 12 November 1800.
Burton WHITFORD bur. 12 November 1800.
John DISNEIGH m. Margaret HUNT 13 November 1800.
Thomas WILFORD bur. 16 November 1800.
Ignatius DIGGES m. Charlotte MURPHY 16 November 1800.
Mrs. Capt. STEEL bur. 17 November 1800.   {R-III-56}
Thomas CLOUDSLEY m. Jane SUMMERS, alias COOPER, 18 November 1800.
Evan EVANS m. Delia GORDON 18 November 1800.
John TILDEN m. Eliza BARRERE 20 November 1800.

Thomas MONTECUE m. Anne WATSON 23 November 1800.
George Washington s/o Robert & Eliza SPENCER b. 27 September &
bapt. 23 November 1800.
William FICKEY bur. 23 November 1800.
Richard COOKE m. Elizabeth VAN WYCKE 23 November 1800.
Eliza Mary Ann Price d/o James & Eleanor COOKSEY b. 6 September &
bapt. 23 November 1800.
Ellen WIGNELL bur. 24 November 1800.
Mary d/o Margaret BAILEY bur. 25 November 1800.
George POWELL m. Jemima ABLE 26 November 1800.
Thomas CORCKHILL m. Anne COLE 27 November 1800.
Joseph s/o Anthony & Elisabeth REEVES b. 20 & bapt. 28 Nov. 1800.
William Henry s/o William & Elisabeth VAN WYCK b. 20 & bapt. 28
November 1800.
Richardson Stuart s/o Richard FRANCIS bur. 29 November 1800.
Mary MILLER bur. 29 Novembr 1800.
Mary Anne d/o George & Jane JACOB b. 1 April & bapt. 1 Dec. 1800.
Joseph s/o Anthony REEVES bur. 2 December 1800.   {H-396}
Henry s/o Larkin YOUNG bur. 4 December 1800.
Henry s/o John & Sarah DENMEAD b. 16 Sept. & bapt. 4 Dec. 1800.
Robert Lloyd s/o Thomas & Matilda NELSON b. 14 September & bapt.
4 December 1800.
Thomas DIVINE m. Jane SUTER 4 December 1800.
George s/o George & Jane CROOK b. 30 Nov. & bapt. 5 Dec. 1800.
John s/o John JERVIS bur. 7 December 1800.
Frances d/o Christopher HUGHES bur. 10 December 1800.
John DAWSON m. Nancy COX 10 December 1800.
A child of William Young LEWIS bur. 11 December 1800.
George ELY m. Catharine DAVIS 11 December 1800.
Dutton RICHARDS m. Margaret BOWEN 11 December 1800.
Mary wife of John STANSBURY bur. 12 December 1800.
Anne b. 30 September 1795; Joshua b. 10 November 1797; Catharine
b. 4 February 1800; children of William & Martha LOGUE all
bapt. 12 December 1800.
Lettice d/o John & Lydia HILTON b. 6 April & bapt. 12 Dec. 1800.
Elisabeth d/o Henry & Mary BISHOP b. 21 March 1797; bapt. 12
December 1800.
Joseph STEWART m. Rebecca WADE 13 December 1800.
Michael MC MAHON m. Elisabeth BOYD 13 December 1800.
Charles HAW m. Jane HOWARD 17 December 1800.
Edward H. STALL m. Martha AITKEN 17 December 1800.
Robert MORETON m. Anne GROVES 17 December 1800.
Isaac WESTOVER m. Mary BERRY 18 December 1800.
George PAINTER m. Nancy THOMPSON 18 December 1800.
John CLARKE m. Anne HOSGOOD 19 December 1800.   {R-III-56}
Anne d/o Joseph & Anne ARMAID b. 1 Sept. & bapt. 21 Dec. 1800.
Mary d/o William & Anne MARTIN b. 12 August & bapt. 21 Dec. 1800.
Levin GALE of Somerset County bur. 21 December 1800.
An unbaptized child of Mrs. GWYNN bur. 22 December 1800.
Charlotte Sarah d/o Samuel & Hannah CHURCH b. 30 September &
bapt. 23 December 1800.
Thomas s/o Cornelius & Sarah MC CARTHY b. 22 January 1799; bapt.
23 December 1800.
George Charles s/o John & Mary FOWNES b. 25 January & bapt. 23
December 1800.
Mary wife of Samuel HUTCHINS bur. 25 December 1800.
Mary Elisa d/o Peter & Deborah HOFFMAN b. 29 May & bapt. 25
December 1800.
James s/o Robert & Eve THOMAS b. 17 Sept. & bapt. 28 Dec. 1800.

ST. PAUL'S PARISH

This information was taken from Box #7, MS 1727, Manuscript Divsion, Maryland Historical Society Library, Baltimore, Maryland, and is a list of accounts kept by the church on monies received and paid out for various years in the late 1700's.

While many of the account books available for this time period contain many original signatures, this particular account book does not.

Money Recev'd from Pews by M. DORLING since 25 Sept 1784 to 14 January 1787: (Only the names have been copied, not the amounts paid, which are listed in pounds, shillings & pence.)

William MC CROY; Luther MARTIN, his order on Philip GRAYBELL; George LUX and (?) GRUNDAY of George GRUNDAY; Hesd. COURTENAY; William STAYTON; Daniel BOWLY; John MOALE; Thomas FUSSELL; Thomas USHER; Nicholas ROGERS; Thomas YATES; Walter ROE; James HUTCHINGS & HUGHES; John DORSEY; John STERETT & LAMING; M. HELM; R. RIDGELY & BUCHANAN; Stephen STEWARD Junr.; Charles RIDGELY of John; Alexander W. DAVEY; William HAYES, E. JOHNSON and VANBIBBER; Margaret CARROLL; Jeremiah YELLOTT; Thomas LANGTON; Uriana SOLLERS and GIBSON; Thomas WORTHINGTON and Co.; Richard CURSON; Thomas and Samuel HOLLINGSWORTH; J. E. HOWARD; RIDELY and PRINGLL; Thorowd. SMITH and Co; William JACOB; Elinor FULFORD; J. DONALDSON and Co.; Ezekeil Jno. DORSEY; John PROCTOR and Co.; William JACOB of Z.; Joseph GREEN; R. Horace PRATT and Co.; James TRIPPE and Co.; John MC ALESTER and Co.; Thomas CONSTABLE; Gab'l. KINGSBURY; John HAMMOND; Charles BIRKBECK; William TINKER and Co.; Robert DE SILVER; William GRAHAM; STERLING and DORLING; James TEBBITT; William ADAMS; Mary K. GODDARD; Frederick FOLGER; William PATTERSON; Jonathan HANSON; John BARNEY; Elizabeth FERGUSON; George James L. ARGEAW; William YOUNG; Brian PHILPOT; Aw. Skinner ENNALLS; Caleb HALL; Richard CULVERWELL; Johnzee SELLMAN; Robert PORTUSE; George VAUGHAN; Daniel GRANT; Thomas JOHNSON; Margaret SANDERSON; Francis SMITH; William JOHNSON; Benjamin ROGERS; Rosein CLIFTON; John NUTBROWN; Brittm. DICKINSON; Charles RIDGELY of William; William DANCER; Richard BURLAND; Jno. WEATHERBURN; Amos LONEY; Charles CARLINE; John SMITH; & William HAMMOND.

Pews rented from the first & what Rec'd. To J. E. GESTE from 25 September 1786; To James EDWARDS from 25 March 1786; To John HALL from 25 March 1785; To Richard LAWSON from 25 Septembver 1785; To William GRAYHAM from 25 March 85 Insolvent; To Jonas PENNINGTON from 25 September 1784, Mr. William ASKEW to be charged with 1 years rent of above pew; To John HALL from 25 March 85; to Thomas PILKENTON from 25 March 85; give up 25 September 86, not rented; To James DAVERSON from 25 September 84; To Andrew ELECOT from 25 March 85; to David HELLIN from 25 September 1785.

1786:   Money Expended for Wall

June 23   To Mathew DAVIS cash
     29   To Henry NOGLE for 10,000 bricks
      "   Mr. MACUBINGS for his bill
      "   To John NUTBROWN
      "   To Henry TOMALTY for Lime House, locks, hinges, etc.
July 10   To George FAUS on Account, Stone Hauling 20 perches
      "   To Henry LINHART, ditto

147

1786:   Money Expended for Wall (con't)

July 10   To Mathew DAVIS, in full
     11   To Robert STEWARD for boundary stones
      "   To Christopher BECHAM on account.
      "   To A. W. DAVEY 5,000 bricks
      "   To John DONALD for drayage stones
      "   To Mathew DAVIS
      "   To James EARL for Drayage
      "   To Henry LINHARTE on account, stone
      "   To Henry NOGLE for 14500 bricks
      "   To George FAUS on account, stone
      "   To Phil. of Henry EBHARTE, stone hauling
      "   To George HELM for 10,000 bricks
Aug 12   To Christ. REEHAM cash on account
      "   To Samuel JOHNSON 42 B. lime
      "   To Robert WILMOT
     16   To James HARR 11 1/2 perch Stone Hauling
     25   To John LENHARTE 37 1/2 per. Stone
      "   To Robert BUTTON
     26   To William YASH(?)
      "   To Richard HOSKINS 4 day laboring
     28   To Christ. REEHMS, order of John MOALE
     29   To Mathew DAVIS digging trench
Sep   2   To John DORD for lime
      6   To John FORD 26 b. lime
     28   To William LOUGE, lime
     29   To Math. DAVIS of Co, @ different times
      "   To Ett. LEAD, drayage of stones
      "   To John POGE
      "   To Richard HARKINS 12 1/2 days
      "   To John HICKEY 10 days
      "   To Henry FULSERD 3 days
Oct   6   To John POGE
      "   To Edward LYNTCH 4 days labour
      "   To Richard HOSKINS 3 days labour
      "   To Otto LEAD
      "   To Robert STEWARD on Account, stones
      "   To Richard HOSKINS 4 days
      "   To William STAR drayage of stone
      "   To Luke WHITE 27 1/2 Lime
      "   15,000 Bricks of Charles RIGDLE[Y]
     21   To Richard HOPKINS 16 days
      "   To William NASH
     23   To John POGE
      "   To William NASH for old windows
     26   To HOPKINS & WILSON's bill for planke
     28   To Joseph HARTE for Lime
      "   To John HICKEY for 4 1/2 days
      "   To George FROST "   "   "   "
      "   To Richard HOSKINS 5 days
      "   To Cash for Rum
      "   10,300 bricks of J. E. HOWARD
     31   To John POGE
      "   To Henry LINHART on account for stone
Nov   1   To Jnath. DAVID by SCATES
      4   To Greenbury COE, lime
      "   To Robert STEWARD on account, stones
     17   To Henry Cronke WEALING, 5,000 bricks

ST. PAUL'S PARISH

```
1786                    Money Expended for Wall (con't)
Nov  18  To Martin FREEPORT
     "   To Richard HOSKINS
     "   To John HICKEY 3 days
     "   To Thomas SCATES 4 days
     "   To Joseph Inay (May ?) WEALING 9,500 bricks & laboring
     "   To Joseph Bradband WEALING 19,500
     "   To Mathew DAVIS, digging foundation
     25  To Robert WILMOT for lime
Dec  22  To Hewey NEAL 2 days
     30  To George FOSS on account stone hauling & to John
         WEATHERBURN
1787 Jan 1  To Light GOLD(?)
Feb   1  To William NASH on account
     "   To George CHILDS on account, stone hauling
      6  To Thomas F. DIXON for Vestry Order
     "   To John MARYMAR for POGUE order
     16  To John JEFFERY, hauling nails
     "   To Ap. LOOK for Church Gate
     21  To William STAR for drayage, stones
     24  To Richard HOSKINS filing up graves
     26  To Robert STEWARD on account stone balls
Apr   4  To Jnrs. WOSLER to cash
     "   To Joseph BARKER cash
     15  To James TOLBERT 7 days worke
     21  To 35 bush. lime of Greenbury COE
     25  To 30 b. Lime of Henry HOWARD
     27  To John REEM
June  5  To Larn WRIGHT
July 30  To Edmond HOGAN for fees
Aug  24  To Mrs. WOSLER
Sep   3  To A. J. POPER for Redgester
     "   To Joseph BARKER to an order of sermons
     16  To John WEATHERBURN for 3 water casks.
```

St. Paul's Church by money from first subscriptions by cash from
Pews: May 15, 1786:
George GRUNDEY;   Samuel Thomas HOLINGSWORTH; Thomas USHER; Robert
SLATER;   John NICKOLSON; Ambrose CLARKE; Mr. Mohn LAUGHLING; Mrs.
FULFORD;   Mr. MC AULESTER; Capt. YELLOT; Walt. ROE; John HAMMOND;
John RICHARDSON;   James STERLING;   John MOWTON; Col. ROGERS; Wil-
liam HAMMOND; Thomas USHER Junr,; Thomas PRATTON; William GIBSON;
Thomas USHER Senr.;   Philip ROGERS;   Edward MURRY;   Thomas R.
TILGHMAN;   Ridly PRINGLE;   James CAMBELL;   James CROXAL;   Samuel
JOHNSON;   Samuel OWINGS;   Amos LONEY;   William MATHEWS;   William
WEST;   William YOUNG;   Dr.   COLE; A. Leiner ENALLS; Thomas SMITH;
John MOOLE;   Edmund KELLY;   William SLAYTON;   Joseph GREEN; David
MC MACKIN;   William ADAMS;   Francis ELERTON;   Hercules COURTENAY;
Archibald MONCRESS;   Rev.   William WEST; William BUCHANAN; Thomas
CONSTABLE (in Nails);   John E.   HOWARD; Antoy. NOBLE; John HALL;
James EDWARDS; Tinker STONSTAT; William MURPHEY.
1787, February 16: Capt. Philip WATTERS; MARRYMAN & SHEBY.
```
  "      March 28:  William EVENGS
  "      April 3:   Thomas RUSSEL; George MC CANDLESS
  "      April 14:  Byron PHILPOT; Richard RIGDLEY
  "      April 23:  Richard MOALE
  "      September 18:    Thomas LITTLEJOHN;  William  HAMMOND;  John
                         CROCKITT & J(?) WATTERS
```

ST. PAUL'S PARISH

St. Pauls Church by Second Subscription (no year given):
Hollingsworth YELLOTT; Mr. CROCKSHANKS; Mr. LINTINGBURG; Richard
BURLING, Archibald CAMBILL; Capt. YELLOTT; Thomas B. USHER; Col.
Nicholas ROGERS; Isaac VANBIBER; William GIBSON; James DONALDSON;
William HAMOND. (April 14) Capt. Henry JOHNSON; (April 23)
William MC CREREY; (Sept 15) Dr. James WYNKOOP; (Oct 9) William
STAYTON; Ambros CLARKE.

St. Paul's Church - Expenses paid:

```
1784 Oct  3   To Nicholas ROGERS & YELLOT
     Nov 23   To Rev. William WEST
     Jun  7   To John YOUNG, orders of vestry
1785 Mar 29   To Thomas CONSTABLE, orders of the vestry
      "       To cash paid to Thomas DIXON
1786 Nov  9   To Mr. DONALDSON bil for velvet & silk lining &
              Stephen STEWARD's bills & John MARTON's order on
              P. GRABLE
1787 Oct  9   To John BROWN for house rent
```

On the above accounts there are many repetitive entries for
various dates. To save space, names were not repeated.

Church Money Credit:
```
1787 Oct 22   Christopher HUGHES
         23   Cash of Andrew BUCHANON
         27   Cash of Samuel JOHNSON
     Nov  1   Cash for Joseph GREEN, Richard LAWSON, Richard(?)
              CURSON
          3   Cash for Thomas COPER
          6   Cash for John NUTBROWN on account of GRAVES & PELL,
              William TINKEN
         17   Cash Mabory HELM
         19   Cash USHER of DONALDSON
         20   Cash Mr. ROE
         26   Cash Mr. DAVY & Samuel JOHNSON
     Dec  4   Cash of John PRENGAL
          8   Cash of George ROBERTS
         17   Cash of Col. Nicholas ROGERS & William EVINGS
         20   Cash of Thomas EDWORD
         29   Cash of Christopher HEWES
1788 Jan  9   Cash of Mr. Britingon DICKINSON for wall
              subscriptions
              House
1789 Sept 8   Joseph BACKER, William MITCHELL, William SHEPARD,
              Negro Benn, Negro Phillip & James TALBERT (cash).
     Oct 13   Cash to William BROWN.
     Dec 20   Agreed with Mones DORLING to furnish stone steps
              for the churchyard.
```

ACCOUNTS OF LAND SOLD BY M.D. (MARYLAND DIOCESE)
1787 May 28 & June 7 James STERLING; June 8 & 10 Peter MACKEN-
HORN & Jonathan RUTTER; June 28 & July 2 Capt. RYLEY; July 2
Francis DAWS; July 7 Peter MACKENHORN; July 14 John HARBEAUICK;
August 6 Joseph BARKER; August 23 John STIGER; September 3 John
CUMINGS; November 23 John RUSK; December 4, A. CARTER & Thomas
LITTLEJOHN(?).

ST. PAUL'S PARISH

1788 March John MOON(?) & Joseph TOWNSOND; May 14 Benjamin WITTEKEN; May 15 Thomas SHIPPEN; July 14 Filty NELSON; October 16 James STERLING.

1789 June 21 Joseph STONE; June 26 Thomas SKIPPER; August William MORRIS.

The above account books are in good condition, but the handwriting is very poor.

ACCOUNTS PAID OUT

1787 Jan To Christopher KEEHM(?) on account of works.
          To John POGUE to cash
     Also January 1787 for stone hauling Philip Henry ELHART, George FAUS; Henry LINHART; James KARR, Martin RUPERT; George CHILDS & to William NASH for cash.
     1788 Dec To William FOSTER - 6 days work; James TALBERT 2 days; Ben --- 6 days; James SIMONS 6 days; Benjamin WITHER; Joseph BARKER; John KELPW(?); Jacob KIMMERLY; & John PHILIPS.

151

CHURCH WARDENS & VESTRYMEN - ST. PAUL'S PARISH

This list was taken from Appendix I, Volume II, of Rev. Allen's two volume set of St. Paul's Parish history that he intended to publish. This was never done because funds that been had accumulated to do so were given to the church to rebuild after a fire. Copies of these handwritten volumes can be seen at the Maryland Historical Society (MF 236.SP 1A4). The entries below are taken directly from Rev. Allen's notes, which contain genealogical material as well as dates of offices held.

Appendix II of this volume contains a list of the taxables in St. Paul's Parish, Baltimore County 1774, from the sheriff's book and also additions on Rev. Dr. West's list in the year 1786/7. The list includes communicants and taxables for the following Hundreds. Baltimore West, Baltimore East, Deptford, Westminster, Back River Lower, Middlesex, Patapsco Upper and Patapsco Lower. This is a considerable list and will be published soon in a book of lists of the Baltimore area by Family Line Publications.

Vestry notes for the years 1693 through 1720 have not been found. There is no explanation for the letters BL, PL, etc. used below, but it is assumed that they stand for Back River Lower, Patapsco Lower, etc.

V denotes vestrymen, CW denotes church wardens:

George ASHMAN V 1692. Buried 31 January 1669. From 1672 he was the presiding Justice of Baltimore County.
John TERRY V 1692. Called Captain, died 4 March 1698.
Francis WATKINGS V 1692. Called Senior, from Back River. He was buried 3 or 10 April 1696.
Nicholas CORBAN V 1692-1695 Called Senior, of Bear Creek. He was buried 31 December 1696.
Richard SAMPSON V 1692. 1695.
Richard CROMWELL V 1692. 1965.
John FORNEY V 1695
John GAY V Clerk 1692.
William WILKINSON V 1695.
John HAYS V 1695.
The records from this point to 1721 have not been located.
Thomas BIDDESSON V 1721.
John EAGER V 1721.
John ISRAEL V 1722. A visitor of the country school 1723.
John ORRICK V 1722. P. L., Patapsco, Lower Hundred.
Joseph MURRAY V 1722.
John DORSEY of Edward V 1722. In 1713 High Sheriff, 1723 a visitor of the country school, called Colonel.
Luke TROTTEN V 1722 through 1724. Took up lots in Baltimore PL Town in 1730.
James MOSE V 1722.
John EAGLESTONE CW 1722 through 1728 & 1731. BL or PL
Christopher RANDALL CW 1722-1723, V 1724 through 1726 & 1741 through 1743. In 1742 a commissioner for St. Thomas Chapel & Register of that parish in 1744.
Richard OWINGS V 1722 & 1723.
Thomas HINES V 1722, 1729 & 1730.
Edward NORWOOD V Clerk 1722.
Hugh JONES V 1722 & 1723.

Tobias STANSBURY V 1722 & 1723. BI or PL

Thomas SHEREDINE V 1722 through 1724, 1726 through 1728 & 1730 & 1731; V. 1734 through 1736, 1740 through 1742. Called Major, delegate to General Assembly, died 1754.

John MERRYMAN V 1723 through 1725. PL

John BOERING V 1723 through 1725. In 1582 presiding Justice of the County, bought land in Patapsco Neck 1679.

Henry BUTLER V 1723 through 1725.

William HAMILTON V 1723 & 1724; V 1732 through 1734. Purchased land 1710. A visitor to the country school 1723. Commissioner to lay out Baltimore Town & Town Commissioner 1729. In 1734 he was called Colonel and was the Presiding Justice of the County. In 1736 he was High Sheriff. In 1742 he was a Commissioner of St. Thomas Chapel.

John COCKEY V 1722, 1723, 1728, & 1733 through 1735. Purchased land near the Patapsco. In 1732 was County Justice & Town Commissioner.

Edward NORWOOD V Clerk 1722.

Edward COOKE, V Clerk 1723 through 1725.

James POWELL V 1724, 1725, 1730. Took up lots in Baltimore Town.

Philip JONES V 1724 through 1726. In 1730 County Surveyor & a (?) of lots in Baltimore Town.

Thomas TAYLOR CW 1724.

William BUCKNER V 1725 through 1728. In 1729 a Commissioner to lay out Baltimore Town. In 1730 took up lots.

Thomas STANSBURY V 1725 through 1727 BL

Richard GIST V 1726 through 1728, CW 1731. Son of Christopher GIST, who lived on the south side of the Patapsco as early as 1682. In 1729 Deputy Surveyor of the Western Shore & a commissioner to lay out Baltimore Town. Died before 1730[sic].

Richard LENOX V 1726 & 1727. PL

Samuel MERRYMAN V 1726 through 1728.

James RIDER CW 1726.

William BARNEY CW 1726 through 1728 & 1735.

James MOORE Clerk 1726 through 1733.

Luke STANSBURY V 1727 through 1729.

John BOWEN V 1727 through 1729. PL

Charles RIDGELY V 1728 through 1730, CW 1732, 1735 & V 1736 through 1738. General Assembly.

Buckler PATRIDGE(?) V 1728 through 1730. BL near Bear Creek.

Benjamin BOWEN V 1729, 1730; CW 1732.

Lloyd HARRIS V 1729 through 1731; CW 1736 through 1738. In 1730 took up Town Lots.

James ROBERSON CW 1729.

Jonas ROBERSON CW 1729.

William HAMMOND V 1730 & 1731. Called Colonel, probably s/o John HAMMOND, who settled north of the Patapsco upon land as early as 1695. He was one of the County Justices. In 1729 a commissioner to lay out Baltimore Town & took up town lots. In 1735 High Sheriff. Died 1754.

John MOALE V 1730 through 1732. Merchant from Devonshire, owned land & carried on business near the Parish. 1728 delegate to General Assembly. Died 1740 leaving 2 sons, John & Richard.

George WALKER CW 1729 & 1735; V 1736 through 1738. A Thydecan(?) House near Pennsylvania Avenue called Chatsworth, in with his brother James WALKER from Petershead, Scotland; 1725 came from Anne Arundel County to Baltimore County. 1730 a Town

Commissioner & took up lots. Sold this lot to the Vestry, on which the St. Paul's Church stands. Died 1743.

John RISTEAU CW 1739; V 1742 through 1744. Called Captain.

Thomas TODD V 1731 through 1733. Son of Capt. Thomas TODD, possibly of Virginia, who purchased land at North Point as early as 1664.

George BUCHANAN V 1731 through 1733; CW 1734; V 1737 through 1739. A physician, came from Scotland & purchased land as early as 1723. 1729 a Commissioner to lay out Baltimore Town. Died 1750.

William FELL V 1733 through 1735 & 1740 through 1742. Has brother Edward, a Quaker. 1730 bought Copus (?) Harbour, the point. In 1745 a Town Commissioner. Died 1746. Built on Lancaster Street a house standing in 1822.

Robert NORTH CW 1735; V 1738 through 1740. Called Captain, carried freight as early as 1723. In 1730 took up town lots & built NW Baltimore & Calvert Streets. In 1732 Town Commissioner. Died before 26 December 1749.

Frances HINCKLEY Clerk 1734 through 1737.

Richard GIST V 1734 through 1736; CW 1738, Register 1739 & 1740; Presiding Justice of the County 1736.

Edmund STEVENSON CW 1734.

Nicholas HAILE V 1735 through 1737. Commissioner of St. Thomas 1742 thorough 1744.

Samuel OWINGS V 1735 through 1737. In 1741 in St. Thomas Parish. He was a County Justice 1758.

John ENSOR CW 1736.

Alexander LAWSON CW 1737. Town Commissioner 1746. Died before 1760.

John EDWARDS CW 1737.

Christopher GIST V 1737 through 1739 & 1742 through 1747. In 1742 a commissioner of St. Thomas Chapel.

John HEDDEN Clerk 1738 & 1739.

Joseph CROMWELL V 1739 through 1741; 1748 through 1750 & 1758.

George ASHMAN V 1739 through 1741. Lived in St. Thomas Parish & a vestryman there. In 1750 Inspector of Tobacco.

John MERRYMAN V Clerk 1739 & 1741. In 1765 a Town Commissioner.

John GILL CW 1739. In 1745 one of the vestrymen of St. Thomas.

John HANSON CW 1740; V 1747 through 1749.

Josephus MURRAY Jr. CW 1740.

Edward FOTTERAL V 1741. Died that year. Was from Ireland. Built the first house in Baltimore Town with free(?) stone.

Nathaniel GIST CW 1741.

James GARDNER Clerk 1741 through 1749.

Nathaniel STINCHCOMB V 1742 through 1744. Was one of the vestrymen of St. Thomas Parish 1745 & died in 1746.

John MERRYMAN Senr. CW 1742 & 1746.

John BAILEY CW 1742.

John MERRYMAN Jr. V 1743 through 1745; CW 1748. One of the Committee of Safety 1774.

Solomon HILLEN V 1743 through 1745. Died 1747. BL

Darby LUX CW 1743; V 1744 through 1746; CW 1749; V 1750. Died 1750. Called Captain. In 1733 commanded a ship in the London Trade. Purchased lots on Light Street, where he resided. In 1745 Town Commissioner & 1748 Delegate to General Assembly.

Job EVANS CW 1743. PL

Abraham RAVEN CW 1744.

Mayberry HELM CW 1744; V 1748 & 1749; CW 1750; V 1751 through 1753.

Thomas HARRISON CW 1745. A Merchant from England. In 1742 built near the SE corner of South & Water Streets. In 1745 a Town Commissioner. In 1746 made an addition to the town. In 1757 (67?) the largest subscriber to improving the town. Market House built on his ground. 1774 one of the Committee of Delegates. Died 14 October 1782 leaving half his estate to the Rector of St. Pauls.

William LYON CW 1745. Declined as not qualified by a residence of 3 years. V 1753 through 1755. A physician. He was a Scotch Presbyterian & one of the first organizing the Presbyterian Church in 1764.

Charles RIDGELY CW 1745; V 1750 through 1752. Called Captain. In 1774 on the Committee of Observation, In 1776 one of the framers of the State Constitution. In 1786 a delegate to the General Assembly. Died 1798. PL

Lyde GOODWIN CW 1745.

Alexander LAWSON V 1746 through 1748. Removed from the parish.

Tobias STANSBURY V 1746 through 1748. BL

Nicholas ROGERS CW 1746 & 1752. In 1756 the owner of a vessel, in 1753 lottery manager to build a wharf; aid to Gen. D------- & afterwards to Gen. De KALB.

Sabret(?) SOLLERS V 1747 & 1748. Last excused.

Thomas FRANKLIN V 1747, 1749 through 1751. In 1750 Presiding Justice for more than 20 years; 1751 delegate to General Assembly, called Capt. BL

John RIDGELY CW 1747; V 1752, 1753, 1758 through 1760; in 1742 was High Sheriff.

William GREEN CW 1747.

William LYNCH V 1747, 1748, 1750, 1754 through 1756; 1766 through 1768 & 1772.

Abraham EAGLESTONE V 1748 through 1750; 1754 through 1756.

Philip JONES V 1748 through 1750. Called Captain.

George HARRIMAN V 1748 through 1750. BL

John STINCHCOMB V 1748 through 1750; 1754 through 1756. Called Captain.

Robert GREEN V 1748 through 1750.

Patrick LYNCH CW 1748. PL

William MACKUBIN V 1749 through 1751.

John WALKER Clerk 1749 through 1751.

Thomas BOONE V 1757.

John LONG V 1751 & 1752.

Edmund TALBOT CW 1751, clerk 1751 & 1752; V 1764 through 1766.

Moses RUTTER CW 1751. M

William MACLEAN Register 1751, died.

William ROGERS V 1751 & 1752; V 1756 through 1758; CW 1760. Innkeeper corner NE Baltimore & Calvert Streets. 1753 Lottery Manager.

N. Ruxton GAY V 1752 through 1754; 1754 City Commissioner; 1753 Lottery Commissioner & County Surveyor.

William LUX V 1752 through 1754; 1759 through 1761; CW 1762-1772. 1753 Lottery Commissioner; 1774 member of Constitutional Convention at Annapolis; one of Committee of Observation & a County Justice.

Lyde GOODWIN CW 1745 & 1752. 1783 Surgeon of the independent infantry; 1786 lectured on the theory & practice of medicine in the Medical Society; a County Justice.

James CARY CW 1752.

Richard CHASE V 1753 & 1754. Declined being an attorney at law; 1753 Lottery Commissioner.

Darby LUX Register 1753; CW 1768. 1774 Commission of Observation & of Trade & Army.

John MOALE CW 1753, 1758; V 1761 & 1762; W 1765 & 1767; V 1770, 1771, 1782, 1783, 1785 through 1788. Son of John. 1753 Lottery Commissioner. Built a house which stood in the wall(?) of St. Peter's Church. Sketched a view of Baltimore Town 1763; 1763 Town Commissioner; 1765 delegate to the General Assembly; 1768 Commissioner for board of Court House; 1773 Trustee of the Poor. Added to land of the Town; 1774 on the committee of Observation. A county Justice; died 1798.

Mayberry HELM V Register 1754; CW 1757-1760; V 1772 through 1774 & 1777 through 1781. M

Thomas ENSOR Jr. CW 1754.

Brian PHILPOTT V 1754, CW 1759, 1763. An English Merchant lately arrived in 1750-51. City Commissioner; 1753 Lottery Commissioner; 1760 purchased land between the Harford Run & James FALL (?) & built at the NE corner of the bridge; 1762 laid out the ground in lots; 1775 held a Commission in Col. SMALLWOOD's Regiment.

Tobias STANSBURY of Tobias V 1754.

John CARNAN CW 1754; v. 1760 & 1761.

Capt. Tobias STANSBURY V 1754. BL

John WOODEN, Jr., V 1754 M

John FRAZIER V 1754. Had a shipyard.

Joseph BANKSON V 1754.

William WELLS V 1754 through 1756.

Zechariah MACKUBIN V 1755 through 1757 & 1759. P.U. 1775 on the Committee of Observation.

Hithe SOLLERS V 1755 through 1757. PL

Alexander LAWSON CW 1775; V 1763. Clerk of the County Court; on the Committee of Observation.

Nicholas MERRYMAN of Samuel CW 1755.

Samuel MERRYMAN CW 1756.

R. King STEVENSON V 1756 through 1758.

Edward LEWIS Jr. Register 1756 through 1758.

Thomas JOHNSON V 1757 through 1760.

Edward BOWEN V 1757 & 1758.

Charles CROXALL V 1757. PU

Christopher CARNAN CW 1757.

Joan MOALE, Jr. CW 1758.

Andrew BUCHANAN CW 1759, V 1762 through 1764 & 1767 through 1769. 1768 Committee for building the Courthouse; 1774 one of the Committee for Observation; County Justice; 1776 Commander of the Militia; died 1786.

John ENSOR, Jr. V 1759 through 1761.

John ORRICK V 1760 & 1761.

Alexander STEWART V 1761 & 1762, CW 1768; died that year. Called Captain.

Robert ALEXANDER CW 1762, V 1768 through 1774. One of the Committee of Observation; 1776 delegate to the Convention.

Richard MOALE CW 1761, V 1763 through 1765. 1774 one of the Committee of Observation.

William OTTY CW 1761.

Benjamin ROGERS V 1762 through 1764 & 1771 & 1772.

Thomas JONES V 1762 & 1763. Member of the 1776 Register of Wills; 1778 Judge of the Court of Appeals; served at North Point.

John MERRYMAN, Jr. CW 1763, V 1765 through 1767. President of the Com. Council.

Edmund STANSBURY V 1764 through 1766. BL

William ASQUITH CW 1764, V 1767 through 1769 & 1773. 1774 Committee for Observation.

Robert ADAIR CW 1764, V 1768. 1765 Delegate to the General Assembly & High Sheriff; 1768 Committee on building the Court House; lived SE Corner of Baltimroe & Lombard Streets.

George HOWARD V 1765. Elder brother of Gen. John E. HOWARD.

Thomas SOLLERS V 1767 through 1769 & 1781. 1773 County Justice. Died 1783.

Sabret(?) SOLLERS V 1770.

Thomas TODD V 1770. PL

Nicholas JONES V 1770 through 1772.

Edward HANSON CW 1770, V 1775 & 1778.

Harry Dorsey GOUGH V 1772 & 1773.

Owen ALLEN V 1772 through 1774.

A. S. ENNALS CW 1772.

William RUSSELL V 1773 through 1775 & 1782 through 1784. Came to Baltimore 1771; 1787 Judge of the Criminal Court; 1791 Judge of the Orphans Court; 1792 Judge of the District Court.

James LAWSON V 1773 & 1774. Went to Europe.

Thomas USHER CW 1773.

George WOOLSEY CW 1773.

William GOODWIN V 1774 & 1775. 1797 member of the City Council.

Matthew RIDLEY CW 1774. A merchant, came to Baltimore about 1771.

John PHILPOTT CW 1774.

Charles RIDGELY of John CW 1775.

Daniel HUGHES CW 1774, 1775 & 1781.

Daniel BOWLEY V 1775, 1779 through 1781 & 1784. 1774 an officer in the Militia; 1782 Town Commissioner; 1783 Port Warden; 1786, 1789 & 1802 Elected to the State Senate; one of the wharves in the City built by his executors is called after him. Died 12 November 1807.

James EDWARDS V 1776 & 1777. One of the committee to get up the Bank of Maryland; 1790 to 1796 a member of the City Council.

George PRESTMAN V 1776.

James CLARK CW 1776. One of the Board to Examine Pilots 1787.

Philip ROGERS CW 1776. 1774 one of the Committee of Observation; a gentleman of landed estate. 1778 formed the Army; 1789 President of the Society of the abolition of Slavery & for the relief of free negroes and others unlawfully held in bondage.

Charles CARROLL V 1779 through 1781. Called the barrister Carroll of Mount Clare, SW of the City on the Washington Road. 1775 on the Committee of Safety; 1776 one of the framers of the State Constitution; first State Senator & reelected 1781; appointed Chief Justice of the General Court but declined; died 28 March 1782 at age 59.

George LUX V 1779 through 1781. 1774 Secretary of the Committee of the County; 1775 he with Gen. HOWARD gave a lot in Washington Town for a common burying ground.

Thomas DONELLAN V 1779, CW 1780 through 1782, V 1783.

John DORSEY CW 1779. 1781 on the Committee to welcome General Washington to Baltimore Town.

Samuel Stringer COALE CW 1779, V 1780. A physician. 1790 lectured on chemistry.

Richard RIDGELY V 1779 through 1782 & 1784. A member of the Bar. 1782 Town Commissioner; 1782 a Port Warden; 1784 first delegate to the first Conventon; was appointed one of the Committee to form a place of Ecclastical government; 1785 delegate to Congress; 1786 was Senator of Maryland & a Presidential

Elector; 1811 a judge of the Judicial District Court in which he continued till his death 21 February 1824 dying at 68. A most Christian death.

Thomas GATES V 1780 through 1782. Called Major.

Hercules COURTENAY V 1781 through 1785. A merchant in 1770; 1774 one of the Committee of Observation; a County Justice; 1782 Town Commissioner; 1796 a member of the City Council & President thereof.

Mones DORLING V 1782, CW 1784 through 1787, 1789 & 1791. A doctor.

Walter ROE CW 1782, V 1783, 1788 & 1790.

William JACOB Register 1782 through 1784.

William GIBSON V 1783 & 1784 & 1791 through 1793. 1776 Register of the Court of Admiralty & Clerk of the County Court. Was an officer in the Army; 1783 built on Price (Paca?) Street West of the Town; 1788 High Sheriff as well as Clerk of the County; 1797 Treasurer of the County.

James ALCOCK V 1782. 1774 a teacher of languages.

Jeremiah YELLOTT V 1784. Captain. 1774 lately from England; Commanded the "Antelope" 14 guns; 1787 one of the board to license pilots; 1790 one of the Bank of Maryland; 1794 Navy Agent; died in 1805 leaving the interest of $10,000 for the Free School of St. Peter's Church, Sharp Street.

Nicholas ROGERS V 1784 & 1795 through 1797, 1799 through 1801. Colonel. 1781 one of a committee to prepare for the defense of the Town against Arnold; 1788 a County Justice on the Criminal Court; 1791 Justice of the Orphans Court; 1797 one of the City Council; 1802 Commissioner to build the new Jail; 1800 delegate to Diocesian Convention; died 1822.

John HAMMOND CW 1784, V 1787 through 1789.

John WEATHERBURN V 1785 through 1789.

Samuel JOHNSON V 1785 through 1793. 1783 a member of the Bar; in 1789 & 1791 chosen delegate to the Diocesian Convention; delegate to Convention 1786.

John MERRYMAN V 1785 thourgh 1791. 1788 & 1791 appointed delegate to the Convention; 1797 member of the City Council; 1801 Commissioner to build new jail.

John Eager HOWARD V 1785 through 1799; 1792 through 1794; 1803 through 1805 & 1809 through 1812. 1788 & 1792 appointed Delegate to Convention & 1812. He removed to Baltimore Town during the Revolution from St. Thomas Parish, previous to which 1774 one of the Committee of Observation; 1775 one of a Committee to license law (?); 1775 & 1776 a vestryman of St. Thomas; 1776 entered the Army under Washington; was Lt. & was in the battle of Cowpens SC 1781 & at Eutaw, where he was wounded & was complimented by Congress with a Silver Medal; 1782 lots East of Eutaw Street & annexed them to the town; 1785 with George LUX, Esq., gave a lot for a common burying ground South of the City; 1786 an Elector for County & Town; 1787 a member of Congress. In 1788 he was elected Governor & also in 1789 & 1790. In 1792 he was a Judge of the District Court; 1791 a Senator in the U.S. Senate; 1794 appointed Major General of the Maryland Militia but declined. In 1797 he was reappointed to the U.S. Senate; 1798 designated by George Washington to be a Brigadier General in the U.S. Army. In 1794 he gave the lot to the parish for the Parsonage, on which it now stands; 1809 gave the ground for the Washington Monument (Baltimore City); 1813 one of the Committee for Supply in Defense of Baltimore; 1816

Elected to the Senate of Maryland; 1817 President of the Maryland Colonization Society. He died 12 October 1827, aged 75.

Edward JOHNSON V 1785 through 1787. Delegate to Convention 1788 & 1789; was a judge of the County Court; 1797 a member of the City Council; 1804 Presidential Elector; 1811 an Elector of the Senate; 1812 Presidential Elector; 1816 Elector a 3d time; 1822 Elected Mayor of the City.

William MC CREARY CW 1785; V 1791. 1801 Baltimore Dispenser; 1802 Member of Congreses; 1811 Senate of Maryland.

William BUCHANAN of George V 1787 & 1787, 1790 through 1792. 1774 one of the Committee of Observation; a County Justice; 1775 on the Committee to Trade & Arms; 1777 Commissary of General Purchase for the Army; 1778 Register of Wills. He was a member of the bar. Died 19 September 1804.

Alexander W. DAVIS CW 1786.

Andrew S. ENNALS V 1788 through 1793.1790 Delegate to Convention.

George GRUNDY CW 1788, V 1789 through 1792.

Robert DORSEY 1787 delegate to the Convention.

Charles CROOKSHANKS V 1789, 1794. Died 1794.

Alexander FURNIVAL CW 1798. Captain. 1776 held a Commission with Col. SMALLWOOD's brigade; 1789 Postmaster.

Larn WRIGHT Register 1789, 1791 through 1793.

William WINCHESTER V 1790. An associate Judge in the District Court; 1804 President of the Union Bank of Maryland.

Richardson STUART CW 1791 through 1793.

Thomas JOHNSON V 1792 through 1795. Died 1795. 1781 on a committee to prepare for defense; 1787 one of the board to examine & license pilots; 1789 Judge of the Electoral Court of Maryland (appointed); 1791 appointed Judge of the Supreme Court of the United States; 1794 one of the board of health.

Robert COURTNEY CW 1792.

Thomas USHER V 1793 through 1795. Delegate to Convention 1795.

William VAN WYKE V 1793 & 1794.

John STEELE CW 1793, 1802 & 1803.

Henry NICOLS V 1795 through 1797, 1800 through 1702, 1815 through 1817. Delegate to Convention 1795 & 1801 through 1805 & 1808, 1816 & 1817. 1797 a member of the City Council.

Thomas HOLLINGSWORTH Jr., V 1797 through 1815. Died in 1815. 1785 spoken of having a wharf & 1789 as one of the first in the Bank of Maryland.

William LORMAN CW 1794, V 1797 through 1804. Had resided here about ten years in 1793.

Thomas BAILEY CW 1794 & 1795. In 1803 he was a Sheriff.

Thorowgood SMITH V 1794 through 1796, 1803 through 1809. Died 13 August 1810. In 1789 on the committee for the Bank of Maryland. He was a County Justice & Mayor of the City.

George ROBERTS V 1794 through 1796.

Archibald CAMPBELL V 1794 through 1796. From Great Britain 1783.

Samuel CHASE, Delegate to Convention 1794, 1801 through 1804 & 1813. Register 1794.

William CLEMM CW 1795. Colonel. Held a commission in the Army & Baltimore Town 1783; In 1794 one of the officers detached to quell the insurection near Petersburg.

Richard LAWSON V 1795 through 1799. 1797 Member of the City Council.

William SMITH V 1795. 1781 on the Committee to address General Washington; 1782 a Town Commissioner; 1785 an owner of a wharf; 1789 Representative in Congress; 1801 member of the Maryland Senate. Died 27 March [1801?] at 85.

CHURCH WARDENS & VESTRYMEN - ST. PAUL'S PARISH

Dixon BROWN V 1796 through 1798.
James DAVIDSON CW 1796 & 1797.
William SINGLETON CW 1796 & 1797.
Richard CARSON Jr. V 1797 through 1799.
William COLE V 1798.
George BUCHANAN V 1798. Doctor; 1796 member of City Council.
Peter MILLER CW 1798.
William BRANSON CW 1798.
Benjamin BAKER V 1799 & 1800 & 1801.
Hezekiah CLAGETT V 1799, 1813 & 1814. Delegate to Convention 1806.
William COOKE V 1800 through 1802. Delegate to Convention 1810 & 1811; 1814 Captain of a Company at Bladensburgh; 1821 Secretary to the (?).
George LINDENBERGER CW 1800, V 1802 & delegate to Convention. 1777 held a commission in the army; 1780 Special Commissioner of the Town; 1781 Justice.
James CORRIE CW 1800 & 1801. Merchant. Died 180(?). Came to Baltimore about 1783. Left more than $10,000 to St. Peter's Free School, but by defect of the will it was lost.

The following information was taken from the first of two volumes at the Maryland Historical Society (MF 236.SP1A4) handwritten by the Rev. Ethan Allen in 1855, which he intended for publication. It was not published due to "want of volunteer patronage." As the original vestry books have not been located, this work has been used to abstract genealogical information.

In 1629 the Territory of Maryland was part of Virginia, Kent Island and the only minister assigned was the Rev. Richard JAMES. There was a settlement for the purpose of Indian trade at Palmer's Island (now Watson's 1855) near the mouth of the Susquehanna opposite Havre de Grace (Md) made by the Kent Islanders. In 1632 Lord Baltimore obtained a patent and in 1634 St. Mary's City was settled under Leonard CALVERT. This colony was settled in the larger part by Protestants with no clergy, and in the smaller part by Romanists (Catholics).

Under the Act of 1692, the freeholders of Patapsco Parish were directed to meet and make choice of 6 Vestrymen. From the Baltimore Court Records for 1693, folio 126, "The Vestry met at the house of John THOMAS when it was determined that Pettites OLDFIELD's was the most convenient place to erect a church and appointed John GAY to be the clerk of the vestry, Mr. WATKINGS being absent." George ASHMAN, Nicholas CORBIN of Bear Creek, John TERRY, Richard SAMPSON, Francis WATKINGS, Richard CROMWELL present. From a book of Ministerial Records "Marked A" [not found today] 1695-1717, "Francis WATKINS, Senior of Back River was buried April 3 or 10, 1696. Nicholas CORBAN [sic] Senior of Bear Creek buried December 31, 1696. Capt. John TERRY died 4 March 1698. Col. George ASHMAN buried 31 January 1669." Rev. Allen remarks that in his time the first Vestry book (1692-1722) was not known to be in existence.

1676 The Rev. John YEO was the first Church of England clergyman who officiated in Baltimore County in the parishes of St. Pauls as well as St. Johns and St. Georges (the latter two now Harford County). Rev. YEO died in 1686, leaving a married daughter and a son, John; Miles GIBSON was his administrator.

1694 The parish church of St. Pauls was on the Patapsco Neck, adjoining Mr. PATRIDGE's land near Bear Creek. A description of the location was given by General Tobias STANSBURY aged 90 years in July 1852 when he said that old St. Paul's Church stood about 30 or 40 rods this side (west) of where the Sollers Point Road leaves the North Point Road, on the left side as you go East. It was built of brick. In 1765 it was in ruins and the bones of the dead who had been buried were moved to Baltimore Town. No remains of the church were to be found when Rev. Allen visited the spot in 1849.

1702 The Vestry purchased of Col. John THOMAS a glebe of 124 acres. This tract was known as "Good Luck" and was on the north side of the Patapsco at the head of Clopper's; now (1855) Colegate's Creek. A parsonage was built. The Rev. Mr. TIBBS had been in the parish more than 13 years in 1715.

In 1720 the Friends had a Meeting House at John GILES on Whetstone Point (now Ft. McHenry) and were the only denomination besides the Church of England to have sufficient numbers to establish a public worship house.

4 December 1722 the Vestry agreed with Mr. WILMOTT to clear the woods 30 yards square from the church, for which he was paid 300 pounds of tobacco, or about $5.00

In 1722, at the petition of the Wardens, Vestrymen and others, Westminster parish, lying south of St. Pauls in Anne Arundel County, the Rev. TIBBS not objecting, all that part of St. Pauls south of the Patapsco from the Bay to the lower wading place on the Patapsco Falls-some little distance above Elk Ridge Landing-was set off and given to Westminster Parish (St. Margaret's). The Vestry Records of Westminster Parish were burned with the church in a fire of 1802.

11 June 1723 Edward COOK was Vestry Clerk. Land was secured for a chapel from Col. James MAXELL who died before the title was made out to the parish. In September it was agreed with James RIDER to make a floor for the vestry house and to make latches for the doors. This dwelling was very primitive and it is believed that the chimney was built of sticks and filled with clay. The vestry reported that year that they had visited the library, which they found in good order and a catalogue was given which included books entitled: Hebrew Bible, Bloomes Geography, Wingate's Arithmetic, Heroic Poetry, Measures of Christian Obedience, Dr. Wake Concerning Swearing, the Greek Bible and other religious sermons. Most of these books were gone by Rev. Allen's time.

18 May 1824 Patrick NEAL was asked to, but could not qualify as schoolmaster and was admonished. In August John EAGLESTON agreed to repair the seats that were falling apart in the church.

5 January 1725 Philip JONES was ordered to provide the body of laws of the General Assembly, the latest print, for the use of the vestry. In May the vestry heard Richard LEWIS, on account of the orphan daughter of Philip and Mary PITSTON, to whom LEWIS was guardian. William SMITH was High Sheriff.

2 January 1727 the vestry met to discuss building a new church due to progress of the population further west, in that direction going more than 20 miles and to the northwest 12 to 14 miles from the church; the church being at that time located not more than 2 miles from the parish's southern boundary. In May that part of Baltimore County south of the Patapsco River (which had been given to Westminster Parish) and that part southwest of the Patapsco Falls was given to Anne Arundel County. Six hundred taxables that had been part of Baltimore County for 67 years were now in Anne Arundel County. In October the vestry was empowered to purchase land to build a church and Thomas SHEREDINE, Richard GIST and later Richard BUCKNER were appointed to purchase 2 acres "as near the northeast part of John MERRYMAN Senr's land." This was not possible, and they purchased land from Moses EDWARDS. This land was on the York Road near WALSH's Tanyard and at that time surrounded by land of Harry Dorsey GOUGH, Esq. The land was never used to build a church and was rented to Richard RUTTER for 21 years in 1743.

October 1728 Queen Caroline Parish, Anne Arundel County, took the territory west and southwest of the Patapsco Falls, which reduced the population of St. Pauls further.

8 August 1729 the General Assembly passed an Act for erecting a town on the North side of the Patapsco, where John FLEMMING then lived, known as Coles Harbor, directing 60 acres to be made out in 60 lots and to be called Baltimore Town. (Coles Harbor, a tract of 550 a. surveyed in 1667 by George YATES and afterwards assigned to David POOLE, 30 acres of which was included in the land of Baltimore Town. The tract known as Mountenays Neck bounded Coles Harbor.)

In 1730 the vestry agreed with Doct. George WALKER for lot #19 on the town plat to place the church on; (where the church stands today-1988) the corner of Saratoga and Charles (then Forrest) Streets. 28 July it was agreed with Thomas HARWELL to build the walls of the new church and agreed with Charles WELLS to provide 100,000 bricks. 3 November the vestry agreed with John MOALE and William HAMMOND to get the rafters and door and window frames.

2 February 1731 the vestry agreed with Mr. HAMMOND to build a vestry house and with Charles RIDGELY to draw the brick and Jonas ROBINSON to furnish 1500 bushels of lime.

9 April 1731 agreed with John BABCOCK build walls, Mr. HARWELL failing to fill his contract. 4 May the vestry sent a letter to the Rev. Mr. TIBBS saying they desired him to come oftener to his church. John HALL, Sheriff showed 913 taxables in 1731, an increase of 170 since 1728.

In 1731 the below were individual subscribers to finance the new church, these names found in the Treasurer's book: George WALKER; Francis HINKLEY, William ROGERS, Walter DALLAS, Jonas ROBINSON, Lloyd HARRIS, Richard LEWIS, Christopher RANDALL, Charles DORSEY, John TOWNSHEND, George BAILEY, John CROMWELL, Christopher RANDALL Junr., John PARRISH, Hyde HOXTON, George OGG, William HAMMOND, John MOALE, Elizabeth HUELL, William BUCKNER, George BUCHANAN, R. GIST, Joseph CROMWELL, John JIMKIN, David REISTER(?), Joshua HOWARD, John WOOLEY, John RISTEAU and Edward RIESTER(?). The church was not paid for only by people of the parish but contributions in small portion were made by Friends and Romanists. In July it was agreed with Samuel COTTRELL to joint, round and lay shingles on the church.

2 May 1732 it was agreed with John DE BUTTS to do the joiner work and Mr. HAMMOND to furnish the lumber. 18 June it was agreed with John WILLIAMS to level the floor of the new church. On 11 October 1732 Rev. Mr. TIBBS died, "our old shepherd." He had been incumbent for over 30 years, was not married, but left his property to his sister, who is not identified by a first name. He had not resided within his parish, but had a farm by the farm of Col. BOULDER called "Tibbs United Inheritance," east of the head of Middle River near the old Philadelphia Road, not far from Orems Chapel location in 1855 in St. John's parish. Rev. Mr. HOOPER succeeded him, and he was the first minister that bought lots and settled in Baltimore Town.

ST. PAUL'S PARISH

15 April 1734 Francis HINKLEY, Vestry Clerk, was ordered to bring up chest and communion table from the old church, but the pews were not ready. 10 September Joshua HALL was engaged to build a gallery.

26 April 1736 Doct. George WALKER presented a punch bowl.

1 May 1738 it was agreed with John HANDS to build pews at 4.60 per yard and to lay the floor at 2d per foot. Mr. FELL was appointed to give the joiner instructions and furnish plank. Joshua HALL was to plaster the church. And in 1739 the church was finished, 8 years after it was started.

On Friday, 12 July 1739 Rev. Joseph HOOPER, Rector, died and was buried in the church on Tuesday following. He was followed by the Rev. Benedict BOURDILLON (his wife was Gertruij JANSSEN and they had a son Andrew Theodore born 24 March 1737/8; baptized in Monie Church by his father 14 May 1738. The parents stood proxy for Andrew JANSSEN and Amy BOURDILLON, godfathers [sic]). In 1737 Rev. BOURDILLON was the incumbent of Somerset Parish, Somerset County and in 1739 he was Rector of St. Johns for 6 weeks. By this time the population was moving into the forest to the northwest.

1 January 1740 Mayberry HELM was to "pale in the church yard and to put up horse blocks."

26 May 1741 A chapel of ease was proposed in Garrison Forest. Capt. John RISTEAU, High Sheriff of the County, was living on his land about a mile north of the present (1855) U.S. Arsenal, and he was obliged to have a garrison of soldiers there to protect the settlements from Indian depredating. The same year the General Assembly passed an act to purchase 2 acres of land for a Chapel of Ease for the forest inhabitants, which is St. Thomas Parish, Garrison Forest.

Vestry Records 1726-1781 contain original signatures of John EAGER, Tobias STANSBURY, John MERRYMAN, John COCKEY, William BARNEY, Charles RIDGELY, John MOALE, George WALKER, John RISTEAU, William FELL, Robert NORTH, George BUCHANAN, Richard GIST, J. EVANS, Edmund TALBOT. This volume is available at the Maryland Historical Society Manuscript Division (MSS 1727, Box 7). Because of its string binding it cannot be xeroxed, but can be photographed.

In 1756 through 1762 the following bachelors show as taxed for worth of 300 pounds and over: Of Baltimore Town: Thomas HANSON, Doct. J. STEVENSON, John MOALE, Edward PARISH, Andrew BUCHANAN, William BAXTER, Daniel CHAMIER Jr., Thomas DICK, James FRANKLIN, John MERCER, Jonathan PLOWMAN, Mark ALEXANDER, John SHULE.
Upper Hundred: McLain BAILY, John WELCH, John ORRICK, James RICHARDS, Edward POULANY, Jabez BAILEY.
Lower Hundred: Joseph TAYTON(?), Samuel, Josias and Edward BOWEN, Moses MACKUBBIN, William WOOD, Nathaniel WILLIAMS, John HOWE, Thomas SOLLERS, Jona. HANSON Jr., Thomas JONES, Edmund STANSBERRY, Jonathan HARRISON Jr., William PATRIDGE and John ADMETH.
Those taxed as worth 100 pounds and under 300 pounds:
Lower Hundred: Christopher DUKES, Lawrence WATSON, Christopher STRANGESH(?), Edmund STANSBERRY, William PATRIDGE.

Upper Hundred: Elijah OWENS, Solomon WOODEN, John HOOD(?), John FLOYD, Benjamin BANNEKER, Samuel and Edward BOWEN, Jabez BAILEY, Josias BOWEN, McLain BAILY, Samuel HOWE, Jonathan HANSON Jr., William HADELIN, James RICHARDS, Daniel and Richard STANSBURY, David RUSK and David STEWART. The French War was terminated in 1763, and the Bachelors ceased to be taxed.

An entry in 1763 shows that H.L. married M.S. who was but twelve years old, but she refused to abide by the marriage, so he brought the case before the Vestry. Decision was not recorded.

19 July 1763 entry shows "Rev. Thomas CHASE and Miss Ann BIRCH, eldest daughter of Mr. Thomas BIRCH, Chirurgion, and a man mid-wife, in the town of Warwick in the County of Warwick, in that part of Great Britain called England, were married by the Rev. William WEST, minister of Westminster Parish, the ceremony performed at St. Paul's Church. Mr. CHASE had lived a widower 23 years."

The Easter Monday 1772 entry shows John ISRAEL, John ORRICK, John COCKEY, Joseph MURRAY, John DORSEY of Edward, Luke TROTTEN and James MOSE elected Vestrymen, and John EAGLESTONE and Christopher RANDALL elected Church Wardens. The above and Rector Thomas SHEREDINE, Hugh JONES, Tobias STANSBURY, Thomas HINES and Richard OWINGS constituted the Vestry at the meetings at this time. On the same date Samuel DORSEY was ordered to deliver up all the books and papers of St. Pauls to Richard OWINGS on sight. Edward NORWOOD was Vestry Clerk.

1 August 1772 - The vestry agreed of John WILMOT to build a new vestry house.

10 May 1784, being 83 in number, pews were distributed by lot to pewholders in the old church and were occupied as follows, the first being number one, the last number 83: William MC CREARY, Luther MARTIN, George LUX and George GRUNDY, Henry COURTENAY, William SLAYTON, Daniel BOWLEY, John MOALE, Thomas RUSSEL, Thomas USHER, Nicholas ROGERS, Thomas YATES, Walter ROE, James HUTCHINS, John DORSEY, John STERRETT and Benjamin LAMING (LARNING?), Mayberry HELM, Richard RIDGELY, Stephen STEWART Jr., Charles RIDGELY of John, Alexander DAVIS, William HAYES, Matthew TILGHMAN Jr. and Mr. and Mrs. CARROLL, Jeremiah YELLOTT, Thomas LANGTON, Ariana SOLLERS, Thomas WORTHINGTON, Richard CURSON, Thomas and Samuel HOLLINGSWORTH, John Eager HOWARD, Mark PRINGLE, Thoregood SMITH, William JACOB, Eleanor FULFORD, Joseph DONALDSON, Ezekuel John DORSEY, John PROCTOR, William JACOB, Joseph GREEN, R. Horace PRATT, James TRIPPE, John MC ALISTER, Thomas CONSTABLE, Gabriel KINGSBURY, John HAMMOND, Charles BIRBECK, William TINKER, William DESILVER, William GRAHAM, James STERLING and Mones DORLING, James TIBBETT, William ADAMS, Mary GODDARD, Frederick FOLGER, William PATTERSON, John BARNEY, Elizabeth FERGUSON, George James L'ARGEAU, William YOUNG, Brian PHILPOT, A. Skinner ENNALS, Richard CULVERWILL, Johnzie SELLMAN, Caleb HALL, George VAUGHAN, Daniel GRANT, Thomas JOHNSON, Margaret SANDERSON, Francis SMITH, Benjamin ROGERS, Rossen CLIFTON, John NUTBROWN, William DANCER, Richard BURLAND, John WEATHERBURN, Amos LONEY, Charles CARLINE, John SMITH, WIlliam HAMMOND. (Pew # 55, 62, 71, 75 and 76 being shown with no names.)

ALLEN, Catherine Elizabeth
  (HAWKINS) 53
 Christiana 59
 Christiana (PENNY) 55
 Dorcas 65
 Elisabeth 128
 Jane 50
 Jesse 128
 John 53, 55, 59, 66
 John Long 113
 Lucas 106
 Mary 55, 59
 Owen 157
 Reuben 94
 Richard 24
 Robert 45, 55, 67
 Sally 67
 Sarah (DEAN) 55
 Sinah 71
 William 55
 Zachariah 113
ALLENDER, Elizabeth 95
ALLEY, Eliza. 53
 George 53
 Nancy 53
ALLISON, Ann (SHEPPERD) 98
 Elisha 98
 Patrick, Rev. 53
ALWARD, Azel 144
 Sally (MC CAMMON) 144
ALWELL, Rebecca 78
 Sarah 78
 William 78
AMELUNG, Eliza Caroline 117
 Frederick John Magnus 117
 John Frederic Magnus 139
 Sophia Elisabeth Anspach 139
 Sophia Louisa 117, 139
AMLER, John, Capt. 14
AMONSCOARS, Elizabeth 94
 John 94
 Mary 94
AMOS, (?) 47
ANDERSON, Ann 38
 Elisabeth 110
 Elizabeth 33, 86
 Elizabeth (GOCOGHEGAN) 94
 Jabez 94
 John 36, 39, 84
 Kitty 134
 Lydda (RICHARDS) 36
 Mary 66
 Mary (ROE) 126
 Sarah 66, 73
 Susanna (BROWN) 39
 William 84, 126
ANDREW, Cassandra 76
 Elenor (TOBY) 85
 Robert 85

ANDREWS, Elizabeth 26
 Patrick Read 26
 Ruth 40
 William 26
ANGLEING, Mary 29
ANGLEN, Barbary 5
 Cornelious 5
ANNIS, Margaret (THOMPSON) 73
 William 73
ANSPACH, Elisabeth 135
 Elizabeth (FURNIVAL) 125
 Henry Nicholas 125, 129
ANTHONY, Joseph 104, 111
 Mary Anne 104
 Sarah 104, 111
ANTONIE, Joseph 121
 Mary 121
APPLE, Anne (FOWLER) 121
 Christian 65, 121
 Margret (HERNS) 65
 Mary 74
APPLEBY, Ann (CREAGUE) 36
 Conrad 36
 Elenor Fair (JACOB) 101
 John 101
APPLEMAN, Mary 74
ARBACK, Henry 26
 Mary 26
 Penelope 26
ARGEAW, George James L. 147
ARMAID, Anne 146
 Joseph 146
ARMER, Samuel 52
 Susanna (SWAN) 52
ARMISTEAD, Eleanor B. 136
ARMITAGE, (?) 47
 Anne 140
 Eleanor 140
 Elenor (JONES) 90
 James 133
 John 47, 90, 140
 Margaret 122
 Roger 66
 Sarah 66
ARMOR, Mary 64
 Samuel 64
 Susanna 64
ARMSTEAD, Lucy 104
ARMSTRONG, Anne 78
 Elisabeth (DOUGLAS) 145
 Isabella 70
 James 145
 Jane 133
 Lydia 128
 Margaret (GRIFFIN) 66
 Patience 74, 84
 Patty 67
 Richard Revel 74
 Sarah 78

ARMSTRONG, Solomon 66, 70
  William 78, 133
ARNALL, Benjamin 13
  Joseph 13
  Susannah 13
ARNEST, Margaret 123
ARNOLD, (?) (TUMBLETON) 31
  Francis 121
  George 31
  Joseph 33
  Mary 121
  Rebecca 143
  Richard 121
  Ruth 38
  Sarah (LEE) 34
  Susannah (CHAPMAN) 33
  William 34
ARROWSMITH, Elizabeth 24
  Mary 24
  Samuel 24
ARRUNDAL, William 2
ARTHINGTON, Richard 90
ASHBURNER, Anna (GIBSON) 141
  Elisabeth 132
  John 141
  Mary 119
  Samuel 82
ASHLEY, Benjamin 87
  Catharine 87
  Elizabeth 87
ASHMAN, (?) 47
  George 33, 152, 154, 161
  George, Col. 161
  Jemina (MURREY) 33
  Margaret (LEATHORN) 100
  Thomas 100
ASHMORE, Nancy 81
ASKEW, Anna Maria 124
  Catharina 83
  Elizabeth 68
  Hannah 131
  Jonathan 75, 83, 124
  Joseph 131
  Josias 131, 136
  Mary 83, 124
  Mary (PORTER) 75
  Robert 131
  Susann Porter 83
  William 68, 147
ASKIN, Catharine 63
  Elenor 63
  James 63, 67
  Sarah 67
ASQUITH, Edward 29
  Elizabeth 29, 43
  Elizabeth (CONNELL) 40
  John 29, 43
  Tabitha 29
  Thomas 29

ASQUITH, William 29, 40, 43,
  157
ASTERMAN, Catharine 85
ATCHINSON, (?) 48
ATKINSON, Mary 125
  Sarah 65
ATMORE, Lilian (MORROW) 137
  William 137
ATTORTH, Charles 131
ATWORTH, Charles 131
AUGHENBAUGH, John 139
  Susanna (LITTLE) 139
AVELIN, Louisa 69
AVERLY, George 10
  Passtohr 10
  Pattey 10
AVERY, Archibald 84
  Lucretia 118
  Mary (MC BRIDE) 79
  Robert 79, 84, 118
AVIS, James 32
  Mary (STEVENS) 32
AYERS, Jeremiah 33
  John 13
  Mary (FRANKLIN) 33
  Nathaniel 13
  Rhoda 13
  Ruth 13
  Thomas 13
AYRES, Elizabeth 65
BABCOCK, Clark 95
  John 163
  Margaret (FLINN) 95
BABINGTON, Mary 38
BACKER, Joseph 150
BADCOCK, (?) 144
BAER, William 114
BAGFORT, Elizabeth 92
BAHLER, Andrew 70, 97, 120
  Hezekiah 97
  John 70
  Martha 70, 97, 120
  Sarah 120
BAILEY, Amos 101, 104
  Anne 101, 119
  Benjamin 14
  Elam 90
  Elane 14
  Elijah 11
  Elizabeth 66
  Enoch 42
  George 4, 11, 14, 42, 163
  Helen 14
  Jabez 164, 165
  James 96
  Jane 75
  John 14, 154
  Juliana 110
  Kerenhappuck 4

BAILEY, Levin 85
  Margaret 110, 146
  Margaret (LOWDER) 85
  Mary 14, 101, 104, 146
  Ruth 14
  Sarah 4, 11, 14, 129
  Sarah Nevett 96
  Thomas 96, 129, 159
  William 14, 110
  William Nevett 129
BAILY, Amos 95
  Anne (REAMS) 95
  McLain 164, 165
BAKER, Alexander 14, 16
  Ann 44, 51
  Anne 137
  Benjamin 69, 125, 137, 160
  Carey 103
  Cathrine 13
  Charles 145
  Delilah 13
  Elizabeth 32, 36
  Endimion 13
  Ephraim 96
  Hannah 35
  Hannah (BAKER) 35
  Helen 64
  James Chapman 69
  John 31
  Keturah 7
  Manning 101
  Mary 125
  Mary (CREBS) 145
  Mary (HILLIARD) 31
  Mary (STEVENS) 35
  Maurice 16
  Mesha 7
  Morris 7
  Nicholas 35
  Nicholson 14
  Obed 16
  Rebecca (CLAIR) 101
  Robert 44
  Sacey (REIMY) 96
  Sarah 37, 69, 141
  Zebediah 7, 35
  Zipporah 14, 16
BALABREGA, Jacob 80
  Mary 90
  Susanna 90
BALDEN, Elizabeth (JONES) 118
  John 118
BALDRY, Mary (GREEN) 53
  William 53
BALL, Anna Pamela (GREEN) 105
  Elizabeth 25
  Judith (MAGACY) 128
  Samuel 25, 128
  William 105

BALLARD, Elizabeth 62
  Elizabeth (PAGE) 55
  Michael 55, 62
  Rebecca 74
  Robert 71, 74
BALLEBRAGA, Jacob 57
  Juliana Catherine 57
  Mary 57
  Rossanna 57
  Sarah 57
  Solomon 57
BANKS, Elizabeth 12
  John 12, 81
  Mary 12
  Susanna 81
  William 12, 81
BANKSON, Elizabeth 20, 22, 35
  James 20, 22, 114
  John 115
  Joseph 20, 22, 35, 82, 156
  Joseph, Jr. 142
  Lloyd 115
  Louis 82
  Mary 20, 22, 36
  William 115
BANKSTON, Hannah 32
BANNAKER, Katherine 32
BANNCKER, Esther 36
BANNEKER, Benjamin 165
BANNERMAN, John 138
  Susanna 138
BANNING, Priscilla 48
BANSLEY, Elizabeth 11
  James 11
  William 11
BARBARIN, Elisabeth 140
  Elisabeth (MOORE) 111
  Louis 83, 109, 111, 140
  Maria 109
  Maria (CORBET) 83
  Theresa 140
BARBARY, John 138
  Louisa 138
  Mary 111, 138
BARBER, James 39
  John 131
  Margaret (RICHARDS) 131
  Sarah (ROGERS) 39
BARCLAY, Margaret (COLE) 35
  Thomas 35
BARDLEY, Mary 68
BARDWELL, Jane 16
  Joseph 16
BARKER, (?) 49
  Amelia 58, 75, 128
  Bettsy 58
  Charlotte 75
  Conrad 58
  Eliza 58

BARKER, Elizabeth 27, 105
  Emilia 143
  Joseph 58, 75, 105, 128, 143,
    149, 150, 151
  Sarah 58
  William 27
BARKITT, Ann 54
  John 54
BARLETT, Anne 94
  John 94
  Rachel 94
BARLOW, (?) 44
  Elizabeth 52
BARNABY, Charles 24
  Elias 24, 52, 93
  Elizabeth 24
  Margaret 93
  Pleasance 24
  Rachel (RIFFETT) 52
BARNANCE, Richard 66
BARNARD, (?) 47
  John 28
  Priscilla 28
BARNES, Adam 40
  Mary (OSBURNE) 128
  Ruth (SHIPLEY) 40
  William Parker 128
BARNET, James 100
  Margaret 34
  Polly (FITZGERALD) 100
BARNETT, Archibald 119
  Catharine 76
  Catherine (HISSEY) 52
  Jacob 52
  Mary 32
BARNEY, Absalom 2
  Anne 108
  Charity 108
  Elizabeth 10, 22
  Evelina 108
  Frances 18
  Frances Holland 22, 42
  Frances Holland (WATTS) 35
  Harriot 113
  Hebe Holland 108
  John 147, 165
  John Holland 22, 108
  Joshua 22, 140
  Margret 42
  Margrett 22
  Maria Frances 108
  Mary 2, 5, 6, 9, 22, 35, 42
  Peggy 18, 22
  Rebecca 140
  Rebecca (RIDGLEY) 127
  Ruth 6
  William 2, 5, 6, 9, 10, 18,
    22, 35, 42, 127, 153, 164
  William Bedford 140

BARNEY, William Stevenson 22
BARNHOUSE, Catharine 22
  Mary Elizabeth 22
  Philip 22
BARNSLEY, Elizabeth (HALL) 65
  Joseph 65
BARNSWELL, Thomas 126
BARRANCE, Deborah 137
  Elisabeth 137
  James 137
BARRATT, Dorcas 37
  John 35
  Margarett (NEWELL) 35
BARRERE, Eliza 145
BARRET, Catharine (RUKE) 134
  John 101, 134
  Mary (HAGERTY) 101
BARRETT, Elizabeth 82
  John 50, 120
  Margery (BRAITHWAITE) 50
  Mary 120
  Thomas 82
BARRISSON, Alexander Bradford
    63
BARRY, David Andrew 51
  Mary 51
  Michael 51
  Nancy (THOMPSON) 52
  Standish 52
BARTLEMAY, Catharine 135
BARTLETT, John 105
  Rachel 105
BARTON, Ann 25
  Cealidge 25
  Comfort 16
  Comfort (ROBERTS) 31
  Edward Hall 85
  Elizabeth Mary Trippe 68
  Greenberry 16
  Hazael 16
  James 16
  Joshua 16
  Kathrine 16
  Lewis 16
  Lydia Agness Monkhouse 75
  Mary 16
  Michal 39
  Rachel 25
  Rebecca (BEDDESON) 30
  Sarah 25, 85
  Sarah Emerson 68, 75, 94, 95
  Selah 16, 30, 31
  Seth 68, 75, 85, 94, 95
BARTRAN, Marianne 84
  Pierre 84
BARWELL, Jesper 42
BASDIL, Rebecca 137
  William 137
BASEMAN, Ann 52

171

BOND, Elinor 6
Elisa 142
Elisabeth 108
Elizabeth 9, 12
Ellin 24
Frances (PATRIDGE) 34
Jacob 34
James 139
Jemima 14
Juliana 139
Kerrenhappuck 15
Kitty 137
Luke Stansbury 12
Mary 6, 9, 12, 13, 14, 15, 24
Mary (JONES) 31
Nelly 142
Nickodemus 15
Oliver 139
Pamela 108
Peter 11, 15, 32
Phebe 15
Phebe (THOMAS) 32
Prescilla 9
Richard 6, 9, 12, 13, 14, 15,
   31
Ruth 9, 108, 142
Samuel 11
Sarah 15, 31, 108
Sophia 15
Susanna 11, 15
Susannah (BUTTLER) 32
Thomas 15, 24, 32, 108
Urath 15
William 9, 12, 15
BONE, Ann 34
Eleanor 141
BONER, Hugh 139
Mary 139
Rosanna 139
BONNER, Ann Maria (NICHOLSON)
   39
Matthias 39
BONUS, William 98
BOOKER, Priscilla 74
BOON, Elizabeth (HALE) 64
John Cockey Robert Burley 64
BOONE, Thomas 155
BOOTH, Edward 80
Jane (KAYL) 65
William 65
BOOVEY, Abraham 62
Isaac 62
Jacob 62
Thomas 62
BORDLEY, Catharine (STARCK) 120
John 120
John Melchor Keener 133
Margaret (KEENER) 109, 119
Margaret Keener 133

BORDLEY, William Clayton 109,
   119, 133
BOREING, Elizabeth 10, 11, 23
Elizabeth (WELCH) 31
James 31, 33
John 23
John, Capt. 42
Joshua 23
Martha (WHEELER) 33
Mary 7, 41
Mary (HAILE) 30
Presotia 42
Rebeckah (GAIN) 31
Thomas 7, 10, 11, 30, 31, 41
William 10, 11
BOSLER, Anne Maria 106
John 106
Mary 106
BOSLEY, Elizabeth 5
James 5
Patience 5
BOSLINE, Elizabeth (PARISH) 30
James 30
BOSS, Eleanor 120
Hayes 120
Rebecca Perrigo 120
BOSTON, Henrietta 142
Hillard 17
Hilyard 17
James 32
Katherine (BANNAKER) 32
Keziah (PEAKS) 125
Lucy 142
Mary 17, 33
Rachel 17, 35
Richard 125
Sarah 17, 35
Thomas 142
BOSWELL, Ann 25
Flora 25
William 25
BOTNER, Eliza (SHERWOOD) 97
John 97
Rachel 137
BOUGHTON, Daniel 108
John 108
Molly 108
BOULDER, (?), Col. 163
BOURDILLON, Amy 164
Andrew Theodore 164
Benedict, Rev. 14, 164
David 14
Gertruij (JANSSEN) 164
Jacob, Rev. 14
Johanna Gertruy (JANSSEN) 14
Thomas 14
William Benedict 14
BOUTE, John 100
Louise (GUERSOIS) 100

174

BOVEY, Rachel 62
BOWEN, Ann 30
  Benjamin 1, 2, 5, 9, 41, 153
  Edward 156, 164, 165
  Eliza 131
  Elizabeth (WHITH) 35
  I. M. 47
  James 39
  Jehu 68
  John 23, 153
  Jonas 41
  Jons 35
  Joseph M. 48
  Josias 68, 164, 165
  Josious 5
  Magarte (MURPHY) 71
  Margaret 146
  Margaret (ROBISON) 39
  Martha 29
  Mary 1, 2
  Naomah 20
  Samuel 23, 164, 165
  Sarah 1, 2, 5, 9, 23, 41, 68
  Solomon 2, 20
  Sophia 131
  Susanna 68, 135
  Temperance 20
  Tobitha 5
  William 131
  William Jones 71
BOWLAND, Jane 139
BOWLEY, Ann 61
  Anne Lux 116
  Daniel 46, 61, 157, 165
  Daniel, Jr. 71
  Elizabeth 61
BOWLIN, Ally (HOBBS) 95
  John 95
BOWLING, Thomas 126
BOWLY, Ann 68
  Daniel 68, 147
  Elizabeth 68
BOWYER, George 129
BOYCE, Eleanor 128
  Eleanor (MOONEY) 112
  Elisabeth 128
  Hugh 112, 128
BOYD, Adam 101, 117
  Elisabeth 146
  John 117
  Mary 136
  Sarah (KEATLY) 139
  Violet 101, 117
  Violet (BOYD) 101
  William 139
BOYE, Anthony 81
  Sarah (BROWN) 81
BOYED, Ann 30
BOYES, Elisa 142

BOYES, Hugh 142
BOYLE, Anne 90
  Hugh 90
BOYS, Frances 31
BRADBURN, Mary 116
BRADFORD, Sarah (SNIDER) 50
  William 50
BRADLEY, Elizabeth (JONES) 34
  John 34
BRADSHAW, Catharine 114
  George 93
  Mary 131
  Nancy 101
BRADY, Elizabeth 60
  Joseph 60
  Sarah 60
  Winy 101
BRAITHWAITE, Margery 50
BRANCH, John 52
  Rebecca (STRAWBLE) 52
BRANNEN, Mary (SHEPPARD) 37
  Thomas 37
BRANSON, Elizabeth 61, 84
  Joseph 97
  Margaret 61, 79, 97, 117, 141
  Margaret (SMITH) 57
  Mary 117
  William 57, 61, 79, 84, 91,
    97, 117, 141, 160
BREESET, Sarah 34
BRENAN, Elisabeth (BLAKE) 134
  John 134
BRERETON, (?), Capt. 45
BREWER, Jacob 77
  John 77
  Rebecca 77
  Rhoda 129
BRIAN, Catherine 38, 39
  Elisabeth (POTTER) 135
  John 50
  Mary (DREEVES) 50
  Mary (MILLER) 113
  Michael 113
  Richard 135
BRIANT, Cissill 8
  Edward 8
  Elliner 8
  James 8
  Providence 8
  Turler 8
BRICK, Lydia 110
BRICKHEAD, Matilda 133
BRICKS, Charlotte 143
BRIGHTMAN, John 131
  Polly (PITTAY) 131
BRISCOE, Elizabeth 76
BROAD, Barbary 30
  Barbary, Sr. 41
BROADBURN, Eleanor 118

BROADSHAW, Anne 101
BROOKE, Daniel 23
  Rachel 23
  Sarah 23
BROOKS, Sarah (JONES) 31
  William 31
BROOME, Henry 112
  John 112
  Mary 112
BROTHERS, Elizabeth 37
  Hannah 7
  Nathael 7
  Thomas 7
BROTHERTON, Blanch 91
  Blanche 61, 77
  Joseph 44
  Thomas 61, 77, 91, 102, 105
  Thomas Woodley 77
  Walter 91, 102
  William 61
BROW, Catharine (PERKINS) 75
  John 75, 103
  Mary (KELLY) 103
BROWN, Ann 46
  Anne (TURNER) 30
  Anne Demillion 115
  Aquila 101
  Barbara 113
  Bathia 138
  Catharine 85, 91, 117, 129
  Dickson 20, 34
  Dixen 17
  Dixon 20, 21, 160
  Edward 141
  Eleanor 110
  Elisabeth 134, 137, 138, 140
  Elisabeth (MORRIS) 122
  Elizabeth 17, 20, 21, 142
  Elizabeth (SMITH) 55
  Elizabeth (TROTTON) 34
  Frances (CHARTRES) 33
  Francis 21, 91
  Frederick 52
  Harriot Mangin 101
  Henry 138
  Isaac 44
  James 33
  Jane (CAMEL) 82
  Joanna 77, 142
  John 20, 23, 30, 91, 117, 122,
    129, 137, 138, 142, 150
  John, Dr. 41
  Maria Charlotte Sophia 101
  Martha 23
  Mary 41, 50, 75, 133, 138
  Matilda 117
  Nancy 95
  Perry 90
  Philadelphia 134

BROWN, Philip 95
  Rebecca 51
  Richard 20
  Robert 59, 66, 77
  Sally 95
  Sara 101
  Sarah 59, 77, 81
  Sarah (WILLSON) 52
  Susanna 39
  Thomas 55, 82
  William 23, 59, 134, 150
  William Dalrymple 129
BROWNE, Dickson 20
  Elizabeth 20
  Richard 20
BROWNING, Daniel 46
  William 50
BRYAN, Benjamin 2
  Biddy 112
  Cicelia 2
  Frances 65
  James 22
  Kitty (HUNT) 132
  Mary 22, 73, 75, 79, 101
  Nicholas 22
  Richard 85
  Sarah (TIMBRELL) 85
  Thomas 132
  Thurlo 2
BRYANT, Eleanor 33
BRYSEN, Elizabeth (STEVENSON)
  93
  James 93
BUCCKNER, William 41
BUCHANAN, (?) 147
  Alexander Pitt 23
  Andrew 15, 23, 25, 36, 127,
    135, 156, 164
  Anne 85, 91, 127, 135
  Archibald 15, 25, 144
  Dorothy 23
  Eleanor 15, 16, 20, 34
  Elenor 79
  Elinor 7
  Elizabeth 25, 59
  Frances Pearsall 132
  Georg 98
  George 15, 16, 23, 59, 63, 91,
    127, 160, 163, 164
  George Anderson 100
  George, Dr. 7, 15, 154
  James 16, 59, 68, 85, 91, 100,
    132
  Katherine 16
  Letitia 59, 63
  Lloyd 7, 20, 25
  Mary 135
  Mary Ann 63
  McKean 127

177

BUSH, Greenbury 100
  Hannah 78
  John 62, 99
  Rhoda (DAVIS) 100
  Thomas 99
  Thorny 33
BUSHER, Hannah 78
BUSK, Anne 137
  Eleanor 109
  Elenor 101
  Elizabeth 18
  Greenbury 117, 137
  Helen 80
  James 18, 117
  John 18, 80, 101, 109
  Rhoda 117, 137
  Ruth 18
  Thomas 80
  William 18, 117
BUSSEY, Margaret 130
  Thomas 130
  Thomas John 130
BUSSY, Henry Ashpaw 119
  Margaret 119
  Thomas 119
BUTHAEY, Elizabeth 36
BUTLER, Absolom 4
  Alice 36, 76
  Amon 1
  Charles 75
  Charles Henry 84
  Charlotte Elizabeth 75, 84
  Christian 128
  David 127
  Elizabeth 1, 75
  Henry 1, 3, 4, 15, 153
  Margaret 86
  Samuel 36
  Sarah 15
  Sophia 1
  Susan Maria (JOHNS) 127
  Susanha 3, 4
  Susanna 1
  Susannah 15
  Temperance 3
  Youroth 1
BUTTERWORTH, Sarah 31
BUTTLER, Ann 31
  Mary 32
  Susannah 32
BUTTON, Harriot Robert 101
  Jane 101
  Jane (MATTHEWS) 85
  Magdalen 37
  Reine Guillaume 85
  Robert 148
  William 101
BYRON, Angelina 88
  Mary 88

BYRON, Y---- 88
BYWATERS, Eddy (WOOD) 31
  Thomas 31
CABEL, Humphrey 110
CABLE, Adam 93
  Elisabeth 139
  Elizabeth 70, 118
  Henry 70, 93, 118, 139
  Robert 118
  William 70
CABLES, Mary 125
CADERMAN, Biddy (BRYAN) 112
  Francis 112
CADLE, Anne 139
  Elizabeth 39
CAFFREY, Anthony 32
  Johannah (HEARN) 32
CAIN, Alexander 142
  Jane 40
  Michael 38
CALBERSON, Harriot 84
  William 84
CALDRON, Mary 39
CALDWELL, Amelia 141
  Elizabeth 23
  George 141
  James 23
  John 95, 112
  William 112
CALEB, Henry 50
CALEF, Achsah 77, 100
  James 77
  John 77, 100
  Juliana 100
CALELF, Eisch 54
  John 54
  Samuel 54
CALF, Achsah 61
  John 61
CALLAHAN, Catherine 40
  Frederick William 102
CALLEGAN, Daniel 28
  Elenor 28
  Mary 28
CALVER, (?) 44
CALVERT, Cecilius 24
  John 24
  Sarah 24
CAMBEL, Margaret 29
CAMBELL, James 149
CAMBILL, Archibald 150
CAMEL, Jane 82
CAMPBELL, Altha (WILKINS) 125
  Ann 43
  Archibald 45, 63, 107, 122,
    159
  Biddy (O'DONNELL) 101
  Elisabeth 107
  Elizabeth 63

179

CHAPMAN, Isaac 31
  John 34
  Joseph 143
  Lyke 19
  Mary (FITCHPATERICK) 31
  Mary (HALL) 34
  Nilhel 102
  Nuthill 134
  Robert 33
  Sophia 19
  Susanna 102
  Susannah 33
CHARD, Ann 23
  George 23
CHARFINCH, Mary 30
CHARTRES, Frances 33
CHARTRESS, Betsey (LUCA) 135
  John 135
CHASE, Ann 23, 24
  Ann (BIRCH) 36, 165
  Anna 63
  Caroline 67
  Catharine 22
  Francis 22
  George Birch Russell 24
  Jeremiah Townley 22
  Maria 63
  Mary 63, 71
  Richard 22, 155
  Samuel 45, 76, 159
  Thomas 23
  Thomas, Rev. 23, 24, 25, 36,
    37, 38, 39, 40, 165
  Thorndick 67
  Thorndyke 63
  William Jacob 63
CHATTEL, James 93
  Mary 87
  Thomas 93, 94
  William 87
CHATTLE, Thomas 71
CHAWFINCH, Elizabeth 32
CHAYTOR, James 127
  Sarah 127
CHENEY, Drusilla 111
  Joseph 111, 114
  Priscilla 114
  William 111
CHESTER, Elizabeth 87
  Mary (COURSEY) 37
  Samuel 37
CHETTLE, Hanner 35
CHEVES, Daniel 92
  Mary (CARNES) 92
CHICARD, Baptista 83
  Rachel (EYRES) 83
CHILCOAT, Elisabeth 5
  Elizabeth 1
  Humphrey 1

CHILCOAT, James 1, 5, 15
  John 15
  Margaret 15
  Robinson 15
CHILCOTE, Humphry 17
  Mary 17
  Sarah 17
CHILD, (?) 66
  George 66
CHILDS, Benjamin 25
  George 24, 25, 149, 151
  Hannah 24, 25
  James 135
  Martha 24
  Polly (NEWCOMER) 135
  William 25
CHILGORE, James 66
CHINEA, Rachel 40
CHINN, John Yates 103
  Sarah Farfax (CARTER) 103
  William 90
CHINOARTH, John 11
  Mary 11
CHINWORTH, Jane (WOOD) 33
  John 33
CHISHOLM, Elisabeth 116
  Sarah 116
  Thomas 116
CHOATE, Austain 6
  Catharine 133
  Christopher 6
  Edward 32
  Flora 6
  Jane 133
  Mary 6
  Richard 6
  Thomas 133
  Zabrit 6
CHRISTE, James 26
  Mary 26
  Thomas 26
CHRISTIAN, Anthony 119
  Elisabeth (WELSH) 119
CHRISTIE, Bridget 85
CHRISTOPHER, Ann 24, 27
  Anne 117
  Elijah 27
  James 27
  John 24, 26, 27
  Nickloss 26
  Susanna 27
  Susannah 24, 26
CHURCH, Anna Maria 113
  Charlotte Sarah 146
  Hannah 113, 146
  Samuel 113, 146
CILESTIN, Mary 38
CLAGETT, Fanny Caroline 126
  Frances 89, 126

COOK, Catharine 30, 65
  Columbus 124
  Daniel 66
  Edward 100, 162
  Elizabeth 32, 58
  George 100
  Greenbury 52
  Hannah 43
  Jacob 58
  James 91
  Jane 100, 136
  John 18, 19, 34
  Judeth 33
  Katherine 42
  Kiturah 58
  Louisa 83
  Margaret 83, 91, 104, 124
  Mary 18, 19
  Mary (PRICE) 34
  Mathew 19
  Rebecca 66
  Thomas 19, 35
  William 18, 19, 83, 91, 104,
    124
  William Gregory 104
COOKE, Edward 41, 153
  Elizabeth (VAN WYCKE) 146
  Richard 146
  William 160
COOKSEY, Eleanor 146
  Eliza Mary Ann Price 146
  James 146
COONEY, Elizabeth 100
COOPER, Ann (SOUTHERN) 37
  Calvin 136
  Elisabeth (MC LANE) 107
  George 37
  Jane 145
  John 60, 78, 107
  Margaret (PALMER) 136
  Margaret (SUMMERS) 39
  Martha (ROBERTS) 43
  Rebecca 60
  Samuel 43
  Sarah 38, 113
  Susanna (BEACH) 78
  Thomas 39, 60
COPE, Susannah 32
COPER, Thomas 150
COPPER, Harriot 119
  Jane 119
  Samuel 119, 130
CORBAN, Abraham 2
  Edward 2
  Jane 2
  Nicholas, Sr. 152, 161
  Phillis Anna 2
CORBEN, Edward 3, 4
  Jane 3, 4

CORBEN, Providence 3
  Unity 4
CORBET, Maria 83
CORBETT, Sarah 133
CORBIN, Mary 85
  Nicholas 161
  Vincent 85
  Zany 85
CORBITT, Elisabeth 141
  Jane 141
  John 141
CORBY, Jane (GORDON) 132
  John 132
CORCKHILL, Anne (COLE) 146
  Thomas 146
CORD, Sarah 73
CORDIMAN, Ann (SAMPSON) 32
  Philip 32
CORKRAM, Elliner 11
  Mary 11
  Thomas 11
CORNER, Adam 26
  Grabill 26
  Gratvill 26
  Sarah 26
CORNISH, Levin 73
  Milly (GOVARE) 73
  Rachel 88
CORRIE, Elizabeth 98
  James 160
CORVALL, Elizabeth (DAVIDSON)
    55
  Thomas 55
COSDEN, Elenor (BUCHANAN) 79
  Jeremiah 79
  Jeremiah, Jr. 95
COSSETT, Catharine 104
COTHERNE, (?), Rev. 31
COTTER, Catharine 37
  Catherine 66
COTTRELL, Samuel 163
COUGHLAN, Frances 27
  Mary 27
  Richard 27
COUHNS, Jacob 140
  Polly (SALWAY/TALWAY) 140
COULSON, Louisa 63
  Martha 63, 90, 109, 119
  Thomas 63, 82
COULT, (?) 47
COULTER, Alexander 115
  Jane 115
  Peggy 115
COUNNS, Elisabeth 134
COURSEY, Mary 37
COURTENAY, Ann Boyd 61
  David Stewart 138
  Henry 138, 165
  Hercules 61, 88, 135, 149, 158

185

CROCKSHANKS, (?) 150
CROMLY, Mary 83
CROMWELL, Anne 139
  Betsy 137
  Hannah 31
  John 163
  Joseph 154, 163
  Richard 152, 161
CRONMILL, Jacob 75
  Jane 75
  John 75
CROOK, Charles 81
  George 88, 121, 146
  Jane 121, 146
  Jane (MORROW) 88
  John 121
  Mary 81
  Walter 81
CROOKSHANKS, Charles 80, 159
  Mary 76, 82
CROSGROVE, Elisa 145
CROSS, Bridget 113
  Charlotte (LEWIS) 79
  Elisabeth 6
  Elizabeth 53
  Henry 14
  John 24
  Joseph 6, 30
  Kessia 55
  Levinah 66
  Mary 6, 14
  Rachel 53
  Robert 79
  Samuel 24
  Sarah 57
  Susanna 24
  William 53
CROUCH, Eleanor Clemaretta 116
  Elisa 144
  Elisabeth 116
  Ellen 144
  Joseph 29
  Mary (LYNCH) 29
  Thomas 116
CROW, Jane 129
  Sarah 43, 74
  Thomas 43, 102
  William 43, 68, 74, 102
CROWDER, Elizabeth 57, 84
  Joseph 54, 57, 68, 84, 110,
    114, 120
  Judith (CLASSAY) 110, 120
  Mary 54, 57, 114
  Sarah 54, 68
CROXAL, James 149
CROXALL, Charles 34, 156
  Eleanor (BUCHANAN) 34
  Eleanor (GITTINGS) 52
  Elenor 63, 96

CROXALL, James 52, 63, 96
  Rebecca (MOALE) 34
  Richard 34, 63
CROZIER, John 132
  Margaret 132
  William 132
CRUMP, Jane 34
CULLEE, Jesse 140
  Rachel (RICKETTS) 140
CULLEN, Betsy 118
  Cassandra 118
  John 118
CULLESON, Anne 37
CULVERWILL, Richard 147, 165
CUMINGS, John 150
CUMINS, John 74
CUMMINGS, Margaret 135
CUMMINS, Alexander 80
  Elizabeth 84, 87
  Mary 109
  Thomas 84
CUNNINGHAM, Catharine 97
  Catharine (LEARY) 83
  John 83, 93, 97, 104
  Margaret 97, 104
  Mary (PUELY) 93
CUNNYNGHAM, Elizabeth (ADAMS)
    40
  Robert 40
CURFIELD, William 89
CURRAM, Elizabeth (BUCKINGHAM)
    65
  William 65
CURREY, Elizabeth 40
CURRY, Elizabeth (WILSON) 37
  John 37
CURSON, (?) 47
  Anna Maria 114, 121
  Elisabeth 114, 139
  Elizabeth 86, 103
  Elizabeth (MOALE) 78
  Elizabeth Rebecca Baker 103
  Ellen Moale 139
  Richard 103, 114, 147, 150,
    165
  Richard, Jr. 78, 86, 121, 139,
    141
  Samuel 86, 141
CURTAIN, (?) 47, 48
  Anne 134
  Eliza. 58
  James 53, 58, 119, 134
  John 145
  John Kelly 145
  Mary 53, 58
  Mary Ann 53
  Sarah 145
CURTIS, Abarillah 18
  Benjamin 18, 85, 91

187

CURTIS, Bridget (HARNES) 52
  Deborah 85
  Edmund 95
  Eleazer 52
  Eliza Maria 108
  Elizabeth (KIRBY) 95
  Francis 108, 134
  Henrietta Perigo 85, 91
  John 18, 48, 55, 114
  Mary Anne Catharine 108
  Peggy (EDWILLS) 55
CUSHION, Catharine (SMITH) 88
  Thomas 88
CUSTIS, Abiather 35
  Benjamin 35
  John 35
CUTFIELD, Mary 89, 92
CUTLER, Eleanor (WOODEN) 34
  Francis 34
DAFFIN, George 36
  Mary (BANKSON) 36
DAGG, Ann 26
  James 26
  William 26
DAILY, Margaret 88
  Mary 114
DALEY, Ally (KEEFE) 115
  Daniel 124
  Elisabeth (KILLEN) 124
  John 115
DALL, Charlotte 59, 66
  Elenor Addison 92
  Eliza Bradford 92
  James 59, 66, 92, 106, 123
  Jams 66
  John Heathcote 59
  John Robert 123
  Sarah Brook 92, 106, 123
  William Henry 106
DALLAS, Walter 163
DALRYMPLE, Elizabeth 73, 87
  John 66, 73, 87, 96, 98, 115
  Jonn. 102
  Maria 115
  Mary 73, 96, 115
  Richard 102
  Richard Pickett 96
  William Picket 73
DALY, Susanna 36
DANCER, (?) 46
  William 45, 48, 128, 147, 165
DANIEL, Anne 126
  Nicholas 126
DANILY, Dolly 39
DARBEY, Alice 11, 12
  James 11, 12
  John 11, 12
DARBY, Ailce (GAY) 31
  Alice 8, 12

DARBY, Daniel 8
  Elizabeth 1
  Elizabeth (DEMITT) 29
  John 8, 12, 31
  Mary 36
  Nathaniel 1, 29
  Rachel 125
DARLEY, Caroline (MILLER) 52,
  55
  Michael 52, 55
  Rachel 125
DARLING, Jane 58
  Robert 58
  Thomas 58
DARLINGTON, Ann (HIND) 33
  William 33
DARRINGTON, James 75
  Mary Charlotte 75
  Rebecca Harriet 75
DASHIELL, Allyfair 120
  Benjamin 133
  Charles Kilbern 120
  Christy 90
  Daniel 101
  George Washington 136
  Henry 125
  James 120, 136, 143
  Mary (LEEKE) 125
  Polly 101
  Polly (DASHIELL) 101
DAUGHERTY, Catharine 110
DAVERSON, James 147
DAVEY, A. W. 148
  Alexander W. 147
  Charlotte 87
  George 87
DAVIDSON, Benjamin 36
  Elizabeth 21, 35, 55, 72
  Elizabeth (BAKER) 36
  Elizabeth Key 21
  Harriot 72
  James 68, 160
  Job 72
  Robert 21, 68, 82
  Samuel 68
  Sarah 105
  Susanna 82
DAVIES, Ann 52, 55
  Catherine 60
  Edward 12, 55, 60
  Elizabeth 89
  Esther 12
  Kitty 55
  Margret 55
  Susanna 12
DAVIS, (?) 45
  Alexander 165
  Alexander W. 159
  Ambrose 40

189

DEHAY, Sarah 13
Sarah (TILBURY) 33
DEITER, Margaret 88
DELAHAYE, Sophia 76
DELANAP, Jesper 95
DELISLE, Elizabeth (LAROCHE)
107
John Godart 107
DELISLLE, Hilliare 53
Marie Rose (POIRICE) 53
DELL, Edward 100
Ezekiel 100
Joshua 100
Sarah 100
DEMITT, Elizabeth 29
Hannah 26
Joshua 26
Mary 29
Rachel 26
DEMMETT, John 4
Rachell 4
Richard 4
DEMMIT, Burch 114
Catharine 114
John 13
Joshua 13
Louisa 114
Rachel 13
Richard 13
DEMMITT, Anne 21
Athaliah 12
Barbara 12
James 12
Joshua 21
Presbury 15
Richard 21
Sophia 15
Stansbury 15
Thomas 15
DEN, Ann 25
Anne 24
Charlotte 24
Thomas 24, 25
William 25
DENASKEY, John 41
DENICE, Catherine 30
DENMEAD, Adam 104, 114, 128,
140
Henry 146
John 105, 127, 146
Mary 104, 105, 128
Sarah 104, 127, 146
Sarah (DAVIDSON) 105
William 128, 140
DENNIS, Daniel 46, 61, 68, 73,
93, 99
Eliza. 73
Elizabeth 61
John 68

DENNIS, John Washington 93
Margrett 42
Martha 61, 106
Susanna 128
DENNY, Hannah 55
DENROCHE, Lewis 49
DENT, George 38
Susannah (DAVIS) 38
DENTON, John 40
Margaret (MAY) 40
DERBIN, Rachel 66
DERMOTT, Elisabeth 144
Jane 144
Thomas 144
DERRY, Margaret 52
DERYDOR, John James 4, 41
Mary 4
Sarah 4, 41
DES CHAMPS, Frances 129
DESHAW, Mary (DAILY) 114
Peter 114
DESILVER, (?) 48
William 165
DESMOND, Catherine 43
DETLIFF, Christian 65
Mary (KENLY) 65
DETLISS, Christian 65
Mary (KENLY) 65
DEVALL, Thompsa 95
DEVER, John 37
Rebecca (TALBOT) 37
DEVERIS, Elizabeth 37
DEVINE, Elizabeth 82
DEVITT, (?) 46
DEW, Ann 25
Elizabeth 36
Thomas 25
William 25
DEWITT, Catherine 70
Elizabeth 70
Thomas 70, 77
DIBLEY, John 72
DICE, Elisabeth (WINSTANLY) 131
Henry 131
DICK, Elizabeth 54
Isaac 54
Isaiah 46
Thomas 22, 164
William 114
DICKES, Elizabeth 81
Isaac 81, 102
Mary 81
DICKESON, Priscilla 65
DICKINSON, Britingham 23
Britingon 150
Brittm. 147
Catharine 23
Elizabeth 23
William 23

191

193

EASTON, Elizabeth 94
  George 80, 93, 94, 111
  Hannah 94
  Kathrine 25
  William 93
  William Bowen 25
EBDIDGE, Anne (DAVIS) 135
  William 135
EBHARTE, Henry 148
EDENFIELD, Orpha 36
EDES, Anne 91
  Joseph 91
  Nary Anne 91
EDGAR, Eliza 102
EDGEBURY, Dorothy 119
  Mary 119
  William 119
EDMINSTON, William, Rev. 38
EDMONSON, John 136
EDMONSTON, Robert 50
EDNEY, Constant (PENINGTONE) 34
  Thomas 34
EDWARD, William 130
EDWARDS, (?) 48
  Alice 5, 41
  Ann 127
  Ann (RAWINGS) 69
  Anne 85
  Carolina 140
  Charles 23
  Dorcas 64
  Edward 9
  Elizabeth 20
  Ephraim 23
  Henrietta Maria 85
  James 27, 37, 49, 147, 149,
    157
  John 4, 5, 9, 14, 20, 29, 47,
    154
  Lusanah 20
  Lusandy 23
  Maria Charlotta Sophia 127
  Martha 14
  Mary 4, 5, 9, 14
  Mary (MERREMAN) 29
  Moses 4, 41, 162
  Nancy 140
  Philip 69, 85
  Robert 90
  Ruth 27
  Ruth (STANSBURY) 37
  Sarah 90
  Sophia 140
  Sophia (LERONETT) 125
  Thomas 20
  William 20, 23, 27, 76, 125,
    127, 140
EDWILLS, Peggy 55
EDWORD, Thomas 150

EGAN, Ann 69
EGELSTONE, Abraham 26
  Richard Diver 26
ELBERT, Elisabeth 137
ELECOT, Andrew 147
ELERTON, Francis 149
ELHART, Philip Henry 151
ELLEDGE, Ruth 31
ELLERTON, Anne 73
ELLIOTT, George 30, 124
  Harriot 121
  James 115, 120, 135
  John 122
  Juliana 142
  Mary (SLAUGHTER) 135
  Patience (BUCKNER) 30
  Prudence 124
  Robert 121, 142
  Sarah 115
  Sophia 115
  William 124
ELLIS, John 70, 121, 127
  Mary 92
  Sarah 36
  Susanna 71
  Thomas 121
ELLISON, Basil Baily 111
  Daniel 111
  Priscilla 111
ELLSAM, Jane 12
  Robert 12
  Thomas 12
ELLSOM, Jane (TAYLER) 32
  Robert 32
ELMORE, Catharine 133
ELMS, Ann (PUNTANY) 31
  Mabry 31
ELPHINSTON, David 57
  Lydia (HAMBLETON) 57
ELVINS, Elizabeth 121
  Jane 121
  William 121
ELWOOD, Elizabeth (DEVINE) 82
  Thomas 82
ELY, Catharine (DAVIS) 146
  George 146
ELZEY, Rachel (CORNISH) 88
EMMERT, Catharine 106
EMORY, Elisabeth 134
EMPEY, Ann 31
ENALLS, A. Leiner 149
ENGLE, Joseph 142, 143
  Margaret 70, 116, 145
  Margaret (HURST) 81
  Margret 22
  Mary Anne 116, 143
  Massy 82
  Sally 94
  Sarah 70, 94

197

198

FREELAND, Juliet 76
FREELOCK, John 121
  Sidney (WALKER) 121
FREEMAN, Ann 35
  Catharine (FARMER) 81
  Charles Wentworth 79
  Mary 79
  Patrick 81
  Priscilla 128
  Richard 142
  Samuel 79
  Sarah Anne 79
  Sidney 142
FREEPORT, Martin 149
FREER, Chloe 117
  Chloe (LEAGUE) 113
  John 113, 117
  Peter 117
FRENCH, Hannah 36
  John 87
  Mary 88
FRENCHES, Samuel 49
FRIETS, Anne 113
  Joseph 113
FRIETZ, Anne 100, 123
  John Benjamin 100, 102
  Joseph 100, 102, 123
FRINCHAM, Henry 87
  Rebecca 130
FRIOR, Catherine (CALLAHAN) 40
  John 40
FRISBY, Ann 26
  Francis Norton 26
  John 26
FROST, Ann 89
  Francies (TYE) 30
  George 89, 148
  Kitty 89
  Robert 30
  Soloman 89
FRY, Elisabeth 108
  John 108
  William 43
FULFORD, (?) 149
  Catharine 103
  Eleanor 165
  Elinor 147
  Mary 78
FULHAM, Dorothy 87
FULKS, Joseph 42
  Sarah 42
FULLER, Elizabeth 97
  Samuel 97
  Thomas 97
FULSERD, Henry 148
FURGUSON, James 42
FURLONG, Lawrence 138
  Sarah 138
  William 138

FURNIVAL, Alexander 58, 75, 159
  Elizabeth 58, 75, 125
  Louisa Georgina 75
  Sarah 58
  Washington 75
FUSBURY, Eleanor (GEANY) 53
  George 53
FUSSELL, Thomas 147
GAIKES, Anne 84
  Elisabeth 104
  Elizabeth (FLOOD) 89
  James 104
  Samuel 84, 89, 104
GAILE, Joanna 76
GAIN, Catherine 2, 41
  Elizabeth 4
  John 4
  Mary 30, 31
  Rebecca 4
  Rebecca (HARKENS) 30
  Rebeckah 31
  Rebekah 8
  Samuell 41
  William 2, 4, 8, 30, 41
GAITER, Ralph 52
  Sarah (ROWLES) 52
GALE, Alexaner 56
  Kessiah 56
  Levin 146
  Matthew 84
  Milcah 133
  Rachael 56
GALF, Margaret 65
GALLAGHER, Daniel 126
  Jane (HIGGINBOTTOM) 126
GALLAHER, Francis 144
  Margaret (DOLAN) 144
GALLION, William 67
GALLOWAY, Elizabeth 23
  Helena Maria 130
  James 23, 36
  Jane 70
  Judy (MC KAFFERTY) 132
  Mary 23
  Mary Ann (GOOCH) 36
  Robert 132
  William 130
GAMBLE, Mary (MC PILLON) 92
  Thomas 92
GANER, Hugh 80
GANTIER, Edward 119
  Thomas 119
GARDENER, Catherine 39
  Easter 26
  John 26
GARDER, Sarah 29
GARDINER, Deborah 68
  Elizabeth 106
  Mary 71

200

GOSSTWICK, Elisabeth 30
GOSTWICK, Aberilla 1
  Anne 2, 41
  Betty 10
  Ebarilla 2, 10
  Ebarilla (YANSTONE) 29
  Elizabeth 2
  Elizabeth (YANSTONE) 29
  George 10
  Joseph 10
  Mary 1
  Nicholas 1, 2, 10, 29, 41
  Thomas 2, 29
GOSWICK, Aquila 35
  Elizabeth 4
  Elizabeth (STANSBURY) 35
  John Oystain 4
  Joseph 41
  Thomas 4
GOTT, Anthony 7
  Cassandra 7
  Elizabeth 7
  Martha 39
  Richard 7
  Ruth 7, 32
  Samuel 7, 48
  Sarah 7
GOUGH, Frances Philips 79
  Harry Dorsey 25, 53, 157, 162
  John 145
  Martha (LOWRY) 145
  Prudence 25
  Sophia 25, 53
GOULARD, John 117
  Margaret 117
  Thomas 117
GOULD, John 96
  Margaret (WHEELER) 96
GOVARE, Milly 73
GOVEN, Gerard 69
  Sarah (GILES) 69
GOVER, Gerard 94, 120
  Mary Hammond 94
  Sarah 94, 120
  William 120
GOWDY, James 98
  William 98
GRABLE, P. 150
GRACE, Edward 32
  Patience (FOSTER) 32
GRAHAM, Elizabeth 88
  William 90, 147, 165
GRAINGER, Elizabeth 66
  Joseph 68, 134
  Sarah 68
GRANDY, George 45
GRANGER, Barbary 52
  Joseph 52
  Samuel 52

GRANT, (?) 48
  Alexander 7, 30
  Caroline (GLEDE) 85
  Daniel 147, 165
  Daniel, Jr. 92, 102
  Eleanor (REILEY) 37
  Elisabeth 7
  Elisabeth (COLE) 30
  Eliza Harwood 92
  Isabella 92
  Jane 52
  Marmaduke 37
  Mary 7
  Nancy 105
  Susanna (DENNIS) 128
  William 85, 128
GRAVES, (?) 150
  Ann 26
  Anne 95
  Duret 26
  John 26
  Matthew 104
GRAY, (?), Capt. 42
  Absalom 8
  Ann 27, 52
  Anne 1, 21
  Catharine 78
  Chloe 105
  Cloe 62
  Comfort 27
  Elizabeth (WILSON) 92
  Ephraim 21
  George 88
  Jane 68, 70
  John 65, 68, 105, 127, 129
  Joseph 88, 92, 111
  Joseph Berry 62
  Joshua 102
  Lucy (FOSTER) 65
  Lynch 78
  Margart 88
  Martha 31
  Mary 1, 21, 68, 112
  Mary (BRADBURN) 116
  Mary (DEMITT) 29
  Mary (LINCH) 34
  Nancy 81
  Peter 116
  Rebecca 5
  Rebekah 8
  Richard 112
  Samuel 11
  Sarah 53, 78
  Sophia (HOLMES) 40
  William 62, 105, 111, 129
  Zachariah 1, 5, 8, 29, 34
  Zackariah 5
  Zarack 27
  Zechariah 40

HAMILTON, Jane 13
 John 2, 13, 15
 Maria (SELMAN) 128
 Mary Anne 94
 Rachel (WILLIAMS) 97
 Ruth 2
 Sarah 2, 13, 121
 Sidney 13
 Sydney 15
 William 2, 13, 15, 128, 153
HAMMER, Ann (CAPOST) 55
 Peter 55
HAMMETT, Mary 145
HAMMILTON, William 41
HAMMOND, (?) 44, 46, 68
 Ann 10
 Anne 79, 103
 Avis 65
 Benjamin 10, 32
 Caroline 35
 Charles 93
 Eballia 8
 Ebarilla (SIMPKINS) 31
 Eliza. (RAVEN) 32
 Elizabeth 16, 51, 103
 Elizabeth (ANDERSON) 86
 Elizabeth (MC CONNELL) 50
 Elizabeth Anne 97
 Esther 23
 John 45, 50, 51, 86, 93, 101,
  103, 147, 149, 153, 158, 165
 John Barnett 51
 John Mc Connell 51
 Larkin 16
 Laurance 8, 31
 Margett (TALBOTT) 32
 Margrett 10
 Mary 19, 35, 94, 97, 127
 Matthew 79
 Nancy (JOYCE) 66
 Rachel 8
 Rebecca 16, 94
 Rezin 66
 Sarah 16
 Sarah (SHEREDINE) 33
 Thomas 16, 48, 79, 127
 William 16, 23, 32, 33, 68,
  94, 97, 127, 147, 149, 163,
  165
 William, Col. 153
HAMMONDS, John 65
HAMOND, William 150
HANCOCK, Honour (STRINGER) 35
 William 35
HANDLEN, Catharine 130
HANDS, John 164
HANEY, Elizabeth 65
HANKEY, Mary 105
 Mary Anne 116

HANNAH, Edward 74
 Elizabeth 74
 Teressa 74
HANNAN, Elizabeth 65
HANNS, Mary 35
HANSON, Airy (ROLLS) 39
 Christopher 24, 39
 Cuzsiah 11
 Edward 157
 Edward Spicer 18
 Elizabeth 14
 Hannah 36
 Jemima 36
 John 154
 Jona., Jr. 164
 Jonathan 6, 7, 11, 12, 13, 14,
  30, 82, 147
 Jonathan, Jr. 165
 Joshua 18
 Mary 13, 30, 82
 Molly 14
 Nancy (CLAY) 122
 Sarah 7, 11, 12, 13, 14, 18,
  111
 Sarah (SPICER) 30
 Theodore 122
 Thomas 164
 Timothy 12
HANWAY, Belinda (CANE) 73
 Francis 73
HARBEAUICK, John 150
HARBONG, Charles 55
 Fanny 55
 Nancy 55
HARBORD, Susanna 125
HARCOURT, Mary 39
HARDEN, Honor 29
HARDING, Abraham 88, 115
 Anne (LEE) 145
 Charles 135
 Christopher 145
 John 129
 Mary 88, 115
 Polly (MARCHANT) 126
 Rebecca 115
 Thomas 126
 William 88
HARDY, James 39, 62
 John 143
 Mary 62
 Mary (CALDRON) 39
 Rachel 129
 Sarah (EVANS) 143
 William 62
HARGROVE, Margaret (BUCKLEY)
  124
 Thomas 124
HARISON, Partick 130
HARKENS, Rebecca 30

207

HARKINS, John 132
  Peggy (POWELL) 132
  Richard 148
HARN, Elisabeth 6
  Honnor 6
  Patrick 6
HARNEL, Christiana 127
  John 127
HARNES, Bridget 52
HARO, Juliana (ROLORS) 93
  Samuel O. 93
HARP, Elenor 79
HARPER, Harriet 102
  John 82, 102
  Margaret 36
HARR, James 148
HARRIMAN, Alis 2
  Ann 15
  Anne (WILKINSON) 29
  Eliza. 35
  Elizabeth 14
  George 15, 18, 29, 155
  Jane (SMITH) 29
  Jemimah 2
  John 2
  Pricilla 14
  Rachel 14, 18
  Robert 14
  Ruth 35
  Samuel 29
  Sarah 18
HARRINGTON, Nancy 138
HARRIS, (?), Dr. 46
  Ann 3, 67
  Anne 139
  Benjamin 106
  Cathreen 27
  Daniel 67
  Eleanor 2
  Elenor (MOORE) 85
  Eleoner (ROGERS) 29
  Hannah 117, 139
  James 85, 117, 122
  James Lloyd 2
  John 117, 122, 139
  Lloyd 2, 29, 42, 153, 163
  Margaret 2
  Margrett 33
  Mary 3, 144
  Moses 106
  Roseana 27
  Ruth 106
  Sarah 2
  Thomas 3
  William 2, 27
HARRISON, (?), Dr. 48
  Abraham 65
  Alexander 86
  Anne Caroline 133

HARRISON, Daniel 96, 131, 133,
  140, 143
  Edward 78, 80, 92, 116, 139,
  142, 144
  Eleanor 133
  Elisabeth (GAULT) 137
  Elizabeth 86, 96
  Elizabeth (LANGAM) 33
  Elizabeth (TILLINGSWORTH) 96
  Hall 137
  Henry 92, 133
  James 130
  Jane Maria 133
  Jesse 131
  Johannah (MORRIS) 31
  John 31
  Jonathan 133
  Jonathan, Jr. 164
  Joshua Kirby 133
  Letilla 133
  Lilly (MADKINS) 65
  Lily 86
  Margaret 78, 92, 116, 130
  Margery 133
  Mary (WHITE) 37
  Otho 133
  Sarah 34
  Thomas 37, 155
  William 33, 91
HARRISSON, Benjamin Kirby 63
  Daniel 62, 63
  John 14
  Johnathan 62, 63
  Margaret 62
  Margery 63
  Mary 14
HARROWSMITH, Martha 33
HARRY, Demaris 129
HARRYMAN, Alice 10, 12
  Allinor 6
  Ann 8, 11
  Anne 4
  Charles 5
  Comfort 6, 8, 12
  Comfort (TAYLOR) 29
  Ebarilla 10
  Eleanor 34
  Elizabeth 10, 12
  Elizabeth (SIMKINS) 31
  George 4, 8, 11
  Jane 41
  John 5, 10, 12, 40
  Mary 33
  Mary (EAGLESTONE) 40
  Patience 8
  Prudence 12
  Robert 10, 12, 31
  Ruth 6
  Samuel 6, 8, 12, 29, 41

HARRYMAN, Sarah 12
  Thomas 10, 12
  William 11
HART, Araminta 139
  Elisabeth 136
  John 135
HARTE, Joseph 148
HARTEGIN, Mary (SAWELL) 34
  William 34
HARTER, Hannah 44
  James 44
  John 44
  William 44
HARTWAY, Elizabeth (PARNETSON)
  33
  Feiters 33
HARVEY, Anne 143
  Eleanor (JACKSON) 52
  Elizabeth 8
  Hannah (THORNTON) 43
  James 143
  Jonathan 104
  Joseph 103
  Lucy (ARMSTEAD) 104
  Margaret (BURNS) 112
  Margarett 12
  Margrett 8
  Mary (THOMPSON) 103
  Thomas 8, 43
  William 8, 12, 52, 71, 112
HARWAY, Margrett 7
  Mary 7
  William 7
HARWELL, Thomas 163
HARWOOD, Henry 83
  Jane (BUCKLER) 83
HARYMAN, Elizabeth 8
HASE, Eleanor 37
HASHAM, Josiah 137
  Mary (KNUPWOOD) 137
HAUFMAN, Philip 102
HAW, Charles 146
  Jane (HOWARD) 146
HAWK, Sara (BROWN) 101
  Thomas 101
HAWKENS, Nathen 4
  Rebecca 4
HAWKINS, Alleridge 2
  Ann 33
  Ann (SHIPLEY) 40
  Anne 2
  Becky 128
  Benjamin 7
  Catherine Elizabeth 53
  Elizabeth 2, 7, 15
  Henry 128
  John 6, 8, 30
  Joseph 40
  Mary 2, 8, 34

HAWKINS, Mary (SIMKINS) 30
  Matthew 2, 7, 15
  Prescilla 8
  Ralph 66
  Samuel 128
  Susanna (JACOBS) 66
  William 7
HAY, James 106
  Mary (COMICAL) 106
HAYDN, Elizabeth (MAHONEY) 85
  Samuel 85
HAYES, Edward 122
  Elizabeth 90
  Isaac 98
  James 98
  Margaret 96
  Maria (O'BRIEN) 122
  Mary 80
  Mary V. 79
  William 90, 147, 165
HAYLY, Kitty (ANDERSON) 134
  Samuel 134
HAYNAM, Mary 63
  Thomas 63
HAYS, John 38, 152
  Rebecca (WILLIAMS) 38
HAYWARD, Harriot (BARNEY) 113
  Henry 113
  Rachel 38
HAYWORTH, Jonathan 51
  Rebbecca (RANDALL) 51
HAZE, Catharine 105
  Hugh 105
  Mary Anne 105
HAZLETON, Ann 129
HAZZARD, Eleanor (BURGHES) 57
  George 57
HEAD, Ann 55, 61, 82
  Anne 74
  Elenor 74
  George 61, 68
  John 47, 55, 61, 68, 74, 80,
    82
HEALY, Leah 65
HEARN, Johannah 32
HEARNS, William 50
HEATH, Eleanor (JOYCE) 53
  Jane 53
  Jesse 118, 143
  Martha 118
  Samuel 53
HEATHRINGTON, Eliza Vaughn 117
  Sarah 117
  Sarah (POLLOCK) 66
  Thomas 66, 117
HEDDEN, John 154
HEDDINGER, Catharine (HERMAN)
  71
  Michael 71

HEDRICK, John 65, 67, 81
  Margaret 81
  Margaret (GALF) 65
  Robert 67
  William 81
HEDRICKS, Anne (FISH) 81
  James 81
HEIDE, Elisabeth 130
HEINER, Esther 69
  Frances 88
  Jacob 69
  Nicholas 69
HELLEN, Ann King 130
  Anne King 123
  Arcajah 123
  Mary King 83
  Peter 130
  Peter Y. 132
  Peter Young 123
  Susanna Aisquith 123, 132
HELLIN, David 147
HELLING, (?) 46
HELM, George 148
  M. 147
  Mabory 150
  Mayberry 154, 156, 164, 165
HELMES, Margaret 88
HELMS, (?) 48
  Anne 12
  Catharine (CLARK) 73
  Elizabeth 35
  John 73
  Mary 35
  Mayberry 12
  Mayberry, Jr. 35
HENDER, Nancy (TOWNSEND) 109
  Thomas 109
HENDERSON, Elizabeth 33
  Isabella 141
  Jane 79
  Jemina 31
  John 39
  Michal (BARTON) 39
  William 130, 141
HENDON, Henry 53, 54, 62
  Josias 54
  Mary 53, 54, 62
  Sarah Susanna 62
  William Westfield 53
HENDRICKSON, Ruth 52
HENESY, Elizabeth (WARRINGTON)
  64
  Michael 64
HENLEY, Elenor (FLOOD) 81
  Robert 81
HENNESSY, Hannah 43
HENRY, Bridget (CROSS) 113
  Elizabeth 52
  Samuel 113

HENRY, Sarah 65
  William 101
HENSELLER, Ann 51
HENSHAW, Nancy 71
HEPBURN, Thomas 67
HERBERT, Charles 59, 77, 140
  Fanny 59, 77, 140
  James 59
  John 77
  Peter 140
  Sarah 31
HERMAN, Catharine 71
HERMES, (?) 46
HERNS, Margret 65
HERONBORN, Catharine Isabella
  134
  Robert 134
  Susanna 134
HERRIS, James 122
  John 122
HERRON, Eleanor 110
  Robert 88
  Susanna 88
  William 88
HESSY, Charles 12
  Jane 12
HEWES, Christopher 150
HEWETT, Amelia 93
  Elisabeth 30
  Richard 41
HEWITT, Eli 106, 123, 134
  Jacob 123
  Martha 123, 134
  Martha (DENNIS) 106
  Thomas 134
HEWLETT, John 27
  Margaret 27
HEWLING, Ann (BOWEN) 30
  Jonas 30
HICK, Ann (LOWE) 23
  Elizabeth Margaret 23
  William 23
HICKES, Elizabeth 104
  Robert 104
  William 104
HICKEY, John 148, 149
  Margaret (AIRES) 112
  Peter 112
HICKINGBOTTOM, George 26
  Joel 26
  Mary 26
HICKLEY, Charles 113
  Elizabeth Ann 67
  James 67, 87, 104, 129
  Mary Anne 140
  Sarah 113, 129, 132
  Thomas James 129
HICKS, Elizabeth 43
  Elizabeth (HENRY) 52

HICKS, Robert 52
HIGDON, Jane 107
HIGGINBOTTOM, Jane 126
HIGGINS, Ann 45
  Anne (ELLERTON) 73
  Edward 73
HIGINBOTHOM, (?), Rev. 138
  Isabella 138
  Margaret 138
  Ralph, Jr. 138
  Susanna (BLUNDELL) 136
  Thomas 136
HIGNOTT, Elizabeth 27
  Sarah 27
  Thomas 27
HILAND, Catherine (SMITH) 39
  George 39
HILL, Anna (WILLIS) 140
  Asa 67
  Caroline 37
  Deborah 80
  Elizabeth 56
  Hannah 26, 56, 76
  James 88, 90
  Jane (BOWLAND) 139
  John 50, 56, 80, 139
  John C. 126, 129
  Joseph 26, 98
  Judith 129
  Judy (FENNER) 126
  Margaret 67
  Mary 38
  Nancy 80
  Rebecca 111
  Richard 26, 140
  Robert 87
  Rosanna 26
  Ruth 26
  Sarah 26, 78, 88
  Thomas 88, 90, 98
HILLEN, Elizabeth 4, 14, 15, 34
  Elizabeth (RAVEN) 30
  Johanna 15
  John 41
  Lydia 64
  Mary 4
  Nathaniel 14
  Soloman 4, 30
  Solomon 14, 15, 42, 154
HILLIARD, Mary 31
HILLING, Elizabeth 7, 9
  John 9, 42
  Solomon 7, 9
HILMAN, Alexander 141
  Elisabeth (WHIPPLE) 141
  Reubin 136
HILSDEN, Catherine 56
  John 56
  Samuel 56

HILTON, Abraham 79
  Catharine (THOMPSON) 79
  John 96, 146
  Lettice 146
  Lydia 96, 146
  Mima 96
HINCKES, Mary 117
HINCKLEY, Frances 154
HINCKS, Nelly 53
HIND, Ann 33
HINDMARSH, John 70
HINDON, Lidia 3
  Richard 3, 29
  Sarah 3
  Sarah (GARDER) 29
HINES, Mary 30
  Thomas 152, 165
HINGDON, Mary 50
HINKLE, Anthony 137
  Kitty (BOND) 137
HINKLEY, Francis 163, 164
HINNER, Nicholas 47
HIPKINS, Thomas 80
HIPSLEY, Benjamin 52
  Elizabeth (BISHOP) 52
HIPWELL, Barbara 102
  Hum. 102
  Humphrey 86, 123
  Humphry 113
  James 86, 123
  John 113
  Sarah 86, 113
HISCA, Eade Rebecca 122
  Nicholas 122
  Sarah 122
  Sophia 122
HISER, Charlotte (SWEETING) 89
  David 89
  John 16, 20
  Mary 16, 20
  Samuel 16
  Sarah 20
HISLET, Mary 92
HISS, Ann 54
  Catura 54
  Charles 54
HISSEY, Catherine 52
  Charles 17
  Elizabeth 17
  Henry 17
  James 143
  Jane 17
  Keturah 17
  Mary 17, 119
  Mary (MILLER) 143
  Sarah 17
HITCH, John 140
  Polly Collins 140
HITCHCOCK, Presotia 32

211

213

216

217

222

MANLY, William 23
MANNELL, James 132
  Mary (DOLY) 132
MANSON, Catharine (DAUGHERTY)
  110
  William 110
MANSPEAKER, Henry 93
MANWARING, James 95
MARCHANT, Mary 8
  Polly 126
  Richard 8
MARCHENT, Ellinor 4
  Mary 4
  Mary (SWEETING) 29
  Richard 4, 29
  William 4
MARGAR, Mary (ANDERSON) 66
  William 66
MARKLAND, Orpha (EDENFIELD) 36
  William 36
MARLER, Sarah 33
MARR, Aney (OWINGS) 39
  Catharine 119
  William 39
MARRYHAN, Sarah 45
MARRYMAN, (?) 149
  Charles 30
  Milleson (HAILE) 30
MARSH, Ann 7
  Comfort 17
  Elizabeth 17, 33, 94
  Gilbert 7, 34
  Jane 105, 127, 142
  John 7, 17
  Josiah 34
  Lavina (BUCKNAM) 34
  Mary 84
  Prudence 34, 102
  Sarah (BREESET) 34
  William 84, 94, 105, 127, 142
  William George 105
MARSHAL, John 64
  Mary 64
  Phebe 49
  Susanna 64
MARSHALL, Elizabeth 25
  Eve (ROTHROCK) 117
  George William 25
  Henry 117
  James 112
  John 120
  Mary Sophia 25
  Orpha 25
  Susan 120
  Thomas 25
  William 25
MARTEN, Frances 26
  John 26
  Margrete 26

MARTIN, Anne 136, 146
  Araminta (HART) 139
  Betsy (LINDSAY) 129
  Catharine 77
  Catherine 54
  Ed. 102
  Eliza Sophia 58
  James 82, 95, 97, 125, 139
  John 45, 109, 110, 129, 136
  Julia 125
  Luther 48, 58, 67, 102, 147,
    165
  Maria 58, 102
  Mary 146
  Mary Anne 136
  Nancy 109, 128
  Nancy (MAHONEY) 88
  Richard 128
  Sarah 95, 97, 125
  Sarah (ROUSE) 82
  Thomas 102
  William 54, 66, 77, 88, 97,
    109, 110, 128, 146
MARTON, John 150
  Sinah 95
MARYMAR, John 149
MASE, Jane 55
  John 55
  Susanna 55
MASH, James 33
  Margrett (HARRIS) 33
  Mary 30
  Rosehannah 30
MASHAM, Mary (NEWMAN) 33
  Philip 33
MASON, Benjamin 111, 112, 113,
    137
  Catharine 97
  Elisa 116
  Jacob 97
  James 54, 70, 116
  John 105
  John Washington 137
  Mary 54
  Michael 97
  Rebecca 40
  Sarah 54, 70, 116, 137
  Sarah (COOPER) 113
  Sarah (REDING) 105
  Susanna 112
MASS, Anna 114
  John 81, 88, 114
  Mary 88
  Mary Essek 114
  Mary Essig 81
  Samuel 88
MASSEY, Elisabeth 115
  Joseph 115
MASSY, Anna 105

227

MASSY, Elisabeth 105
  Joseph 105
MASTER, Legh, Rev. 108
MATHEWS, Catharine 24
  Cathreene 36
  James 24
  Robert 24
  William 149
MATHISON, John 126
  Mary (GILBERTHORP) 126
MATTHEWS, Anne (GILL) 85
  Catharine 123
  Elizabeth 33
  Elizabeth (SHORTERS) 40
  Francis 135
  James 123
  Jane 85
  Margaret 65
  Margaret (O'DONNELL) 135
  Martha 123
  Mary 31
  Sarah 119, 123
  Thomas 33, 85
  William 40
MATTHIAS, James 37
  Magdalen (BUTTON) 37
MAUCABY, William 66
MAXELL, James, Col. 162
MAXFEILD, Margrett (JARVISS) 30
  Robert 30
MAXFIELD, Hannah 7, 41
  James 7
  Joseph 7
  Margrett 4, 6, 12
  Mary 12
  Moses 4
  Rechal 6
  Robert 4, 6, 12
  Samuel 7, 41
MAXWELL, Elizabeth 40
  Margaret 40
  Marion 52
  Mary 94
MAY, Cathrine (BEAMER) 39
  James 133
  John 48
  Margaret 40
  Sarah (CORBETT) 133
  Thomas 39
MAYBURY, John 24
  Martha 24
  Richard 24
MAYCOCK, Phebe (MILES) 40
  William 40
MAYDWELL, Hannah 40
MAYHAM, Elliner 32
MAYHEW, Eleanor (MC KENSIE) 55
  William 55
MAYJORS, Esther 10

MAYJORS, Mary 10
  Peter 10
  Rachel 10
MAYNER, Henry 8
  Sarah 8
  Susannah 8
MAYO, Eleanor 122
  Elenor 75
  Elizabeth 75
  William 75, 122
MC ADUE, Anne (SPENCER) 92
  Samuel 92
MC ALESTER, John 147
MC ALISTER, John 165
MC ALLISTER, Ann (SAMPSON) 40
  Charles 40
MC AULESTER, (?) 149
MC BLAHERTY, Margaret 103
MC BRIDE, Hugh 102
  Mary 79
  Mary (PHILE) 66
  Roger 66
MC CAMMON, Sally 144
MC CANDLESS, George 149
MC CANNON, Alexander 132
  George Burke 145
  Joseph 145
  Sarah 145
MC CARTER, (?) 48
  Robert 45
  Sarah 96
  William 91
MC CARTHY, Cornelius 114, 146
  Margaret 61
  Margret 55
  Mary 61
  Mary Anne 114
  Nicholas Sluby 61
  Sarah 114, 146
  Thomas 146
MC CARTY, Lucy 38
  Winifred 127
MC CLASKEY, John 107
  Mary (WHEELER) 107
MC CLURE, Ann 25
  Daniel 25
  John 25
  Margaret 86
MC COLLUM, Alexander 33
  Elizabeth (BEESTON) 33
MC CONEKY, (?) 46
  John 46
MC CONIKIN, Eleoner 36
  John 36
MC CONKEY, Ann 123
  Jane 133
  John 123
  Nancy 123
  Thomas 102, 123

228

MC CONNELL, Elizabeth 50
  James 94
  John 94, 128
  Sarah (LERET) 128
MC CONNICAN, John 36
  Mary (DARBY) 36
MC CORD, Isaac 102
MC CORMICK, Francis 125
  Jane (GRAYDY) 121
  John 121
  Martha (MOORE) 125
MC COY, Anne 108, 118
  Catharine (HOGAN) 100
  Charlotte 106
  Richard 100
  William 68
MC CRAY, John 92
  Mary (ELLIS) 92
MC CREARY, William 159, 165
MC CREERY, Susanna 80
  Thomas 80
MC CREREY, William 150
MC CROY, William 147
MC CUBBIN, Elisabeth 108
  Elizabeth 118
  Mary 22
  Sarah 22
  Zachariah 22
MC CURDY, Catherine 52
  John 47
MC DOE, Elizabeth (RIDDLE) 73
  William 73
MC DONALD, Alexander 108
  Edward 43
  James 38
  John 67, 102
  Mary Ann Dorsey 65
  Polly (DAVIS) 108
MC DONNEL, Andrew 131
  Anne 131
  Samuel 131
MC DONNELL, Anne 81
  John 73, 80
  Margaret 81
  Mary 80
  Peter 73
  Samuel 81
  Sarah 81
MC DOO, Ann 127
  Elisabeth 127
  Samuel 127
MC DOWELL, Elisabeth 107
  Thomas 107, 131
  Thomas Kennedy 90
MC EUEN, Ann (WALKER) 34
  Christopher 34
MC EVOY, James 140
  Mary Anne (HICKLEY) 140
MC FALL, John 96

MC FALL, Margaret (HAYES) 96
MC FEE, Ann 57
MC FEEL, Mary 83
MC GARVEY, Rachel 139
MC GAUGHY, Edward 129, 139
  Eleanor 139
  Jane 139
  Jane (WILSON) 129
MC GEE, Elizabeth 71
MC GILL, Carvel Bell 110
  John 110
  Martha 110
MC GINNISS, Edward 58
  Jane 58
  Roger 58
MC GOWAN, Eleanor 112
MC GRATH, John 136
  William 136
MC GREGORY, Anne 125
  Catharine 141
  Edward 141
  Margaret 141
  Mary 38
  Patrick 125
MC GROGGEN, Charlotte (OWINGS)
  84
  Patrick 84
MC GUIRE, Anariah 79
MC HARRY, John 126, 128
  Margaret (FITZGIBBON) 126, 128
MC HENRY, Dennis 110
  Joyce (WHILTON) 110
MC INTYRE, Elizabeth 88
  Patrick 88, 131
  Sarah 88
MC KAFFERTY, Judy 132
MC KEAG, William 110
MC KEAN, Peggy 116
MC KENNY, Daniel 126
  Mary 126
  Rebecca 126
MC KENSIE, Eleanor 55
  Mary 113, 117
  Polly 113
  Susanna 123
MC KENSY, (?) 48
MC KENZIE, Archibald 118
  Benjamin 62, 77, 99, 129
  Dillon Benjamin 94
  Elizabeth 70
  Elizabeth (DOYLE) 118
  George 123
  Mary (JACKSON) 123
  Rebecca (BEETLE) 129
  Susanna 94
  Sussana 62
  Sussanna Margaret 62
  William 94, 99
MC KENZIES, Benjamin 48

MERCHANT, Elizabeth 140
 Elizabeth (HARRISON) 96
 John 96
MERCIN, Sussanna 52
MEREDITH, Elizabeth 11, 15
 Elizabeth (COOK) 32
 Jemima (TAYLOR) 34
 Rachel 15
 Samuel 11, 15, 32, 34
 Sarah 11
MEREKIN, Ann 54
 Charles 54, 60
 Elizabeth 60
 James 54
 John 54
 Joshua 54
 Sarah 54, 60
 William 54
MERIMAN, Kedermath 2
MERREDITH, Actia 13
 Elizabeth 13
 Samuel 13
MERREMAN, Mary 29
MERRICK, Anne 39
 Catharine 81
 Henry 84
 Patrick 84
MERRIKEN, Charles 76, 112, 145
 Sarah 76
MERRIMAN, Alice 1
 Charles 2, 7, 41
 Elizabeth 1, 18, 29
 Jane 2, 18, 29
 John 1, 3, 29
 Joseph 3
 Martha 3
 Mary 2, 35
 Milison 7
 Nicholas 3, 18
 Sarah 3
 Sarah (ROGERS) 29
MERRIT, Anne 132
MERRY, Robert 124
MERRYMAN, Action 19
 Anne (PRESBURY) 136
 Benjamin Rogers 28
 Charles 1, 9, 11, 41
 Cloe 14
 Deborah 28
 Elisabeth 30
 Elizabeth 8, 18, 51
 George 9
 Jane 15
 Jane (Jean) 19
 Jemima 42
 Jemina 32
 Johannah 11
 John 1, 8, 12, 18, 28, 39, 51,
 153, 154, 158, 164

MERRYMAN, John Ensor 28
 John, Jr. 5, 154, 156
 John, Sr. 41, 154, 162
 Joseph 18, 21
 Keturah 31
 Margaret 6
 Margret 6
 Margrett 9, 11, 14, 42
 Marice 19
 Martha 1
 Mary 1, 3, 9, 19, 21, 31, 41
 Milisant 9
 Millisant 11
 Moses 21
 Nicholas 3, 28, 156
 Nicholas Rogers 51
 Rachel 15
 Rebeckah 32
 Samuel 1, 3, 15, 19, 41, 153,
 156
 Sarah 5, 8, 12, 34, 51
 Sarah (ROGERS) 39
 Sarah (SMITH) 28
 Sarah Rogers 51
 William 6, 9, 11, 14, 42, 136
MESHAW, Achsah 103
MESSER, Mary 105
METCALFE, John 15
 Mary 15
METZLER, Daniel 97
 Margaret 97
 Rebecca 97
MEYER, Patty 108
MEYERS, John 90, 92, 95, 99
 Mary 81
 Sarah 92, 99
 Thomas 90
 William 92, 95
MIER, Anne 21
 Eliza (COLE) 35
 Elizabeth 21
 George Henry 21
 John Henry 21, 35
MIERKEN, David 117
 Louisa 117
MIFFORD, Sussanna 65
MILAM, Elizabeth 31
MILBY, Rachel (PORTER) 118
 William 118
MILDEW, Aquila 57
 Zena (GERMAN) 57
MILES, Daniel 50, 52
 Margaret 77
 Mary (GORMAN) 50, 52
 Phebe 40
 Samuel 77
MILL, (?) 46
MILLAR, Elizabeth (SMITH) 38
 William 38

232

234

NAGLE, Edward 65
 Margaret (MILLER) 65
NAILOR, Hannah 100
NANTZ, Hanah 69
 Henry 69
 Martha 69
NANTZE, Hannah 92, 114, 130
 Henry 92, 114, 130
NANVORRUCK, John 115
NASH, Anne 109
 Catherine 60
 Charles 89, 98, 109
 Elsbeth 90
 Grace 89, 109
 Joseph Chick 60
 Samuel 67
 Thomas 60, 67
 William 89, 98, 148, 149, 151
NAUBONUCK, John 115
NEAL, Eleanor 29
 Eleoner 2
 Hewey 149
 James 2
 Jeremah 2
 Margaret 2
 Patrick 2, 162
 Sarah 2
NEALE, (?) 145
NEEDHAM, John 145
 Nancy (COLE) 145
NEFTLAND, Hannah 103
NEIGHBORS, Sarah Edmondson 116
NEIL, Mary 65
NELSON, Filty 151
 Henry 48
 Mathilda (JOHNSON) 70
 Matilda 83, 146
 Robert Lloyd 146
 Susannah 65
 Thomas 70, 83, 146
 William 83
NEWBY, Godfrey 104
 Sarah 104
NEWCOMER, (?) 47
 Polly 135
NEWEL, Susanna 86
 Susanna (MOREHEAD) 78
 William 78
NEWELL, Margarett 35
NEWMAN, Ann 63
 Francis 99
 Harriet 88, 94
 Henry 60, 91, 95
 John Holly 60
 Lydia 99
 Mary 33
 Mary (GAIN) 31
 Rebekah 33
 Sarah 60, 91, 95

NEWMAN, William 31
NEWSTER, Ann (FREEMAN) 35
 Thomas 35
NEWTON, Joseph 102
 Joseph James 108
NICHOLAS, John 138
 Mary (BEAR) 138
NICHOLS, (?) 50
NICHOLSON, (?) 45
 Ann Maria 39
 Elisabeth 107
 Elizabeth 90
 John 107, 131
 Mary 35
 Mary Anne 131
 Rachel 100
 Susanna 107, 131
 William 42
NICKELL, Gressey 65
NICKOLDSON, Mary (CONNELL) 35
 William 35
NICKOLSON, John 149
NICOLS, Charlott 97
 Charlotte 84
 Henry 75, 159
 James 68, 84, 97, 102
 Jarnes 90
 Maria 68
 Mary 84, 90
 Rebecca (SMITH) 75
NICOLSON, Sarah 69
NINDE, Catharine 115
 James 115
NIXON, Ketty 97
NOBLE, Antoy. 149
 Catherine 61
 John 61
 Peggy 61
 Phillis 31
NOEL, (?) 44
 Margarett 22
 Ruth 22, 43
 Septimus 22, 43, 80
NOGLE, Elizabeth 86
 Henry 147, 148
 Mary 86
 Peter 86
NOON, William 47
NORRIS, Delia 125
 Elizabeth 125
 James 125
 Jane (PETERKIN) 134
 John 142
 Lloyd 134
 Maria 145
 Sarah 73
 William 73
NORTH, Elisabeth 5
 Eliza 35

236

ORRICK, Mary (GARVEY) 84
  Nancy 133
  Nicholas 38
  Rebekah 7
  Richard Wilson 120
  Sarah 65
  Susanna 7
ORSLER, Edward 31
  Ruth (OWENS) 31
OSBAN, John 10
  Joseph 10
  Mary 10
OSBORN, Eliza 98
  Jonas 99
  Martha 100
  Robert 98
  Samuel 100
  Susanna 100
OSBORNE, Jonas 105
  Joseph 129, 142
  Mary 105
  Sarah 129
OSBURN, John 30
  Joseph 72
  Mary (SULLIVAN) 30
  Samuel 55, 57, 72
  Susanna 57, 72
  Sussanna (AKELS) 55
  Thomas 112
OSBURNE, Mary 128
OTTWAY, Nicholas 43
OTTY, William 156
OWEN, Elisabeth 138
  Solomon 138
  William 138
OWENS, Elijah 165
  Elliner 32
  Ruth 31
OWINGS, Achsah 83
  Aney 39
  Bail 7
  Caleb 13
  Charlotte 84
  Hannah 13, 15, 42, 139
  Hannah (FORQUER) 30
  John 13, 42
  John Cockey 12
  Joshua 12, 13, 32
  Mary 12, 13, 122
  Mary (COCKEY) 32
  Rachel 10, 13
  Richard 13, 122, 152, 165
  Robert 30
  Ruth 13
  Samuel 7, 10, 13, 14, 15, 30,
    149, 154
  Sarah 13, 15
  Sophia 13
  Stephen 15

OWINGS, Thomas 14
  Urath 7, 13, 14, 15
  Urath (RANDALL) 30
  Ureth 10
OXFORD, Mary 34
OYSTON, Henry 40
  Margaret (POUTANEY) 40
OZARD, Anne (JOHNSTON) 103
  Robert 103
PACKER, William 40
PAGE, Bennet 74
  Daniel 108
  Elizabeth 55
  Esther (MILLER) 34
  John 67, 74
  Mary 67
  Polly (HUGHES) 108
  Sarah 74
  William 34
PAINE, Elizabeth 96
  Mary 96
  William 96
PAINTER, George 146
  Nancy (THOMPSON) 146
PALLEN, Benjamin 1
  John 1, 41
  Sarah 1
  William 1
PALMER, Alice 105
  Ann 57, 84
  Anne 105
  Edward 50
  Eleanor 57
  John 57, 105
  Margaret 136
  Martha Curtain 84
  Mary (NOWLAN) 50
PALSER, Thomas 42
PAMPHILION, Edward 60
  Elizabeth 69
  Rebecca 60, 69, 124
  Thomas 60, 69, 93, 124
  William 93
PANNELL, Elisabeth B. 136
PAR, Charles 3
  Daniel 3
  John 3
  Margaret 3
PARAGY, Flora (RYDER) 32
  Joseph 32
PARAN, Jane 72
PARISH, Edward 164
  Elizabeth 27, 30
  Jemima 59
  John 27, 59
  Richard 37
  Sarah 27, 59
  Sarah (BAKER) 37
PARKER, Anne 76

237

PARKER, Anne (CRAIN) 30
  James 145
  Mary 145
  Thomas 30
PARKINSON, Diana 64
  Edward 101
  Mary (WARD) 101
PARKS, Charlotte 39
  Ealy 65
  Frederick 52
  John 34, 52, 97, 119, 120, 124
  Mary 118, 119, 124
  Mary (COLLINS) 98
  Mary (STEWART) 97
  Mayberry 118
  Rachel 52, 119, 120
  Rachel (PARKS) 52
  Ruth (HENDRICKSON) 52
  Sally 118
  Sarah (LINCHFIELD) 34
  Sophia 70
PARLET, Mary 34
PARLETT, Elisabeth 6
  Elizabeth (DEW) 36
  Martin 3
  Mary 3, 6, 32
  Mertin 6
  William 36
PARLOT, Mary 18
  Sarah 18
  William 18
PARNETSON, Elizabeth 33
PARREGOY, Flora 13
  Joseph 13
  Nathan 13
PARRISH, Edward 32
  Elizabeth (GILL) 32
  Elizabeth (THOMAS) 31
  John 31, 163
PARROTT, Abner 129
  Benjamin 94
  Sarah 129
PARSONS, Ann 50
PARTERIDGE, Buckler, Dr. 10
  Flurre 10
  Jemima 10
PASSEY, Anariah (MC GUIRE) 79
  James 79
PASSMORE, Joel 144
PATE, Elizabeth 123
PATERSON, Anne 111, 141
  Anne (BROADSHAW) 101
  Elizabeth 99
  James 73
  John 27, 99, 101, 111, 124,
    141
  Mary 27
  Mary Anne 103, 124
  Nancy 73

PATERSON, Nancy (CRAIG) 89
  Rebecca 103
  William 27, 65, 89, 103, 111,
    124
PATRIDGE, (?) 161
  Buckler 153
  Elizabeth 20
  Frances 34
  Joseph 20
  Sarah 20
  William 164
PATTEN, Frances 137
  John 137
PATTERSON, Anne 127
  Elisabeth 120
  James 49, 53, 82, 120, 127
  Jane (HEATH) 53
  John 43, 101, 127
  Nancy (BRADSHAW) 101
  Robert 43
  William 147, 165
PATTON, Mathew 38
PATTY, Ruth 130
PAUL, Henry 132
  Mary 132
  Rebecca 132
  Sliter 132
  Zachariah 132
PAULIN, Elizabeth 13
  Robert Newman 13
PAULING, Aquiler 3
  Sarah 3
PAYAN, Alexander 76
PAYNE, (?) 49
  Christina 138
  Elizabeth 36
  George 36
  James 89
  John 65, 119, 138
  Letitia (MILWARD) 89
  Mary 103
  Mary (GLENN) 65
PAYSON, Nancy 106
PEACHEY, Amelia 133
  Elizabeth 96
  Mary Anne 133
  Pamela 96
  William 96
  William Traverse 133
PEACHY, Amelia 107
  Thomas Griffin 107
  William Traverse 107
PEACOCK, Elizabeth (SMITH) 38
  Honor 1
  Honor (HARDEN) 29
  Jacob 1, 29, 71
  John 38
  Mary (GARDINER) 71
  Ruth 1

PEAKE, (?), Capt. 115
PEAKS, Keziah 125
PEALE, Elisabeth 113
 Elizabeth (BERRY) 101
 Elizabeth Ann 84
 George Allison 113
 Mary 84
 William 84, 101, 113
PEARCE, Elizabeth 96
 Elizabeth (CUMMINS) 87
 Mary (CRAWFORD) 32
 Thomas 87, 96
 William 32, 96
PEARSE, Mary 16
 Thomas 16, 98
 William 98
PEARSON, Andrew 98
 Bridget 39
 Daniel 125
 Elizabeth 97
 Patty (SMITH) 98
 Sally Anastatia (HOLDEN) 125
PEATHERS, Elizabeth 89
PECK, Charlotte 63
 Elizabeth 63
 John 63
 Lydia 60, 64
 Nathaniel 60, 64
 Rebecca 64
PECKARD, Elizabeth 74
PECKER, Mary 92
PEDDICOAT, Ann (JACKS) 32
 Nicholas 32
PEIRCE, Humphrey 117
PELL, (?) 150
 Anna 133
 Elisabeth 107
 Elizabeth 79, 133
 Mary 79
 Thomas Hayley 107
 William 79, 107, 133
PELLING, Jonathan 40
 Margaret (KEYS) 40
PELTON, William 76
PEMBERTON, Mary (MAXWELL) 94
 William 94
PENDERGRASS, Margaret 56
 Mary 56
 Patrick 56
PENINGTON, Edward 26
 Elizabeth 17
 Jemima 26
 Jemima (HANSON) 36
 John 17
 Josiah 26, 36
 Martha 17
 Mary 17
 Urath 17
PENINGTONE, Constant 34

PENN, Anna 129
 Deborah (CONNOWAY) 82
 Resin 112
 Rezin 83
 Ruth 83, 112
 Shadrack 112
 Susanna 83
 William 82
PENNINGTON, James 59
 Jemima 27, 111
 John 19
 Jonas 147
 Joshua 27
 Josias 27, 111
 Keturah 59
 Mary 19, 98
 Pricilla 59
 Rebecca 70
 Sarah 106
PENNY, Alexander 26
 Christian 26
 Christiana 55
 Elisabeth 93
 Elizabeth 25, 26
 Henry 25, 26, 93
 Prudence 25
PENRICE, Mary (WEBB) 93
 Thomas 93
PEOT, Louisa (AVELIN) 69
 Peter 69
PEPPER, Pamela 85
PEPPERMAN, Anthony 122
 Mary (CLAYTON) 122
PERDUE, Martha (WATSON) 37
 Walter 37
PEREGOY, Amey 1
 Amy (GREEN) 29
 Ann 1
 Frances 29
 Henry 1, 29
PERET, Barbara 78
 Elizabeth 78, 92
 James 92
 Valentine 78, 92
PERIGO, Deborah 24
 Eleanor (SHERMEDINE) 37
 Flora 22
 John 24, 25, 95
 Nathan 22, 35
 Nicholas 37
 Rebecca 22, 24, 25
 Rebecca (EVANS) 35
 Sarah 25
PERINE, John Simon 115
 Margaret 115
 Simon 115
PERKINS, (?) 50
 Catharine 75
 Mary 60

PILLY, John 33
  Mary (WHEELY) 33
PINDALL, Charles Ridgely 145
  Mary (LANDERMAN) 145
PINE, Eleanor 65
  John 132, 143
  Juliana 144
  Susanna 132
  Susanna (CREMAR) 112
  Thomas 112, 132, 143, 144
PINFIELD, Anne 113
PINKERTON, James 145
  Mary (SHORT) 145
PINKHAM, Phillis (NOBLE) 31
  Richard 31
PINSTON, Thomas 84
PIPER, Grace 105
PITSTON, Mary 162
  Philip 162
PITT, Anne 121
  Hannah 93
  Rebecca Maria 121
  William 93, 121
PITTAY, Polly 131
PITTRING, Deborah 58
  Elizabeth 58
  Peter 58
PLACE, Celices 26
  Elizabeth 26
  Thomas 26
PLEWMAN, Anne 1
  Jonathan 1
  Rachel 1
PLISHO, Mary (MILLER) 39
  Nicholas 39
PLOOM, Rachel (MC GARVEY) 139
  William 139
PLOWMAN, John 32
  Jonathan 164
  Sarah (CHAMBERS) 32
PLOWRIGHT, Mary 31
PLUMBER, Ann 36
PLUNKETT, Elizabeth 78
POALING, Mary Ann 31
POCOCK, Abraham 126
  Ann 43, 54
  Anne 120
  Anne (LISTON) 90
  Bendeict 56
  George 120
  George Adwell 90
  James 43, 56, 63
  Jemima 43
  Jemima Barton 54
  John 52
  Joshua 43, 54
  Lydia (FOSTER) 126
  Margaret 37
  Rebecca 43, 56, 63

POCOCK, Susanna Somers 120
  Temperance (ISGRIG) 52
POE, Christian 109
  Jane 94, 109
  Mary Anne Fitt 109
POGE, (?) 45
  John 148
POGUE, John 151
POIRICE, Marie Rose 53
POLLOCK, Cullen 93
  James 87
  Jane 62, 118
  Margaret 62
  Sarah 66
  William 62, 118
POMFREY, Rachel 43
PONTANEY, Sarah (WOODEN) 33
  William 33
POOL, Joseph 144
  Rachel (DERBIN) 66
  Sarah 67
  William 66, 67
POOLE, David 163
  Joseph 119
  Sarah 119
POPER, A. J. 149
PORTER, Anne 96
  Catharine 83, 113
  Catharine (BROWN) 85
  Elliner 12
  Jesse 118
  Lewis 85
  Martha 30
  Mary 75
  Nathaniel 40
  Polly 134
  Rachel 118
  Rebecca (MASON) 40
  Robert 75
  Susanna (BUCK) 75
  Thomas 12
  William 118
PORTUSE, Robert 147
POTEE, Charlotte 119
  Mary 33
POTTER, Elisabeth 135
  Susanna 77, 78
  William 67
POTTS, (?) 46
POULANY, Edward 164
POULSTON, George 90
POULTON, Ariana 92
  Thomas 92
POUTANY, Alnar 20
  Mary 20
  Rosanah 20
  Rosanna 40
  William 20
POUTENAY, Margaret 40

241

246

ROW, Michael 142
  Rebecca 142
ROWE, Mary Anne 106
  Thomas 50
ROWLAND, Elizabeth 95
ROWLES, Anne 21
  Anne (GORSWICK) 35
  Anne (LYNCH) 29
  Constance 4
  Constance (SAMPSON) 29
  Elizabeth 21, 29, 51
  Elizabeth (DUNGAN) 81
  Jacob 4, 21, 29, 34, 81
  Mary 31
  Mary (SCARF) 34
  Rachel 21
  Richard 4, 21, 35
  Sarah 52
ROWLS, Ann 41
  Jacob 41
  Patience 31
ROYAL, John 65
  Mary (SHEELS/SKEELS) 65
ROYSTON, Abraham 12
  Ann 33
  John 12
  Mary 12
RUKE, Catharine 134
RUMAGE, Elizabeth 53
  Nicholas 53
  Priscilla 53
RUNDLET, Elizabeth 103
  Francis 103
  Mary 103
RUPERT, Martin 151
RUSH, Daniel 82
  Patience 142
RUSK, David 165
  Elisabeth 125
  John 112, 121, 150
  Robert 112
  Thomas 67
RUSSAEL, John 64
  Rebecca 64
  William 64
RUSSEL, (?) 48
  Alexander 28, 54
  Ann 28
  Elisabeth (HOBBS) 110
  Elisabeth (TOWNSEND) 139
  Elizabeth 53
  Frances Moale 28
  Jane 54
  John Moale 28
  Lewis 53
  Louisa 53
  Rachel 54
  Rebecca 28
  Rebecca (MOALE) 40

RUSSEL, Robert 110
  Sarah 53
  Thomas 28, 40, 45, 47, 139,
    149, 165
  William 48
RUSSELL, Charlotte 55
  Elisabeth (HOBBS) 120
  Elizabeth (WILLIAMSON) 85
  Frances 74
  Michael 55
  Racheal 55
  Rebecca 77
  Robert 120
  William 74, 85, 157
RUST, Ann 54
  Charles 63
  George 63
  John 121
  Mary 63
  Paul 54
  Thomas 54
RUTER, Elizabeth 20
  Henry 20
  Sarah 20
RUTLEDGE, Jane 1
  John 1
  Ruth 1
RUTLIDGE, Abraham 34
  Penelope 34
RUTTER, Ann 8, 9, 10, 42
  Anne 30
  Christiana 59
  Easter 2, 3, 4
  Easther 42
  Edward 135, 141
  Edward Hanson 86
  Edward Pennington 142
  Elisabeth 111, 135
  Eliza. 53
  Elizabeth 8, 21, 62, 81
  Henry 21, 59
  John 53, 62, 81, 111, 135
  Johnathan Hanson 53
  Jonathan 150
  Josias 98, 142
  Margaret (MC CLURE) 86
  Mary 142
  Mary (BARNEY) 35
  Mary (PENNINGTON) 98
  Mary Anne (RIPPER) 141
  Mary Hanson 81
  Moses 2, 23, 155
  Mosts 10
  Richard 9, 21, 23, 35, 42, 162
  Sarah 111, 138
  Soloman 4
  Sophia 9, 23, 42
  Thomas 2, 3, 4, 59, 62
  William 8, 10

248

RUTTOR, Esther 7
  Thomas 7
RYAN, Eleanor (MURPHY) 130
  Elisabeth B. (PANNELL) 136
  John 130
  Mary 144
  Sara 94
  Timothy 136
RYDER, Ann 14
  Elizabeth 14
  Flora 32
  Francis 14
RYE, Gustavus 131
  John 111, 131
  Mary (BARBARY) 111
RYLAND, John Burke 106
  Mary 139
  Richard 92
  Sarah 92
  Sarah (JONES) 106
  Sylvester 139
RYLEY, (?), Capt. 150
RYSTON, Benjamin 10
  John 2, 10
  Mary 2, 10
  Robert 2
RYSTONE, John 1
  Mary 1
SABEL, Anne Christiana 123
  Catharine 123
  John 123
SADLER, Anne 129
  Elisabeth 128
  Eliza 134
  Leonard 115
  Samuel 48
  Thomas 128, 134
SAITH, John 41
  Joyce 41
SALISBURY, Matthew 83
  Prudence (TRAVIS) 83
SALTONSTALL, Jane 135
  Joseph L. 135
  Sarah 135
SALWAY, Polly 140
SAMPLE, William 45
SAMPSON, Ann 32, 40
  Ann (EMPEY) 31
  Constance 29
  Jacob 50, 62
  Martha 62
  Mary 29
  Richard 31, 42, 152, 161
  Tench Tilghman 62
SANDEL, David 20
  Elizabeth 20
  Jacob 20
  William 20
SANDERS, James 40

SANDERS, Ruth (ANDREWS) 40
SANDERSON, Margaret 147, 165
SANDS, Alexander 52, 89
  Dalilah 89
  Delilah (BURK) 52
  William 89
SANK, Action 26
  Elizabeth 26
  George 26, 131
  Hannah (VANSANDT) 131
SANSOM, Anna (KIMS) 133
  Henry 133
SAP, Daniel 55
  Margaret 55
  Mary 55
SARGEANT, Elizabeth 12
  John 12
  Samuel 12
SARGENT, Adelina Alice 68
  James 79
  John 68
  Mary (YOUNG) 79
  Ruth 68
SARJANT, Benjamin 15
  Elizabeth 15
  John 15
SARTER, Elizabeth 13
  Jane 13
  Mary 13
  Peter 13
SAUL, Christopher 121
  Sarah (DAVIS) 121
SAUNDERS, Dorcas 73, 95
  Dorcas (ALLEN) 65
  George 95
  John 65, 73, 82, 95
  Mary 65, 73, 82
SAVAGE, Elizabeth (CORRIE) 98
  Elliner 32
  Hill 15, 94
  Patrick 98
  Sarah 15, 94
SAWELL, Mary 34
SAWYER, Anthony 126
  Sarah (SPALDING) 126
SAYTH, John 32
  Sarah (RICH) 32
SCAGS, Lydia (HILLEN) 64
  Thomas 64
SCANLAN, Catharine 105
SCANTLAN, Lucy 98
SCARF, Mary 34
SCATES, (?) 148
  Thomas 149
SCHAEFFER, Eleanor 138
SCHIVELY, Eleanor 121
SCHREIBER, John H. 143
  Maria F. (YEISER) 143
SCHUNK, Elisabeth 141

S INDELL, Sussana 43
S ING, Benjamin 4
  John 4
  Margrett 31
  Mary 4, 5, 33
  Ruth 5
S INGDALL, Mary 30
S INGLETON, Alice 98
  Charles 81
  Elisabeth 112
  Elizabeth 81, 131
  Elizabeth (SLATER) 69
  Robert 131
  Thomas Slater 112
  William 69, 81, 98, 112, 131,
    160
S INKLEN, Mary (HINES) 30
  William 30
S ISSLER, Anne 80
  Kitty (SMITH) 140
  Philip 80
  Samuel 140
S ISSON, Joseph Benjamin
    Christopher Hughes 126
  Mary 126, 143
  Mary (INGRAM) 89
  Mary Anne Davis 143
  Richard 89, 126, 143
SITH, Thomas 34
SITLER, Catharine 100
SKEEL, Ann (STAPLE) 65
  William 65
SKEELS, Mary 65
SKEWSE, Nancy 87
SKILEHORN, Frances 39
SKIPPER, Thomas 151
SKUSE, Anne 88
SLADEN, Eleanor (MURPHY) 43
  James 43
SLAMEKER, John 60
  Mary 60
SLATER, Alice 93
  David 72
  David Harris 79
  Diana 99
  Elizabeth 69
  Hannah 57, 99, 128
  Joseph 79
  Lydia Ball 128
  Robert 82, 93, 149
  Sally James 57
  Sarah 79
  William 57, 99, 128
SLATON, (?) 45
SLATOR, Charles 59
  Henry 59
  Joseph 59
  Sally James 67
  Sarah 59

SLATOR, William 67
SLAUGHTER, Mary 135
  Susanna (JONES) 140
  Thomas 140
SLAUN, Elizabeth 125
SLAYMAKER, Elizabeth 22
  James 22
  John 22
SLAYTON, William 149, 165
SLEMAKER, Elizabeth 35
  Elizabeth (GILES) 33
  James 33, 35
SLEMAN, Mary Agnes 90
SLIDER, Mary 30
SLIGH, Sophia 9
  Sophia (WILKISSON) 31
  Thomas 9, 31
  William 9
SLY, John 122
  Mary 122
SLYDER, Christopher 10
  Mary 10
SMALL, Jacob 83, 139
  Nancy (FLEETWOOD) 83
SMALLWOOD, Anne Margaret 141
  John Richard 141
  Margaret (KEITHOLTZ) 100
  Robert 100, 141, 145
SMART, Esther (DUNN) 131
  Zachariah 131
SMEWING, Drewey 55
  John 55
SMITH, Abby (THOMAS) 128
  Abner 12
  Addison 24, 28
  Agnes 52
  Alexander 143
  Alice 9, 26, 29
  Amos 81
  Andrew 109
  Ann 27, 38, 65
  Ann (CONNELL) 34
  Anne 75, 88, 96, 145
  Basil 75
  Bazil Lowman 145
  Beddy 40
  Benjamin 144
  Caleb 144
  Catharine 88, 94
  Catherine 27, 39
  Catherine Rogers 24, 28, 43
  Charity (LETT) 34
  Charles 34
  Charles Merryman 11
  Chloe 27
  Cloe 26
  Daniel 22
  Edward 22
  Eilce 29

SOLLERS, Sarah 68, 118, 135
  Sarah (PENNINGTON) 106
  Thomas 23, 106, 118, 135, 157,
    164
  Uriana 147
  William 19, 138
SOLOMON, Elizabeth 68
  Elkin 68
SOMELIN, Fanny 71
SOMMERS, John 36
  Mary (LASHFORD) 36
SORTER, Hannah 6
  Jane 6
  Peter 6
SOULSBY, John 88
  Matthew 83, 88
  Prudence 88
  Prudence (TRAVIS) 83
SOUTHALL, Ann 51
SOUTHERN, Ann 37
SOUTHWOOD, Mary 103
  Thomas 103
SOUTHWORD, Mary (SPECK) 140
  William 140
SOWERS, Kitty 138
SPALDING, Sarah 126
SPANSBY, Nancy 132
SPARKS, Elizabeth 121
  James 133
  John 27
  Maria 27
  Samuel 27, 121
  William 121, 133
SPARKSMAN, Leah 126
SPEAR, Catharine 139
  James 139
  Mary 139
SPECK, Mary 140
SPENCE, Elisabeth (JARVIS) 134
  Peter 134
SPENCER, (?) 45
  Anne 92
  Benjamin 49, 50, 63, 142, 143
  Eliza 146
  Elizabeth 24
  George Washington 146
  Georgiana 142, 143
  Mary 24, 27
  Mary (WHITACKER) 36
  Rebecca 39
  Richard 24
  Robert 146
  Sarah 63, 142
  Stephen 27
  William 24, 27, 36
SPENSE, Catherine (MOONEY) 36
  Dogulass 36
SPENSER, Benjamin 83, 102
  Joseph 83, 102

SPENSER, Sarah 83
SPICER, Amon 18
  Anne (CADLE) 139
  Elisabeth 5
  Elizabeth 54
  Elizabeth (LLOYD) 39
  Elizabeth (SCOVEY) 39
  Hannah 142
  James 39
  Jane 39
  John 5, 11
  Jonathan 18
  Juliatha 34
  Julytha 5
  Peregrine 54
  Rebeckah (MERRYMAN) 32
  Rebekah 11
  Sarah 30, 142
  Thomas 11, 32, 39, 54, 139
  Valentine 142
SPIERS, Elisabeth (KEMP) 141
  Thomas 141
SPRAY, John 44
  Mary (SUMMERS) 44
SPRINGFIELD, Leah 51
SPURR, James 32
  Judeth (WILLIAMS) 32
SPURRIER, Anne 126
  Elisabeth 126
  John 126
  Sophia 126
  Thomas Green 126
  William 126
  William, Jr. 95
ST. CLAIR, Celia Anne
    (CONNOLLY) 85
  George 85
STACEY, Ann 72
  Anne 76
  Catharine 25
  Jane 57, 72
  John 25, 72
  Matthew 57, 72, 76
  William 25, 57
STACY, Kitty 93
  Mathew 93
STAFFORD, (?), Capt. 144
  Bridget 112
  Catharine 125
  James 125
  Patrick 112, 125
STAHL, Andrew 61
  Mary 61
STAINES, Susanna (HUGHES) 116
  William 116
STAINSBUAREY, Danel 26
  Sarah 26
STALL, Edward H. 146
  Martha (AITKEN) 146

STANDSBURY, Thomas 42
STANLEY, John 40
  Margaret (MAXWELL) 40
STANSBERRY, Edmund 164
STANSBERY, Benjamin 19
  Hannah 19
  Thomas 19
STANSBURY, (?) 68
  Abarillah 2
  Angian 19
  Ann 11, 13
  Ann (ENSOR) 31
  Anne 12
  Anne (CULLESON) 37
  Blanche 22
  Casandra 22
  Cathrine 19, 22
  Charles 11, 24, 76
  Daniel 1, 3, 5, 11, 20, 63,
    76, 77, 124, 165
  David 19, 77
  Deborah 130
  Dixon 2, 124
  Edmond 2
  Edmund 27, 157
  Elenor 68
  Elisabeth 5, 124
  Eliza. 63
  Elizabeth 1, 3, 5, 13, 17, 24,
    35, 66, 77
  Elizabeth (ENSOR) 35
  Ezekiel 54
  Frances Philips 118
  Frances Philips (GOUGH) 79
  George 5, 21, 24
  Hanah 20
  Hannah 11, 13, 15, 18, 22, 79,
    124
  Hannah (GORSUCH) 32
  Hanner 35
  Henrieta Maria 16
  Henrietta 19
  Henrietta Maria 77
  Hesia 54
  Honnor 5
  Honor 2, 3
  Isaac 68
  James 64, 74
  Jane 2, 4, 5, 11, 18, 27
  Jane (LONG) 36
  Jean 19
  Jemima 5, 34, 64
  Job Garretson 63
  John 11, 12, 13, 31, 42, 76,
    118, 146
  John Dickson 35
  John Dixon 68
  John E. 103

STANSBURY, Joseph 25, 36, 68,
    79, 118, 124
  Joseph Ward 18
  Joshua 42, 63, 76
  Kezia 100
  Keziah 27
  Luke 4, 18, 19, 42, 153
  Mary 16, 18, 19, 20, 21, 22,
    24, 126, 146
  Mary (HAMMOND) 19, 35
  Mary (PROCTER) 103
  Mary Fowler 77
  Nathaniel 22
  Patience 54
  Rebecca 19
  Richard 1, 3, 24, 25, 64, 74,
    165
  Richard Gardner 20
  Richardson 18, 22
  Robert 20
  Ruth 4, 17, 21, 37, 68
  Samuel, Sr. 37
  Sarah 13, 19, 22, 24, 25
  Sarah (GARDNER) 20
  Sophia 31
  Susan 114
  Thomas 2, 5, 11, 13, 15, 18,
    19, 20, 22, 24, 32, 35, 77,
    153
  Tobias 2, 3, 5, 16, 20, 22,
    153, 155, 156, 164, 165
  Tobias, Capt. 156
  Tobias, Gen. 161
  Tobies 20, 35
  Tobois 19
  William 17, 22, 35
STAPLE, Ann 65
STAR, Elizabeth 61
  James 61
  Mary 61
  William 148, 149
STARCK, Catharine 120
STARKINS, Catharine (COSSETT)
    104
  Thomas 104
STARR, (?) 46
  Ann 44
  Benjamin 103
  Dorcas 103
  James 44
  John 144
  Joseph 102, 103
  Mary 44
  Thomas 103
  William 102, 103
STATIA, Jane 54
  Mary 54
  Matthew 54
  William 49

256

STAYTON, William 147, 150
STEARNES, Catharine (ASTERMAN) 85
　William 85
STEEL, (?), Capt. 145
　Frances Allanby 143
　John 143
　Nancy 143
　Peter 115
STEELE, Frances 81
　John 159
　Sarah 104
STEELL, Anne 118
　John 106, 118
　Nancy (DAWSON) 106
STENCHCOME, John 30
　Katherine (MACCLEANE) 30
STEPHENSON, Eleanor 56
　Henry 44
　John 44
　Kessiah 56
　Margaret 44
　Margret (MC CARTHY) 55
　Moses 55, 56
STERETT, John 147
STERLING, (?) 147
　James 149, 150, 151, 165
STERRETT, Dummone 50
　John 165
　Joseph 144
　Mary (HARRIS) 144
　Mary Bourdieu 137
　Phillips 50
　Rebecca 137
　Samuel 137
STEUART, James 89
　Margaret 89
　Rebecca 89
STEVEN, George 138
STEVENS, (?) 48
　Achsah (OWINGS) 83
　Anne 82
　Jennet 104
　John 83
　John M. 104
　Lydia 82
　Mary 32, 35
　Rachel 33
　Sophia 76
　William 76
STEVENSON, (?) 93
　Anne (CAULK) 82
　Anne Henry 85
　Charles 136
　Charlotte 53
　Edmund 154
　Edward 7, 8, 9, 12
　Eleanor 52, 53
　Eleanor (SHAW) 52

STEVENSON, Elizabeth 7, 93, 125
　Elizabeth (PEATHERS) 89
　Esther (JONES) 78
　Henry 12, 13, 17, 19, 22, 32, 82
　J., Dr. 164
　Jacob 52
　Jane 22
　Jemima 12, 13, 17, 19, 22
　Jemina (MERRYMAN) 32
　Jesse 53
　John 32, 52
　Mary 9
　Mary (BOYD) 136
　Mary (TIPTON) 32
　Meshach 78
　Meshack 52
　Moses 52, 53
　R. King 156
　Rachel 7, 125
　Richard 7
　Ruth 17
　Samuel 52, 89, 125
　Sarah 8
　Shedrack 52
　Susan 12
　Susanna 8, 9
　William 8, 19, 52
STEWARD, (?) 47
　Catherine (MUMFORD) 39
　Elizabeth 40
　Frances Haly 40
　Henry 39
　Mary 37
　Robert 148, 149
　Stephen 40, 150
　Stephen, Jr. 147
STEWART, (?) 47
　Alexander 20
　Alexander, Capt. 156
　Ann 20, 60
　Catharine (ENSOR) 135
　Catherine 38, 43
　Charles 55, 60
　David 165
　Diana 108
　Eleanor 53
　Elizabeth (YIELDHALL) 135
　Ezekiel 135
　Hanna 86
　Isaac 108
　James 53, 127
　John 135
　John Hooper 92
　Joseph 146
　Mary 55, 92, 94, 97
　Mary Helen 92, 94
　Nancy 55
　Patty 60, 120

259

261

WALSH, Edward 43
 John 104
WALTEEN, Achsah 25
 David 25
 Elizabeth 25
WALTER, Ferdinand 87
 Henry 72, 145
 John 111
 Juliana 111
 Letitia 111
 Philip 87
WALTERS, Agnes 64, 86
 Ann 64
 Benjamin 64, 86
 Charles 130
 Elisabeth (HEIDE) 130
 Philip 47
 William 86
WALTON, Caroline 128
 Elizabeth 80
 Elizabeth (WILLIAMS) 34
 John 121, 128
 Juliana 121
 Letitia 128
 Nancy 80
 Thomas 34
WANN, Edward 34
 Prudence (MARSH) 34
WARD, Ann (BOYED) 30
 Betsy 91
 Charles 76
 Daniel 30
 Ebenezer 99
 Elisa 139
 Elisabeth 116, 137, 139
 Elizabeth 27, 99, 123, 128
 Irene 79, 99, 123, 127
 James 54
 John 36, 116, 139, 143
 Joseph 71, 79, 99, 123, 127, 128
 Katherine 33
 Leonora 99
 Margaret (LOBB) 29
 Martha Charles 99
 Mary 27, 38, 54, 101
 Mary (KELLEY) 36
 Mary Anne 116
 Robert 49
 Sarah 54
 Simon 29
 Sophia (DELAHAYE) 76
 Sophia Elizabeth 99
 Thomas 99
 Urania 79
 William 91, 99, 137
WARDEN, Ann (FISHER) 57
 John 57
 Matilda 120

WARDEN, William 120
WARFIELD, (?), Dr. 130
 George Fraser 103, 129
 Lewis 129
 Margaret 119
 Rebecca 103, 129
 Susanna 103
WARIN, Eleoner 29
WARRELL, Mary 37
WARREN, Bethia 123
 Bethia (HOWARD) 85
 Eleanor 123
 Elisabeth (SHIELDS) 132
 Henry 132
 Martha 33
 William 85, 98, 123
WARRILL, Henry 34
 Juliatha (SPICER) 34
WARRINGTON, Elizabeth 64
WATERS, Abigail (WILLIAMS) 64
 Anne 122
 Anne (fALLOWS) 101
 Charlotte 135
 Elenor 69, 96
 Elisabeth 111
 Eliza 69
 Elizabeth 91, 98
 George 64
 J. 149
 James 69, 91, 98, 102, 111
 Joseph 69
 Martin 46
 Mary 103, 145
 Mary (IRELAND) 37
 Matilda Elenora Anne 102
 Matilda Eleonora Anne 91
 Nelly (HINCKS) 53
 Philip 53, 68, 69, 96, 102, 111, 122
 Philip Zacharie 68
 Prudence 111
 Robert 37
 Stephen 111
 William 96, 101, 102, 122
WATERSON, Grace (CAMPBELL) 140
 James 140
WATKIN, Maria 85
 Susanna 85, 95
 Susanna (MINSKIE) 65
 William 65, 85, 95
WATKINGS, (?) 161
 Francis 161
 Francis, Sr. 152
WATKINS, Betsey 70
 Elisabeth (SPURRIER) 126
 Francis, Sr. 161
 James 47, 52
 John 70
 Joseph 109

WATKINS, Margaret 105
  Maria 87
  Mary 70
  Polly (SHANEY) 109
  Rebecca (MILLER) 52
  Richard 95
  Thomas 126
  William 87, 105, 110
WATSON, Anne 135, 146
  Anne (OGDEN) 86
  David 72
  Elizabeth 47
  Fanny (MOODY) 52
  Joseph 52
  Lawrence 164
  Martha 37
  Mary Magdalen (ROORBACH) 72
  Polly 136
  Thomas 86, 135
WATTERS, Philip, Capt. 149
WATTS, Adeline 126
  Ann 18
  Anne (BODY) 35
  Beale 21
  Benjamin 81
  Dickerson 21
  Edward 1, 3, 4, 5, 21, 29,
    125, 126
  Edward Allison 18
  Elinor 5
  Elisa 126
  Elisabeth 145
  Elisabeth (GARNONS) 113
  Elisabeth Sarah 145
  Frances Holland 4, 35
  John 1, 5, 11, 18, 21, 35
  Josias 21
  Mary 1, 3, 4, 5, 30
  Mary (MORGAN) 29
  Penellope 21
  Robert 5
  Sarah 5, 11, 21
  Sarah (EAGLESTONE) 35
  Susanna (GRIFFIN) 81
  Thomas 113, 145
  William 11
WEALING, Henry Cronke 148
  Joseph Bradband 149
  Joseph Inay 149
WEARER, John 83
  Mary (MC FEEL) 83
WEARY, Anne 107
  Anne (MERRIT) 132
  Joseph 110, 120
  Lenora 142
  Mary 124
  Rebecca (PERRIGO) 110, 120
  Sarah 111
  Thomas 111, 132

WEARY, William 132
WEASON, Mary (STANSBURY) 126
  Thomas 126
WEATHERBOURN, Catherine 60, 66
  John 60, 66
  Mary Ann 60
WEATHERBURN, Catharine
  (LITTLEJOHN) 37
  Jno. 147
  John 149, 158, 165
  John Dixon 37
WEATHERBY, Jesse 131, 133
  Matilda 131, 133
  Sarah 131
  Urith (SCINDALL) 88
  William 88
WEATHERS, Ann (COATES) 52
  Ann (COATS) 40
  Zebulon 40, 52
WEAVER, (?) 50
  Elizabeth (NICHOLSON) 90
  Jacob 90, 118, 145
  John 49, 131
  Mary 142
  Sarah 145
  Sarah (LAUDERMAN) 118
WEBB, Eleanor 116
  Eleanor (ROW) 39
  Elenor 62
  Henry 62, 74, 102, 116, 121
  James 39, 62, 102
  Jane 103, 121
  John 74
  Margaret 116, 121
  Mary 93
  Nancy 124
  Williamson 87
WEBSTER, (?) 50
  Amelia 64
  Elisabeth (THOMBURG) 140
  John Skinner 140
WEEKINS, Martha 115
WEEKS, Sarah 66
  Thomas 41
WEGLEY, Edward 35
  Jane (FISHER) 35
WEIR, John 109
  Sarah (MADDEN) 109
WEISENTHAL, (?), Dr. 114
WELCH, Ann 32
  Elizabeth 31
  Elliner 31
  John 164
WELLER, Andrew 78
  Mary (RHODE) 78
WELLS, Alexander 12
  Alice (WIGNALL) 36
  Ann 7, 12, 52
  Charles 4, 143, 163

266

WELLS, Charlotte (CRAIGHEAD) 39
  Cornelius 39
  Eliza. (HOWARD) 33
  Elizabeth 12
  Francis 12
  George 47
  Honour 12
  James 12
  Jane 138
  Joseph 7
  Mary 67, 108, 138
  Prudence 12
  Rebecca 74
  Richard 12, 67
  Sarah 4, 100
  Thomas 12, 33, 36, 95, 108,
    138
  Thompsa (DEVALL) 95
  William 7, 156
WELSH, Ann 9
  Elisabeth 119, 120
  Elizabeth 100
  Laban 9
  Margaret 37
  Martha 120
  Thomas 120
  William 100
WENDLAKE, Lawrence 114
  Margaret (CONLEY) 114
WESCOTT, John 43
  Sarah (JOHNSON) 43
WEST, (?) 45
  Ann (PUE) 83
  Anne 114
  Edward 82
  Elijah 57, 71, 85, 107, 108
  George 99
  George William 90
  Joel 119
  Juliana Francisca (REPP) 119
  Margaret 39, 85
  Mary 57, 71, 85, 107, 108, 138
  Nancy (JOHNSTON) 82
  Polly (CLASBY) 106
  Sarah 107, 108
  Simeon 106
  Stephen 83
  William 149
  William, Rev. 28, 40, 50, 149,
    150, 165
WESTCOTE, James 138
  Mary (WEST) 138
WESTMINSTER, William, Rev. 36
WESTOVER, Isaac 146
  Mary (BERRY) 146
WHALEY, Mary 70
WHAN, George 109
  James 109, 123
  Ruth 109

WHEATLY, James 44
  Mary 44
WHEEDER, James 134
  Sarah 134
  Susanna 134
WHEELER, Ann 8, 14, 35
  Ann (HAWKINS) 33
  Benjamin 14
  Catherine 18
  Charlotte 72
  Eleanor 61
  Elizabeth 51, 55, 73
  Elizabeth (HILLEN) 34
  Hannah 52
  Harriet 79, 90
  Isaac 8, 47, 48, 51, 55, 58,
    79, 90, 107, 138
  John 44, 45, 58, 61, 101
  Katherine (GARDNER) 34
  Margaret 61, 96
  Margret 44
  Maria 107
  Martha 8, 14, 33
  Mary 18, 72, 107
  Moses 8, 18, 34
  Pleasant 55, 79, 107, 138
  Plesant 58
  Rebbecca 51
  Richard 29
  Sarah 61
  Solomon 8
  Stephen 72
  Thomas 14, 33, 34
  William 8, 44, 101, 138
WHEELY, Mary 33
WHELER, Rebeccah 29
WHETFORD, Barton 143
  Pamela 143
WHETTS, Rachel (FLOYD) 32
  Thomas 32
WHIFFIN, Joseh 64
  Susanna (KNIGHT) 64
WHILTON, Joyce 110
WHIP, Benjamin 3
  John 3
  Margaret 3
  Mary 3
  Samuel 3
  Susanna 3
  Uroth 3
WHIPLE, Elizabeth (PATE) 123
WHIPPLE, Dolly Williams 140
  Elisa 117
  Elisabeth 140, 141
  Polly 140
  William 123, 140
WHITACKER, Mary 36
WHITAKEY, David 131
  Elizabeth 131

WHITE, (?), Capt. 48
  Andrew 24
  Anne 2, 94, 123
  Anne Parren 139
  Catharine 100
  Catharine (MERRICK) 81
  David Hellen 123
  Eleanor 24, 55
  Elizabeth 91, 112
  Elizabeth (ROBERTS) 65
  Frances 77, 112
  George 55, 77
  George Griffith 106
  Griffith 55, 77, 106
  Hannah 102
  Isabella 90
  James 81
  Jane 91
  John 2, 29, 47, 65, 114
  Joseph 50
  Julian (LARY) 115
  Juliana 136
  Luke 148
  Mary 2, 37, 112
  Mary (ALEXANDER) 36
  Mary (RENCHER) 29
  Michael 115, 136
  Nancy 100
  Patty (WILSON) 114
  Priscilla 113
  Roanna 77
  Robert 77
  Samuel 94, 123
  Samuel, Jr. 33
  Sarah 24, 55, 106
  Sarah (WITCHCOAT) 33
  Sharper 100
  Sidney Hellen 94
  Susanna 136
  Thomas 90, 112
  William 91, 102
WHITESIDES, Bamber 115, 125
  Martha (WEEKINS) 115
WHITFORD, Burton 145
WHITH, Elizabeth 35
WHITNEY, Susanna (NEWEL) 86
  Thomas 86, 102
WHITTERFIELD, Margaret
  (WARFIELD) 119
  William 119
WICKINS, Jemima (HOLAWAY) 33
  Robert 33
WIESENTHAL, Andrew 24
  Charles Frederick 24
  Elizabeth 24
WIGNAL, William 66
WIGNALL, Alice 36
WIGNELL, Elizabeth 64
  Ellen 146

WIGNELL, James 91
  Jane 91
WILCOCKS, James 113, 145
  Mary (MC KENSIE) 113
  Polly 145
  Polly (MC KENSIE) 113
  William 145
WILCOXON, Esther (TAYLOR) 39
  William 39
WILEY, George 75
  Jane (SMITH) 75
  Margrett (SING) 31
  William 31
WILFORD, Thomas 145
WILK, Catharine (MAGUIRE) 136
  Peter 136
WILKENSON, Elizabeth 33
WILKES, (?) 46
WILKESSON, Jethro Linch 8
  Philles 8
WILKINS, Altha 125
WILKINSON, Anne 29
  Barbara 24
  John 24
  Rachel 12
  Rachel (LENORE) 33
  Rebecca 24
  Robert 12, 33
  William 12, 152
WILKISON, Ann 26
  Thomas 26
  William 26
WILKISSON, Rachel (LENOX) 32
  Robert 32
  Sophia 31
WILLCOCKS, James 53
  Sarah (GRAY) 53
WILLCOX, Elisabeth 134
  James 134
  Sarah 134
WILLESS, Ann 101
WILLIAM, John 47
WILLIAMS, Abigail 64
  Alice 10, 14
  Ann 27, 51, 56, 71
  Ann (SEYMER) 36
  Ann (WELLS) 52
  Anne 86, 98
  Catharine 85
  Catherine (TUCKER) 40
  Charity 22
  Charles 47, 85
  Edward 106
  Eleanor 58
  Elisabeth 10, 129
  Elizabeth 22, 27, 34, 85
  Elizabeth (PERSON) 36
  Ellen 51
  Frances 85

WILLIAMS, Hannah 10, 53, 80, 106
Jacob 132
James 51, 71, 99, 108
Jane (MORRISON) 52
John 26, 27, 36, 40, 48, 51, 52, 53, 56, 58, 68, 71, 74, 87, 109, 129, 163
Joseph 51
Judeth 32
Kitty 99
Lucy 135
Martha 5
Martha (HOGGINS) 109
Mary 5, 26, 27, 33, 85
Nancy (HUMPHRIES) 142
Nancy (SMITH) 132
Nathaniel 164
Owen 129
Phineas 144
Rachel 97
Rachel (MAID) 108
Rebecca 38
Richard 26, 27
Roland 10
Rowland 14
Sally 80
Silby 93
Tamar 114
Thomas 10, 142
William 22, 47
WILLIAMSON, (?) 46
David 135
Elizabeth 85
Lucy (WILLIAMS) 135
Mary 29
WILLIBY, Jane (CAIN) 40
William 40
WILLING, Matthew 121
WILLIS, Ann (BAKER) 51
Anna 140
George 132
John Winfield 51
WILLMOTT, Ruth 30
WILLOX, Dorcas (BARRATT) 37
William 37
WILLS, Colin C. 90
Elenor (REED) 78
Luke 78
Susanna (ROBBERDS) 90
WILLSON, Elizabeth (SHIPWAY) 92
Hannah 61
Isabella 53
James 61
Jane 64
John 52, 53, 61, 65
Joseph 61
Margaret 40
Margaret (DERRY) 52

WILLSON, Margret 43
Maria 75
Mary 50
Milcah (TAYLOR) 65
Nathaniel 92
Robert 53
Sarah 13, 52
William 13, 47
WILMANS, Charles 111
Charles Henry 99, 116
Charles John Stricker 116
Elisabeth Grant 116
Elizabeth Grant 99
Herman 111
Sophia 111
Sophia Bankson 99
WILMEN, Mary (MORRIS) 86
Richard 86
WILMER, William 77
WILMOT, Hannah (WHEELER) 52
John 52, 165
Robert 34, 148, 149
Sarah (MERRYMAN) 34
WILMOTT, (?) 162
WILSON, Andrew 107
Darcus (TOON) 93
Edward 17
Elenor (RIDDLE) 94
Elisabeth 107, 126
Elizabeth 37, 68, 92, 126
Francis 124
Garret 34
Garrett 17
George 123
Hannah 87, 94, 113, 118, 120, 143
Hannah (DUFFY) 144
Hannah (HILL) 76
Hugh 76, 94, 118, 143
Isaac 68
Isabella 87
James 140
Jane 129
John 68, 87, 93, 107, 124, 144
Joseph 87, 113, 114
Leah (SPARKSMAN) 126
Margaret 124
Martha 118
Mary 66, 68, 87, 94, 107
Mary (DAVIS) 140
Nathaniel 126, 144
Patty 114
Rosanna 17, 143
Rosanna (SMITH) 34
Susanna (WOLFE) 143
Thomas 17, 143
William 17, 94, 126, 143
WILY, George 86
Jane 86

269

Other Heritage Books by Bill and Martha Reamy:

Erie County, New York Obituaries as Found in the Files of
The Buffalo and Erie County Historical Society

Genealogical Abstracts from Biographical and
Genealogical History of the State of Delaware

History and Roster of Maryland Volunteers, War of 1861-1865, Index

Immigrant Ancestors of Marylanders, as Found in Local Histories

Pioneer Families of Orange County, New York

Records of St. Paul's Parish, [Baltimore, Maryland], Volume 2

St. George's Parish Register [Harford County, Maryland], 1689-1793

St. James' Parish Registers, 1787-1815

St. Thomas' Parish Register, 1732-1850

The Index of Scharf's History of Baltimore City and County [Maryland]

Other Heritage Books by Martha Reamy

1860 Census Baltimore City: Volume 1, 1st and 2nd Wards
(Fells Point and Canton Waterfront Areas)

Abstracts of South Central Pennsylvania Newspapers
Volume 2, 1791-1795

Early Families of Otsego County, New York, Volume 1

Early Church Records of Chester County, Pennsylvania, Volume 2
Martha Reamy and Charlotte Meldrum

Abstracts of Carroll County Newspapers, 1831-1846
Martha Reamy and Marlene Bates

CPSIA information can be obtained at www.ICGtesting.com
Printed in the USA
BVOW06s1034100516

447494BV00023B/342/P